To the Reader

In publishing ANNUAL EDITIONS we recognize the enormous role played by the magazines, newspapers, and journals of the public press in providing current, first-rate educational information in a broad spectrum of interest areas. Many of these articles are appropriate for students, researchers, and professionals seeking accurate, current material to help bridge the gap between principles and theories and the real world. These articles, however, become more useful for study when those of lasting value are carefully collected, organized, indexed, and reproduced in a low-cost format, which provides easy and permanent access when the material is needed. That is the role played by ANNUAL EDITIONS.

New to ANNUAL EDITIONS is the inclusion of related World Wide Web sites. These sites have been selected by our editorial staff to represent some of the best resources found on the World Wide Web today. Through our carefully developed topic guide, we have linked these Web resources to the articles covered in this ANNUAL EDITIONS reader. We think that you will find this volume useful, and we hope that you will take a moment to visit us on the Web at *http://www.dushkin.com* to tell us what you think.

Welcome to the second edition of *Annual Editions: Social Welfare and Social Work 00/01*. This book provides an overview of the social welfare system in the United States as well as an introductory look at how the profession of social work functions within that system. These are important topics to study, even if you do not plan to become a social worker. As a responsible citizen you are very much involved in the social welfare system whether you realize it or not. In fact, every time you vote on issues or choose a political candidate, every time you pay your taxes, which fund social programs, and every time you receive some benefit from any one of a number of federal, state, or local programs, you are interacting with the social welfare system in the United States. So, it seems to make sense that everyone have at least a basic understanding about social welfare.

At the outset, let's define a couple of terms for clarification: *Social Welfare* relates to organized efforts of any society that are designed to assist individuals, families, and groups when they have needs. Those needs can be economic, medical, social, or educational in nature, and they can be needs that arise quite naturally, like the need to get an education, or the need to find employment, or the need to be healthy and safe in one's own community. Sociologists tell us that there are four very basic components or foundations of a society: the family, the economy, the political system, and organized religion. All of these societal components (also called "institutions" in the theoretical sense) provide a series of benefits to individuals, to families, to groups, and to society itself. Another way to look at social welfare is to see it as a *fifth institution* in society, which acts as a "safety net" to catch anyone who is not being adequately served (for whatever reason) by the other four institutions. That is to say, for example, if the family structure breaks down for a child, or if one is poor because of unemployment or lack of basic skills, or if one feels disenfranchised or discriminated against, or if one feels isolated and vulnerable—that is when the social welfare system should enter with some program or some service to help.

Social work is a profession that one prepares for through specialized education in a college or university setting. Social workers work within the social welfare system and serve as staff in the many social agencies and organizations that provide services to people who need help in the areas mentioned above. Social workers are not the only professionals providing the benefits and social services that we have been discussing. Other professionals who also provide service throughout the social welfare system would include advocates, case managers, counselors, lawyers, physicians, nurses, occupational and physical therapists, teachers, and a wide range of professionals who describe themselves as "human service" or "social service" workers.

The articles in this edition of *Annual Editions: Social Welfare and Social Work* were chosen from a wide range of journals because of their ability to provide you with current and "real life" examples of issues that you are studying this semester. Your other textbooks and readings are probably presenting the material in a highly organized and comprehensive manner. Since formal textbooks are usually written by one or two authors, you can expect the same style of writing and structure throughout the entire book. There is certainly nothing wrong with that—in fact, that "sameness" is one of the most attractive features that textbooks offer both to instructors and to students. This book is different, and it is intended to be used in conjunction with any of the more formal textbooks that provide introductory material regarding social welfare and social work. It is hoped that this book will take up where the textbooks leave off in order to offer you some current facts, some different perspectives, and some fresh ideas on the material that you are studying.

Annual Editions: Social Welfare and Social Work 00/01 is divided into five distinct sections: (1) the history of social problems and social welfare; (2) current social problems: poverty and discrimination; (3) Social Security and welfare reform; (4) social services in family and child welfare; and, (5) social services in health, mental health and mental retardation, and corrections. Generally, these major sections should be consistent with the way your textbook divides the material for this course.

Also, in this edition we have included a *topic guide* and a list of selected *World Wide Web* sites that relate to areas of traditional concern to students and professionals in the field of social welfare. They should be very useful for locating interrelated articles and Web sites through our *Dushkin Online* support site at *http://www.dushkin.com/online/*.

If you have suggestions for articles or topics to be included in future editions of this series, please let us know. You are also invited to use the postage-paid *article rating form* provided on the last page of this book. Your ideas and input would be appreciated.

Vincent E. Faherty, DSW
Editor

A·N·N·U·A·L E·D·I·T·I·O·N·S

Social Welfare and Social Work   00/01

Second Edition

EDITOR

Vincent E. Faherty
University of Southern Maine

Vincent E. Faherty, DSW, is a professor of Social Work at the University of Southern Maine in Portland, Maine, where he teaches Introduction to Social Welfare and Research Methods courses. He received his MSW from Fordham University in 1970 and his DSW from the University of Utah in 1976. Dr. Faherty also earned an MBA degree in 1984 from the Internal Management Institute at the University of Geneva in Geneva, Switzerland. Prior to coming to the University of Southern Maine in 1988, Dr. Faherty taught at the University of Missouri–Columbia and at the University of Northern Iowa. He has published and presented papers in the areas of child welfare, social work administration, and social work education, and he has been the recipient of several federal and state grants in public child welfare. In 1984 he was the recipient of a Fulbright award and was in residency in Italy. Having served as Department Chairperson since 1988, Dr. Faherty returned to full-time teaching in the spring of 1998.

Dushkin/McGraw-Hill
Sluice Dock, Guilford, Connecticut 06437

Visit us on the Internet
http://www.dushkin.com/annualeditions/

Credits

1. History of Social Problems and Social Welfare
Unit photo—Family of Arkansas sharecroppers, © 1932, courtesy of the Library of Congress.
2. Current Social Problems: Poverty and Discrimination
Unit photo—© 1999 by Cleo Freelance Photography.
3. Social Security and Welfare Reform
Unit photo—United Nations photo by Michael Tzovaras.
4. Social Services in Family and Child Welfare
Unit photo—© 1999 by Cleo Freelance Photography.
5. Social Services in Health, Mental Health & Mental Retardation, and Corrections
Unit photo—© 1999 by PhotoDisc, Inc.

Copyright

Cataloging in Publication Data
Main entry under title: Annual Editions: Social welfare and social work. 2000/2001.
1. Social service—United States. 2. Social problems—United States I. Faherty, Vincent E., *comp.*
II. Title: Social welfare and social work.
ISBN 0–07–235074–1   361.3'973   ISSN 1520–3964

© 2000 by Dushkin/McGraw-Hill, Guilford, CT 06437, A Division of The McGraw-Hill Companies.

Second Edition

Cover image © 1999 PhotoDisc, Inc.

Printed in the United States of America   1234567890BAHBAH543210   Printed on Recycled Paper

Contents

UNIT 1

History of Social Problems and Social Welfare

Five articles in this section examine some of the history that social welfare has played in society.

The concepts in bold italics are developed in the article. For further expansion please refer to the Topic Guide and the Index.

UNIT 2

Current Social Problems: Poverty and Discrimination

Nine unit selections discuss the problems of poverty, discrimination, and affirmative action. The pressure these forces have placed on the welfare system have done a great deal to shape the delivery of social support.

vi

The concepts in bold italics are developed in the article. For further expansion please refer to the Topic Guide and the Index.

UNIT 3

Social Security and Welfare Reform

Twelve articles in this section
examine the current state of social
welfare and its effect on various
parts of the U.S. population.

The concepts in bold italics are developed in the article. For further expansion please refer to the Topic Guide and the Index.

UNIT 4

Social Services in Family and Child Welfare

Six selections in this section examine the impact that the social service system has on the citizens who benefit from this safety net.

The concepts in bold italics are developed in the article. For further expansion please refer to the Topic Guide and the Index.

ix

UNIT 5

Social Services in Health, Mental Health and Mental Retardation, and Corrections

Ten unit articles address the social system's involvement with many aspects of today's society.

The concepts in bold italics are developed in the article. For further expansion please refer to the Topic Guide and the Index.

The concepts in bold italics are developed in the article. For further expansion please refer to the Topic Guide and the Index.

Topic Guide

This topic guide suggests how the selections and World Wide Web sites found in the next section of this book relate to topics of traditional concern to students and professionals involved in the field of social welfare and social work. It is useful for locating interrelated articles and Web sites for reading and research. The guide is arranged alphabetically according to topic.

The relevant Web sites, which are numbered and annotated on pages 4 and 5, are easily identified by the Web icon (◎) under the topic articles. By linking the articles and the Web sites by topic, this ANNUAL EDITIONS reader becomes a powerful learning and research tool.

TOPIC AREA	TREATED IN	TOPIC AREA	TREATED IN
Abortion	34. Safe to Talk ◎ *11, 19, 30, 31*		14. Homosexuality across Cultures 24. Left Behind ◎ *8, 9, 10, 11, 12, 14, 17, 18, 21, 23, 24*
Adoption	*See* **Child Welfare**	**Drugs**	29. Youth at Risk 32. Beyond the Boundaries ◎ *27, 29, 32, 33, 34*
Affirmative Action	11. In Defense of Affirmative Action ◎ *11, 12, 13, 22*	**Economics**	16. Critique of the Case for Privatizing Social Security 17. Don't Go It Alone 21. Welfare's Fatal Attraction 22. Beyond the Welfare Clock 26. Now, The Hard Part of Welfare Reform 32. Beyond the Boundaries ◎ *14, 15, 16, 18, 20, 21, 22, 23, 24, 25*
Aged	36. Religion/Spirituality and Health among Elderly African Americans and Hispanics ◎ *28*
Alcohol	*See* **Drugs**
Cash Programs	18. Welfare Reform Legislation 19. Why Welfare Reform Is Working 20. Welfare to Work 23. Welfare and the "Third Way" 25. Welfare to Work: A Sequel 26. Now, the Hard Part of Welfare Reform ◎ *20, 21, 22, 23, 24, 25*	**Education**	29. Youth at Risk 30. Weapon-Carrying and Youth Violence ◎ *13, 14, 19, 31, 32, 34*
		Ethnic Diversity	*See* **Minorities**
Child Abuse & Neglect	*See* **Child Welfare**	**Family**	19. Why Welfare Reform Is Working 21. Welfare's Fatal Attraction 26. Now, the Hard Part of Welfare Reform 27. Q: Are Single-Parent Families a Major Cause of Social Dysfunction? 32. Beyond the Boundaries ◎ *11, 18, 19, 20, 21, 23, 24, 25*
Child Welfare	27. Q: Are Single-Parent Families a Major Cause of Social Dysfunction? 29. Youth at Risk 30. Weapon-Carrying and Youth Violence 32. Beyond the Boundaries ◎ *11, 14, 19, 20, 21, 22, 23, 24, 25, 26, 27*
		Health Care	15. Missed Opportunity 32. Beyond the Boundaries 36. Religion/Spirituality and Health among Elderly African Americans and Hispanics ◎ *27, 28, 29, 32, 33*
Civil Rights	*See* **Human Rights**
Crime	40. Pay per Plea 41. Unequal Justice 42. Private Prisons ◎ *13, 31, 32, 34*
		HIV/AIDS	32. Beyond the Boundaries ◎ *27, 29, 32*
Culture	14. Homosexuality across Cultures 24. Left Behind 36. Religion/Spirituality and Health among Elderly African Americans and Hispanics 39. Cultural Diversity and Mental Health ◎ *2, 12, 14, 17*	**Homosexuality**	14. Homosexuality across Cultures
		Human Rights	5. When the Laws Were Silent 9. Counting Race and Ethnicity 10. Of Race and Risk ◎ *5, 8, 10, 17, 30*
Day Care	*See* **Child Welfare**
Delinquency	*See* **Crime**	**Immigration**	2. Roslyn's Mutual Aid Lodges 7. D.C.'s Indentured Servants 24. Left Behind ◎ *7, 8, 9, 10*
Discrimination	5. When the Laws Were Silent 7. D.C.'s Indentured Servants 9. Counting Race and Ethnicity 12. Service Redlining 13. War between Men and Women	**International**	5. When the Laws Were Silent 7. D.C.'s Indentured Servants

AE: Social Welfare and Social Work

The following World Wide Web sites have been carefully researched and selected to support the articles found in this reader. If you are interested in learning more about specific topics found in this book, these Web sites are a good place to start. The sites are cross-referenced by number and appear in the topic guide on the previous two pages. Also, you can link to these Web sites through our DUSHKIN ONLINE support site at *http://www.dushkin.com/online/*.

The following sites were available at the time of publication. Visit our Web site—we update DUSHKIN ONLINE regularly to reflect any changes.

General Sources

1. Library of Congress
http://www.loc.gov
Examine this extensive Web site to learn about resource tools, library services/resources, exhibitions, and databases in many different fields related to social welfare and social work.

2. Social Science Information Gateway
http://sosig.ac.uk
This is an online catalogue of thousands of Internet resources relevant to social education and research. Every resource is selected and described by a librarian or subject specialist.

3. The Society for Applied Sociology
http://www.appliedsoc.org
Browse through this SAS site to explore and debate issues of interest in applied sociology, and to learn points to consider when thinking about a career in applied sociology.

History of Social Problems and Social Welfare

4. Geocities.com
http://www.geocities.com/Athens/4545/
This site addresses various topics related to President Franklin D. Roosevelt and his New Deal. While some of the materials are geared for younger students, the summaries of various related topics are useful for people of all ages. Links to the texts of 30 Fireside Chats are included.

5. Human Rights and Humanitarian Assistance
http://info.pitt.edu/~ian/resource/human.htm
Through this site, part of the World Wide Web Virtual Library, you can conduct research into a number of human-rights concerns around the world.

6. The Hunger Project
http://www.thp.org
Browse through this nonprofit organization's site to explore the ways in which it attempts to achieve its goal: the sustainable end to global hunger through leadership at all levels of society.

7. The International Center for Migration, Ethnicity, and Citizenship
http://www.newschool.edu/icmec/
The Center is engaged in scholarly research and public-policy analysis bearing on international migration, refugees, and the incorporation of newcomers into host countries. Explore this site for current news and research resources.

8. Latino On-Line
http://www.latinoonline.org
The purpose of this site is to empower Latinos. The site and its links address such topics of concern to Latinos as immigration, housing, employment, ethnicity, and income.

9. National Immigrant Forum
http://www.immigrationforum.org/index.htm
The pro-immigrant organization offers this page to examine the effects of immigration on the U.S. economy and society. Click on the links for discussion of underground economies, immigrant economies, race and ethnic relations, and other topics.

10. The National Network for Immigrant and Refugee Rights (NNIRR)
http://www.nnirr.org
Visit this site and its many links to explore the NNIRR, which serves as a forum to share information and analysis, to educate communities, and to develop plans of action on important immigrant and refugee issues.

11. University of Amsterdam/Sociology Department
http://www.pscw.uva.nl/sociosite/TOPICS/Women.html
Open this enormous sociology site to gain insights into a number of issues that affect both men and women. It provides links in affirmative action; gender, family, and children issues; social welfare and social work; and much more.

12. University of Pennsylvania/Library
http://www.library.upenn.edu/resources/subject/social/sociology/sociology.html
This site provides a number of indexes of culture and ethnic studies, population and demographics information, and statistical sources. Open the site at *http://www.library.upenn.edu/resources/social/socialwork/socialwork.html* for resources specifically applicable to social work.

13. Wacker Foundation/Crime Times
http://www.crime-times.org/titles.htm
This site lists research reviews and other information regarding causes of criminal, violent, and psychopathic behavior. It consists of many articles that are listed by title.

Current Social Problems: Poverty and Discrimination

14. American Studies Web
http://www.georgetown.edu/crossroads/asw/
This eclectic site provides links to a wealth of resources on the Internet that are related to prominent social issues, from gender issues, to education, to race and ethnicity.

15. Grass-Roots.Org
http://www.grass-roots.org
Various resources and models for grass-roots action and a summary and samples of Robin Garr's book, *Reinvesting in America*, are available on this site.

16. Marketplace of Political Ideas/University of Houston Library
http://info.lib.uh.edu/politics/markind.htm
Here is a valuable collection of links to campaign, conservative/liberal perspectives, and political-party sites. There are "General Political Sites," "Democratic Sites," "Republican Sites," "third-party" sites, and much more.

17. Patterns of Variability: The Concept of Race
http://www.as.ua.edu/ant/bindon/ant101/syllabus/race/race1.htm

This site provides a handy, at-a-glance reference to the prevailing concepts of race and the causes of human variability since ancient times.

18. Poverty in America Research Index
http://www.mindspring.com/~nexweb21/povindex.htm
At this site find definitions and tables related to poverty and poverty areas, answers to FAQs, facts about poverty, discussion of poverty myths vs. realities, and welfare reform.

19. The University of Minnesota's Children, Youth and Family Consortium
http://www.cyfc.umn.edu/Parenting/parentlink.html
Click on the various links for organizations and other resources related to divorce, single parenting, and stepfamilies.

Social Security and Welfare Reform

20. Economic Report of the President
http://www.library.nwu.edu/gpo/help/econr.html
This report includes current and anticipated trends in the United States and annual numerical goals concerning topics such as employment, real income, and federal budget outlays. The database notes employment objectives for significant groups of the labor force.

21. HandsNet on the Web
http://www.igc.apc.org/handsnet2/welfare.reform/index.html
This HandsNet site serves as a clearinghouse for information about current welfare-reform efforts at the national, state, and local levels. Updated frequently, there are fact sheets on legislation, and more.

22. National Center for Policy Analysis
http://www.ncpa.org
Through this site you can access an array of topics that are of major interest in the study of American politics and government from a sociological perspective, from regulatory policy, to affirmative action, to income.

23. Policy.com
http://www.policy.com
Visit this site of the "policy community" to examine major issues related to social welfare, welfare reform, social work, and many other topics. The site includes substantial resources for research, including a glossary.

24. The Urban Institute
http://www.urban.org/welfare/overview.htm
This organization offers lengthy discussions of issues related to welfare and its reform. This page starts with the assertion that "No one likes the current welfare system."

25. WWW Virtual Library: Demography & Population Studies
http://coombs.anu.edu.au/ResFacilities/DemographyPage.html
A definitive guide to demography and population studies is provided here, as well as global poverty links.

Social Services in Family and Child Welfare

26. The National Academy for Child Development
http://www.nacd.org
This international organization is dedicated to helping children and adults reach their full potential. Its home page presents links to various programs, research, and resources.

27. U.S. Department of Health and Human Services (HHS)
http://www.os.dhhs.gov
This home page leads to information about what HHS does, updates on news and public affairs, rundowns on policies and administration of various programs, and gateways to statistics, facts about Social Security, help for families and senior citizens, and so on.

28. U.S. National Institute on Aging (NIA)
http://www.nih.gov/nia/
The NIA, one of the institutes of the U.S. National Institutes of Health, presents this home page that leads to a variety of resources on health and social issues of the aging.

29. U.S. National Institutes of Health (NIH)
http://www.nih.gov
Consult this site for links to health information and scientific resources. Comprised of 24 separate institutes, centers, and divisions—including the Institute of Mental Health—the NIH is one of eight agencies of the Public Health Service.

Social Services in Health, Mental Health and Mental Retardation, and Corrections

30. Carnegie Mellon University/Center for the Advancement of Applied Ethics/Philosophy Department
http://caae.phil.cmu.edu/caae/home/Multimedia/Abortion/IAIA.htm
Reading the pages of this site will give you an introduction to important social perspectives, legal issues, medical facts, and philosophical arguments in the abortion debate.

31. Justice Information Center (JIC)
http://www.ncjrs.org
Provided by the National Criminal Justice Reference Service, this JIC site connects to information about corrections, courts, crime prevention, criminal justice, statistics, drugs, law enforcement, and victims, among other topics.

32. National Institute on Drug Abuse (NIDA)
http://165.112.78.61
Use this site index of the U.S. National Institute on Drug Abuse for access to NIDA publications and communications, for information on drugs of abuse and their effects on individuals, families, and society, and for links to related Web sites.

33. National Mental Health Association (NMHA)
http://www.nmha.org/index.html
The NMHA is a citizen volunteer advocacy organization that works to improve the mental health of all individuals. Consult this site for information on institutionalization.

34. University of Alaska at Anchorage/Justice Center
http://www.uaa.alaska.edu/just/just110/
At this site is an excellent outline of the causes of crime, including major theories, prepared by Professor Darryl Wood. It provides an introduction to crime, law, and the criminal justice system, police and policing, corrections, and more.

We highly recommend that you review our Web site for expanded information and our other product lines. We are continually updating and adding links to our Web site in order to offer you the most usable and useful information that will support and expand the value of your Annual Editions. You can reach us at: *http://www.dushkin.com/annualeditions/*.

www.dushkin.com/online/

Unit Selections

1. **Bethlem/Bedlam: Methods of Madness?** Roy Porter
2. **Roslyn's Mutual Aid Lodges: Between Assimilation and Cultural Continuity, 1887–1940,** Deborah Jo Burnham
3. **"Hallelujah, I'm a Bum,"** James R. Chiles
4. **Every Picture Tells a Story,** Daniel D. Huff
5. **When the Laws Were Silent,** William H. Rehnquist

Key Points to Consider

❖ As you review the history of social welfare, identify and describe trends or patterns regarding how society treats people in need.

❖ How have the various immigrant groups been socialized into American society over the years and up to the present day?

❖ Why do you think we tend to romanticize certain aspects of our nation's history, like the life of the hobo during the Great Depression years? Describe any other examples of this attempt to gloss over historical facts.

❖ Why do you think the ethnic Japanese were singled out for detention during World War II while ethnic Germans or ethnic Italians in the United States were not? What does this tell us about the patterns of racism and discrimination in our nation?

❖ Describe evidence of the continuing influence of the English Poor Laws of 1601 on the social welfare system in the United States.

 **Links**   **www.dushkin.com/online/**

These sites are annotated on pages 4 and 5.

The social welfare system of any society exists, basically, as a response to the variety of social problems that affect that society. In the United States, two of the most intractable social problems against which the social welfare system is aligned are poverty and discrimination. Obviously, these are not simple problems, for they contain within themselves several related problems, such as poor health, inferior education, crime, and so forth. The organized responses of society to these problems is rarely, if ever, completely effective, since so much depends on the available financial resources and on the values and attitudes that a society believes are important.

This first unit provides selective glimpses into the history of some of the problems and some of the societal responses. The articles are arranged in roughly chronological order and cover material within historical time frames from nineteenth century Europe up through the World War II era in the United States.

Mental illness has existed for centuries, but until rather recently, it was viewed in horror as possession by evil forces. Roy Porter, in "Bethlem/Bedlam: Methods of Madness?" chronicles the beginnings of inpatient care for the mentally ill in nineteenth century England.

In discussing nineteenth and twentieth century society in the United States, Deborah Jo Burnham offers a unique snapshot of one of the lesser-known, but highly effective, components of the social welfare system: the self-help, mutual aid organization. Burnham's article, "Roslyn's Mutual Aid Lodges: Between Assimilation and Cultural Continuity, 1887–1940," describes one such organization, in Roslyn, Washington, which can serve as a prototype for the thousands of similar associations that helped immigrants to adapt to and fit into American society.

The next two articles offer some vivid and poignant descriptions of what it was like to be poor, or homeless, or oppressed before and during the years of the Great Depression of the 1930s. James Chiles, in "Hallelujah, I'm a Bum," presents a gritty depiction of the life of the "hobo" during this period, while Daniel Huff recounts the invaluable service provided by the "social photographers" of the early twentieth century in "Every Picture Tells a Story."

Finally, William Rehnquist reminds you, in "When the Laws Were Silent," of one of our country's most recent and chilling examples of officially sponsored racial discrimination: the internment of ethnic Japanese living in the United States during World War II.

History of Social Problems and Social Welfare

An oasis of insanity: 'Bedlame' pictured (top left) near Bishopsgate in Aggas' 1563 'Plan of London'.

BETHLEM/BEDLAM

METHODS OF MADNESS?

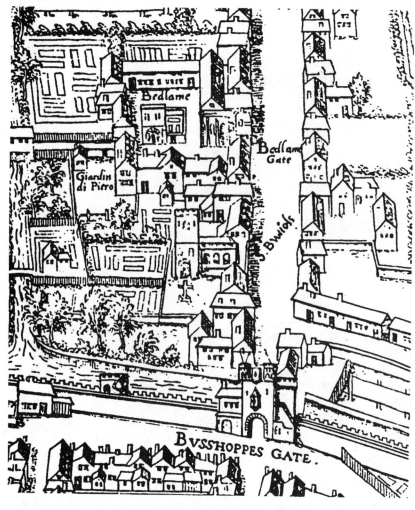

Illustration by Guildhall

'Bedlam' has become a by-word for a wild and crazy place, but what is the historical reality behind a distinguished London institution? **Roy Porter** offers an anniversary portrait.

Bethlem is 750 this year, possibly oldest psychiatric facility in Europe. Founded in 1247 by Simon fitzMary, an alderman and twice Sheriff of London, it arose out of the dealings of that first great multi-national, the Roman Catholic Church. The crusading movement needed friends across Europe, and its sponsors were active in establishing outlets to aid in fund-raising. The foundation of the priory of St Mary of Bethlehem was a contribution to that network, an outpost of the Bishop of Bethlehem. FitzMary had been involved in perhaps shady property deals and probably liked the idea of a pious donation to salve his conscience, not least as

his own name—fitzMary, son of Mary—was immortalised in the priory of St Mary.

The buildings arose on lands in the parish of St Botolph without Bishopsgate, just beyond London's wall. The priory was meant to pray for the souls of the founder, his friends, family and the king; to act as a base for those collecting for the Order of Bethlem; to provide hospitality for passing church ecclesiastics; and to offer sheltered accommodation for those who could pay for it or were recipients of charity. Initially there was no hint that Bethlem should be for the insane.

The first Bethlem lunatics are recorded in 1403, possibly transferred from an existing site at Charing Cross. Bethlem then

housed six deranged men: an inventory listed four pairs of manacles, eleven chains, six locks and two pairs of stocks (though these may not all have been for the lunatics). These links with lunacy, accidental at first, proved lasting. Early records note various donations for 'the sick and insane', and in 1436 a tailor gained exemption from watch and jury service by pleading that he was required to attend 'on the poor frenzied and demented creatures'. There was no obligation for the Master to be a medical man.

Bethlem became embroiled in the political wranglings between corporation and king, and between crown and papacy—at one stage the House was seized by Edward III as an alien priory. Such diplomatic manoeuverings formed a prelude to the Dissolution, when all such religious houses were grabbed by Henry VIII. The City of London petitioned for the continuation of certain hospitals; Bethlem was spared, along with St Bartholomew's and St Thomas', and on December 27th, 1546, the king granted that the said 'Mayor, commonalty, and citizens, and their successors should be masters, rulers and governors of the hospital, or house, called Bethlem'. By the mid-1570s, Bethlem was placed under joint governance with Bridewell, with a common president, treasurer and governing body, though not much is known of its day-to-day affairs.

Our knowledge of the patients is also bitty, and the darkness becomes visible only when something went wrong. In 1619 Dr Hilkiah Crooke, a Cambridge graduate and physician to James I, was appointed Master. Evidently ambitious, he urged that Bethlem should be made independent from Bridewell. But he proved negligent and grasping, and complaints were laid before the governors. In 1632 Charles I launched an investigation and, not for the last time, Bethlem won unwelcome exposure. Funds were flooding into the eponymous Crooke's pocket; accused of absenteeism, he countered that he had originally cured seventeen lunatics but had ceased because 'the governors of Bridewell doe refuse to pay him his Apothecaries bills'—a charge they denied. Crooke was dismissed; the scandal led to reorganisation; record-keeping improved and, from then on, light dawns.

Bethlem escaped the fire of 1666, but the rebuilt City highlighted the dilapidation of the old house. The governors acted, a site was chosen in Moorfields, and a palatial building in the French style was run up in 1675 at a cost of £17,000 to house just over a hundred patients. Reports on this new accommodation were mixed, but despite the madhouse stereotype foreign visitors routinely praised Bethlem's conditions as better than those back home.

Patients were accepted from all over the country. They would be brought on a Saturday to be viewed by the committee and the physician. A bond had to be made out, guaranteeing that he or she would be removed on discharge, and burial charges met if death ensued. A patient was standardly admitted for one year, then to be discharged as cured or

as incurable—though an incurables' wing was added from 1725.

Bethlem acquired physicians of some standing, including Edward Tyson, pioneer anatomist of the orang-utan. Despite modern assumptions about malpractices, Bethlem's committee, comprising City worthies and meeting weekly, performed quite conscientiously. If all too often it had to reprimand the porter or steward or to sack the basket-men and gallery-maids, it was at least energetic in hounding endemic abuses. Standards were set, and within the hospital orders were posted, including the following:

V. That no Person do give the Lunaticks Strong Drink . . .
VI. That such of the Lunaticks as are fit, be permitted to walk in the Yard till Dinnertime . . .
VII. That no Servant, or other Person whatsoever, shall take any Money given to the Lunaticks . . .
X. That some of the Committee go weekly to the said Hospital, to see the Provision weighed . . .

These rules were, of course, broken—a pamphlet published in 1818 by an ex-patient, Urbane Metcalfe, documented bullying and pilfering; but they contradict those historians who have claimed that Bethlem regarded the madmen as beasts, and accordingly the insane were chained and whipped. On the contrary, the committee forbade violence, insisting that patients were there for treatment not punishment.

Between 1728 and 1852, Bethlem's physicians all came from the Monro family—James, John, Thomas and Edward Thomas—their dynasty outlasting the Georges. Continuity was the keynote. They brought in a few therapeutic innovations—cold and hot baths for instance—but Bethlem's mainstays were the familiar purgatives and emetics, with a routine spring bloodletting, and manacles for the troublesome. Therapeutics got set in a rut—when quizzed in 1815 by a House of Commons committee, Thomas Monro finially declared he was still using his father's methods, since he knew none better. Aside from sporadic scandals, what most damaged Bethlem was its air of stagnation at a time when the founding of superior asylums like St Luke's and the York Retreat was sparking optimism and new treatments, notably moral therapy.

Some reforms occurred, however, including the ending of casual public vis-

iting in the 1770s; but the consequent secrecy perhaps created new abuses. When Bethlem was visited in 1814 by the philanthropist, Edward Wakefield, he was shocked on encountering one patient, James Norris:

A stout iron ring was riveted round his neck, from which a short chain passed through a ring made to slide upwards and downwards on an upright massive iron bar, more than six feet high, inserted into the wall. Round his body a strong iron bar about two inches wide was riveted; on each side of the bar was a circular projection; which being fashioned to and enclosing each of his arms, pinioned them close to his sides.

Norris had been thus immobilised for twelve years.

When Wakefield publicised this outrage, a committee of the governors was convened, who came up with the hot air which institutions have perfected:

Every attention has . . . been paid in the Hospital to the cleanliness, the health, and the comfort of the patients confined therein, and . . . every degree of indulgence consistent with the security of the patients and the safety of those employed has been observed.

Norris' contraption, they flannelled, 'appears to have been upon the whole rather a merciful and humane, than a rigorous and severe imposition'. To no avail. On April 28th, 1815, a Parliamentary committee was set up to investigate madhouses.

Evidence heard before the Commons committee revealed shocking, horrifying facts. 'We first proceeded to visit the women's galleries', testified Wakefield:

One of the side rooms contained about ten patients, each chained by one arm or leg to the wall, the chain allowing them merely to stand up by the bench or form fixed to the wall, or to sit down on it. The nakedness of each patient was covered by a blanket-gown only.

Monro sought to reassure the gentlemanly MPs by stating that chains and fetters were 'fit only for the pauper lunatics: if a gentleman was put in irons he would not like it'.

The hearings revealed comprehensive medical mismanagement. Monroe was a supine absentee. The surgeon, Bryan Crowther, lately deceased, had been an alcoholic—the apothecary, John Haslam stated that for ten years he had been 'generally insane and mostly drunk. He was so insane as to have a strait-waist-coat'. George Wallet, the steward, was cross-examined:

How often does Dr Monro attend?
I believe but seldom . . . I hear he has not been round the house but once these three months.

Thus the staff ratted on each other. The Committee carpeted Bethlem; Haslam was sacked, and Monro resigned—to be replaced by his son, Edward Thomas Monro.

This allowed some semblance of a new start, not least because Bethlem also gained a new building. The old Moorfields structure was by 1800 a crazy carcass with no wall still vertical—a veritable Hogarthian auto-satire. Rebuilding was begun in 1812 on a site in St George's Fields, Southwark, just south of the Thames, and completed by 1815—the dome was added in the 1840s. An important development was the addition of blocks for criminal lunatics. This followed from the successful insanity plea of James Hadfield, the would-be assassin of George III. An Act for the Safe Custody of Insane Persons Charged with Offences, hastily passed in 1800, required that such persons be kept in custody at His Majesty's Pleasure. The state paid up, and the Home Secretary assumed overall responsibility for the criminal lunatic department.

Minor reforms followed the move to Southwark and a second physician, the distinguished Alexander Morison, was recruited. But all was not well. In 1835 Bethlem's accountant absconded to the Continent, having defrauded the hospital of £10,066. 6s. 9d, and he was shortly followed by the treasurer who had filched a further £14,473. 12s. 7d. In 1851, a scandal blew up over the death of a patient, a fresh inquiry was opened, nasty cases came to light, a report condemned the hospital for ill-treatment, and concluded that the duties of the physicians and the resident apothecary 'are not fully performed'. Another official cover-up followed, but the upshot was that for the first time Bethlem was placed by Parlia-ment under the Lunacy Commissioners, on the same footing as other asylums. Morison retired, as did the last of the Monros, and Dr Charles Hood was appointed as a reformer.

The time was ripe for change. Thanks to the establishment of county asylums in 1845, which mopped up pauper luna-tics, Bethlem ceased to be a general na-tional charity asylum. And with the opening of Broadmoor in 1860, it also lost its criminally insane. Hood reorgan-ised. A head nurse was appointed re-spectively to the female and male sides, and abuses by the keepers were tackled. Civilising the institution was Hood's chief goal. He set bourgeois standards: patients should be neat, clean and polite, and the interior homelike. 'It is, there-fore, proposed to abolish *all* those *gloomy* appendages which characterised of old the external appearance of the madhouse, and which diffused *gloom* and despondency through the interior of the building', he informed the gover-nors. The trappings of restraint became less conspicuous, skittles and other games were introduced, and the pro-posal that:

Social parties shall take place on the female side, twice-a-week, at which rational amusements will be encour-aged—a practice which has been adopted with very great advantage at Hanwell, Colney Hatch and other large asylums.

The library was enlarged; pictures and canaries brightened the wards; fire-places, carpeting, wooden bedsteads, a new airing-ground with lawns, flower-beds and a bowling-green—all were added. Gone forever were the chains and manacles of Norris. As is evident, Hood was much influenced by the Tuke's moral therapy and John Conolly's desire that middle-class mad folks should be catered for.

In their 1876 report, the Lunacy Commissioners praised the embour-geoisement that Hood had accom-plished, the facilities, attendants, nurses, amusements and atmosphere. Reform had been belatedly put the hospital on a par with its peers; and from then on it acquired the image of a conventional superior psychiatric establishment, cul-minating in 1880 in the adoption of the name Bethlem *Royal* Hospital.

Bethlem thus laid the ghost of 'Bed-lam' to rest. Still independently gov-erned and financed—its estates were large and profitable—it had become, the *Daily Telegraph* noted in 1920, 're-moved largely from the public eye'—surely an unspeakable relief to the governors. Although an incurable list was maintained, the governors acquired a better class of patients—the percent-age of paying patients growing and chronics declining. With the 1930 Men-tal Treatment Act, the number of volun-tary patients increased. In 1900 they had formed 8 per cent of admissions, by 1947 this had risen to 83 per cent. With a 'recovery' rate of above 50 percent, Bethlem was regarded by the Board of Control as one of the nation's successes.

Visitors to early twentieth-century Bethlem came away with the impression that it was less like an asylum than 'a first-class hotel or a hydro'. Particular attention was paid to a good supply of pianos and trips to the Derby. Yet wards were still rigorously locked; padded cells were in regular use, and although mechanical restraint declined, the medi-cal chief, Dr. John Porter Phillips, a man of the old school, still found it necessary to have 'secure rooms'.

Southwark had grown seedy, the building aged, and from 1923 efforts were made to find a new home. A site at Monks Orchard, Beckenham, ten miles to the south-east, was bought, and the new hospital, on the villa plan, was opened by Queen Mary in July 1930. But there were costs as well as benefits to the move. The outpatients' depart-ment, founded as a subsidiary in 1918 for the treatment of early cases, had been closed, ostensibly because it was not attracting the right type of patient, and it never reopened. And Bethlem's new medical school languished as a re-sult of the move to the commuter belt.

Bethlem remained open throughout the Second World War, despite serious bomb damage in 1944; but immediately afterwards the proposed National Health Service presented a new threat to the hospital's independence—the possibility of being absorbed into the wider mental health system, something that was anathema to the governors. The only way to protect its autonomy lay in gain-ing recognition as a teaching-hospital, and this could be achieved only through a merger with the Maudsley, which had gained teaching-hospital status within the University of London. There was irony in this, for Bethlem had seen the

Maudsley as its chief rival ever since its opening in 1923.

The Maudlsey and London County Council were approached and a committee formed to discuss a merger. The governors were gloomy, but at the Maudlsey the ambitious professor of psychiatry, Aubrey Lewis, was eager, as Bethlem would bring a large dowry. It was recognised that the Maudsley would dominate the teaching side but anticipated that Bethlem should control the administration and continue to run the hospital's estates. This is what happened.

On the 'appointed day' in 1948, Bethlem severed its age-old link with Bridewell, opening a new era in the hospital's history as the Bethlem Royal and Maudsley Hospitals or the 'Joint Hospital', a striking marriage of convenience—in psychiatrist Denis Hill's words, 'Royal Bethlem was very old and very rich . . . the Maudsley was very young and very poor.' Since then Bethlem has been overshadowed by the Maudsley and its connected Institute of Psychiatry.

✵

After this flying visit to Bethlem let me raise certain issues posed by its history. First, the question of image. Why did Bethlem become 'Bedlam', a metaphor for madness? It was not primarily because of what actually went on inside—the daily grind was pretty uneventful. It was because of the mystique madness acquired as a religious and cultural symbol—the image of Folly, the court jester, moody melancholy, Crazy Jane, the mad genius, the holy fool. Being so long the only public receptacle for the insane, Bethlem became equated with madness itself. It might be a kingdom—Bethlem and Britannia confederated—or an academy of wise fools: such tropes of irony and inversion ran and ran. In Thomas Tyron's words around 1700:

> To speak truth, the World is but a great *Bedlam*, where those that are *more mad*, lock up those that are *less*.

If Bethlem had not existed, it would have had to be fantasised. Within the Elizabethan and Jacobean *theatrum*

mundi, the madhouse no less than the playhouse staged the dramas of being and seeming, truth and fiction, wisdom and folly. No fewer than five plays written between 1600 and 1625 contain 'Bedlam' scenes: Dekker's *The Honest Whore* and *Northward Ho;* Webster's *The Duchess of Malfi;* Fletcher's *The Pilgrim* and Middleton and Rowley's *The Changeling*. Stage lunatics provided spectacle, comic diversion and a morality play. Bethlem offered a peepshow, displaying the 'types' of lunatic, as in the Bedlam scene forming the finale of Hogarth's 'Rake's Progress' (1732).

What was crucial was that for centuries Bethlem was unique. And it spilled over onto the streets through the Abram-man or Tom o'Bedlam, blanket-covered, filthy and with elfin-knotted hair like Edgar in *King Lear*, wandering the lanes, haunted by the foul fiend Flibbertigibbet, or gaudily dressed and supposedly singing Bedlamite ballads that told mad tales and perpetuated the Bedlam myth.

The idea of Bedlam and its Poor Toms long flourished. A century later, in Jonathan Swift's time, Scribleran satire harped upon the proximity of Bedlam to Grub Street, while cartoonists gave Bethlem its visual twists. Teasing the Bedlamites eventually gave way to a late Georgian sentimentality that created a more tearful set of motifs. But it was only after the ending of public visiting put paid to the spectacle, and scores of other asylums sprang up, that the currency of 'Bedlam' became discounted.

This suggests a second concluding point. Bethlem achieved its high profile because it was unique and therefore a universal signifier. But it further attracted attention because it grew synonymous with scandal. As early as 1403, commissioners were inquiring into the evil deeds of Peter the Porter, charged with stealing thirty-three coverlets, thirty-four blankets, twenty-five sheets, six mattresses, five brass pans, one axe, one spade, three shovels, one pair of tongs, eight platters, eight wooden dishes, two trivets, four tubs and much more. He was the first in a gallery of Gothic sensations: Hilkiah Crooke, James Norris, James Tilly Matthews, Urban Metcalfe, the 1815 House of Commons committee, the criminal lunatics.

In truth, Bethlem probably had no more than its share of abuses; but scandal *did* play a key part, because Bedlam could always be made to serve, like the Inquisition, as the bogey image of the bad old days and ways: Gothic horror, the black myth, the antithesis of psychiatric progress. Bethlem's scandals were gold-dust to reformers. We hear a lot these days about the mad person as scapegoat, but Bethlem itself was stigmatised.

A further explanation of the Bethlem/Bedlam double lies in the institution's public role. The hospital was overseen by the crown, and on its governing board sat the Lord Mayor and other office-holders. By consequence, Bethlem had a virtual obligation to receive patients sent by both the crown and the city authorities, not least would-be regicides like Margaret Nicolson and James Hadfield. It admitted patients committed by the House of Lords and the Privy Council, by the Board of Green Cloth, the Sick and Wounded Seaman's Office and the War Office. Political undercurrents might be present. One Elizabethan journal described how on June 5th, 1595:

> A certain citizen, being a silkweaver, came to the Lord Mayor's house, using some hard speeches concerning him and in dispraise of his government. The Lord Mayor said he was mad and so committed him to Bedlam as a madman.

A series of notorious trouble-makers or politically embarrassing individuals were lodged at Bethlem. After Lady Eleanor Davies conducted her prophesying campaign against the court of Charles I, forecasting the deaths of his ministers, she was committed to what she called 'Bedlam's loathsome Prison'. Another was Richard Stafford, who, denouncing William III as a usurper, published numerous tracts as a Scribe of Jesus Christ, only to be declared insane and sent to Bethlem in November 1691. The politicisation of lunacy in Early Modern England has been under-estimated, and in that process Bethlem played a prime role.

But does this mean Michel Foucault was right? Should we see Bethlem as a key instrument of control, was it the English expression of 'that great confinement' which, Foucault claimed, shut up the mad, along with all other sorts of unreasonable and troublesome folks, in the classical age? Paris' Hôpital

Général, according to Foucault, turned the old madness that had a truth to tell into an unreason that was silenced; and folly, which had always mingled in society, into an Other which had to be sequestered from rational society. Did Bethlem do the same?

In truth it makes little sense to liken London's Bethlem to Paris' Hôpital Général—Bethlem was tiny, and it was a specialist institution not a general dump for society's flotsam and jetsam; and whereas Foucault's very point was the *exclusion* of the mad from the public, Early Modern Bethlem was a show. For Bethlem, the term 'Great Confinement' is hopelessly inappropriate: far better to call it the Great Exhibition.

What is it that makes institutions perpetuate themselves, assuming a life of their own? And how does that affect those associated with them? We need all sorts of histories. We need archeo-logical digs into institutions at particular moments, structural analyses of thin slices of time. But, as this survey hopes to have shown, institutional history studied over the longue durée also offers rewards of its own.

FOR FURTHER READING:

Patricia H. Allderidge, *Bethlem 1247–1997: A Pictorial Record* (Phillimore, 1996) and 'Bedlam: Fact or Fantasy?', in W. F. Tynum, Roy Porter and Michael Shepherd (eds), *The Anatomy of Madness*, vol. 2 (Tavistock Publications, 1985); T. Bowen, *An Historical Account of the Origin, Progress and Present State of Bethlem Hospital* (London, 1783); Michael Foucault, *La Folie et la Déraison: Histoire de la Folie à l'Age Classique* (Librairie Plon, 1961); abridged as *Madness and Civilisation: A History of Insanity in the Age of Reason*, translated by Richard Howard (Random House, 1965 and Tavistock Publications, 1967); Natsu Hattori, '"The Pleasure of Your Bedlam": The Theatre of Madness in the Renaissance', *History of Psychiatry*, vi (1995); A. Masters, *Bedlam* (Michael Joseph, 1972); E. G. O'Donoghue, *The Story of Bethlem Hospital from Its Foundation in 1247* (T. Fisher & Unwin, 1914); R. R. Reed, *Bedlam on the Jacobean Stage* (Harvard University Press, 1952); David Russell, *Scenes from Bedlam: A History of Caring for the Mentally Disordered at Bethlem Royal Hospital and the Maudlsey* (Baillière Tindall, 1997).

Roy Porter is Professor of the Social History of Medicine at the Wellcome Institute and co-author, with Jonathan Andrews, Asa Briggs, Penny Tucker and Keir Waddington, of The History of Bethlem, *published by Routledge [in 1997], from which this article has been adapted.*

Roslyn's lodges provided an opportunity for ethnic groups to retain ties to their ancestral cultures, while entering the culture of the United States. Two bands and members of several lodges parade through Roslyn in 1899.

Roslyn's Mutual Aid Lodges
Between Assimilation and Cultural Continuity, 1887–1940

Deborah Jo Burnham

THE 19th-century waves of immigrants into the United States involved one of the largest population transfers in history. The outcome, rather than resembling the American folk ideology of the "melting pot," has, at times, been more of a *bouillabaisse*, with each individual ethnic group floating in very hot soup and rubbing up against each other, often as not, in the wrong way.

Roslyn, a small mining town in north-central Washington State, was a microcosm for this period of American history. There, as well as in other parts of the nation, mutual aid societies (also called lodge, fraternal benefit organization, and national ethnic insurance association) played many roles in the blending of the American ethnic soup.

From *Journal of the West*, Vol. 36, No. 4, October 1997, pp. 13-19. © 1997 by Journal of the West, Inc. Reprinted by permission of Journal of the West, P.O. Box 1009, 1531 Yuma, Manhattan, KS 66505-1009, USA.

These societies filled the role of the missing extended family in times of joy and sorrow, afforded a place of socialization that recognized the individuals' cultural heritage, while still working toward the goal of assimilation (defined as " . . . the incorporation or integration of different ethnic and racial groups in the mainstream of society"[1]), and gave the immigrant financial security in very insecure circumstances. Despite the public disapproval of European communalist groups, the immigrants were forced to create economic institutions that would work for them as a group. This required adaptive strategies, since the normal routes were closed to them. Because the idea of fraternal orders was acceptable to white male Americans, the immigrants were able to adapt that social institution within an ethnic framework and use it at least to survive, if not to succeed.

Anthropology and sociology authorities disagree on how true assimilation should be accomplished to be successful. But they have proposed several theories, including the following:

- *Anglo-conformity*, which devaluates alien cultures to promote the dominant Anglo one;
- the *melting pot*, where cultural blending and intermarriage among different ethnic groups produce a new distinctive "American" group;
- and *cultural pluralism*, which argues that the preservation of distinct ethnic variation has been the true source of American cultural vitality. This paradigm calls for assimilation without the destruction of the

individual cultural differences, something not easily accomplished, according to Michael S. Bassis and his fellow authors. For many immigrants, including those of Roslyn, the various lodges performed the delicate balancing act between assimilation and cultural continuity.

One of the primary ways the lodges aided the immigrant was by teaching English. The previously established English-speaking community in Roslyn promoted only English-speaking immigrants. It was impossible to obtain employment in management without speaking English. Banks and other financial institutions would not approve loans to immigrants without naturalization papers, and these were not available without passing language tests. The English-speaking social groups, including those with a religious affiliation, limited their membership to people from similar backgrounds. The Italians assimilated rapidly, learning the language and rising into the ranks of business owners and into management positions. But the Balkan immigrants clung to their cultural heritage despite the hardships this brought them.

Very few marriages took place among the different ethnic groups. In this social situation the lodges played a role in resisting the *melting pot* method of assimilation. By arranging marriages through the various lodge affiliations, a cultural mix was avoided. Ironically, though, there were some instances where the parents would approve a marriage to a person of another country, or to a natural-born American, before allowing one between

Roslyn in 1889. Development was rapid after the railroad arrived. Virtually all of the original buildings were frame structures.

Local History Collection, Ellensburg Public Library

This school photograph reflects the multi-cultural nature of Roslyn's population in 1913. Mrs. Adelina Laudinsky identified the ancestry of some of the children in this photograph: Africa, Croatia, Czechoslovakia, Dalmatia, England, Finland, France, Germany, Ireland, Italy, Norway, Poland, Russia, Scotland, Sweden, Syria, and Wales.

Local History Collection, Ellensburg Public Library

children from neighboring European towns. Historical hatreds had followed the immigrants to the new world.

Roslyn's ethnic make-up was constantly in flux, due to new groups of miners coming and going with the rise and fall of the mines' fortunes. Each new wave of miners brought its own specific problems for them in identifying themselves as "American." Thus, Roslyn's society finally settled on the *cultural pluralism* pattern of assimilation. The sequence of lodge formations easily identifies the ethnic composition of new immigrants.

The earliest immigrants to work the mines were from the British Isles and Canada. They, along with American-born miners, chartered the first lodge, Welcome Lodge No. 30, Knights of Pythias, on November 15, 1887, two years before the territory became Washington State, and three years before Roslyn was incorporated. Its charter membership of 39 included names like Wright, McDonald, O'Brien, Lynch, Miller, Adams, Fleming, and Anderson. Three of the charter members, Thomas Fleming, Archie Anderson, and W. J. Thompson, were members of the original Northern Pacific Railroad team that had discovered the Roslyn coal field in 1886. While there were a few members of the lodge and the community that were not of British extraction, they were in the minority.

The Knights of Pythias had been founded in 1868, in Washington, D.C., as a fraternal order. Its goal was to form an all-white male society where the attributes of friendship, charity, and benevolence could be fostered by ritual behavior and through peer pressure. In 1877, the KOP added a fraternal insurance department, the Endowment Rank. The department acted as an insurance group so that by the time Roslyn's lodge was chartered,

the Welcome Lodge was able to pay sick and death benefits from the start, including funeral charges. Later, the lodge would offer distress aid for those areas suffering a calamity, such as an earthquake. The lodge also operated camps for poor children; promoted driving safety, blood banks, and homes for the aged members and their families; and awarded scholarships.

By 1888, Roslyn had grown to a community of 1,200. Two new groups had moved into the town: an influx of Italian immigrants and the trainload of black miners brought in to break the strike instigated by the Knights of Labor Union. This ethnic mix was reflected in the charter membership of the Independent Order of Odd Fellows lodge, instituted in nearby Ronald, January 16, 1888, which later consolidated with the Lake Valley Lodge No. 112 in Roslyn. While the charter application was signed by members with the names Ross, Nelson, Brigg, and Giles, the general membership included names such as Pessette, Bruno, Giovanini, Paletto, Zucea, and Musso.

The IOOF had originated in England, with evidence of its existence as early as 1745, under the name United Order of Odd Fellows. The first groups met at local taverns, with this "odd man or that" joining in an evening of conviviality, hence the name. Later, in 1813, those members who were unhappy with the drunkenness associated with the organization broke away under the name Independent Order of Odd Fellows to become a temperance lodge, although not all locals followed this rule. The IOOF came to America in the late 1810s, the first American lodge to offer its members financial benevolencies such as relief to the sick, distressed, and orphans, and burial of members and families. Between 1830 and 1895, the IOOF initiated over two million members,[2] a striking number considering that the total U.S. population in those years fluctuated around 50 million.[3] The Roslyn lodge still maintains its cemetery for members and families, and over the years it has been involved in many community service projects including the Red Cross and polio drives.

In the 1800s, several black lodges existed in the United States, including the blacks-only Masonic Temple, founded under the name of Prince Hall, and the Grand United Order of the Odd Fellows. While there are no black lodges recorded in Roslyn, there are indications of lodge activity to be found in Mt. Olivet, the black cemetery. The new entry sign states that Mt. Olivet, started in 1888, is the final resting place for 300 black-American miners. It goes on to relate that James Shepperson founded the first Free Mason lodge in Roslyn, Knights of Tabor, and two black-American churches. According to the white-produced histories of Roslyn, James Shepperson merely owned "Big Jim's Colored Club." There is some evidence to suggest that the "club" was cover for a black Masonic lodge. Considering the hard feelings between the white population and the black miners, who had been brought in to break one of several strikes, it is viable to assume that the blacks might have kept this information to themselves to avoid being considered "uppity," particularly since this charge was usually followed by racial violence.

On July 5, 1986, Shepperson's grave was covered with a full-length plaque engraved with the insignia of the Masonic Temple, which reads

In Memory of
P.G.M. [Past Grand Master] James E. Shepperson
Dedicated this 5th day of July 1986
M. W. Prince Hall Grand Lodge, Washington.

Another headstone is decorated with two converging roads that meet over three interlocking rings with the initials F, T, and L inscribed, one letter inside each. This is the symbol of the Odd Fellows Organization, the rings and initials representing the three degrees of the fraternity, Friendship, Love, and Truth. Only a member of the highest degree may use this completed symbol on his headstone.

While the black miners were not immigrants per se, they were considered "foreigners" by the other townspeople. A photograph from the 1920s shows a class that is supposed to represent different nationalities. The one black child, Hanna Green, is referred to as "African." Also, a Washington State publication of the period refers to the blacks as a "foreign race." It appears that they used the lodges in a manner similar to that of the immigrants—for survival within a hostile environment.

As many as 45 lodges existed at one time in Roslyn, some over a 50- to 75-year period.[4] The majority of these groups were, like the Masons and the Odd Fellows, local affiliations of national and international mutual benefit societies. The two main exceptions appear to be the Italian lodges, *Societá Silvio Pellico* and the *Cacciatori D'Africa* (Hunter of Africa). While these may have been associated with other lodges, there is nothing in any of the fraternal organization references or directories that indicates this was the case, However, this was not an unusual occurrence within Italian communities. Cleveland, Ohio, had 35 different Italian mutual benefit lodges at the turn of the century. The major factor in this fragmentation was the provincialism of Italian immigrant groups. National identity was not of paramount importance to them; rather they identified with smaller regional or village affiliations, often restricting membership to applicants from specific towns.

The lodges represented a middle ground, where members could meet to interpret the new country, or in the case of the black families, the white culture, while allowing them to maintain active ties with their own cultural or ethnic backgrounds. Pragmatically, they also acted as insurance companies by providing sickness and death benefits. They also gave the members a place to acquire capital, something difficult to do at a regular financial institution without the benefit of naturalization papers. In lodges, members could borrow cash against their policy, using its value as collateral. Even had the banks and loan companies been willing to finance them, they would not have trusted a firm with whom they could not converse in their own language. They had heard horror stories of immigrants in financial distress being pressed into making their mark on pieces of paper that essentially enslaved them.

The next wave of immigration was slow but steady, and occurred between the late 1880s and early 1910s. These immigrants came from the Balkan lands that would make up Yugoslavia. Most were uneducated, unskilled, and socially insular. Like the Italians before them, these immigrants were caught up in village loyalties, but there were also ethnic and religious disputes among the Croats, Slavs, Slovenes, Serbs, Protestants, and Muslims, as well as the various Catholic denominations, Roman, Greek Orthodox and Russian Orthodox, each with its own prejudices and hatreds.

The various Catholic churches played a major role in the Slavic and Italian immigrants' lives. Sometimes they worked *with* the lodges, such as when the various ones held religious parades to the church to have their native and American flags blessed, or as they took their food to the church for the traditional Easter blessing. At other times, they competed for the scarce immigrant dollar. Many of the immigrant churches were built with funds raised through the lodges. For several years the Croats, Serbs, and Slavs all worshipped at the same church, but when the Croats began to feel that the Serbs were trying to take over, they broke away, instituted their own church, and sent for a Croatian-speaking priest. He never came.[5]

There were several Balkan lodges; some existed for only a short time. Several went through name changes along with their national lodge organizations, so that the records seem to show several different lodges, but merely reflect those modifications. Others lost too many members to keep their local going, so they merged with another in similar straits. The original Dr. David Starcevich Lodge became a place of contention, and so it was split into two independent lodges, #1 and #2.[6] The histories of many of the fraternal groups cannot be traced because their records have been lost or destroyed in the various fires that cursed Roslyn. However, histories can be patched together, from a variety of sources, for the following lodges.

The Roslyn lodge of the Fraternal Union of St. Barbara #39, an affiliate of the American Fraternal Union, was organized in 1902 by Slavic émigrés Anton Janacek, Lucas Motar, and John Gresnik, who named it for a legendary Greek Orthodox martyr.[7] There were 25 charter members, mostly Croatian, with some Slovenes taking part. At one time there were over 300 Slavs active in this lodge, but when Frank Bole died in 1955, he was the only Slav left on the roster. Cross-referencing the membership roster with the 1920 U.S. census we learn that several of the members listed in the census as Austrian were in reality of Serbian, Slovakian, or Croatian ethnicity.[8] Before 1918, Serbia was associated with the Austro-Hungarian Empire.

The St. Barbara lodge was organized nationally in 1898 under the name South Slavonic Catholic Union. Its principal activity was selling fraternal insurance, although as it grew, the Union branched out into orphan and dread-disease benefits, old-age assistance, and disaster relief. Also involved in the immigrants' social life, the Union sponsored baseball teams and other youth-oriented activities. Charitable work, abolitionist activities, and the fight against disease, hunger, and illiteracy were among its contributions to the greater community.

The start of World War II was a time of great stress, particularly for the Balkan immigrants. There was a growing antagonism toward "foreigners" in the United States, and various members of the ethnic community, including many Germans, Anglicized their names. Shortly after the Yugoslavian government adhered to the Tripartite Pact of the Axis Powers in 1941, Balkan immigrants became targets for ethnic harassment. As a consequence, in a paroxysm of American nationalism, the various lodges held patriotic parades and promoted the buying of war bonds by their membership. It was at this time that the South Slavonic Catholic Union became the American Fraternal Union.

While most of the lodges sponsored social activities that emphasized ethnic and cultural relationships, at the same time, they offered instruction on American naturalization in both English and the immigrants' native tongues. The lodges were the principal owners and caretakers of the various fraternal graveyards in Roslyn, en-

suring the lodge member a place of burial without impoverishing his family. In some cases, the lodge members carried out the funeral ceremonies and rituals traditional to their native culture, which was a comfort to a grieving family. Lodge members would prepare the grave while the body lay in state at the family home, until 1897, when Washington state law required a licensed undertaker care for the remains.[9] Fraternal members still prepared the graves and escorted the body to the undertaker, reversing their lodge badges as a sign of respect and mourning. The lodge would then conduct a funeral procession through town and sponsor a funeral service in the native language. Death and injury benefits were paid to the worker or his family, providing the funds needed to survive until other arrangements could be made.

The Sokol Lodge was organized in 1914 by a Mr. Sabich, who came to Ronald that year. It began as the Croatian Lodge, but soon changed its name to reflect its interest in supporting physical education in the form of gymnastic teams or *sokols*. The Yugoslavian children were unfamiliar with American sports such as football and baseball, and were thus often left out. The lodge organized a gymnastic team consisting of 23 Yugoslavian youths. This sokol toured the Pacific Coast performing routines to traditional Balkan music. During World War I, this team, along with the rest of the lodge, organized fundraisers to help send medical supplies and other necessities to the "old country."[10]

The Improved Order of the Red Men Lodge, organized in July 1898, had primarily British, American, and Italian members. Their costume consisted of "Indian" regalia, including a feather headdress, duck-skin suits, and pipes. The lodge claimed to be a continuation of the pre-Revolutionary War–America fraternities, the Sons of Liberty and Sons of Tamina. The Red Men's avowed purpose was to preserve American traditions and provide sickness, accident, and death benefits. Interestingly, until 1974 neither Native Americans nor Amerindians (anthropological term short for American Indian) could join. In 1976, the lodge began supporting the American Indian Development program, which is designed to help Native American children with health care and education. However, the Roslyn lodge had disbanded in 1950.

Several other Roslyn fraternal organizations also supported cemeteries and disaster benefits. Ethnic societies included the Dr. David Starcevich lodges, #1 and #2, the National Croatian Society, the Ancient Order of Foresters (Great Britain), a Serbian mutual aid society, the United Ancient Order of Druids (international British, which the Italians took over), the Lithuanian Alliance of America, a Slavonian lodge, and a Polish union. Non-ethnic groups that offered death and burial benefits included the Veterans of Foreign Wars, Moose, and Eagles.

Besides providing insurance, the national fraternal orders assisted ethnic continuity by acting as an informal matrimonial service. Lodge contacts replaced the familial involvement in arranging marriages. Most of the immi-

Membership badges from Roslyn lodges.

grants had come from large, interactive families in the old country, and the lodge members often took the place of blood kin in the celebration of weddings, anniversaries, birthdays, and other events of significance.

While there were no defined ethnic neighborhoods in Roslyn, some immigrants never moved out of their native circles. Instead of forming ethnic communities and living "among their own kind," they settled for socializing strictly within their own ethnic organizations.

The second generation, while retaining ties to its ethnic heritage, felt pressure to conform to American standards and practices. Experiencing cultural conflicts between what they were taught in the American education system and what they learned at home, they usually accepted the American set of norms and values. *Norms* are those explicit or implicit standards or principles accepted by the society as appropriate behavior; *values* are conceptions of the desirable principles that guide human choice. Each makes up what today's politically correct ideology calls "moral standards." Thus, they gained admission into the major businesses and professions.

While the first generation of Roslyn's immigrants had worked side by side with the original townspeople, they very rarely rose to the supervisory level in a company. It took the second generation to attain this.

A few first-generation and most of the second-generation German and Italian Roslynites moved into the private "American" clubs and friendship cliques, which led to management and business opportunities. However, they also remained active within their own ethnic circles. For the Balkan immigrants, it took until the third generation to fully assimilate into both the public and private arenas.

When discussing these cultural processes, it would be wise to remember that Roslyn is not the norm. Roslyn's high population of recognizable ethnic groups was unusual enough to engender government comment. While a 1920 pamphlet from the State of Washington Bureau of Statistics and Immigration for investors, homebuilders, and travelers, praises Kittitas, Ellensburg, Ronald, Cle Elum, and Thorp for their financial possibilities and wonderful facilities, it also takes note of Roslyn's cultural pluralism.

> Altitude 2,218 feet. Population 1910 census, 3,500. Located on the Roslyn branch of the Northern Pacific railway, 29 miles northwest of Ellensburg. The city is supported almost entirely by coal mining and the population consists principally of foreign races attracted by that enterprise. They include Austrians, Hungarians, Italians, Germans, Russians, Poles, Danes, Scandinavians and Negroes. Over 500,000 tons are taken yearly from two mines beneath the city itself and over 700,000 tons mined at neighboring towns are shipped through. The city is provided with two grade schools, a four year high school, weekly newspaper and a public library.[11]

Roslyn continued to be a town of immigrants. The school census of 1922–1923 showed the percentages of nationalities that were represented: Croatians 23%, Americans 11%, English 11%, Austrians 10%, Slavs 7%, Italians 7%, Finnish 4%, Swedes 2%, Lithuanians, Russians, Scots, Polish 1% each, and non-specific ethnic groups, 21%.

During research on the various lodges as a whole, one thing became clearer: While social contacts, ethnic identification, and cultural activities were major factors in the part lodges played in the immigrant life, economics was the greatest influence on the consistency of lodge participation. In times of economic trouble, when buying coal for the stove and food for the table became difficult, people still found the money for lodge dues, despite these hardships. They would not have done this for ethnic or social participation alone. The lack of alternate economic security in the face of probable disaster necessitated this behavior, especially since mining was such a dangerous occupation, with death or injury an everyday possibility.

Mary Osmonovich Andler, speaking about her reluctance to cancel her lodge insurance, made this economic point very clear. She stated that she would not get as much out of the policy as had been put in, but she remembered how much her parents scraped to pay that premium each month. No matter what had to be left out of the budget, that premium was always first on the list. Her parents could not imagine a time when Mary would not need the security of that policy. Mary felt that to cancel it now (1994) would be to ignore her parents' sacrifices.[12]

Mutual aid fraternities offered the immigrant a collective strategy, which was acceptable within the Anglo-American culture, for surviving within, and yet outside of, a dominant culture rife with exclusionary social and financial practices. At the same time, the lodges facilitated the immigrant acculturation process and even helped toward naturalization. They were a place where both the alien and naturalized citizen could enjoy ethnic and American social practices. They provided financial security to a group ignored by regular financial organizations, and they served as the agent of change in the evolution needed—between where the immigrant came from and where he hoped to go. For the immigrant, the lodges were a place where he felt at home, even in a strange, often hostile land.

NOTES

1. Michael S. Bassis, Richard J. Gelles, and Ann Levine, *Sociology: An Introduction* (New York: Random House, 1988), 312.
2. Albert Stevens, *The Cyclopedia [sic] of Fraternities: A Compilation of Existing Authentic Information and the Results of Original Investigation as to the Origin, Derivation, Founders, Development Aims, Emblems, Character and Personnel of More than Six Hundred Secret Societies in the United States* (New York; E. B. Treat and Co., 1907), 247–262.
3. Edith Abbot, *Historical Aspects of the Immigration Problem* (New York: Arno Press and *The New York Times*, 1969), 401–405.
4. *Roslyn Cemeteries* (Roslyn, WA: Roslyn Historical Society, n.d.), brochure in the Roslyn Museum.
5. Oral interview by Deborah Jo Burnham with Mary Andler, May 19, 1994.
6. Anne Chenoweth, "Roslyn Cemetery" (unpublished manuscript for the Central Washington University Anthropology Department, Ellensburg. WA, Dec. 1978), 25–26.
7. *Spawn of Coal Dust: History of Roslyn 1886–1955* (Roslyn, WA: Operation Uplift, 1955). 49–52.
8. *Ibid.*, 64.
9. Chenoweth, "Roslyn Cemetery," 39.
10. Chenoweth, "Roslyn Cemetery." 25–26; *Spawn of Coal Dust*, 50–78; and the individual information signs at the Roslyn Cemetery, provided by each lodge or organization.
11. Harry F. Giles, Deputy Commissioner, State of Washington, Dept. of State, J. Grant Hinkle, Secretary of State, Bureau of Statistics and Immigration, eds., *The Advantages and Opportunities of the State of Washington for Homebuilders, Investors and Travelers* (Olympia: Frank M. Lamborn, Public Printer, 1920), 102.
12. Andler interview, April 26, 1994.

ADDITIONAL SOURCES

Because these groups were part of the larger national society, I have used several manuals, books, and articles dealing with the goals and historical workings of the national lodges.

Barton, Josef J., *Peasants and Strangers: Italians, Rumanians, and Slovaks in an American City, 1890–1950* (Cambridge, MA: Harvard University Press, 1975), 75–80.

Bodnar, John, *Immigration and Industrialization: Ethnicity in an American Mill Town, 1870–1940* (Pittsburgh, PA: University of Pittsburgh Press, 1977), *passim*.

Gordon, M. M., *Assimilation in American Life: The Role of Race, Religion, and National Origins* (New York: Oxford, 1964), 113–125.

Greenbaum, Susan D., "A Comparison of African American and Euro-American Mutual Aid Societies in 19th Century America," *The Journal of Ethnic Studies*, 19, 3 (Fall 1991): 107.

Roslyn Cemetery Historical Society Reader Board. This board was created by the Roslyn Historical Society in a manner similar to a museum exhibit and contains several photographs of Roslyn life. Under each photograph is a narrative caption written from material found on the back of the photos and other sources.

Schmidt, Alvin J., *Fraternal Organizations: The Greenwood Encyclopedia of American Institutions*, vol. 3 (Westport. CT: Greenwood Press, 1980), 183–186.

Shideler, John C., *Coal Towns in the Cascades: A Centennial History of Roslyn and Cle Elum, Washington* (Spokane, WA: Melior Publications, 1986), *passim*.

Stoianovich, Traian, "Yugoslavia," in *Collier's Encyclopedia*, 1972 ed.

Deborah Jo Burnham studied American history at Central Washington University in Ellensburg. During this time, she began her research on the community of Roslyn. She resides with her husband in the small agricultural town of Ephrata, Washington. In her spare time, she is now studying European history.

"Hallelujah, I'm a Bum"

They took to the road in jobless thousands
to escape failure, seek work—or find a kind of freedom.

BY JAMES R. CHILES

BOB LOGAN'S JOB WAS TO FURROW HIS family's cotton fields. One day Logan, 16 years old and with nothing but cotton and more cotton in sight, obeyed an impulse and jumped into an empty boxcar on a train passing through his Texas town. On the floor of the car, he found a piece of board, and cut this message into it: "Bob Logan Gone West." As the train got under way, he tossed the board out at a road crossing in the hope that someone would see it and tell his mother.

It was fitting: a message in a metaphorical bottle, from a man gone adrift. This was the spring of 1933 and all across the country, desperate young men were reaching for the grab irons of boxcars. For a time during the Great Depression, more than a million men entered the world of the American hobo. There were thousands of boys, and some girls and women, too. They flipped freights, rode the rods, decked rattlers and ditched bulls.

Their dusty epic forms the final chapter to the story of that peculiarly American figure, the rail-hopping hobo. He's part documented history, part legend, part clown. Americans prize success, so it might be tempting to write all hoboes off as losers who couldn't find a place in the national dream, simply another addition in the lexicon of America's outcasts, whom we know as bums and drifters, as vagrants and the homeless. Yet the ranks of hoboes and of rail-riding laborers during the lean years included such future notables as novelist Louis L'Amour,

TV host Art Linkletter, oil billionaire H. L. Hunt, journalist Eric Sevareid and Supreme Court Justice William O. Douglas, to name a few. Whether celebrities or among the forgotten, oldtime hoboes deserve our thanks as the men (and women) who cut the wheat in Nebraska and Kansas, raised railroad beds in Utah, felled timber in Washington, worked as roughnecks in Texas oil fields, picked fruit in California, built the raw towns, and moved on. They did it for very little pay, at great danger to themselves and for virtually no recognition.

Much of the information that comes down to us about hoboes in casual reading is a caricature of the good and the bad, like the twin masks of joy and sorrow that symbolize the theater. In Preston Sturges' classic 1941 film *Sullivan's Travels,* a lightweight film director played by Joel McCrea suffers a brief but brutal experience as a hobo. Once again warm, safe and fed, he wistfully tells those gathered around him why laughter is so important: "Did you know that's all some people have?" And in fact it is the shoesole-flapping, dog-evading hobo that we laugh at, as portrayed in the old film comedies.

I'll show you the bees in the
cigarette trees, And the soda
water fountain
And the lemonade springs where the
blue bird sings
In the Big Rock Candy Mountains.

DOROTHEA LANGE/LIBRARY OF CONGRESS

In 1939 Dorothea Lange photographed two hoboes waiting for a ride in California.

While I don't rank myself as an ex-hobo, I did briefly ride the freights in Montana and western Canada in 1976 to see what it was like, and what I saw persuaded me out of many of these stereotypes. I was a 21-year-old, traveling with my two brothers and three friends. We encountered hoboes along the way who called themselves "fruit bums," after the harvests they worked. We saw the danger of the life; we huddled out of the mountain wind that whipped through the big doors and we gagged in a blue haze of diesel fumes trapped inside long tunnels. We enjoyed the panoramic view. Such travel is grimy; each day on the road left us coated with a fine brown dust from the boxcar floors, as if we had been bronzed en route. Rail riding is not one of my finest achievements—it's against the law and I don't endorse it to my children—but those days made vivid memories.

Even with a little firsthand experience, I still had to jettison plenty of wrong notions during my months of digging into what it was really like to take the hobo road during the darkest years of the 1930s. Depression-era men like Bob Logan spent months and even years on the road, looking not for the Big Rock Candy Mountains but for just a decent job that would get them out of the jungle. Far from dissolute and depraved, these hoboes relied on courage and unimaginable fortitude to face danger, hardship and humiliation. Most were just trying to get along and get by in the grim backdrop of a depressed economy. They used their wits to find work, stay one step ahead of the law and fight off the constant stabs of hunger.

The image of the hobo as a happy go-lucky, fancy-free bum emerged long after hoboes first hit the rails. Rail-borne transient men first appeared on the American scene in the 1870s (SMITHSONIAN, November 1977) They were foot-loose veterans of the Civil War, and they scratched a bare existence out of the short-term labor market of the West. They also scared the breath out of many law-abiding citizens. It was all made possible by the growth of the railroads; by 1870, some 53,000 miles of track laced across the nation. This grew to 200,000 miles in 1890, and hit 230,000 miles by 1930. The railroads hauled cattle to Chicago, wheat to Eastern bakers and cereal makers, coal to feed the furnaces of Michigan's mighty River Rouge auto plant, and crude out of the East Texas oil patch.

Hoboes took to the rails the way itinerant raftsmen took to the rivers before the Civil War and hitchhikers would take to the highways after World War II. The origin of the term "hobo" remains obscure and disputed; some say it's a corruption of *homo bonus,* Latin for good man. If so, most Americans had little tolerance of these good men, who looked to be able-bodied beggars living off the fat of the land. As the hobo ranks doubled and doubled again, when the economic panics of 1873 and 1893 threw hundreds of thousands out of regular jobs, the public's fear of these nameless, hollow-eyed men grew in proportion. And rightly so, as many gave up on finding work, becoming instead tramps and bums and yeggs, that is, those who traveled, those who didn't and those who preyed on the honest traveling laborers. A dean of the Yale Law School dismissed them all as "depraved savages"; short stories painted these men as symbols of primitive evil. Popular magazines warned that demented vagrants were derailing trains and commandeering locomotives. Yet many people did help them. The rural communities of America, as elsewhere, had relied on the itinerant for generations to bring much-needed skills, news and gossip, and extra hands during harvest time. A familiar sight was the mushfakir, a hobo who repaired umbrellas. But, instead of a handful of vagrants passing through, their numbers kept growing. Little towns could be overrun when freight trains pulled in.

Public alarm hit a peak about 1914 as Europe descended into world war. Press reports portrayed the Industrial Workers of the World as a rebellion in the making, a subversive tide that threatened cherished American freedoms. IWW members, or Wobblies, often rode the rails in a campaign to organize and recruit hoboes and downtrodden workingmen into their dream of the One Big Union. The *Little Red Song Book,* filled with Wobbly labor songs, included the hobo favorite, "Hallelujah, I'm a Bum," which became something of an IWW anthem. Its decidedly anti-work lyrics did little to help the Wobblies' cause. The IWW faded, a casualty of over-

Though Lange's hoboes were mostly "itinerant single men," she met this family traveling by freight train to find work in Yakima, Washington.

patriotic zeal that came about after the United States got involved in the war.

By the 1920s the scary image was changing. The public had learned that some pretty famous literary folk had ridden the freights–like Jack London and Carl Sandburg, for instance–and they turned out all right. Now the message coming across was that hoboes weren't all that bad; and neither was life on the open road. Maybe they were just grown-up Huck Finns, defiantly independent. The upgraded image got help from Charlie Chaplin as the Little Tramp and from master clown Emmett Kelly. Kelly created Weary Willie, a figure who, with his sad face, ratty clothing and melancholy worldview, appeared in the Ringling Brothers circus and in cartoons, films, on Broadway and, later, television. Hoboes had newspaper comics, tuneful ballads, vaudeville skits and movie melodramas on their side. The New Hobo was becoming a romantic rogue, unchained and unkempt. "Freedom is the one God I worship," hobo poet Harry Kemp wrote. Brutes no longer, now they were rebelling against fate, if haplessly.

Do you know how a hobo feels?
Life is a series of dirty deals.
This is the song of the wheels.

This freedom came at a cost. Rather than spending their days alternating between filched-pie feeds and harum-scarum misadventures with railroad cops, real hoboes of the Depression spent long days searching and begging for scraps of food and scraps of work made doubly scarce by the fact that many thousands of others were out scouring for the same thing. Hoboes sometimes went days without food.

A good job might offer a week of 12-hour days of hard labor, at a wage of one or two dollars a day, or might pay nothing more than a place in a bug-ridden bunkhouse and meals boiled out of spoiled food. Bob Logan of Texas spent his months on the road digging potatoes in Idaho, harvesting Dakota grain and picking fruit in New Mexico. A couple of days' work, then more days looking for the next wage; that was as much as hoboes could expect.

While the drifting and desperate army of Depression-era young men may have looked like so much slag off the melting pot, the appearance was deceptive. Actually, they were more promising than unemployed men of similar age back at home. Gen. Pelham Glassford, chief of police in the District of Columbia in 1932 when the Bonus Marchers arrived to pressure Herbert Hoover for their long-awaited WWI bonuses, reported to Congress the next year that young men who were idling back in their hometowns lacked the "intelligence, resourcefulness, and the spirit of the boys on the road."

Before the Depression, the average hobo was an older man who didn't want permanent employment; but with the upheaval, these old pros were far outnumbered by young men with no prospects, and others who had held good jobs but lost them. The old hoboes adapted by teaching the newcomers about survival on the road. These young men fell into a subculture, fashioned by several generations of rail-hopping hoboes, replete with its own lingo, poetry, code of ethics and honor. The hub of hobo life was the camps, or "jungles," which had much in common wherever they were located. Thomas Minehan, a sociologist at the University of Minnesota who visited many hobo camps while studying juvenile transients of the Depression, said they usually were on the sunny sides of hills, near a source of water, and within walking distance of switchyards and coal bunkers. Trees and brush offered shelter from cold winds. A town dump for scavenging made the happy picture complete.

Hoboes living in jungles didn't offer their real names and didn't ask yours; it was enough to travel under monikers such as Toledo Red, Boxcar Bertha or Fry Pan Jack. An unspoken set of rules governed hobo gatherings. The pots were to be left clean; no hobo was to rob a fellow hobo in camp. In the same way that guerrillas must cultivate the generosity of the locals, hoboes lived under a powerful code outside the jungle as well, to avoid angering the townspeople who were the source of odd jobs and handouts. Thievery was to be avoided or at least kept to a minimum: perhaps a pie lifted here and there, some

Falling asleep, even for a moment, could—and often did—mean an instant and gruesome death.

vegetables snitched from a garden, or a clean shirt hurriedly unclipped from a clothesline. But breaking into a house or threatening the local people was an extremely serious offense among the hobo fraternity, and might well bring death.

Walking in on a jungle, a visitor would find fires lapping at old pots or tin cans while hoboes whittled knickknacks and swapped information about good eats and bad railroad police, known as bulls. Everyone was expected to contribute to dinner, most often a Mulligan stew. According to young Graydon Horath, who watched an old hand one day in 1937, preparing such a dinner was as simple as putting water to a boil in a can, dumping in some cornmeal and slices of bologna, salt meat, onions and potatoes, and tending the fire for several hours to keep the food cooking at a low simmer.

Mingling in with the hoboes in the jungles were other kinds of wanderers. While the distinctions between them often were blurry to outsiders, the differences were clear enough to jungle residents. "Bums loafs and sits," explained one hobo to hobo chronicler Godfrey Irwin. "Tramps loafs and walks. But a hobo moves and works, and he's clean." William O. Douglas never had any intentions of bumming. "I rode the rails," he said, "not as a sightseer," but to get to places where he hoped to find work. Douglas liked to find a dark corner in a boxcar where he could protect his back. Mixed in with the hardworking stiffs, and indistinguish-

able at a glance, was a sprinkling of fugitives and hardened criminals ever alert for any whiff of cash. During the boom years of manual labor in grain harvesting, robbers, called yeggs, had formed gangs to reap money from hoboes who were departing jobs in the wheat fields, and they stole thousands of dollars a season. Art Linkletter recalled that two such men held him and a friend up in a boxcar in Washington State, and came within a trigger-pull of killing both of them.

Most important among a hobo's survival skills was learning the finer points of how to "flip" a train—boarding a train, riding it safely, and staying on by avoiding bulls. Hoboes stole rides on both passenger trains and freight trains. And although they would have preferred to board their chosen cars at leisure in the yards, railroad police tried to keep them off any property bounded by the "yard limit" signs. That left hoboes to jog alongside a train as it pulled out, then swing aboard while trying not to slip under the wheels. Of the 216 trespassers who died on the Missouri Pacific's property in 1931-32, most were men who met with accidents getting off and on the trains. Hobo author Tom Kromer describes sprinting along the track to catch a train, reaching for the side of the car, and feeling a step hit his fingers. "I grab it as tight as I can. I think my arms will be jerked out of their sockets. My ribs feel like they are smashed. I hang on. I make it."

Jack London describes a time at the turn of the century when a friend didn't make it. He and a fellow teenager flipped a 10:20 P.M. Southern Pacific going east out of Sacramento. London jumped and pulled himself aboard. His buddy "French Kid" stumbled, and fell under the train, and the wheels took both his legs off. Not aware of his friend's tragic mishap, London decked a "rattler," riding flat and spread-eagled atop one of the cars on an eastbound train. "Only a young and vigorous tramp is able to deck a passenger train," he would later write. "The young and vigorous tramp must have his nerve with him as well."

While passenger trains were fast, they offered few perching possibilities. Some daring hoboes scrunched atop part of the brake assembly that was built into the wheel trucks of passenger coaches, ending up with their heads just inches from the spinning steel wheels. In one variation of rod riding, hoboes seized on the iron truss rods used to strengthen wooden railroad cars. The rods hung about two feet apart, 18 inches underneath the car and only about 10 inches from the ground. "The trick," confided William O. Douglas, "was to get a couple of boards and lay them across the rods to form a small platform. We'd lie on the boards, on our stomachs, our heads on our arms and our eyes tightly closed. It was a miserable place to ride because the suction of the train kept dust and cinders constantly swirling." Falling asleep, even for a moment, could—and often did—mean an instant and gruesome death. Carl Sandburg and Art Linkletter both fell asleep while riding on couplings and the tops of cars, and came within a breath of falling beneath the wheels.

Boxcars got a 'Bo out of the wind and were hard to beat for all-round comfort, but they held dangers.

Over the years hoboes could be found on or in just about every location aboard a freight train. At various times they were reported riding on the cowcatcher, hiding under coal in the tender, standing on the couplings, hanging on the grab irons that served as ladders, sitting on top of the cars and nestled in gondolas of scrap iron. Boxcars got a 'Bo out of the wind and were hard to beat for all-around com-

fort, but they held dangers just like anyplace else on a freight train. When my friends and I rode the boxcars, hoboes and rail workers warned us not to sit on the edge of the doorway and dangle our legs out the side; it was bad form not just because it drew the law's attention but because the massive side doors could roll shut in a sudden stop and lop off our legs. Hoboes in boxcars also ran the risk of being crushed under poorly secured cargo, dying in train wrecks or asphyxiating in insulated "reefer" (refrigerator) cars, which were sometimes locked from the outside after an unsuspecting hobo had climbed aboard. At the peak of the Depression, 6,500 illegal railroad riders were killed or injured in a single year.

Accidents might or might not befall, but bad weather was a certainty for hoboes long enough on the road. The triple factors of traveling through the winter, being broke and risking jail are what earn people the right to say they have truly lived the hobo life. Amateurs like me, sometimes called scenery bums, had money to avoid begging, didn't stay long and got off the road well before frigid weather. "It is a very serious thing for a tender individual not properly clothed, to ride outside in winter weather. I do not see how they can escape pneumonia," R. S. Mitchell, chief special agent for the Missouri Pacific Railroad, told a congressional hearing in 1933. The obvious solution of running south for the winter could be dangerous because Cotton Belt police chiefs and sheriffs were alert against penniless snowbirds looking to roost until the arrival of spring. Beatings, chain gangs and often death awaited the hobo who strayed into the wrong small town.

Of course hoboes' campfire stories cast hoboes as Davids up against so many iron-fisted railroad bulls. Among the Goliaths, a few loomed over the rest. Jeff Carr of Cheyenne, Wyoming, was ranked as one of the roughest, toughest railroad bulls around. By the early 1920s, Carr was a legend from Texas to Maine, writer Glen Mullin reported in his book of

hobo travels. A drifter nicknamed Runt described Carr this way: "A big goof he was, wid a slouch-down mustash, cowboy hat, coupla guns strapped on im." He said he had seen Carr gallop alongside a freight, and reach out and grab a hobo off the train and sling him across the horse's neck, like a prize deer. The real T. Jefferson Carr, a Cheyenne lawman and railroad detective, had been rough on hoboes and tramps in the 1890s. According to legend, he was beaten to death by hoboes with a coupling pin, but in fact, he died of a lingering illness in 1916 at age 73.

Railroads often did have legitimate gripes against hoboes. In 1932 railroads were hopping mad about riders who would pick out refrigerator cars full of vegetables and fruit; if the car was too cold they'd open up the ventilator doors wide to warm it up, ruining the food. Hoboes were known to build fires inside boxcars during winter, and occasionally the blazes got loose and burned up the cars. Even so, the accidents caused by the hoboes didn't seem to warrant the violence unleashed upon them by many bulls. One railroad bull explained that some yeggs had once started a gunfight during an arrest and shot his pal. "Since then I club all hoboes on general principles," he reported. Other bulls learned to flush out hoboes riding the rods by lowering a piece of iron tied to a rope from between two cars. The bull would pay out the rope and let the iron whip about underneath the car, killing any hobo unlucky enough to be riding below.

Though some policemen kept up the old brutal ways throughout the Depression, no amount of clubbing and shooting could have kept all the hoboes off the trains. The chief special agent of the Missouri Pacific said that by 1930 most railroads had given up even trying to pinch them, explaining at a hearing why hoboes laughed when threatened with arrest: jail would give them a warm place to rest up.

You will eat, bye and bye,
In that glorious land above the sky;

Work and pray, live on hay
You'll get pie in the sky when you die.

By early 1933 the nation was in deep economic trouble, with one out of five able-bodied workers jobless. In the years from 1929 to 1931, the Missouri Pacific's hobo count rose from 13,000 per year to 200,000. As public schools were shuttered for lack of money and banks went bust, even cities with a history of earlier charity to tramps and hoboes before the Crash cut way back on free lodgings and soup lines. Each winter month, the total number of hoboes and highway tramps passing through Deming, New Mexico, equaled the resident population. It would be easy to paint tight-fisted cities as just so many Scroogevilles, but officials felt honor-bound to conserve any spare change and available jobs for needy local people rather than a crowd of grimy strangers dumped off by arriving freight trains. Hoboes called such unfriendly towns hostile, which they pronounced "horse-style."

A survey of transients during the Great Depression suggested that perhaps 8,000 women were on the road as hoboes. One woman told a sociologist that the toughest thing was staying clean. Constant hunger she didn't mind so much, she said: "You don't stay hungry after the second day anyhow." Not all women took to the road out of economic desperation. "Boxcar Bertha" Thompson, probably the best-known woman hobo of the era, said it was restlessness and love of variety that put her on the road at age 15.

Perhaps 200,000 children were loose on American railroads and highways at the peak of the national misery. Sociologist Thomas Minehan lived among them during 1932 and 1933. He found that the boys and girls tended to gather in gangs for safety. Many kept notebooks of their travels. Minehan jotted down this pointed comment from a boy's diary after the writer had visited a mission house: "No use standing up for Jesus. . . . Nothing but beans and misery."

Young people who traveled alone were in real danger from sexual predators. Particularly in the confines of a boxcar cut off from escape or help, hoboes and other transients lived in a strip of land as lawless as the wild frontier. Assaults had always been a problem in the woman-starved hobo life, and well before the turn of the century they had entered the regular hobo lexicon. "Jockers," or male homosexuals, took on boys. Sometimes the relationship required the boys to beg in towns for food or money. Usually it would begin with the older man assisting the boy with advice or food, and then turned into slavery that could last months or years. Some hobo versions of "The Big Rock Candy Mountains" song describe this predator-prey relationship.

And thus another nostalgic image tumbles, that of the noble life of the road. If you spent long enough on the road, you were sure to experience the duality of humankind: some rail workers were brutal, but most were willing to give hoboes a break of some kind. Rail workers' aiding and abetting of hoboes was a quirk of humanity that drove railroad executives wild. Still, it's a pattern that surfaces again and again in hobo accounts and it matches my experience on the road; our group only started riding freights after a railroad employee told us how to manage it.

Take the Santa Fe Railroad's yardmaster at Belen, New Mexico; around 1932 this official ran a water pipe from his house out to the two-acre hobo jungle next door so the dozens of men living there could have clean water to drink and to wash with. Certainly his family was tired of them always knocking on the door, but it was a kinder act than finding enough police to run them out of town.

LIBRARY OF CONGRESS

A hobo gulps coffee on a back porch as a housewife watches; thousands of men traded work for food.

To see how familiarity bred friendship between some trainmen and hoboes, I visited Portage, Wisconsin, the hometown of Pat K. Windus, a retired locomotive engineer. During the Depression this central Wisconsin city was a terminal of the Milwaukee Road rail line and therefore had hundreds of people on the payroll as ice-house workers, baggage handlers, signalmen, car inspectors, repairmen, brakemen, firemen and engineers.

In 1934, at age 9, Pat Windus lived with his mother and two siblings in a frame house about two blocks from the rail yard. Windus' father had just died, and his mother fed the family by taking in washing, cooking meals for others and baking 35 to 50 pies every night for a local restaurant called the Pig-n-Whistle. All that took a lot of stove wood, Windus said, recalling that they always had four or five long rows of wood stacked up and needing to be split. It was too much for the children; enter the hoboes, who could earn a good meal by stopping by Ma Windus' house to split stove wood for a couple of hours. "They started splitting wood at 5 o'clock most every morning," Windus recalled, pausing like he could hear the "ker-chunk" once more. The transients lived at a jungle a few hundred feet away, on the other side of the rail yard in a grove of trees by Mud Lake. "On our birthdays," Windus said, "they'd bring us some book or toy." Some evenings, the hoboes gathered on the Winduses' porch to listen to the radio.

By the start of World War II, the hobo era was fading fast. While the war's end did turn loose large numbers of veterans, a prosperous economy and the G.I. Bill, which offered them free education, kept most young men from hitting the rails. Nothing like the earlier booms developed. Where once detectives on the Santa Fe might find 500 transients on a freight train, by the early 1950s a thorough search would turn up fewer than 10. All the driving forces had run out of steam. The demand for transient harvest work all across the West dropped off to little more than isolated fruit and vegetable picking, and migrant workers in beat-up automobiles could work that market better. Towns and farms didn't offer the odd jobs and fill-in work so essential to the hobo economy. There were jobs for young men now, but employers needed people willing to stay around and learn technical skills, not footloose drifters. And the 1950s saw

William O. Douglas rode the rails, he said, "to get to places where he hoped to find work."

railroads shift from steam to diesel, which hit hobo lifestyles hard. The simpler operation of diesels cost them the outbuildings they used to shelter in, the friendly railroad families who provided handouts, and lumps of coal that fueled jungle fires. There were fewer trains and they took longer runs, with fewer stops where a hobo could get himself aboard.

In the end, you'll have to reach your own conclusions about the real life of hoboes back when they covered the landscape. Statistics show that for thousands of men it was the way to a dusty death and a nameless grave at trackside. But after his hobo trek, Carl Sandburg noted, "Away deep in my heart now I had hope as never before. Struggles lay ahead, I was sure, but whatever they were I

would not be afraid of them." Jack London credited his "realism" and success as a storyteller to his time as a hobo. Perhaps his hobo days colored William O. Douglas' decisions as he sat on the Supreme Court years later and battled for the constitutional rights of all Americans, regardless of their status, wealth or power. Certainly the countless stories from rail-riding hoboes inspired writer Jack Kerouac and the members of the Beat Generation of the 1950s and 1960s.

As for me, I prefer to think of Ma Windus' back porch in Portage, Wisconsin, on a summer evening in 1934. There's a group of men there, weather-beaten but resourceful transients who couldn't fit in, sipping iced tea and listening to the Chicago Cubs on the radio. The whistle of the Milwaukee Road's train No. 263 is sounding in the yards two blocks away. Maybe they'll bid adieu and hop the train for parts unknown; maybe they'll miss the train and catch another one tomorrow. As Pat Windus told me, "It didn't matter. Their ticket was always good."

Frequent contributor James R. Chiles has written about subjects as diverse as radio towers, junkyards and fire fighting.

Every Picture Tells a Story

Daniel D. Huff

In the first few decades of the 20th century, the social work pioneers leaned heavily on the then new technology of the camera. Ironically, the names of even the leading social photographers are far better known among photographers than among social workers. This article examines the contributions of a few avatars of social photography that were closely connected to the social work pioneers. The career of Paul Kellogg, a social work pioneer who was most associated with social photography, is also briefly examined. Finally, the article suggests that today's social workers should follow the lead of the social work pioneers and use modern technology to put images back into social work campaigns.

Key words: images; modern technology; photographs; pioneers; social photographers

Most Americans educated in the last half of the 20th century are familiar with the photographs taken by the early social photographers. The stark, blunt photographs of New York's poor, taken by Jacob Riis, the carefully composed and biting images of working children and Ellis Island immigrants created by Lewis Hine, and the compelling portraits of depression migrants taken by Dorothea Lange, have entered the nation's collective memory through magazines, history books, and films (Trachtenberg, 1989). Many of the more notable social photographers were also avid social reformers who worked closely with many social work pioneers.

One of the strategies commonly used by key figures in social work's history was their effective use of images. In the first few decades of the 20th century, the profession's pioneers leaned heavily on the then new technology of the camera (Squires, 1991). Early social work leaders recognized that wedding the data accumulated through their investigations and surveys to

"Street Arabs in Night Quarters"
Jacob Riis. Library of Congress.

sensitive drawings and photographs made their presentations more powerful (Kellogg, 1914; Squires, 1991). However, the strong links between early social work and social photography is a piece of the profession's legacy that is in danger of being lost.

From *Social Work*, November 1998, pp. 576-583. © 1998 by the National Association of Social Workers, Inc. Reprinted by permission.

"Ellis Island" **Lewis Hine.**
Library of Congress.

Social Photographers

Jacob Riis was a famous author and reform crusader of the 1880s and 1890s, who wrote a poignant description of life in New York's seamier tenements. Riis worked and collaborated with prominent social work reformers including Lillian Wald, Jane Addams, and Paul Kellogg (Chambers, 1971). Lewis Hine, the creator of a remarkable collection of images documenting working class life in the early 20th century, worked for both Florence Kelley at the Child Labor Committee and Kellogg at *Survey,* the social work journal (Gutman, 1967). Roy Stryker, head of the Farm Service Administration (FSA) photography team, worked his way through college as a settlement house resident. Hine taught Stryker how to mix images and text and Kellogg helped Stryker publicize the photographs his team was collecting (Hurley, 1972). Dorothea Lange, a prominent social photographer of the 1930s, was the daughter of a social worker and the wife of a relief official (Curtis, 1989). Consequently, she was well aware that her work with "dust bowl" migrants was a powerful reform tool. Her photographs of the rural refugees were largely responsible for the creation of public services to help these people (Time-Life, 1972). Lange's (1936) early work with migrants was published in *Survey Graphic* and she continued to contribute photo essays for that publication throughout the decade (Curtis, 1989).

By the general definitions of their day, some of the early social photographers were social workers. Ironically, the names of even the leading social photographers are far better known in photography than in social work (Guimond, 1991). This situation needs to be changed. Not only did these individuals play important roles in social work's history, their work exemplified how social work can make its contemporary campaigns more effective through the use of images. What follows is a brief examination of the contributions of some early social photographers who were closest to social work and who believed that their

reform impulses were as much a part of their photographs as were their skills at composition and printmaking (Goldberg, 1991).

Jacob Riis—Camera Crusader (1849–1914)

A man cannot be expected to live like a pig and vote like a man.

—Jacob Riis

Jacob Riis. Library of Congress.

Jacob Riis was a reformer and a pioneer in the field now known as documentary photography. He began using photography in the late 1880s to accompany his descriptions of the sordid conditions in the slums of New York City (Riis, 1890). He took photographs for only 10 years and claimed he was awkward with the techniques of photography. Many say his images project a power and sense of intimacy that is unique (Alland, 1974). Riis's photography becomes all the more remarkable when we remember that his equipment was quite intrusive. All of his images were taken with a bulky tripod camera and many required the use of a flashlight, a dangerous contraption that more closely resembled a flare gun than today's flashlight (Guimond, 1991). His campaigns covered issues that included many of the early social work causes such as public health, child labor, and overcrowded tenements. Eventually he abandoned photography and devoted all of his time to reform activities. At his lectures, Riis used lantern slides of his most convincing photographs to emphasize major points (Alland, 1974).

Jacob Riis immigrated to the United States from Denmark in 1870. After years of extreme poverty and hardship, he finally found employment as a police reporter for the *New York Tribune* in 1877. In the 1880s he began working in New York's most crowded slums (Guimond, 1991). His most popular book, *How the Other Half Lives,* was published in 1890. It was a

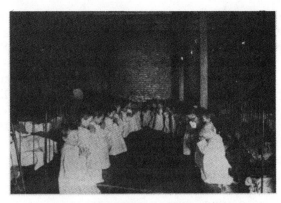

"Prayer-time in the nursery—Five Points House of Industry" **Jacob Riis.** Library of Congress.

pivotal work that precipitated much needed reforms in the tenements and made him famous. Theodore Roosevelt held Riis in very high esteem, calling him, "the most useful citizen of New York" (Alland, 1974, p. 33) and offering him positions of power and influence in his administration. Instead, Riis continued advocating for the less fortunate, producing books on the plight of poor children, immigrants, and tenement dwellers (Goldberg, 1991). When Riis died in 1914, a New York settlement house was named after him (Alland, 1974). The Jacob Riis photography collection is one of the most popular in America and the images are used extensively by writers, educators, and journalists (Alland, 1974).

In viewing these prints I find myself identified with the people photographed. I am walking in their alleys, standing in their rooms and sheds and workshops, looking in and out their windows. And they in turn seem to be aware of me.

—Ansel Adams

Lewis Wicks Hine (1874–1930)

"The Human Spirit is the thing, after all . . ."
—Lewis Hine

Lewis Hine was an unusually gifted photographer whose images conveyed his subjects' individuality and humanity. His pictures project an authenticity that became a highly effective lever for reform (Hine, 1909). Hine was from Oshkosh, Wisconsin. In 1901, after studying at the University of Chicago, he took a position at New York's Ethical Culture School. While he was teaching there, Hine began to explore photography as an aid to his teaching and as an expression of his social conscience (Gutman, 1967). After graduating from New York University in 1905, Hine began his career in "sociological photography" with the National Child Labor Committee where he worked with

such social work icons as Jane Addams, Florence Kelley, and Lillian Wald (Curtis, 1984). In 1907 Hine joined Kellogg's team of social workers on the Pittsburgh Survey, a study funded by the Russell Sage Foundation to report on the daily lives of Pittsburgh's working people. This assignment led to a lifelong collaboration with social workers and the social work journal *Survey* (Chambers, 1971). From this time through the beginnings of World War I, Hine traveled the country for both *Survey* and the Child Labor Committee, documenting industry's exploitation of women and children. His dignified pictures of immigrants and children were used to blunt the early 20th century stereotype of the new immigrants as second-class citizens (Guimond, 1991).

Hine often wrote the reports that accompanied his images and believed strongly that his pictures were but a piece of the puzzle. He felt that his images were most convincing when combined with carefully crafted captions and narratives (Guimond, 1991). At the 1909 National Conference on Charities and Corrections Hine explained, "When a photograph is sympathetically interpreted the result can be a powerful lever for social uplift" (Hine, 1909, p. 356). Hine's work was greatly valued by the young social work profession. He eventually contributed to more than 200 articles for the social work journals *Survey* and *Survey Graphic,* covering a broad array of subjects, including Hull House, steel workers, and African Americans (Gutman, 1967).

After Hine documented the plight of refugees for the Red Cross in World War I, he became an independent social photographer, taking assignments for a variety of agencies and publications. In 1930 Hine was hired to document the building of the Empire State Building. Although Hine's work received a great deal of positive attention from the critics, like many artists, he had a difficult time supporting himself during the Great Depression. Hine died in 1940, destitute and on relief (Gutman, 1967).

"Breaker Boys" **Lewis Hine.** Library of Congress.

Roy Stryker (1893–1975) and the FSA Photography Collection (1935–1943)

What you have here are a bunch of sociologists with cameras.
—Ansel Adams

"Standing in a bread line" **Walker Evans.**
Library of Congress.

Roy Stryker was not a photographer. In fact, he took pride in telling people about his awkwardness with even a simple box camera (Stryker, 1973). Roy Stryker was from a rural Kansas family. He worked his way through Columbia University as a resident of the Union Settlement House (Hurley, 1972). While a student at Columbia, he caught the attention of a prominent agricultural economist and stalwart New Dealer Rexford Tugwell. After graduating, Stryker taught economics at Columbia University and edited the illustrations for one of Tugwell's books. Many of the book's images came from the camera of Hine. Hine also tutored Stryker on how to most effectively use his photographs (Hurley, 1972).

Stryker became a protégé of economist and stalwart New Dealer Rexford Tugwell. The young Stryker was initially assigned the task of publicizing the good

"Dust Storm" **Arthur Rothstein.**
Library of Congress.

deeds being performed by the agency's programs and staff, thereby muting some of the criticisms being mounted against the agency by forces inside and outside the government. Initially, the agency photographers and photographs were only a part of this larger mission (Stryker, 1973). Stryker believed, however, that images were crucial to this assignment and assembled the agency's photographers into a central division. He then began assigning the photographers various scripts, which would give their work a central purpose and perspective. Within a short time, his vision was enlarged to documenting the whole panoply of American rural life (O'Neal, 1976). Working with only a small band of talented photographers, Stryker created one of the richest visual archives of American life ever recorded (Guimond, 1991). In a New Deal reorganization, Stryker's new team of photographers was shifted into the FSA. Consequently, the photographs collected by Stryker and his team have become known as the FSA Photographs (Stryker, 1973).

When Franklin D. Roosevelt took office in 1933, he appointed Tugwell as Assistant Secretary of Agriculture, and in 1935 Tugwell was appointed director of Farm Resettlement Administration, an experimental program designed to help small farmers (Hurley, 1972). After a series of part-time positions helping his mentor, Stryker was appointed by Tugwell to head the Information Division of the FSA. Stryker quickly assembled a talented team of photographers that included Arthur Rothstein, Walker Evans, Carl Mydans, Ben Shahn, Dorothea Lange, Russell Lee, Marion Post Walcott, John Vachon, and Gordon Parks (Curtis, 1989).

Stryker was the team leader. He defended his budget from an often unsympathetic Congress. He provided the photographers with scripts and insisted that the photographers understand the economic and cultural context of their photographic subjects. He also encouraged journalists and social scientists to use the photographs to educate the public (O'Neal, 1976). Stryker's team assembled a collection of images that was a remarkable social commentary. These images quickly became an important tool for social justice advocates during the middle and late 1930s (Trachtenberg, 1989).

As early as 1935 the FSA collection was being used to illustrate articles in *Survey Graphic* (Hurley, 1972). In the summer of 1936, *Survey Graphic* featured a two-page portfolio of Dorothea Lange's pictures of sharecroppers, which included the now famous "Migrant Madonna." Between 1935 and 1940, *Survey Graphic* featured FSA photographs in eight articles. During this same period more than 14 books used illustrations from the FSA collection (Hurley, 1972). Most of the FSA photographers continued their careers in photography and have become icons in their field. The FSA Photograph Collection is one of the most widely used sets of images in the public domain. It continues to be used in documentaries and social commentaries about America's rural past (Trachtenberg, 1989).

"*Migrant Madonna*" "*She said that they had been living on frozen vegetables from the surrounding fields, and the birds that the children killed. She had just sold the tires from her car to buy food. There she sat in that lean-to tent with her children huddled around her, and seemed to know that my pictures might help her, and so she helped me. There was a sort of equality about it.*" **Dorothea Lange.** Library of Congress

Dorothea Lange (1895–1965)

I was compelled to photograph as a direct response to what was around me. It went just absolutely in the blind staggers.

—Dorothea Lange

Often referred to as the mother of the FSA group, Dorothea Lange stands out as the FSA photographer who was most closely connected to the advocacy–reform traditions of Hine and Riis. She was raised in New York City by her mother, who was both a single parent and a social worker (Hurley, 1972). Lange fully understood the social reform implications of her work and frequently collaborated with her husband, Paul Taylor, who was both an administrator and investigator for the California Relief Agency (Curtis, 1989). Her acumen as a portrait photographer was well established before the Great Depression, but as refugees from the nation's dust bowl began appearing in California, Lange turned to illustrating the darker side of the human condition (O'Neal, 1976). Her first such photograph, *The White Angel Bread Line* was taken at a soup kitchen outside her studio. The photograph received so much favorable publicity for both herself and the migrants that she was hired to document rural social problems for the California Relief Agency (Hurley, 1972).

Lange's work with the "other half" appeared in numerous newspapers and magazines, including *Survey*, before she joined the FSA group. Some experts contend that it was Lange's early works that inspired Tug-

well and Stryker to create the photography group and that her early perspective helped shape the FSA viewpoint—stark but dignified—that is a hallmark of the collection (Curtis, 1989). In the middle and late 1930s she and her husband collaborated on several articles for *Survey* (Taylor, 1935) and wrote *American Photographs* (1939), a compelling book on the plight of migrant workers (Trachtenberg, 1989). Lange's photograph *Migrant Madonna* is arguably the most famous of all the FSA photographs and appeared in *Survey Graphic* in 1936 (Lange, 1936). After the Great Depression, Lange continued her commitment to dispossessed people. She photographed the Japanese American internment camps during World War II and after the war documented the complex lives of poor people in Africa, Asia, and South America (Hurley, 1972).

Paul Kellogg—Master of Images (1879–1958)

The common link between early social work and the social photographers was social work pioneer Paul Kellogg, editor of the profession's early publications, *Charity, Charity and the Commons, Survey,* and *Survey Graphic*. Kellogg edited social work's first journal, *Charities,* and took over as chief editor a few years after that publication changed its name to *Survey* in 1912 (Kellogg, 1909). When he was first employed by the journal *Charities,* Kellogg was a young social worker who had been a reporter for a small midwestern newspaper. His early education in social work included courses at the New York School of Philanthropy and a summer tutorial by Jacob Riis (Chambers, 1971).

One of the pivotal events in early social work and in Kellogg's career was the Pittsburgh Survey of 1907. The Pittsburgh Survey, funded by the Russell Sage Foundation, provided a detailed report on the lives of Pittsburgh's working people. The project lasted more than a year. The study was published in six volumes, quickly becoming a model for social work research. The Pittsburgh Survey not only documented city life through written reports, but also relied heavily on the photographs of Hine and the drawings of Joseph Stella (Chambers, 1971). The success of the Pittsburgh Survey raised the prestige of the young social work profession dramatically and was partly responsible for the decision to change the social work journal's name from *Charity and the Commons* to *Survey* (Kellogg, 1909). In 1921 Kellogg created *Survey Graphic,* a reform magazine that used art and images even more extensively than did *Survey* (Devine, 1939).

Browsing through the old issues of Kellogg's publications is a revelation. The early issues of *Survey* and later *Survey Graphic* reflect the breadth and comprehensive interests of the early social workers. Essays and pictorials on unemployment and discussions about issues such as prohibition and international relations are combined with details about child welfare work and adoption. Kellogg carefully avoided using articles that used language he considered too pretentious, setting an example many wish more current social work publications would follow (Chambers, 1971). Kellogg did not only use art and photographs to accompany the text; often the images were the story. He put together photo essays that were decades ahead of their time. He used images in ways that helped tell the story without succumbing to the danger of pandering to the visual senses (Hine, 1936; Kellogg, 1914).

Kellogg's relationship with Hine was strong and lasting. His publications featured both Hine's photographs of industrial workers and pictures of rural life in the 1920s and 1930s (Hine, 1936). In 1939, realizing that the failing Hine was in desperate straights, Kellogg along with Stryker and the famous photographers Paul Strand and Alfred Stieglitz helped Hine organize his most successful exhibit. Although the exhibit was not financially successful, it was highly acclaimed by critics. Kellogg was still sending the old photographer checks right to Hine's death in 1940 (Trachtenberg, 1977). Kellogg also was one of the first to use Lange's photographs of "dust bowl" migrants (Taylor, 1935). As the FSA project began, *Survey Graphic* was an early and dependable outlet for many FSA photographs. Kellogg regularly consulted with Stryker on how to best use the images he was collecting and even about what subjects to assign to his photographers (Hurley, 1972).

As Kellogg's social work publications matured, they were aimed at the center of the profession. There were articles about the "nuts and bolts," as it were, of social work practice, but the bulk of the writing and graphics were devoted to more general issues and reform crusades that related to all social workers—whether they were working in public welfare, psychiatric clinics, or schools (Chambers, 1971). He used his understanding of images and artists to give life and dimension to the problems and events confronting the social work profession (Hine, 1936; Kellogg, 1914; Lange, 1936). Kellogg's masterful use of photographs and art serves as an exemplar for the profession as it prepares to enter the next century.

Implications for Practice

Social work's centennial celebration has been helpful in getting social workers back in touch with the issues and personalities that shaped the profession. There is much to learn from the examples set by the social work pioneers; their sensitivity to injustice, their tolerance for the foibles surrounding the human condition, and their appreciation for the larger context of social

problems are just a few of many admirable characteristics shared by the early social workers that we could all emulate. A re-examination of how early social workers used images in their campaigns can help today's social workers exploit modern technologies, such as video and the Internet, in the profession's current crusades. Social workers today have largely abandoned media-rich presentations, relying instead on statistics, tables, and—all too often—turgid essays. Consequently, much of the emotion is lacking in our appeals, and this diminishes the important mission of educating the public. Most important, our advocacy for such groups as the poor and homeless has been less powerful.

A unique element of the social work profession has been its ability to blend skill technique, and theory with art. The word "art" refers to the emotional component of social work practice that is essential for success. Feelings are just as essential to the understanding of social problems as they are to understanding individual instances of domestic violence or homelessness. For example, local studies of homelessness should include respectful photographs of homeless families and individuals in the same vein as those used by Lange. Reports of local housing problems could include photographs of conditions similar to those used by Riis in his photograph-studded surveys of tenements in New York City. Adding visual elements to our communications will help professional social workers move beyond communicating with other experts and social workers and reach the wider audience that the social work advocacy mission demands.

Social work educators will find unique challenges associated with teaching students how to effectively add images to their work. Students need to be taught how to use video feedback to sharpen their group and individual skills and how to use video images in their reports on local social problems. Students need to learn how to search the Internet and World Wide Web for information about policy and case planning problems, but they should also be taught how to make web pages about their agencies and the problems challenging their clients. This effort will require that social work educators learn new skills in video technology and computers or that they develop interdisciplinary classes and collaborate with such diverse fields as art and communication.

Social workers need to create new ways of communicating with each other and the public. Essays and reports should link to images, sounds, and music media that inject the emotional context that is such a crucial component of all social problems. Fortunately, we have even more tools to work with than the early pioneers enjoyed. We can use photographs, which continue to be robust aids, as well as videos, computers, and the Internet. The World Wide Web has tremendous potential. The Web is capable of integrating tables, text, images, and audio, and it is inexpensive. At the 1909 Conference of Charities and Corrections, photographer Lewis Hine stated, "The greatest advance in social work is to be made by the popularizing of camera work, so these records may be made by those who are in the thick of the battle" (p. 356). His advice rings as true today as it did 90 years ago.

References

Alland, A. (1974). *Jacob Riis: Photographer and citizen.* New York: Aperture.

Chambers, C. (1971). *Paul Kellogg and the Survey: Voices for social welfare and social justice.* Minneapolis: University of Minnesota Press.

Curtis, J. (1989). *Mind's eye, mind's truth: FSA photography reconsidered.* Philadelphia: Temple University Press.

Curtis, V. (1984). *Photography and reform.* Milwaukee: Milwaukee Art Museum.

Devine, E. (1939). *When social work was young.* New York: Macmillan.

Goldberg, V. (1991). *The power of photography.* New York: Abbeville Press.

Guimond, J. (1991). *American Photography and the American Dream.* University of North Carolina Press, Chapel Hill.

Gutman, J. (1967). *Lewis Hine and the American social conscience.* New York: Walker.

Hine, L. (1909). How the camera may help in general uplift. In A. Johnson (Ed.), *Proceedings, National Conference of Charities and Corrections* (pp. 355–356). Fort Wayne, IN: Fort Wayne Printing.

Hine, L. (1936). Rural America. *Survey Graphic, 25,* 669–671.

Hurley, J. (1972). *Portrait of a decade: Roy Stryker and the development of documentary photography in the thirties.* Baton Rouge: Louisiana State University Press.

Kellogg, P. (1909, January). To change the name of charities and the commons. *Charities and the Commons,* pp. 1251–1256.

Kellogg, P. (1914). *The Pittsburgh District, Civic frontage.* New York: Survey Associates.

Lange, D. (1936). Draggin-around people. *Survey Graphic, 25,* 524–525.

O'Neal, (1976). *A vision shared.* New York: St. Martin's Press.

Riis, J. (1890). *How the other half lives.* New York: Scribners.

Squires, C. (1991). The long search for hope: The unending idealism of the committed photojournalist is as strong as ever. *American Photo, 2,* 58–61.

Stryker, R. (1973). *In this proud land.* New York: Graphic Society.

Taylor, P. (1935). Again the covered wagons. *Survey Graphic, 25,* 348–351.

Time-Life. (1972). *Documentary photography.* New York: Time-Life Books.

Trachtenberg, A. (1977). *America and Lewis Hine.* New York: Aperture.

Trachtenberg, A. (1989). *Reading American photographs.* New York: Hill & Wang.

Daniel D. Huff, *is professor, School of Social Work, Boise State University, 1910 University Drive, Boise, ID 83725. Send correspondence to the author at the history station: http://www.idbsu-edu/socwork/dhuff/xx.htm. Professor Huff is the author of a book on social work history to be published by NASW Press.*

When the Laws Were Silent

BY WILLIAM H. REHNQUIST

In the wake of Pearl Harbor, tens of thousands of American citizens were taken from their homes and locked up simply because of their Japanese ancestry. Was their internment a grim necessity or "the worst blow to civil liberty in our history"? The Chief Justice of the United States weighs the reasoning.

THE ENTIRE NATION WAS STUNNED BY THE JAPANESE attack on Pearl Harbor on December 7, 1941, but it seemed much closer to home on the West Coast than elsewhere on the mainland.

Residents became fearful of ethnic Japanese among them. Japanese immigrants had begun to settle on the West Coast shortly before the turn of the century and had not been assimilated into the rest of the population. Under the Naturalization Act of 1790, those who had emigrated from Japan were not able to become citizens; they were prohibited by law from owning land and were socially segregated in many ways. The first generation of Japanese immigrants, the issei, therefore remained aliens. But their children, the nisei, having been born in the United States, were citizens from birth. Californians particularly, including public officials—Gov. Culbert Olson, State Attorney General Earl Warren, and the mayor of Los Angeles, Fletcher Bowron—began to call for "relocation" to the interior of the country of persons of Japanese ancestry.

At the outbreak of the war the military established the Western Defense Command, which included the coastal portions of California, Oregon, and Washington. Gen. John DeWitt, its senior officer, at first resisted the clamor to remove the Japanese. But state and local public officials were adamant, and they were supported by their states' congressional delegations. The chorus became more insistent when the Roberts Commission released its report in late January 1942.

On December 18, 1941, President Roosevelt had appointed a body chaired by Owen J. Roberts, an Associate Justice of the Supreme Court, "to ascertain and report the facts relating to the attack made by Japanese armed forces upon the territory of Hawaii on December 7, 1941." The commission met first in Washington and then went to Hawaii, where the members heard numerous witnesses. The commission found that there had been highly organized espionage in Hawaii: "It has been discovered that the Japanese consul sent to and received from Tokyo in his own and other names many messages on commercial radio circuits. This activity greatly increased towards December 7, 1941 . . . . [The Japanese] knew from maps which they had obtained, the exact location of vital air fields, hangars, and other structures. They also knew accurately where certain important naval vessels would be berthed. Their fliers had the most detailed maps, courses, and bearings, so that each could attack a given vessel or field. Each seems to have been given a specified mission."

In February 1942 a Japanese submarine shelled oil installations near Santa Barbara. The pressure built for forced evacuation. Attorney General Francis Biddle, Secretary of War Henry L. Stimson, and Assistant Secretary of War John J. McCloy were the decision-makers for the two concerned departments. None of them favored relocation at first, but eventually Stimson and McCloy changed their minds in the course of often heated discussions among themselves and their subordinates. Final

From *American Heritage*, October 1998, pp. 76-89. Adapted from *All the Laws but One: Civil Liberties in Wartime* by William Rehnquist. © 1998 by Alfred A. Knopf, Inc., a division of Random House.

approval of course rested with the President. On February 11, 1942, McCloy asked Stimson to find out if Roosevelt was willing to authorize the removal of the nisei as well as the issei. Stimson asked to see the President but was told FDR was too busy; a phone call would have to do. "I took up with him the West Coast matter first," Stimson wrote in his diary, "and told him the situation and fortunately found he was very vigorous about it and told me to go ahead on the line that I had myself thought the best."

must be done to defend the country must be done." Biddle concluded with a remarkably perceptive observation: "Nor do I think that the constitutional difficulty plagued him—the Constitution has never greatly bothered any wartime President. That was a question of law, which ultimately the Supreme Court must decide. And meanwhile—probably a long meanwhile—we must get on with the war."

Executive Order 9066, authorizing the removal of the ethnic Japanese from the West Coast, was signed by

Attorney General Biddle on FDR: "I do not think he was much concerned with the gravity or implications of this step. He was never theoretical about things."

Then, Stimson wrote in his 1947 memoirs, "mindful of its duty to be prepared for any emergency, the War Department ordered the evacuation of more than a hundred thousand persons of Japanese origin from strategic areas on the west coast. This decision was widely criticized as an unconstitutional invasion of the rights of individuals many of whom were American citizens, but it was eventually approved by the Supreme Court as a legitimate exercise of the war powers of the President. What critics ignored was the situation that led to the evacuation. Japanese raids on the west coast seemed not only possible but probable in the first months of the war, and it was quite impossible to be sure that the raiders would not receive important help from individuals of Japanese origin."

Biddle, who alone among the high administration officials involved opposed the evacuation, described the situation in these words: "Apparently, the War Department's course of action had been tentatively charted by Mr. McCloy and Colonel Karl Robin Bendetsen of the General Staff in the first ten days of February. General DeWitt's final recommendation to evacuate was completed on February 13, and forwarded to Washington with a covering letter the next day. Mr. Stimson and Mr. McCloy did not, however, wait for this report, which contained the 'finding' on which their 'military necessity' argument to the President was based, but obtained their authority before the recommendation was received. On February 11 the President told the War Department to prepare a plan for wholesale evacuation, specifically including citizens. It was dictated, he concluded, by military necessity, and added, 'Be as reasonable as you can.' After the conference the Assistant Secretary reported to Bendetsen: 'We have *carte blanche* to do what we want as far as the President is concerned.' " Biddle speculated on Roosevelt's feelings about the matter: "I do not think he was much concerned with the gravity or implications of this step. He was never theoretical about things. What

Roosevelt on February 19. Several weeks later Congress passed a law imposing criminal penalties for violations of the order or regulations that might be issued to implement it. First a curfew was imposed on the ethnic Japanese, then they were required to report to relocation centers, and finally they were taken to camps in the interior of California and in the mountain states. There was no physical brutality, but there were certainly severe hardships: removal from the place where one lived, often the forced sale of houses and businesses, and harsh living conditions in the Spartan quarters of the internment centers. As the war progressed, some restrictions were relaxed. Nisei volunteers made up the 442d Combat Team, which fought bravely in Italy against the Germans. Other internees were issued work permits that allowed them to leave the camp. Finally, most of those who were still interned were released by the beginning of 1945, as a result of the third Supreme Court decision in which the relocation policy was challenged.

GORDON HIRABAYASHI WAS BORN NEAR SEATTLE TO issei parents in 1918, and by 1942 he was a senior at the University of Washington. In May 1942 he disobeyed the curfew requirement imposed by military authorities pursuant to the President's Executive Order, and seven days later he failed to report to register for evacuation. He was indicted and convicted in a federal court in Seattle on two counts of misdemeanor and sentenced to imprisonment for three months on each. He contended that the orders he was charged with violating were unconstitutional, but the federal judge in Seattle ruled against him.

Fred Korematsu, born in the United States to issei parents, was convicted of remaining in San Leandro, California, in violation of a military exclusion order applicable to him. The federal court in San Francisco overruled his claim that the order in question was un-

The men who ruled on Executive Order 9066. Front row, left to right: Justices Reed, Roberts, Stone, Black, and Frankfurter. Back row: Justices Jackson, Douglas, Murphy, and Rutledge.

constitutional, suspended his sentence, and placed him on probation for five years.

The cases were argued together before the U.S. Court of Appeals for the Ninth Circuit in San Francisco, which has jurisdiction over the Far Western part of the United States. Because of procedural variations, they reached the Supreme Court at different times. The case of *Hirabayashi* was sent directly there by the court of appeals and was argued in May 1943.

The Chief Justice at the time was Harlan F. Stone, who had been born in New Hampshire and practiced law in New York following his graduation from Columbia Law School, where he later served as dean. Eight months after Calvin Coolidge became President upon Harding's death in 1923, he appointed Stone Attorney General, with a mandate to clean out the scandal-ridden Department of Justice. Stone obliged and was rewarded by an appointment as Associate Justice of the Supreme Court in 1925. During his sixteen years in that position he was identified as a member of the Court's liberal wing, along with Justices Holmes, Brandeis, and Cardozo. When Charles Evans Hughes retired as Chief Justice in 1941, Roosevelt appointed Stone his successor.

The senior Associate Justice on the Court at the time that the Japanese internment cases were heard was Owen Roberts, a Philadelphia aristocrat who had mixed a successful private practice with occasional stints in public service. He had been a special prosecutor for the United

States in several of the cases that arose out of the Harding administration's Teapot Dome scandals and was appointed to the Supreme Court by President Herbert Hoover in 1930.

Next in seniority was Hugo Black, who, before his appointment, had been a senator from Alabama. During his two terms in the Senate, Black had been a faithful party wheel horse who had supported every piece of major New Deal legislation, including Roosevelt's courtpacking plan. Immediately after the defeat of that initiative, FDR had the opportunity to make his first appointment to the Court, and he chose Black. There was a public outcry when it was revealed that Black had been a member of the Ku Klux Klan, and the newly minted Justice took to the radio to declare that he'd been in the Klan a long time ago, and only as a matter of political expediency when running for an Alabama political office. He was to serve thirty-four years on the Court and be one of the most influential Justices of the twentieth century.

Stanley Reed was born in Minerva, Kentucky, and practiced law in nearby Maysville from 1910 until he went to Washington in 1929 to be general counsel to the Federal Farm Board and then, in 1932, to the Reconstruction Finance Corporation. Roosevelt named him Solicitor General in 1935 and appointed him to the Supreme Court three years later. Considerably less colorful than some of the other Roosevelt appointees, Reed was often the swing man when the Court split 5 to 4 on philosophical questions.

Next in the line of Roosevelt appointees was Felix Frankfurter. Born in Vienna in 1882, and a professor at Harvard Law School for twenty-five years before being named to the Court in January 1939, Frankfurter was a

Roosevelt. Born in Kentucky, he served as a law professor and a judge of the federal court of appeals in Washington before going to the Supreme Court in 1943. He was to serve only six years and during that time joined Murphy as a less fervent, more scholarly champion of the underdog.

Justice Murphy circulated the draft of a caustic dissent chastising the Court for approving a program that "utterly subverts" individual rights in war.

well-known legal scholar and writer and had been identified with numerous liberal causes, among them the trials of Sacco and Vanzetti in the 1920s. A brightly plumaged bird who never gave up his professional mien in his battles for judicial restraint, he would serve on the Court for more than twenty years.

Russell Lee took this photo of one of thousands of hasty liquidations.

LESS THAN THREE MONTHS after appointing Frankfurter, Roosevelt had a fourth Court vacancy to fill. He chose the forty-year-old William O. Douglas, a Yale Law School professor and then a member of the Securities and Exchange Commission. Douglas would serve more than thirty-six years as an Associate Justice—the Court's all-time longevity record—and establish a reputation as a bastion of its liberal wing.

The next year, FDR got yet another opportunity, and this time he picked Frank Murphy, a former governor of Michigan, high commissioner to the Philippines, and briefly the Attorney General of the United States. Murphy would serve only nine years, but that was enough to establish him as a nearly messianic champion of the underdog. When Roosevelt elevated Stone to Chief Justice in June 1941, he appointed Attorney General Robert H. Jackson to fill the vacancy thus created. Jackson, who came from western New York and had served as both the Solicitor General and Attorney General, was an excellent writer, and his opinions showed it. He left his judicial duties immediately after the end of World War II to become the United States prosecutor at the Nuremberg trials, and his experience there had a profound effect on his judicial philosophy.

The ninth member to hear the Japanese internment cases was Wiley B. Rutledge, also appointed by

The Japanese-Americans were represented in the Supreme Court by able counsel, including Edwin Borchard, William Draper Lewis, Brien McMahon, and Osmond K. Fraenkel. Their basic contention was that the President's Executive Order was unconstitutional because it proceeded on the basis that an entire racial group was disloyal, rather than being based on any individual determinations of disloyalty. Briefs supporting these petitioners were filed by the American Civil Liberties Union, the Northern California branch of the American Civil Liberties Union, and the Japanese-American Citizens League.

The government in its brief recited in great detail the calamitous military events of the early days of the war—these ranged from the Pearl Harbor raid to the fall of the British stronghold of Singapore—which it thought justified the orders now being challenged, and went on to catalogue the "concentration of war facilities and installations on the West Coast [that] made it an area of special military concern at any time and especially after the sensational Japanese successes."

The attorneys general of Washington, Oregon, and California filed a brief in support of the government that pointed out that "for the first seven months little occurred to reduce the fear of attack. . . . On June 3, 1942, Dutch Harbor, Alaska, was attacked by carrier-based planes. On June 7, 1942, the Japanese invaded continental North America by occupying the Islands of Attu and Kiska in the Aleutian group. There was an increasing indication that the enemy had knowledge of our patrols and naval dispositions, for ships leaving west coast ports were being intercepted and attacked regularly by enemy submarines." Following the oral argument and conference in the *Hirabayashi* case, Chief Justice Stone assigned the task of writing the Court's opinion to himself. He first greatly narrowed the scope of the opinion by deciding that the Court need pass only on the validity of the curfew requirement and not on the requirement that Hirabayashi report to a relocation center. Hirabayashi had been convicted of both offenses, but his sentences were to run "concurrently"—that is, he would serve only three months in prison even though he had been sentenced to serve three months on each of two different charges. Under established law at that time, if the conviction on one count was upheld, the Court would disregard the conviction on the second count, since it essentially made no difference in the amount of time the defendant would spend in prison. In this case it meant that the Court had to tackle only the easier question of whether a curfew might be imposed, rather than the more difficult one of whether Hirabayashi could be sent to an internment camp.

Stone's task in writing the opinion was not an easy one, because several of his colleagues insisted that there be little or no opportunity to challenge the order later, while Justices Douglas, Murphy, and Rutledge wanted explicitly to leave open that possibility. Indeed, Murphy circulated a draft of a caustic dissent that chastised the Court for approving a program that "utterly subverts" individual rights in war. Douglas circulated a concurrence in which he indicated his view that at some point a person interned under the program should have an opportunity to prove his loyalty. Murphy finally turned his draft dissent into a concurrence but said in it that he thought the program "goes to the very brink of constitutional power." Rutledge also filed a brief concurrence.

Stone's opinion for the Court borrowed a definition of the government's war power from a statement made by Charles Evans Hughes—not while he was a member of the Court but in an article in the *American Bar Association Journal:* The war power of the national government is "the power to wage war successfully," and it was "not for any court to sit in review of the wisdom of their [the Executive's or Congress's] actions, or to substitute its judgment for theirs." If the Court could say there was

NATIONAL ARCHIVES

A grandfather and grandchildren await the bus in Haward, California; he left behind a cleaning business.

a rational basis for the military decision, it would be sustained.

STONE'S OPINION THEN ADDUCED THE FACTS—MOST OF which had been set forth in the government's brief—that showed the threat by the Japanese Navy to the Pacific Coast immediately after the Pearl Harbor bombing. It went on to say: "Whatever views we may entertain regarding the loyalty to this country of the citizens of Japanese ancestry, we cannot reject as unfounded the judgment of the military authorities and of Congress that there were disloyal members of that population, whose number and strength could not be precisely and quickly ascertained. We cannot say that the war-making branches of the Government did not have ground for believing that in a critical hour such persons could not readily be isolated and separately dealt with, and constituted a menace to the national defense and safety, which demanded that prompt and adequate measures be taken to guard against it."

The Court, of course, had to respond to the charge that distinctions based on race alone were not permitted under the Constitution: "Distinctions between citizens solely because of their ancestry are by their very nature odious to a free people whose institutions are founded upon the doctrine of equality. . . . We may assume that these considerations would be controlling here were it not for the fact that the danger of espionage and sabotage, in time of war and of threatened invasion, calls upon the military authorities to scrutinize every relevant fact bearing on the loyalty of populations in the danger areas. . . . The fact alone that the attack on our shores was threatened by Japan rather than another enemy power set these citizens apart from others who have no particular associations with Japan." Stone's opinion upholding the curfew was joined by five of his colleagues. Douglas, Murphy, and Rutledge, while voting to uphold the curfew, wrote separately.

KOREMATSU'S CASE DID NOT COME ON FOR ARGUMENT until October 1944. Here the Court was required to confront not merely the curfew but the far more draconian relocation requirement. The Court upheld relocation, in an opinion by Justice Black, basing its reasoning largely on the earlier decision. This time, however, there were separate dissents by Justices Roberts, Murphy, and Jackson. The flavor of Black's opinion is caught in its concluding passage: "To cast this case into outlines of racial prejudice, without reference to the real

she was a loyal citizen and not charged with any offense. The Court decided that under these circumstances Endo was entitled to be released from confinement. The presidential order and the act of Congress confirming it spoke of evacuation from a military zone but said nothing of detention after the evacuation. While the initial evacuation had been justified in terms of the defense facilities on the West Coast, the detention of a loyal person of Japanese ancestry after the evacuation had taken place was not reasonably necessary to prevent sabotage or es-

In defense of the military, it should be pointed out that these officials were not entrusted with the protection of anyone's civil liberty.

military dangers which were presented, merely confuses the issue. Korematsu was not excluded from the Military Area because of hostility to him or his race. He *was* excluded because we are at war with the Japanese Empire, because the properly constituted military authorities feared an invasion of our West Coast and felt constrained to take proper security measures, because they decided that the military urgency of the situation demanded that all citizens of Japanese ancestry be segregated from the West Coast temporarily. . . . There was evidence of disloyalty on the part of some, the military authorities considered that the need for action was great, and time was short. We cannot—by availing ourselves of the calm perspective of hindsight—now say that at that time these actions were unjustified."

Murphy criticized the military for lumping together with a disloyal few of Japanese ancestry all the others against whom there had been no such showing. Jackson said that the Court was simply in no position to evaluate the government's claim of military necessity: "In the very nature of things, military decisions are not susceptible of intelligent judicial appraisal. They do not pretend to rest on evidence, but are made on information that often would not be admissible and on assumptions that could not be proved. . . . Hence courts can never have any real alternative to accepting the mere declaration of the authority that issued the order that it was reasonably necessary from a military viewpoint."

But in the case of *Endo,* argued and decided at the same time as *Korematsu,* the Court reached quite a different result. Mitsuye Endo had submitted to an evacuation order and been removed first to the Tule Lake Relocation Center in the Cascade Mountains just south of the California-Oregon border and then to another relocation center in Utah. She sued out a writ of habeas corpus, claiming that she was a loyal citizen against whom no charge had been made and that she was therefore entitled to her relief. The government agreed that

pionage. Two members of the Court wrote separately, but all agreed with the result.

Although the Court based its reasoning in *Endo* on the provisions of the act of Congress and the Executive Order, and therefore Congress and the President would have been free to change those to provide for detention, the Court's opinion strongly hinted at constitutional difficulties if that were to be done. And, it should be noted, the military position of the United States was much more favorable in the fall of 1944 than it had been in the spring of 1942. In the Pacific the U.S. Navy won the Battle of Leyte Gulf in October, and American forces were moving steadily closer to the Japanese homeland. There was neither a military need nor a public demand for further restrictions on Americans of Japanese descent, and the entire program was promptly terminated only two weeks after the decision in the Endo case.

There is a certain disingenuousness in this sequence of three opinions—*Hirabayashi, Korematsu,* and *Endo.* There was no reason to think that Gordon Hirabayashi and Fred Korematsu were any less loyal to the United States than was Mitsuye Endo. Presumably they would have been entitled to relief from detention upon the same showing as that made by Endo. But even had Hirabayashi tried to raise that question in his case, he would have failed, for the Court chose to confine itself to the curfew issue. It was not until we were clearly winning the war that the Court came around to this view in Endo. The process illustrates in a rough way the Latin maxim *Inter arma silent leges* (in time of war the laws are silent).

POSTWAR PUBLIC OPINION VERY QUICKLY CAME TO SEE the forced relocation and detention of people of Japanese ancestry as a grave injustice. Writing in 1945, Eugene Rostow, then a professor at Yale Law School and later its dean, declared the program "a disaster" that both represented an abandonment of our traditional subordination of military to civil authority and sanctioned racially based discrimination. Edward Ennis, who as a lawyer in the Justice Department had opposed the program, reappeared nearly forty years later on behalf of the ACLU to testify before the congressionally created Commission on Wartime Relocation and Internment of Civilians. He characterized the program as "the worst blow to civil liberty in our history." In the view of this author, some of this criticism is well justified, and some not; its principal fault is that it lumps together the cases of the issei and the nisei.

The cases before the Supreme Court—*Hirabayashi, Korematsu,* and *Endo*—all involved nisei, children of immigrants, who were born in the United States and thus were American. The basis on which the Court upheld the plan were military representations as to the necessity for evacuation. These representations were undoubtedly exaggerated, and they were based in part on the view that not only the issei but their children were different from other West Coast residents.

In defense of the military it should be pointed out that these officials were not entrusted with the protection of anyone's civil liberty; their job was making sure that vital areas were as secure as possible from espionage or sabotage. The role of General DeWitt was not one to encourage a nice calculation of the costs in civil liberty as opposed to the benefits to national security. Gen. Walter Short, the Army commander in Hawaii, and Adm. Husband E. Kimmel, the Navy commander there, both were summarily removed from their commands ten days after Pearl Harbor because of their failure to anticipate the Japanese surprise attack. The head of the Western Defense command was surely going to err on the side of preparedness.

Moreover, it was not DeWitt and his associates who had first recommended evacuation of the issei and nisei; as we have seen, the principal early proponents of that idea were Governor Olson, Attorney General Warren, Los Angeles Mayor Bowron, and the congressional delegations of the three West Coast states. Public opinion should not be the determining factor in making a military appraisal, but it is bound to occur to those engaged in that task how they will be regarded if they reject a widely popular security measure that in retrospect turns out to have been necessary.

The United States prides itself on having a system in which the civilian heads of the service departments are supreme over the military chiefs, so one might expect that Henry Stimson and John McCloy would have made a more careful evaluation of the evacuation proposal than they appear to have done. Far from the Pacific Coast, they would be expected to have a more detached view than the commander on the scene. But here too there seems to have been a tendency to feel that concern for civil liberty was not their responsibility. There is even more of this feeling in Roosevelt's perfunctory approval of the plan in response to a phone call from Stimpson.

Biddle's protests proved futile even at the highest levels of government, in part because no significant element of public opinion opposed the relocation.

Once the relocation plan was in place, it could be challenged only in the courts. Was the Supreme Court at fault in upholding first the curfew, in *Hirabayashi,* and then the relocation, in *Korematsu*? In *Hirabayashi* the Court could have decided both the validity of the relocation requirement and the curfew requirement, for the "concurrent sentence" doctrine under which it declined to do so is discretionary. But counseling against any broader decision was the well-established rule that the Court should avoid deciding constitutional questions if at all possible, and so the *Hirabayashi* decision left the far more difficult question for another day.

When that day came, in *Korematsu,* a majority of the Court upheld the relocation program. Justice Black's opinion for the Court in *Korematsu* followed the same line of reasoning as had Chief Justice Stone's in Hirabayashi. But this time there were three dissenters, who had voted to uphold the curfew but wanted to strike down the relocation program.

OVER THE YEARS, SEVERAL CRITICISMS HAVE BEEN made of the Court's opinions in these cases. The most general is of its extremely deferential treatment given to the government's argument that the curfew and relocation were necessitated by military considerations. Here one can only echo Justice Jackson's observation that "in the very nature of things, military decisions are not susceptible of intelligent judicial appraisal." But it surely does not follow from this that a court must therefore invalidate measures based on military judgments. Eugene Rostow suggested holding a judicial inquiry into the entire question of military necessity, but this seems an extraordinarily dubious proposition. Judicial inquiry, with its restrictive rules of evidence, orientation toward resolution of factual disputes in individual cases, and long delays, is ill suited to determine an urgent issue. The necessity for prompt action was cogently stated by the Court in its *Hirabayashi* opinion: "Although the results of the attack on Pearl Harbor were not fully disclosed until much later, it was known that the damage was extensive, and that the Japanese by their successes had gained a naval superiority over our forces in the Pacific which might enable them to seize Pearl Harbor, our largest naval base and the last stronghold of defense lying between Japan and the west coast. That reasonably prudent men charged with the responsibility of our national defense had ample ground for concluding that they must face the danger of invasion, take measures against it, and in making the choice of measures consider our internal situation, cannot be doubted."

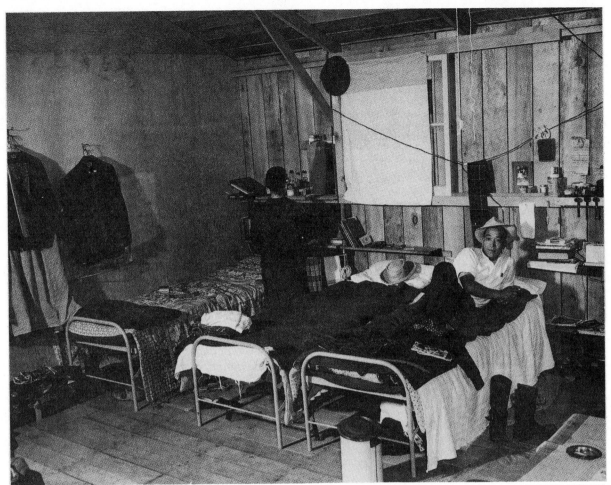

Evacuees in Salinas, according to the caption on this government photo, "enjoy a moment of relaxation."

A SECOND CRITICISM IS THAT THE DECISIONS IN THESE cases upheld a program that, at bottom, was based on racial distinctions. There are several levels at which this criticism can be made. The broadest is that the nisei were relocated simply because the Caucasian majority on the West Coast (and in the country as a whole) disliked them and wished to remove them as neighbors or as business competitors. The Court's answer to this attack seems satisfactory: Those of Japanese descent were displaced because of fear that disloyal elements among them would aid Japan in the war. Though there were undoubtedly nativists in California who welcomed a chance to see the issei and the nisei removed, it does not follow that this point of view was attributable to the military decision-makers. They, after all, did not at first propose relocation.

But a narrower criticism along the same line has more force to it: The nisei were evacuated notwithstanding the fact that they were American citizens. Even in wartime citizens may not be rounded up and required to prove their loyalty. They may be excluded from sensitive military areas in the absence of a security clearance and otherwise be denied access to any classified information, but it pushes these propositions to an extreme to say that a

sizable geographic area, including the homes of many citizens, may be declared off-limits and the residents forced to move. It pushes it to an even greater extreme to say that such persons may be required not only to leave their homes but to report to and remain in a distant relocation center.

The Supreme Court in its *Hirabayashi* opinion pointed to several facts thought to justify this treatment of the nisei. Both federal and state restrictions on the rights of Japanese immigrants had prevented their assimilation into the Caucasian population and had intensified their insularity and solidarity. Japanese parents sent their children to Japanese language schools, and there was some evidence that these were a source of Japanese nationalistic propaganda. As many as ten thousand American-born children of Japanese parentage went to Japan for all or a part of their education. Thus, as Stone put it in his opinion, "we cannot say that the war-making branches of the Government did not have ground for believing that in a critical hour such persons . . . constituted a menace to the national defense and safety . . ."

There is considerable irony, of course, in relying on previously existing laws discriminating against Japanese immigrants to conclude that still further disabilities should be imposed upon them because they had not been assimilated into the Caucasian majority. But in time of war a nation may be required to respond to a condition without making a careful inquiry into how that condition came about.

Were the condition or conditions described by the Court sufficient to justify treating the nisei differently from all other citizens on the West Coast? Under today's constitutional law, certainly not. Any sort of "racial" classification by government is viewed as suspect, and an extraordinarily strong reason is required to justify it.

dislodging of thousands of citizens from their homes on the basis of ancestry.

The issei, however, who were not citizens, were both by tradition and by law in a quite different category. The legal difference dates back to the Alien Enemies Law enacted in 1798 during the administration of President John Adams. The Alien Law is often bracketed together with the Sedition Act passed at the same time, and there is a tendency to think that both were repealed as soon as Thomas Jefferson and his Jeffersonian Republicans came to power in 1801. But only the Sedition Act was repealed;

Were the conditions described by the Court sufficient to justify different treatment of the nisei? Under today's constitutional law, certainly not.

But the law was by no means so clear when these cases were decided. A decade later the Court decided the watershed case of *Brown* v. *Board of Education*, holding that the Kansas legislature had violated the Equal Protection Clause of the Fourteenth Amendment by permitting public schools to segregate students by race. And with *Brown* there was argued a companion case, *Bolling* v. *Sharpe*, challenging similarly imposed segregation in public schools in the District of Columbia. This requirement had been imposed not by a state government but by Congress. The Court in *Bolling*, in a brief opinion not notable for clarity of reasoning, held that the Due Process Clause of the Fifth Amendment imposes on the federal government a limitation similar to that imposed on the states by the Equal Protection Clause of the Fourteenth Amendment. Had this doctrine been the law ten years earlier, the Supreme Court might have found it easier to reach a different result in *Hirabayashi* and *Korematsu*.

The discrimination against the nisei lay in the fact that any other citizen could remain in his home unless actually tried and convicted of espionage or sabotage while the nisei were removed from their homes without any individualized findings at all. The proffered justification—that an attack on the West Coast by Japan was reasonably feared and that American citizens of Japanese descent were more likely than the populace as a whole to include potential spies or saboteurs—was not wholly groundless. A May 1941 "Magic intercept," resulting from the Americans' having broken the Japanese code, contained a message from the Japanese consulate in Los Angeles that "we also have connections with our second generations working in airplane plants for intelligence purposes." But although such information might well have justified exclusion of nisei, as opposed to other citizens, from work in aircraft factories without strict security clearance, it falls considerably short of justifying the

the Alien Enemies Act, with minor amendments, remained on the books at the time of World War II. It provided: "Whenever there shall be a declared war between the United States and any foreign nation or government . . . all natives, citizens, denizens, or subjects of the hostile nation or government, being of the age of fourteen years and upward, who shall be within the United States and not actually naturalized, shall be liable to be apprehended, restrained, secured, and removed as alien enemies.

IN A CASE DECIDED SHORTLY AFTER THE END OF WORLD War II, the Supreme Court, referring to the Alien Law, said: "Executive power over enemy aliens, undelayed and unhampered by litigation, has been deemed, throughout our history, essential to war-time security. This is in keeping with the practice of the most enlightened of nations and has resulted in treatment of alien enemies more considerate than that which has prevailed among any of our enemies and some our allies. This statute was enacted or suffered to continue by men who helped found the Republic and formulate the Bill of Rights, and although it obviously denies enemy aliens the constitutional immunities of citizens, it seems not then to have been supposed that a nation's obligations to its foes could ever be put on a parity with those to its defenders. The resident enemy alien is constitutionally subject to summary arrest, internment and deportation whenever a 'declared war' exists." Thus distinctions that might not be permissible between classes of citizens must be viewed otherwise when drawn between classes of aliens.

The most frequently made charge on behalf of the issei is that the government treated Japanese enemy aliens differently from enemy aliens of German or Italian citizenship when we were at war with all three countries. It appears that there was some removal of Italian enemy aliens for a brief period, but there seems little doubt that the West Coast issei were treated differently from the majority of German or Italian nationals residing in this country. It should be pointed out, however, that there does not appear to have been the same concentration of German or Italian nationals along the West Coast in areas near major defense plants. Japanese emigration to the United States had occurred only within the preceding half-century, and the emigrants resided almost entirely on the West Coast, where U.S. aircraft production was highly concentrated and where attack and possibly invasion were at first feared. Italian emigration had taken place over a considerably longer period, and German since colonial days, and people of German and Italian ancestry were far more spread out in the population in general than were the issei.

These distinctions seem insufficient to justify such a sharp difference of treatment between Japanese and German and Italian aliens in peacetime. But they do seem legally adequate to support the difference in treatment between the two classes of enemy aliens in time of war.

An entirely separate and important philosophical question is whether occasional presidential excesses and judicial restraint in wartime are desirable or undesirable. In one sense this question is very largely academic. There is no reason to think that future wartime Presidents will act differently from Roosevelt or that future Justices of the Supreme Court will decide questions differently from their predecessors. But even though this be so, there is every reason to believe that the historic trend against the least justified of the curtailments of civil liberty in wartime will continue in the future. It is neither desirable nor remotely likely that civil liberty will occupy as favored a position in wartime as it does in peacetime. But it is both desirable and likely that the courts will pay more careful attention to the basis for the government's claims of necessity as a reason for curtailing civil liberty. The laws will thus not be silent in time of war, even though they will speak with a somewhat different voice.

William H. Rehnquist is Chief Justice of the United States. This essay has been adapted from his book All the Laws but One: Civil Liberties in Wartime, *published in October 1998 by Alfred A. Knopf.*

Unit Selections

6. **Poverty 101: What Liberals and Conservatives Can Learn from Each Other,** David Kuo
7. **D.C.'s Indentured Servants,** Martha Honey
8. **Government Can't Cure Poverty,** Robert L. Woodson Sr.
9. **Counting Race and Ethnicity: Options for the 2000 Census,** Judith Lichtenberg, Suzanne Bianchi, Robert Wachbroit, and David Wasserman
10. **Of Race and Risk,** Patricia J. Williams
11. **In Defense of Affirmative Action,** Chang-Lin Tien
12. **Service Redlining: The New Jim Crow?** Chevon Fuller
13. **The War between Men and Women,** Robert Sapolsky
14. **Homosexuality across Cultures: Sensitizing Social Workers to Historical Issues Facing Gay, Lesbian and Bisexual Youth,** David Skiba

Key Points to Consider

❖ Do you agree or disagree that there is some middle ground of facts and solutions regarding poverty upon which both liberals and conservatives could reasonably agree? Defend your answer.

❖ How pervasive is the problem of poverty in terms of absolute numbers and its effect on other problems in society? Do you believe that the federal government can really end poverty if it wanted to? Explain.

❖ In terms of the year 2000 Census, do you agree or disagree that people should be able to identify themselves as multiracial and multiethnic? Why or why not? What, if any, impacts would such a change have on government, on organizations, or on society in general?

❖ Is affirmative action still needed to end discrimination against minorities of color and against women? Defend your position.

❖ Do you believe that "redlining" still exists? In a free market economy, can any community really defend itself against redlining of essential goods and services by corporations? Explain.

❖ As a society, have we become overly sensitive on issues of gender and sexual orientation? Explain your position.

 **Links** **www.dushkin.com/online/**

14. **American Studies Web**
http://www.georgetown.edu/crossroads/asw/

15. **Grass-Roots.Org**
http://www.grass-roots.org

16. **Marketplace of Political Ideas/University of Houston Library**
http://info.lib.uh.edu/politics/markind.htm

17. **Patterns of Variability: The Concept of Race**
http://www.as.ua.edu/ant/bindon/ant101/syllabus/race/race1.htm

18. **Poverty in America Research Index**
http://www.mindspring.com/~nexweb21/povindex.htm

19. **The University of Minnesota's Children, Youth and Family Consortium**
http://www.cyfc.umn.edu/Parenting/parentlink.html

These sites are annotated on pages 4 and 5.

Once you have some historical sense of the problems and responses of the social welfare system, it is time to move forward to the present day. The same problems of poverty and discrimination still persist, and, to no one's surprise, they continue to be complex, multidimensional phenomena that affect a whole range of other, related problems.

This section delves into the problems of poverty and discrimination and assumes that you have already read in your textbooks or discussed in class some of the important introductory material (for example, current statistics on poverty and on people who are poor; the Poverty Index as a measurement of poverty; the causes and consequences of poverty; the civil rights movement; affirmative action legislation; the issue of "reverse discrimination").

There are many ways to define poverty, but perhaps the simplest and most straightforward is to say that it is the situation of not having enough financial resources to pay for the basic necessities of food, clothing, shelter, and whatever else is needed to be a mature, responsible, and active individual in society. In the first reading in this unit, David Kuo reminds us of how complex the problem of poverty really is, and he cautions both liberals and conservatives to look for some middle ground in the debate over how to respond adequately to this critical issue.

In the essay "D.C.'s Indentured Servants," Martha Honey exposes the little-known existence of poverty among foreign-born domestic servants who work for the rich and the powerful. This is followed by Robert Woodson's conservative response to eradicating poverty (see "Government Can't Cure Poverty").

The rest of the articles in this section focus on the problem of discrimination based on a person's race, ethnic heritage, gender, or sexual orientation. There is also an article on affirmative action, which has been generally accepted, until recently, as an appropriate societal response to these problems. You would do well to approach these articles not as "answers" to the problem of discrimination, but rather as "hot buttons" that are designed to get you thinking and discussing in class all of the issues and all of the emotions that this topic tends to generate in most people. Remember that every person approaches the issues of prejudice or discrimination with a unique set of past experiences, family values, personal attitudes, and future hopes. It is vitally important in any discussion of such a sensitive issue to first listen—really listen—before responding with your own experiences, values, attitudes or hopes.

Having said that, the article "Counting Race and Ethnicity: Options for the 2000 Census," by Judith Lichtenberg, Suzanne Bianchi, Robert Wachbroit, and David Wasserman, does not appear to be very controversial. Indeed, it may not be, but it does raise an issue that is sensitive for many people:

How do I wish to be counted if my parents or grandparents share different racial or ethnic identities? The Census Bureau is still struggling with this issue as it develops the survey instruments for the year 2000 Census.

Patricia Williams, in "Of Race and Risk," adds a personal note to the issue of racism by describing the impediments that she encountered as an African American woman applying for a home mortgage.

"In Defense of Affirmative Action," by Chang-Lin Tien, should elicit some diverse reactions in any group discussion. Certainly, affirmative action has become a highly controversial issue, particularly in academic and employment settings. Whether affirmative action has outlived its usefulness or not will undoubtedly be debated into the foreseeable future.

Approaching the subject of discrimination from a community perspective, Chevon Fuller, in "Service Redlining: The New Jim Crow?" challenges you to consider whether minority communities are being further disadvantaged by their lack of access to essential services.

The final two readings in this section relate to discrimination based on a person's gender or sexual orientation. Robert Sapolsky, in "The War between Men and Women," offers a scientific basis as a possible explanation for some of the tension between men and women that might be interpreted as discrimination. Then, David Skiba addresses his article to social workers and provides an overview of issues facing gay men, lesbians, and bisexual persons in cross-cultural contexts.

POVERTY 101

WHAT LIBERALS AND CONSERVATIVES CAN LEARN FROM EACH OTHER

By DAVID KUO

The 21st century has already begun with a radical new welfare system that fundamentally changes how America cares for her poor, dependent, jobless, and abused. The 1996 welfare reform law was the result of a decade of often dramatic and contentious debate about the proper nature of reform. On the one side were conservative reformers who demanded work requirements, illegitimacy prevention, and general de-entitlement. On the other were liberal reformers who also had an interest in work requirements and better job placement but wanted to see the essential characteristics of the social safety net remain intact.

The heat of the last debate was often painfully intense, but perhaps the lull before the next welfare debate begins will afford both camps of reformers the opportunity to learn from each other—especially when it comes to the hard work of recreating civil society and a private sector approach to caring for those individuals in need.

Liberals first. Faith matters. Ironically for a liberal welfare tradition that had its roots in religious revival, many of today's liberals acknowledge that religious faith is certainly a matter of importance, while ignoring—or being actively hostile to—its policy potential as a catalyst for radical change in people's lives.

During the last welfare debate, for instance, Senator John Ashcroft's "charitable choice" provision to allow states to contract with private and religious charitable organizations using federal funds was broadly attacked by many on the left. Yet its basic purpose was simply to level the playing field for faith based not-for-profits.

Overwhelming evidence coming from groups as diverse as the Heritage Foundation and Public/Private Ventures suggests that faith is not only important, it may be *the* factor in determining whether an at-risk child, a welfare mother, or a convicted criminal is able to turn his or her life around. It is vital that political liberals embrace this idea. The next year will give them opportunities to do so: new efforts to encourage this kind of religious element in

David Kuo is president of The American Compass.

welfare include the charity tax credit and further implementation of charitable choice-type measures.

Conservatives next. Governmental programs can do—and have done—good. In just the past few decades, hunger and malnutrition have become far less serious social problems thanks to food stamps. Where once one out of every three elderly Americans was in poverty, today that number has dropped to about one in ten, thanks to the indexing of Social Security benefits and Medicare. These are social policy successes virtually without parallel.

Despite its well-documented failures, particularly vis-à-vis the family, the War on Poverty changed the face of poverty. The lesson for conservatives is that keeping intact a safety net of noncash services for the poor—and especially for the children—is crucial to preventing future welfare dependency. In a recent book, *What Money Can't Buy,* University of Chicago professor Susan Mayer pointed out that the two most important things determining a child's future are, first, that his or her basic needs be met, and, second, that he or she be the child of parents with character. Legislatively, little can be done to ensure the second. Realistically, improving the delivery mechanisms for programs like Medicaid so that those who use the services will have better care and better access should be at the forefront of the conservative agenda.

Liberals need to place more trust in the private sector. Long skeptical of some conservative claims that the private sector could replace decades-old government programs overnight, some liberals appear to believe that the private sector can actually do very little—while clinging to the belief that true compassion is directly related to federal spending on welfare. In fact, free market charity and social entrepreneurism operating without the debilitating effects of government are the real hopes for making a transformational difference.

Looking to examples like the "He Is Pleased" program in Delaware, founded by mutual fund magnate Foster Friess, the evidence is apparent that the social sector is a market like any other—with one difference: here the profit isn't financial, it is personal. He Is Pleased helps homeless men and women transition from the streets into full-time employment. Started with venture capital from Friess several years ago, HIP has already helped about 100 homeless people change their lives. Grounded in hard work—a 90-day cycle of paid work cleaning up the city—and tough rules—tardiness is not accepted, drug tests are mandatory—HIP is a social sector equivalent to micro-corporations like Apple or Sun Microsystems 20 years ago. It is cutting-edge, it is optimistic, and it is providing a challenge to established forms of charity. Scores of programs like these have sprung up across the country—they are the best hope for change and need to be supported.

Conservatives must not trust blindly in the private sector. One temptation to which conservatives sometimes succumb is believing that all government programs are bad and all private charity programs are good. Both are quite untrue.

Conservatives ought not to paint too rosy a picture of private sector charity. Rhetorically, they asked Americans to choose between government and charity, HUD or Habitat for Humanity, HHS or the Red Cross, knowing the answer they would get. But in so doing, they ignored the reality that many of the biggest and best known organizations—groups with multibillion dollar budgets and national recognition—have served as little more than private sector surrogates of the welfare state. Groups like the United Way, the Red Cross, and Catholic Charities receive a substantial portion of their funding from the federal government. Not coincidentally, they also tend to reflect in mission, means, and orientation the government model of impersonal, bureaucratic, and secular assistance that is a far cry from the kind of assistance people need. Conservatives who have been at the forefront of critiquing government should now be at the forefront of critiquing the private sector—of pointing out the good, the noble, and the bad. The recently completed National Commission on Philanthropy and Civic Renewal took a much-needed step in this direction.

Work: The First Step to Beating Poverty

Liberals need to better appreciate the importance of work—all work. Too often liberals have focused on the availability of "good" jobs to the exclusion of encouraging employment. Belittling "low-wage" jobs as demeaning, intentionally or unintentionally they sent a message that work, in and of itself, is not that important—that only "good" jobs count. Conservatives, for their part, need to consider the barriers to moving from welfare to work. Moving to a low-paying job can mean giving up medical benefits for one's children—a clear systemic barrier to work.

Most studies show that getting and keeping a job, any job, is the most essential step to beating poverty. Finding and keeping a job provides more than income. It provides a sense of self-worth and accomplishment. It does something else as well—it almost guarantees raises. While having focused on job training and job opportunities, liberals haven't focused enough on putting people to work—a sort of trial by employment fire. Early evidence from the states seems to suggest that for many people on welfare, the new welfare law provided the impetus to change. This is not to say that all have found work or will be able to, but it is an important lesson—one that, as Governor Thompson of Wisconsin has shown, sometimes requires state spending.

Poverty: A Grinding Reality

A final thought for conservatives. Poverty in America is real. Some on the right seem to suggest that poverty is just an invention of the left, that it is mostly a matter of sloth and bad bookkeeping.

While poverty may not be as life-threatening as it once was, it can still be dark and desperate. As accounts like *There Are No Children Here* and *Turning Stones* have shown, poverty is not just "poverty" though its ravages can turn children into "children"—kids who may be chronologically young but who have seen and experienced life that is beyond the nightmares of many adults.

Coming to grips with the reality of poverty in America may be the most important thing that conservatives can learn from liberals. Certainly it would change the tone of conservatism. Conservatives will have more success undoing the welfare state if they abandon arguments asserting that all of America's poor are either "undeserving" or "nonexistent."

The hope that liberals and conservatives can take the time to learn from each other on matters of poverty springs from the common ground they have already found in the need to strengthen America's civil sector. In just the past half-decade, politicians, pundits, and professors from across the ideological spectrum have come to the recognition that the real hope of reform and the true answers to long-vexing social problems will come from "civil society."

That agreement is rooted in a common appreciation that communities and civic groups and churches have strengths and abilities beyond the dreams of government. They are actively and intimately involved in needy individuals' lives. They share a common code of moral responsibility that provides guidance and guardrails. They have elements of faith that touch people in a far more profound way than a check or a voucher.

If this kind of agreement could find a way to grow in the poisonous atmosphere of the last welfare debate, let us all hope that in this calm after the storm the two sides will come together even more closely and revivify our common lives.

D.C.'S INDENTURED SERVANTS

BY MARTHA HONEY

The brick townhouse with its aluminum front door blends into northern Virginia's suburban sprawl. From the outside it doesn't look like what it is: a modern-day underground railway station for runaway domestic workers imported from the Third World. The smell of spicy food and the sound of high-pitched chatter drifts out of the kitchen. A cluster of about eight women—runaway nannies and housekeepers, most of them from the Philippines— gathers here. Among them is twenty-three-year-old Marilyn Caracas. Here is her story: A distant relative brought Caracas from the Philippines to clean her Fairfax, Virginia, house and care for her three children. Before getting her visa from the U.S. Embassy in Manila, Caracas signed a contract with her employer, who promised to adhere to U.S. labor laws.

But when Caracas arrived in Washington in March 1994, things were not as she expected. On weekends she cleaned the woman's house and took care of her children. Monday through Friday she stayed at the house of the woman's mother-in-law, where Caracas ran an unregistered day-care center for eleven children, in addition to taking care of the older woman. Caracas says she worked from 6:30 A.M. to 11 P.M. seven days a week, and received a mere $230 a month. (Each child at the day-care center paid the mother-in-law $600 a month.) Caracas's employer took her passport and threatened to dismiss and deport her if she complained, Caracas says.

Caracas was exhausted and sick. She says she didn't know where to turn for help. "I was very sad and afraid. I didn't know anyone and didn't know the regulations, the laws," she says. "They told me they don't want me to talk with others, even my co-Filipinos."

One evening she was allowed out to go to the store to buy sanitary napkins. By chance, she met and talked with two other Filipinas who told her about the brick townhouse. For months she plotted her escape. Then, when the mother-in-law went on vacation, leaving Caracas alone, she searched the house and found her passport, which her employer had hidden in the back of a closet. She called the townhouse and one of the residents there came and got her.

For several years, this townhouse has served as a clandestine way-station on a modern-day underground railway. The owner, "Rose" (not her real name), is part of an informal network of people involved in helping foreign domestic servants escape illegal, exploitative, and sometimes abusive employment situations. Rose gives them a place to stay, counseling, and a community.

Scattered around Washington are other way-stations, mainly churches and social-service centers, that have aided hundreds of foreign domestic workers to escape bad situations, find other employment, and get legal help.

In Caracas's case it didn't work. Through a Washington immigration at-

torney, Edward Leavy, Caracas filed a $600,000 suit against her employer. But the employer contacted Caracas's father in the Philippines, protesting that his daughter was making false accusations and bringing shame on the entire family. Under this pressure, Caracas dropped the lawsuit and returned to the Philippines. Nothing happened to the employer, who works for the International Monetary Fund and repeatedly refused to discuss the case. So did officials at the IMF, who argue that this is "a private not an institutional matter."

Caracas and the other runaways are some of the thousands of foreign domestic workers who enter the United States legally to work for diplomats or executives with the World Bank, the IMF, the InterAmerican Development Bank, and other international agencies. Some employers are American. Most are from overseas. Their employees come with the help of special State Department programs that permit international bureaucrats and diplomats to "import" household help (housekeepers, nannies, cooks,

Martha Honey is a journalist and research fellow at the Institute for Policy Studies in Washington, D.C. She wrote "Guatemalan Hit Squads Come to the U.S.A." in the June 1996 issue.

'These women have been virtually under house arrest, forced to work seven days a week basically around the clock, and haven't seen the light of day for two or three years.'

gardeners, drivers, etc.) on either A-3 or G-5 visas. The visas are good for a year, and can be renewed as long as the servant is working for either a diplomat or an international civil servant. In 1994, the State Department issued 3,400 of these visas; 875—or one-quarter—went to Filipino servants.

The domestic servants are mostly women, often single mothers, from poor families in Asia, Africa, and Latin America. "If they come here, it's because they are very poor in their own countries, and they need to support their families. After they made the sacrifice to leave their country, they don't want to go back without money," says Sister Manuela Vencela, assistant pastor at Our Lady Queen of the Americas Church in Washington.

To get the visa, their employers must agree, often with written contracts, to provide "reasonable living and working conditions" as defined under U.S. labor laws. This is supposed to include transportation to and from the United States, wages "no less than" the minimum wage, overtime, fixed hours, time off, sick leave, and paid vacation. Both the IMF and the World Bank (where, according to *Time* magazine, salaries and benefit packages average $123,000 tax-free) have special offices that handle the paperwork involved in importing a domestic servant. But frequently the employers ignore the contracts and illegally force their live-in domestics to work very long hours for little pay. In a few cases, the employers have neglected to pay their servants at all.

"I've been shocked to find that these domestics—they are always women—have been virtually under house arrest, forced to work seven days a week basically around the clock, and haven't seen the light of day for two or three years," says Leavy. "They weren't properly paid, and they were threatened with deportation."

He and other lawyers representing domestics say neither the State Department nor the other institutions involved check to make sure that employers of foreign domestic servants follow U.S. labor laws. One IMF official, who asks not to be identified, describes the Fund as "a facilitator, not a policeman." He says that if the contract is broken, "the IMF really can't

do an awful lot." Even so, he concedes, publicity about these cases is "an embarrassment."

John Connolly, an Alexandria, Virginia, attorney who has handled a number of these cases, blames "the State Department for not following through and attempting to monitor these private-employment agreements" and "the IMF and World Bank for not attempting to ensure that their employees are acting in accordance with U.S. law."

Employers incur the expense of hiring overseas because imported help is considered more controllable. Workers are less likely to quit, run away, or sue, and more likely to endure long hours and low pay without complaint. Employment counselor Celia Rivas, who works at the Spanish Catholic Center in Gaithersburg, Maryland, recalls that a domestic from the Dominican Republic once told her that her employer had proclaimed: "If I ask you to kiss the floor, you have to. You are part of my property. I brought you here and you have to do what I tell you."

Isolation and ignorance are keys to control. Some employers hold their servants' passports and discourage them from leaving the house alone or developing independent friendships. Some even send their servants' pay to overseas bank accounts, according to several former servants and their lawyers. Many servants do not speak English.

If one decides to escape, her route to freedom may begin with a chance meeting with a good Samaritan such as Rose, who fell into her Harriet Tubman-like role by accident. She worked first in Hong Kong and then in Washington for an American diplomatic family whom she says, "thank God," treated her well.

One day at a playground she met another nanny, "Jane," from Guyana, who worked for an Australian woman employed by the IMF. "She was very upset because she was getting only $250 a month" for caring for the woman's son and doing the cooking, cleaning, and laundry, says Rose. Jane told Rose that before leaving Guyana, she had signed a contract with her employer, who agreed to pay minimum wage, give her free room and board, and keep fixed hours of employment.

Based on this contract, the U.S. Embassy issued Jane a one-year G-5 visa. But when Jane reached the United States, her new employer took her passport and ignored the contract, saying "I don't need to give you a higher salary because I did all the work to get you your visa."

Many months later, Jane called Rose to say she was quitting and running away. "She came to my house," says Rose. "Where can she go? She doesn't know anyone. So I had to take her with me." The next day Rose called Ed Leavy, whose name she had gotten through a friend. Leavy succeeded in winning a modest out-of-court settlement for Jane. After that, Rose began assisting other runaway servants, mostly Filipinas.

Leavy first became aware of the problem about fifteen years ago while doing volunteer work at the Spanish Catholic Center in Washington. He has handled several dozen cases. He ticks off a list of his most memorable cases:

• In 1991, Sangita Satyal, a Nepalese domestic servant, was awarded about $40,000 in wages and legal fees from her Nepalese employer, an IMF economist and his wife. Before receiving a visa, Satyal signed the usual contract guaranteeing minimum wage, overtime, and time off. But, unbeknownst to Satyal and the State Department, the economist executed a secondary contract with the woman's father in Nepal in which the economist promised to deposit $50 each month into a bank account. Satyal received room and food, but no salary, and was denied access to the bank account.

• At the McLean, Virginia, home of a Saudi Arabian diplomat, three Filipina women lived, dormitory-style, in the basement. They worked around the clock. Each received only $100 a month. When one of Leavy's colleagues contacted the diplomat, he agreed to an out-of-court settlement rather than undergo the public embarrassment of a trial.

• A Tanzanian analyst at the World Bank brought a registered nurse from his tribe to work as a nanny and domestic, promising that in addition to meeting the terms of the contract, he would allow her to go to university at night. Instead, for two years, she was paid $50 to $100 a week and forced to work seven days a week. Her employer never allowed her to go to school. The

'I could never buy anything new and my shoes had holes in the bottom. When I went grocery shopping I had to put plastic bags on my feet so the snow would not go into my shoes.'

woman finally complained to the World Bank's ethics office, which eventually decided that her employer owed her $13,500. The Tanzanian official refused to pay. The woman then retained Leavy and Connolly, who reached an out-of-court settlement of $21,000.

"At least I had my dignity and I punished them. I showed them that they could not do that," she says. She has since found other employment and succeeded in graduating from college.

In Third World countries, high-level bureaucrats commonly employ household servants for a pittance. Many of these elite seem to see little wrong in doing so when they come to the United States—especially when they believe no one is watching.

Diplomats and foreign executives tend to bring in domestic servants from their own countries. Diplomats who come from the Middle East and Asia often recruit help from the Philippines.

But as the case of Jane and her Australian employer shows, there have also been instances of First World abuse.

A small number of American diplomats or businessmen who are subject to international assignment and are temporarily reassigned to the United States are also permitted to bring in domestic help on a temporary B-1 visa.

One of the most notorious cases to reach the courts involved a Malawian man, Caleb Zintambila, who was brought to the United States by an official with the United States Information Agency. Zintambila says he was paid only $40 a month, which he had to use to buy his own food, and was forced to work up to eighteen hours a day, seven days a week, sleep on a piece of cardboard in the unfinished basement of his employer's Potomac home, and bathe in the backyard with a bucket. "Even in Africa, I didn't wash with a bucket," says Zintambila.

During his two-year employment, Zintambila managed to send $20 a month to Malawi to support his four children. "I could never buy anything new and my shoes had holes in the bottom. When I went grocery shopping I had to put plastic bags on my feet so the snow would not go into my shoes," he explained. He said he managed to

escape with the help of a woman from Trinidad who, by chance, stopped to talk with him while he was mowing the lawn. She found him a good job with a Norwegian family. He brought a lawsuit and eventually was awarded $50,000 in damages.

The lawyers who handle such cases suspect they are seeing just the tip of the iceberg: Many servants either endure exploitation in silence or escape on their own, hiding out in the various multinational communities around Washington.

The State Department has long been aware that servants are being mistreated and labor laws violated. In 1981, Secretary of State Edmund Muskie wrote a memo expressing "deep concern" over evidence that some diplomats based in Washington had "seriously abused or exploited household servants." For six months following Muskie's memo, written contracts were mandatory—even for diplomats. But just six months later, after Muskie left office, the State Department issued a new directive, stating that "requiring employment contracts in each and every case might be unnecessarily burdensome." The State Department dropped the written-contract requirement.

Today, consular officers in U.S. embassies are given the discretion to ensure, either verbally or in writing, that the foreign employers and their servants understand that U.S. labor laws must be followed. This has meant that some servants, particularly those working for diplomats, arrive without a written contract.

In 1995, the State Department submitted a "Statement of Interest" in the case of a Filipina servant, Corazón Tabion, who sued her employer, a Jordanian diplomat. Tabion said that during the two years she worked in the diplomat's home, she was paid only about $50 a week for more than sixty hours of work. The diplomat claimed he could not be sued because he has diplomatic immunity. To the astonishment of John Connolly, Tabion's lawyer, the State Department upheld this claim. The case was dismissed.

"We believe the result is extraordinarily unjust," says Connolly. "The idea that a diplomat can employ someone under the conditions that our client was employed—which were totally unacceptable—and escape any liability is

really an affront to our entire system of jurisprudence and fair play."

State Department officials pledge that they will examine cases brought to their attention.

A May 1996 directive says, "The Department will examine closely any case of alleged abuse by a personal servant, attendant, or domestic that is brought to its attention." The State Department receives only "about one" complaint a year, according to a State Department official, who asks not to be identified.

But abuses continue, as the State Department itself acknowledges. In a May 1996 memo, the State Department again said it was "concerned to learn of problems" including "instances where wages have been withheld from personal domestics for undue periods; where the wages actually paid are substantially less than those stipulated at the time of employment; where passports have been withheld from the employee; where the actual number of working hours weekly is substantially more than those originally contemplated and with no additional pay; and where the employee has been forbidden from leaving the employer's premises even though off duty."

The new immigration law, which came into effect October 1, has further narrowed the options and upped the anxiety of exploited domestic servants.

Lawyers and social workers say foreign workers are now even less likely to come forward to bring legal action because they fear that—even if they win their case—they will be deported.

The problem of abuse is not confined to Washington. Leavy and other lawyers have handled cases of exploited domestic servants working for United Nations officials in New York. In Geneva, the problem led labor activists to form a union to fight for the rights of domestic servants. But U.S. labor-union officials say organizing domestic workers is nearly impossible because they lack a single employer.

Leavy calls such cases "slavery in the shadow of the Capitol." Washington's modern-day underground railway is the best shot many of these workers have.

Government Can't Cure
POVERTY

*".. . Of the more than five trillion dollars that have been poured
into anti- poverty programs and agencies, only 30 cents of each dollar
have made it to the hands of the poor."*

by Robert L. Woodson, Sr.

POVERTY does not create crime, nor does unemployment. In the past, rather than generating social disintegration, times of economic hardship often strengthened the bonds of family, neighborhood, and community. What is it about our response to poverty today that is different from the way we addressed poverty in the past? What is it that has formed a link among poverty, crime, and social deviance? How was it that, in other times, having no money did *not* equate with being in a state of "poverty"? Why do some people recall childhood memories of families pulling together in tightly knit neighborhoods and then remark, "It wasn't until years later that I realized we were poor"?

In the past, where indigenous community support structures were intact, economic hardship was considered to be more of a temporary challenge than an intergenerational condition. Established community associations and church-affiliated organizations historically have functioned to give relief to the needy on a one-to-one basis. It is only within the last 30 years that an institutionalized bureaucracy has developed to administer programs for the poor, complete with a massive standing base of "dependents."

Throughout the history of the black community, for example, grassroots associations such as mutual-aid societies pro-

Mr. Woodson is founder and president, National Center for Neighborhood Enterprise, Washington, D.C. This article is based on a Hillsdale (Mich.) College Center for Constructive Alternatives seminar.

vided relief for those who were in need. The first of these was the Free African Society, founded in Philadelphia in 1787, the members of which contributed one shilling a month for distribution to the needy, with the stipulation that "this necessity is not brought on them by their own imprudence." Throughout the 1800s, mutual-aid societies multiplied throughout the North and, by the 1830s, 100 such organizations were functioning in the city of Philadelphia alone, with an average membership of 75. Mutual-aid societies were a main source of support for blacks in the South, in spite of obstacles of laws that prohibited blacks from assembling. At the end of the 18th century, in addition to providing relief for the needy, mutual-benefit societies and black churches maintained their own schools. As early as 1790, the Brown Fellowship Society provided educational facilities as part of its mutual-welfare program.

As the Federal welfare system took on the roles that formerly had been fulfilled by the indigenous community associations and churches, a major shift occurred. Whereas nearly all previous aid to the poor involved reciprocity—a contribution of work on behalf of any able recipients and a balance of rights and responsibilities—many of the regulations within the Federal welfare system actually functioned as disincentives regarding work, savings, and movement toward self-sufficiency.

For instance, because rates of rent for public housing are calculated as 30% of the household income, as residents make economic progress, they are penalized, in effect, for any increase in income. Without a cap on rents, in some cases payment de-

manded for public housing, units rose above market rates. In addition, regulations stipulated that welfare recipients could have no more than $1,000 in savings. In one case that made headlines, this meant that the mother of a young girl who had taken a part-time job to save for college was fined three times the amount that her daughter had managed to save, and the family was threatened with the termination of all welfare benefits.

Whether or not such regulations consciously were intended to limit the upward mobility of those in the system, they have produced a steady "client base" for what has become a literal "poverty industry." To date, of the more than five trillion dollars that have been poured into anti-poverty programs and agencies, only 30 cents of each dollar have made it to the hands of the poor. Seventy cents of each dollar have been absorbed by those who "serve" the poor. It is not surprising, therefore, that the system itself has been reluctant to embrace reform.

The 30-year rein of the "Poverty Pentagon" has taken its toll on a deeper level than financial stagnation. The system has usurped and weakened the natural indigenous support structures that had existed within low-income communities, such as the family and neighborhood associations. What began as material poverty has evolved to include a spiritual poverty—a sense of hopelessness and rootlessness.

As a steadily growing barrage of programs was generated from "needs analyses" of low-income neighborhoods, a welfare class came to be identified with its deficiencies and was viewed as an isolated,

From *USA Today Magazine*, January 1998, pp. 18-19. © 1998 by the Society for the Advancement of Education. Reprinted by permission.

dependent population. This "ethos of dependency" penetrated the mindset of many of the welfare recipients and, surrendering to the regulations of the system, numerous households found themselves in a cycle of intergenerational dependency.

Who benefits?

There is a danger in trusting the labels of programs or agencies that purport to serve the disadvantaged or poor children. Statistical "portraits" of the poor and minorities have been used continually to justify trillions of dollars in funding. However, the lion's share of such funds has been absorbed by a massive bureaucracy of administrators and service providers.

At the same time, under the false assumption that all members of minorities are equally "disadvantaged," programs and policies have proliferated that primarily have benefited blacks in the upper- and middle-income brackets.

With a massive funding stream at stake, various power centers have struggled to maintain "ownership" of poverty-related problems. A virtual poverty industry has been built on the backs of the poor in which process alone—without regard to product—has been rewarded. Programs and agencies have received funds in proportion to the amount of clients they hold as dependents, rather than the number they successfully have boosted to self-sufficiency.

The nation's 30-year five trillion-dollar anti-poverty campaign should be evaluated primarily in terms of the extent to which it has facilitated the efforts of low-income people to achieve independence. Outcome-based analyses of the facts show that the current approach to poverty has been a dismal failure. Although welfare spending (in constant, inflation-adjusted dollars) has skyrocketed, there has been no significant reduction in America's poverty rate since the War on Poverty was launched.

A true program for reform must go beyond tinkering with various regulations within the system and look to restoring the functions of the indigenous supporting institutions that exist within low-income communities. Throughout the past three decades, these institutions have been weakened severely. The task of revitalizing the "natural immune systems" of low-income neighborhoods is one that will involve effort, investment, and support, rather than benign non-interference.

In addressing the issue of poverty, there are a number of reasons why indigenous activism can succeed where government intervention has failed. Residents of an afflicted community have a firsthand knowledge of the problems, an understanding of the indigenous resources that can be implemented in their solution, and a personal stake in the success of efforts to solve them. Second—and most important—community leaders have proved that they are able to address the problems at their root, rather than simply practice damage control.

The majority of the issues that confront the U.S. today—high rates of crime, teen pregnancy, school dropouts, and drug abuse—are matters of behavior, the results of choices made in the absence of a clear set of guiding values. As a former health commissioner of Washington, D.C., once said, "Thousands of black and Hispanic youths die each year because of the choices they make and the chances they take." Throughout the nation, grassroots leaders have provided living examples of the values they espouse and are proof that it is possible to lead a life of moral integrity, regardless of economic hardships. Through their consistent example, community activists have had the unique capacity not only to change the behavior of youths in their neighborhood, but catalyze an internal change of heart. This results in not merely rehabilitation, but conversion among those they serve.

America is a nation of two economies. The larger society functions with basic market principles under which innovation thrives and rewards are allocated with regard to outcomes and efficiency. Isolated from this world, another portion of the population has been trapped on the treadmill of a command economy, held hostage to the poverty industry that has been immune from outcome-based evaluation. This dualism must be ended, and market principles must be applied as the problems that confront low-income Americans are addressed.

In many cases, simply allowing competition and breaking down the barriers of government regulations will be enough to open realms of opportunity that previously were not accessible to the poor. The Davis-Bacon Act, established in 1931, for example, effectively has taken lesser-skilled workers out of competition for construction jobs that are Federally subsidized, ruling that all workers must be paid "prevailing"—i.e., union—wages. When construction companies that are contracted for this work are forced to pay top-dollar wages, they naturally opt to hire highly skilled union workers. This bill, which was unabashedly discriminatory at its inception, continues to block many minority workers and young laborers from desperately needed job opportunities.

A number of states are blazing trails to tap the skills and talents of residents of their low-income communities. Through creative initiatives, they are beginning a counterattack on dependency-producing policies by applying strategies of empowerment and devolving authority and resources directly to the people. In Virginia, for instance, Gov. George Allen has proposed initiatives which would allow the poor to build assets while reducing government expenditures. In one initiative, multi-layered subsidies that had been awarded to developers and syndicates were eliminated, and the state was able to free 84,000 households of the working poor. One mother of two children, toiling on a poultry farm on Virginia's eastern shore, used this tax savings in conjunction with Virginia's Homestart benefits for the down payment so that she could become, for the first time, a homeowner.

Gov. Allen also has sought ways to tap the energy and skills of low-income citizens to perform building rehabilitation and plumbing installation in their communities that previously had been given to contractors. This move not only provides newfound employment opportunities for the poor, but saves taxpayers' money. In the small Appalachian town of Ivanhoe, for instance, residents have bid to perform basic plumbing jobs for $6,000 to $8,000. Comparable jobs by union professionals formerly had cost the state far more.

These and similar initiatives that look toward low-income communities in terms of their capacities, rather than their deficiencies, hold the key to productive budget cuts and a win-win situation for all citizens. Indigenous to every neighborhood in this nation are individuals, with talent, energy, and will to do more with less. It should be the government's role to support and facilitate their efforts.

Counting Race and Ethnicity: Options for the 2000 Census

Long before Tiger Woods drew public attention to the problem of characterizing Americans of "mixed race," the federal government had begun to reconsider the classification scheme employed by the Census Bureau and other agencies in collecting and reporting data on race and ethnicity. The existing scheme, created in 1977 under Office of Management and Budget Statistical Directive 15, recognizes five basic categories: American Indian or Alaskan Native, Asian or Pacific Islander, Hispanic, black, and white. The use of additional categories in data collection is not precluded by Directive 15, but the reported results must be "organized in such a way that the additional categories can be aggregated" into those on the basic list. On the Census form—surely the most visible instrument for federal data collection on race and ethnicity—respondents must select only one of these basic categories, or else choose the nondescript "Other."

Recently, the Census Bureau has conducted surveys testing alternative schemes, including one that includes a separate "multiracial" category. As this issue goes to press, OMB is preparing to release a report by an Interagency Committee for the Review of the Racial and Ethnic Standards, recommending whether this change or some alternative should be implemented in time for the 2000 Census. After a period of public comment, a final decision will be made this fall.

Much of the impetus for a multiracial category has come from two organizations: PROJECT RACE (Reclassify All Children Equally) and AMEA (Association of MultiEthnic Americans). These groups argue that the current Census form forces those with parents of different races to deny or suppress part of their heritage. For an increasingly large number of Americans, they say, the government's insistence that individuals fit themselves into one of the existing racial categories constitutes an unreasonable or even a repellent demand. On the other side, opponents of a multiracial category argue that the advantages of granting recognition to a small class of

people are far outweighed by its administrative and social costs.

Unfortunately, the debate between these two camps has been governed by the assumption that the *only* alternative to the present scheme is a menu of exclusive categories augmented by the multiracial option. But there is a third alternative, which we believe is preferable to either maintaining the status quo or adding a multiracial category: namely, a "mark one or more" option that allows respondents to check more than one box, but does not offer a new category for mixed race.

To see why this is the best alternative, it will be helpful first to explore the ethical and policy issues surrounding racial and ethnic classification. We will consider the reasons why data on race and ethnicity are collected in the first place, as well as the grounds for assessing the adequacy or appropriateness of a classification scheme. We will then examine the case for creating a multiracial category, sifting through the arguments on both sides of the public debate. While some objections to the multiracial category seem to us misplaced, we conclude that the creation of such a category would have serious drawbacks. We argue finally that the "mark one or more" option avoids these drawbacks and is thus the superior option.

Purposes and Constraints

Any ethical or policy analysis of Directive 15 must begin with the recognition that there is no such thing as *the* correct classification scheme for race and ethnicity (or for anything else, for that matter). A classification scheme based on skin color is not more or less correct than one based on ancestry; a scheme containing a composite category—e.g., Asian or Pacific Islander—is not more or less correct than one that instead breaks the large category into several smaller ones. Classification schemes are constructed for particular purposes, and so there are at least as many classification schemes as there are purposes for classifying.

From *Report from the Institute for Philosophy and Public Policy*, Summer 1997, pp. 18-22. © 1997 by the Institute for Philosophy and Public Policy, University of Maryland at College Park. Reprinted by permission.

It follows that it is impossible to assess a classification scheme without a clear understanding of the purposes for which it is designed and (not always exactly the same thing) the uses to which it is put. Although, in terms of a given purpose, one classification scheme can be better than another, no single scheme can claim to be *the* correct grid that articulates our diversity.

What purposes, then, are served by the collection of data on race and ethnicity? One is statistical or demographic: the government tracks trends and shifts in population growth and distribution, as well as correlations between different racial and ethnic groups and a variety of socioeconomic, health, and educational indicators, to meet the needs of statistical agencies such as the National Center for Health Statistics. A second purpose is legal and political: it is to meet the needs of federal agencies responsible for civil rights monitoring and enforcement. These two purposes are to some extent related; federal agencies are interested in correlations between race and various indicators of wealth or well-being because they want to track the persistence and effects of racism and discrimination. But since differences between racial or ethnic groups in characteristics such as disease incidence may arise from sources other than racism and discrimination, the two purposes are least partially independent.

We shall argue that a change in Directive 15 need not impede agencies in carrying out the statistical and civil rights purposes of collecting data on race and ethnicity. At the same time, it is important to realize that the *significance* of a racial classification scheme extends beyond these purposes. Two considerations lead us to this view. First, the Census is mandatory: all Americans are required to respond to it. Second, there is an obvious sense in which the Census conveys the official view of race and ethnicity—granting recognition to certain categories but not others, establishing a framework for thinking about diversity and social policy. For these reasons, its classification scheme becomes a prominent social fact in its own right. As such, it has *expressive* or *symbolic* significance beyond its explicit purposes.

It is in terms of this expressive and symbolic significance that we can best understand the demand for changes in the present classification scheme by Americans who regard themselves as of mixed racial or ethnic heritages. While we recognize that self-expression is not a purpose of the Census, it is essential that the classification scheme in use not force people to violate their own sense of their racial identity or that of their children. Given the expressive and symbolic role of the Census, members of PROJECT RACE and AMEA are right to insist that official survey forms not compel them to misrepresent their racial self-identification. That an increasing number of people in our society genuinely, and reasonably, feel tied to more than one racial group is a powerful reason for rejecting any framework requiring exclusive identification.

Some have sought to trivialize the failure of Directive 15 to accommodate people who regard themselves as belonging to more than one category by arguing that the number who so regard themselves is insignificant—less than the margin of error in the Census count. But although the number may be *statistically* insignificant, it is not *socially* insignificant. The present classification scheme reinforces a view of racial identity as exclusive and rigid—a view that has serious political and cultural consequences beyond the Census itself.

Enforcement Issues

Defenders of the status quo have argued that the suggested changes to Directive 15 would subvert the purposes of the racial classification scheme and have troubling symbolic implications. One major concern among civil rights advocates and enforcement agencies is that the inclusion of a multiracial category would hamper the government's antidiscrimination efforts. They fear that significantly fewer people would classify themselves as "black," thereby creating a distorted picture of the magnitude of racial discrimination.

The expectation of a large shift may be exaggerated, however. Results of test surveys suggest that only a minute percentage of people who now classify themselves as black would shift to the multiracial category. (The ef-

It is essential that the classification scheme in use not force people to violate their own sense of their racial identity.

fect of including the category is greater on people of other racial mixes, but that is not a primary concern of the civil rights community.) While the shift in self-identification among African-Americans could be greater in future Censuses as people became accustomed to the new category, it would probably have only a very slight impact on the racial data available for civil rights enforcement in the next decade.

Beyond this, we suspect that concerns about lost information rest on a misunderstanding of the multiracial category—one that has not been addressed by its proponents. The public debate would lead one to think that the multiracial category was "opaque"—that it provided *no* information about constituent races. But in fact, the multiracial category being tested asks respondents to list their constituent races. Even if many people who now classify themselves as black switched to multiracial, almost all who did so would list "black" as part of their racial mix. Thus, there would be no lack of information about their racial composition. (The same would be true, obviously, for the "mark one or more" approach, which by definition would allow respondents an opportunity to provide information about all the races with which they identify.)

These facts alone, however, are not enough to assuage civil rights concerns. Even if detailed information about race continues to be *collected*, this will hardly matter for enforcement purposes if this information is not *reported*

Individuals who checked more than one race would, for certain purposes, be assigned to a single race for data presentation.

---

or *presented* in ways that serve those purposes. Unfortunately, proponents of change have had little to say about this critical issue.

Here is one possibility. Suppose that a classification scheme allowed people to list all the racial categories to which they felt they belonged—whether under a multiracial category or by marking one or more. At the data presentation stage, instead of reporting "the number of blacks with household incomes over $60,000," the Census might report "the number of people with household incomes over $60,000 who listed 'black' as *one* of their constituent races," as well as "the number of people with household incomes over $60,000 who listed *only* 'black' as their race." It has been argued that civil rights enforcement requires exclusive, single-race data presentation—that we must be able to assign people who check multiple races to one of the existing categories. But which one? And what about purposes other than civil rights enforcement?

Clearly, the collected data would have to be transformed in some way. Such a transformation would involve "assignment rules," so that individuals who checked more than one race would, *for certain purposes*, be assigned to a single race for data presentation. Thus, for example, a person who listed "black" and "white" as constituent races could be considered "black" for civil rights purposes, but would not need to be reported as black for other purposes, such as health statistics.

Proponents of change might well object to this strategy. They could argue that the government was taking back with one hand what it gave with the other—offering the multiracial category or "mark one or more" as a sop to critics of the present scheme, while continuing to relegate multiracial Americans to the Directive 15 categories. The civil rights community might object just as strongly. For if a strategy classifies people as black for civil rights purposes *either* if they classify themselves as exclusively black *or* if

they list black as a constituent race, that strategy might appear to rely upon a version of the notorious "one-drop-of-blood" rule, which says that a person with even a single black ancestor is to be classified as black.

These objections, however, can be answered. If, in monitoring civil-rights enforcement, a federal agency counted as black those who listed themselves as both "black" *and* "white" or as "multiracial: black/white," it would not be deciding that their self-identification was mistaken—that they *really* belonged to a racial category other than the one they had chosen. It would merely be recognizing that anyone with black ancestry *is at risk* of discrimination because of broad social acceptance of the one-drop-of-blood rule. The pool of at-risk voters or job-seekers should not be regarded as comprised exclusively of blacks, but of people *with black ancestry*. There is no inconsistency in counting a person as a member of this pool while deferring to his self-identification as multiracial, or as white *and* black.

Of course, assignment rules would not be devised only for those who listed "black" as a constituent race. In looking at employment or housing discrimination against Asian-Americans, for example, one would consider all those who listed Asian as one of their races, since "Eurasians" are likely to be subject to the same prejudices and resentments as "pure" Asians.

We believe that it is a virtue, not a flaw, of a proposal for racial classification that it recognizes the legitimacy of grouping people differently for different purposes. For example, a person with one black and one white parent could be counted among the growing number of multiracial Americans for purposes of tracking intermarriage among traditionally segregated groups, but also regarded as being at risk of anti-black discrimination in a society where racial bias still follows the one-drop-of-blood rule. To object to such multiple groupings is to embrace a spurious objectivity about race, which allows classification in only one racial group for any purpose whatsoever. If we become accustomed to employing different groupings for different purposes, we may learn to see racial identity as more fluid, indeterminate, and superficial, with the ultimate effect of reducing race consciousness. In our judgment, that would be a good thing.

Social Impact and Symbolism

Opponents of the multiracial category have raised other objections, however, that are more difficult to dismiss. While some of these objections are overstated, they suggest that inclusion of a multiracial category may have a disturbing symbolism and a divisive social impact. The "mark one or more" option, we will argue, avoids or significantly mitigates these problems.

First, some civil rights leaders argue that the multiracial category would undermine the solidarity of a victimized community. They fear that it would encourage

terms of taint as in terms of hierarchy. It is this racial outlook that helps account for the historic American obsession with miscegenation. And it is *this* outlook, some proponents say, that the multiracial category would symbolically repudiate, since it would defy the principle that any trace of black ancestry defines a person as black.

This disagreement about the symbolic effect of the multiracial category is difficult to adjudicate, since the two sides are emphasizing different aspects of American racism. We believe that an official scheme of racial classification should strive to repudiate *both* the one-drop-of-blood rule and the appearance of a racial hierarchy. In our judgment, the "mark one or more" option succeeds best at meeting this challenge.

The Case for "Mark One or More"

Like the addition of the multiracial category, the "mark one or more" approach would free respondents who regarded themselves as racially mixed from having to choose between their affiliations (or their parents). However, it would *not* offer up a new category that might be construed as intermediate between black and white. It would allow lighter-skinned blacks, or people with one black parent, to opt out of an exclusive identification as black if they wished, but it would not give official status to a new, competing affiliation.

In the public debate, that status is in fact what proponents of the multiracial category have called for: they insist that being multiracial is itself a distinctive identity. "People with a combination of racial and/or ethnic origins *are* multiracial/multiethnic people," leaders of PROJECT RACE and AMEA have written. These groups affirm "the individual's right to be called multiracial/multiethnic." And they specifically reject the "mark one or more" option by insisting that any listing of constituent races on the Census form appear "under the 'multiracial' umbrella." Otherwise, they say, the "multiracial population" will be "under-counted, miscounted, or rendered invisible."

We agree that mixed-race people should be free to identify with every part of their racial heritage. But the insistence on a separate multiracial identity goes too far. A multiracial category would lump together people with very disparate identities. One cannot assume that a multiracial black/white has a great deal in common with a multiracial Asian/American Indian. Even their experiences of dual identity, divided loyalty, and cultural diversity may be significantly different. Admittedly, this could change over time: multiracial people might develop more commonalities, more of a distinctive identity,

African-Americans with mixed ancestry and/or lighter skin to deny their commonality with other black Americans in the hope of acquiring a more privileged status. As we have seen, test surveys suggest that in the short term, inclusion of the multiracial category would not result in widespread defection by people who formerly classified themselves as black. Over time, however, the shift in self-identification could grow more significant.

Critics also fear that the mere inclusion of the multiracial category would symbolically denigrate "unmixed" and darker-skinned blacks. In their view, the multiracial category would be perceived as an insertion into a racial hierarchy in which "black" is negatively valued, and "white" positively valued. Instead of challenging these implicit valuations, it would help sustain them by offering an apparent refinement of the classification scheme—bolstering its spurious claims to objectivity by making it seem more accurate, like the elaborate, "scientific" schemes of overtly racist countries.

One might think that the eclectic composition of the multiracial category—encompassing many different racial and ethnic combinations—would prevent it from contributing to an official or implied hierarchy of racial types. But the history of the "colored" category in apartheid-era South Africa suggests otherwise. A category that includes a variety of combinations might still be viewed as holding an intermediate value between black and white.

Proponents of the multiracial category naturally take a different view of its symbolic import. For them, a central tenet of American racism has been the one-drop-of-blood rule, which conceives of blackness as much in as their ranks swell. And the introduction of a multiracial category could even help *engender* such an identity. But at present, a multiracial category would misleadingly give a single name to an extremely diverse group of people.

Consider those respondents who see themselves as "black *and* white" or "black *and* white, but socially black"—the locutions used by many people with parents of different races. For them, there would be some distortion in choosing the multiracial option from a list of exclusive categories. These people regard themselves as having dual racial identity, not as belonging to a mixed or hybrid group that includes many other racial mixes. Again, the test survey results suggest that few people currently identify as "multiracial" to the extent of checking that category on an exclusive list. This suggests that while the "mark one or more" option would be slightly more procrustean than the multiracial option for a small number of people—those who now identify themselves as multiracial—it would better fit what is likely to be a larger number of people—those who identify with more than one race without identifying themselves as multiracial.

Equally important, by not reifying a multiracial identity, the "mark one or more" option would avoid some of the symbolic and social effects of that dubious refinement in racial categorization. Like the multiracial category, the "mark one or more" option appears to repudiate the one-drop rule. But it does so, we believe, without any suggestion of a more refined racial hierarchy. It can be seen, instead, as decomposing racial identity, by implying the legitimacy of composite descriptions.

Some opponents of any change to Directive 15 worry that a "mark one or more" option, and the plurality of counts of different racial groups that could result, might confuse and anger the public even more than the current system's failure to recognize multiple racial identities. They argue that the American people need and want the federal government to provide one number, one set of racial "facts."

Clearly, public education would have to accompany the change we are proposing. But it is an untested assumption that the public (or the courts or whomever the relevant audience is deemed to be) could not comprehend the complexities of multiple counts for multiple purposes. Social reality is complex. Racial identity is complex. Each generation of Americans is better educated than the one before it, and it is not unreasonable to think that the average American's ability to under-

stand nuance and complexity might also be rising. And if it isn't, then perhaps it is time to improve comprehension of the complexity of racial identity and classification—its meaning, its purposes, and its implications.

In addition to supporting the "mark one or more" option for the purpose of data collection, we believe that federal agencies should have the latitude to tabulate racial data in a way that seems most appropriate to their purposes in gathering that data in the first place. Federal programs would benefit if their racial classifications were more closely tailored to the purposes they were intended to serve, and if agencies had to make explicit the assumptions they used in adopting particular assignment rules. In classifying people differently for different purposes, agencies would be disabusing the American public of the recalcitrant notion that there is an overarching "fact of the matter" about racial identity across the many purposes for which racial data are collected.

—Judith Lichtenberg, Suzanne Bianchi, Robert Wachbroit, and David Wasserman

This essay has been adapted from a memorandum that the authors submitted to the Office of Management and Budget on May 2, 1997, concerning suggested changes to Directive 15. Suzanne Bianchi, professor of sociology at the University of Maryland, joined three Institute members in this research project, which was funded by the National Science Foundation and the Alfred P. Sloan Foundation. Sources: "Standards for the Classification of Federal Data on Race and Ethnicity," *Federal Register*, vol. 59, no. 123 (59FR 29831-35), June 9, 1994; "Standards for the Classification of Federal Data on Race and Ethnicity," *Federal Register*, vol. 60, no. 166 (60FR 44674-93), August 28, 1995; *Spotlight on Heterogeneity: The Federal Standards for Racial and Ethnic Classification*, National Research Council, Committee on National Statistics (National Academy Press, 1996); joint letters to the Office of Management and Budget from PROJECT RACE and AMEA (September 29, 1995, and January 6, 1995); "Coalition Statement on Proposed Modification of OMB Directive No. 15," submitted by Lawyers' Committee for Civil Rights Under Law, National Association for the Advancement of Colored People, National Urban League, and Joint Center for Political and Economic Studies (Nov. 18, 1994); U.S. Bureau of the Census, "Results of the 1996 Race and Ethnic Targeted Test," Population Division Working Paper No. 18 (May 1997).

Of Race and Risk

PATRICIA J. WILLIAMS

Several years ago, at a moment when I was particularly tired of the unstable lifestyle that academic careers sometimes require, I surprised myself and bought a real house. Because the house was in a state other than the one where I was living at the time, I obtained my mortgage by telephone. I am a prudent little squirrel when it comes to things financial, always tucking away stores of nuts for the winter, and so I meet the criteria of a quite good credit risk. My loan was approved almost immediately.

A little while later, the contract came in the mail. Among the papers the bank forwarded were forms documenting compliance with the Fair Housing Act, which outlaws racial discrimination in the housing market. The act monitors lending practices to prevent banks from redlining—redlining being the phenomenon whereby banks circle certain neighborhoods on the map and refuse to lend in those areas. It is a practice for which the bank with which I was dealing, unbeknownst to me, had been cited previously—as well as since. In any event, the act tracks the race of all banking customers to prevent such discrimination. Unfortunately, and with the creative variability of all illegality, some banks also use the racial information disclosed on the fair housing forms to engage in precisely the discrimination the law seeks to prevent.

I should repeat that to this point my entire mortgage transaction had been conducted by telephone. I should also note that I speak a Received Standard English, regionally marked as Northeastern perhaps, but not easily identifiable as black. With my credit history, my job as a law professor and, no doubt, with my accent, I am not only middle class but apparently match the cultural stereotype of a good white person. It is thus, perhaps, that the loan officer of the bank, whom I had never met, had checked off the box on the fair housing form indicating that I *was* white.

Race shouldn't matter, I suppose, but it seemed to in this case, so I took a deep breath, crossed out "white" and sent the contract back. That will teach them to presume too much, I thought. A done deal, I assumed. But suddenly the transaction came to a screeching halt. The bank wanted more money, more points, a higher rate of interest. Suddenly I found myself facing great resistance and much more debt. To make a long story short, I threatened to sue under the act in question, the bank quickly backed down and I procured the loan on the original terms.

What was interesting about all this was that the reason the bank gave for its new-found recalcitrance was not race, heaven forbid. No, it was all about economics and increased risk: The reason they gave was that property values in that neighborhood were suddenly falling. They wanted more money to buffer themselves against the snappy winds of projected misfortune.

Initially, I was surprised, confused. The house was in a neighborhood that was extremely stable. I am an extremely careful shopper; I had uncovered absolutely nothing to indicate that prices were falling. It took my realtor to make me see the light. "Don't you get it," he sighed. "This is what always happens." And even though I suppose it was a little thick of me, I really hadn't gotten it: For of course, I was the reason the prices were in peril.

The bank's response was driven by demographic data that show that any time black people move into a neighborhood, whites are overwhelmingly likely to move out. In droves. In panic. In concert. Pulling every imaginable resource with them, from school funding to garbage collection to social workers who don't want to work in black neighborhoods. The imagery is awfully catchy, you had to admit: the neighborhood just tipping on over like a terrible accident, whoops! Like a pitcher, I suppose. All that nice fresh wholesome milk spilling out, running away . . . leaving the dark, echoing, upended urn of the inner city.

In retrospect, what has remained so fascinating to me about this experience was the way it so exemplified the problems of the new rhetoric of racism. For starters, the new rhetoric of race never mentions race. It wasn't race but risk with which the bank was so concerned.

Second, since financial risk is all about economics, my exclusion got reclassified as just a consideration of class. There's no law against class discrimination, goes the argument, because that would represent a restraint on that basic American freedom, the ability to contract or not. If schools, trains, buses, swimming pools and neighborhoods remain segregated, it's no longer a racial problem if someone who just happens to be white keeps hiking up the price for someone who accidentally and purely by the way happens to be black. Black people end up paying higher prices for the attempt to integrate, even as the integration of oneself threatens to lower the value of one's investment.

By this measure of mortgage-worthiness, the ingredient of blackness is cast not just as a social toll but as an actual tax. A fee, an extra contribution at the door, an admission charge for the high costs of handling my dangerous propensities, my inherently unsavory properties. I was not judged based on my independent attributes or financial worth; not even was I judged by statistical profiles of what my group actually does. (For in fact, anxiety-stricken, middle-class black people make grovelingly good cake-baking neighbors when not made to feel defensive by the unfortunate historical strategies of bombs, burnings or abandonment.) Rather, I was being evaluated based on what an abstraction of White Society writ large thinks we—or I—do, and that imagined "doing" was treated and thus established as a self-fulfilling prophecy. It is a dispiriting message: that some in society apparently not only devalue black people but devalue *themselves* and their homes just for having us as part of their landscape.

"I bet you'll keep your mouth shut the next time they plug you into the computer as white," laughed a friend when he heard my story. It took me aback, this postmodern pressure to "pass," even as it highlighted the intolerable logic of it all. For by these "rational" economic measures, an investment in my property suggests the selling of myself.

In Defense of
AFFIRMATIVE ACTION

"It would be a tragedy if the nation's colleges and universities slipped backward, denying access to talented, but disadvantaged, youth and eroding the diversity that helps to prepare the leaders of the 21st century."

by Chang-Lin Tien

WHEN THE DEBATE over affirmative action in higher education exploded, my open support surprised many. My personal view about using race, ethnicity, and sex among the factors in student admissions has put me at odds with many, including the majority of the Regents of the University of California who govern my campus.

With California voters having decided in November, 1996, to end all state-sponsored affirmative action programs, silence would seem to be a far more prudent course for me to take. Educators already have enough battles to fight—declining public funding, controversy over the national research agenda, and eroding public support for America's academic mission.

Why did I take on the explosive issue of affirmative action? My participation in the debate is inspired both by my role in higher education and my experience as an immigrant of Chinese descent. As chancellor of the University of California, Berkeley, I had seen the promise of affirmative action come true. Today, no ethnic or racial group constitutes a majority among the university's 21,000 undergraduates. Berkeley students enter better prepared and graduate at the highest rate in our history. Through daily interaction in classrooms, laboratories, and residence halls, they develop a

Dr. Tien, professor of mechanical engineering, University of California, Berkeley, was chancellor of the university from 1990 to 1997.

deep understanding of different cultures and outlooks.

As an immigrant, I know the U.S. is the land of opportunity. Unlike any other nation in history, America has taken pride in being built by immigrants and allows foreign-born people like me to participate in the world's greatest democracy.

In 1956, I came here for graduate studies, a virtually penniless immigrant from China with a limited grasp of the language and customs of the U.S. A teaching fellowship was my income. To stretch my frugal budget, I walked across town to eat at the least expensive restaurants and scouted out the lowest-cost washing machines and dryers.

As a result of the wonderful educational opportunities I have enjoyed, I have contributed to America. My research in heat transfer has enhanced our engineering expertise in many critical technologies, including nuclear reactor safety, space shuttle thermal design, and electronic systems cooling. My former students teach and conduct research in America's top universities and industries. I was privileged to head the university with the largest number and highest percentage of top-ranked doctoral programs in the nation.

Yet, along with opportunity, I have encountered the harsh realities of racial discrimination that are part of America's legacy. Like it or not, this history of racial division is linked with the debate over af-

firmative action. Although the U.S. has made great strides, race still divides our society. It is part of the debate over how we afford equal opportunities to everyone.

My first months in the U.S. reflect how opportunity and racial intolerance can be linked. I served as a teaching fellow for a professor who refused to pronounce my name and only referred to me as "Chinaman." One day, the professor directed me to adjust some valves in a large laboratory apparatus. When I climbed a ladder, I lost my balance and instinctively grabbed a nearby steam pipe. It was so hot, it produced a jolt of pain that nearly caused me to faint, but I did not scream out. I stuffed my throbbing hand into my coat pocket and waited until the class ended. Then I ran to the hospital emergency room, where I was treated for a burn that completely had singed the skin off my palm.

My response seems to fit the Asian model minority myth: Say nothing and go about your business. My silence had nothing to do with stoicism, though. I simply did not want to endure the humiliation of having the professor scold me in front of the class.

Today, after four decades of major civil rights advances, members of racial and ethnic minorities like me no longer are intimidated into silence. Still, serious racial divisions remain. Those of us who are of Asian, Latino, or Middle Eastern heritage have become accustomed to having passersby tell us, "Go back to your own country." More typical is the polite query: "What country do you come from?" It makes no difference if you are first-generation or fifth-generation. If you have Asian, Latino, or Middle Eastern features or surname, many Americans assume you were born in another country. The ancestors of a professor in the university's School of Optometry left China to work in California during the 1850s. Even though his roots run far deeper than those of the vast majority of Californians, people invariably ask him where he was born.

Our nation can not afford to ignore the racial strife that continues to divide America. Nor should we forget that the U.S. is a great democracy built by diverse peoples. It is critical to attack the problem of racial division and build on national strengths. The finest hope for meeting this challenge will be America's colleges and universities.

These institutions launched affirmative admissions programs to open their doors to promising minority students who lacked educational and social opportunities. Over time, the composition of America's college students has changed. Campuses are more diverse than at any time in history.

Critics of continuing race or ethnicity as a consideration in student admissions argue that affirmative action unfairly discriminates against white and Asian-American applicants who worked hard in high school and received top grades. They further maintain that it no longer is needed to provide opportunities. Although I agree that affirmative action is a temporary measure, the time has not yet come to eliminate it. Educational opportunities vary dramatically in U.S. public schools.

The inner-city student can find illegal drugs more readily than computer labs and after-school enrichment courses. In contrast, the more affluent suburban student is hooked into the Internet, enrolled in honor classes, and looking forward to summer instruction.

Given this reality, it is fair and equitable to consider race and ethnicity as one factor among many—including test scores and grade-point averages—in admitting qualified youths to highly competitive universities. Such an approach remains the most effective way to make sure America does not turn into a two-tiered society of permanent haves and have-nots.

Assisting promising students is not the only reason for preserving affirmative action. The diversity of students, faculty, and staff that it inspired is one of the most exciting and challenging phenomena in American higher education today. All students stand to gain, whether they are whites, Asian-Americans, or traditionally underrepresented minorities.

I believe students on campuses that lack diversity can gain just a limited, theoretical understanding of the challenges and opportunities in a highly diverse nation. A lecture on Toni Morrison's novels or the theater of Luis Valdez is not enough.

No career or profession will be untouched by the rapid socio-demographic change. For instance, consider how America's diversity will affect those in U.S. colleges and universities. Education students will teach many youngsters born in different countries. Medical students will treat many patients with beliefs and attitudes about medicine that differ from the Western outlook. Students of engineering and business will work for major corporations, where they will be expected to design, develop, and market products that sell not just in the U.S., but in markets around the world. Law students will represent clients whose experience with the judicial system in their neighborhoods and barrios is distinctive from the way middle America regards the law.

A matter of diversity

Diversity in colleges and universities benefits all students, not just the underrepresented minorities. Our experience at Berkeley shows the promise of affirmative action. Every time I walk across campus, I am impressed by the vibrant spirit of our diverse community. Nowhere do you see this better than teeming Sproul Plaza, where dozens of student groups set up tables representing a wide range of social, political, ethnic, and religious interests.

At Berkeley, undergraduates are about 40% Asian-American; 31% non-Hispanic Caucasian; 14% Hispanic; six percent African-American; and one percent Native American, with the rest undeclared. About one-quarter of freshmen come from families earning $28,600 a year or less; another quarter from families that earn more than $90,000. The median family income reported for 1994 freshmen was $58,000.

Young people from barrios, comfortable suburbs, farm towns, and the inner city come together at Berkeley to live and study side by side. Not surprisingly, they find first-time interactions with students from different backgrounds occasionally fraught with misunderstanding and tension.

As chancellor, I made it a point to listen and talk with students. Casual conversations as I walked the campus to meetings, dropped in at the library after work, and sat in on classes gave me greater insight into the day-to-day lives of Berkeley students. They told me about the practical challenges of moving beyond the stereotypes and learning to respect differences.

Some African-Americans and Latinos confided they sometimes believed their professors and white classmates considered them to be inferior academically. This made them feel isolated from the general campus community. Some whites told me they felt like they had been pushed out by less-deserving blacks and Latinos. They also believed that overachieving Asians were depriving them of educational opportunities.

The views of Asian-Americans differed. Some were disturbed by the "model minority" stereotype. They complained that it pits them against other minorities and masks the problem of discrimination they still face. Others were concerned about issues such as affirmative action. They believed it is fair to base admissions on academic qualifications alone—which would open the door to more Asian-Americans.

These differing outlooks are not cause for alarm. Instead, they reflect the views held in society at large. It is important that students of all racial and ethnic groups told me they valued the opportunities on our campus to come together with people of diverse backgrounds. I believe it is this attitude our campus must reinforce as we help them to address differences.

The residence halls are the first place students come together. Because we understand the challenges associated with living together with those who have different values and outlooks, we run programs that encourage students to discuss racial and cultural differences openly.

Our campus tradition of academic freedom is critical. When issues arise where students are divided by race, they don't ignore the matter. We encourage all members of the campus community to air differences freely in forums, seminars, and rallies. Whether the topic is affirmative action, enforcement of the successful California ballot measure that would ban illegal immigrants from public schools, or the organization of ethnic studies, students and faculty passionately debate the pros and cons.

Let me cite an example. In 1995, the long-standing conflict between Israelis and Palestinians led to fiery exchanges between Jewish and Muslim students on our campus. During rallies and counter-protests, an Israeli flag was ripped apart, while Muslim students alleged they were being demonized.

We addressed the issues directly. The campus held meetings to denounce "hate speech," while open debate was encouraged. My top objective was to make sure that discussions on this charged issue did not degenerate into racial epithets. I decided to forego an invitation from Pres. Clinton to attend a White House meeting so I could meet with students who were central to the debate and help them hammer out their differences.

It is this tradition of study and debate that makes American higher education so valuable. Colleges and universities are a haven for open discussion. Only by addressing differences directly can students reach a deeper understanding of the real meaning of diversity.

Today, our campus faces a major new challenge. The University of California Regents have voted to end the use of race, ethnicity, and sex as a factor among many others in student admissions at its nine campuses in 1998. At first, the Regents' decision stunned me. I questioned whether we could preserve the diversity which is so important to our campus after losing an important tool for achieving student enrollments that reflect California's wide-ranging population.

Yet, I quickly realized the importance of the Regents' reaffirmation of their commitment to diversity even though they discarded affirmative action. So, I decided to take the Chinese approach to challenge. In Chinese, the character for crisis actually is two characters: One stands for danger and the other for opportunity. For me, times of crisis present both challenges and opportunities.

The end of affirmative action at the University of California gave us the impetus for trying new approaches to improving the eligibility rates of high school students traditionally underrepresented in higher education. At Berkeley, we set to work right away to turn challenge into opportunity. We realized our efforts would be doomed unless we worked even more closely with the public schools. Within weeks of the affirmative action decision, I joined the superintendents of the San Francisco Bay Area's major urban school districts to announce our new campaign to diversity: The Berkeley Pledge.

The announcement made it clear that our campus would not shirk its commitment to diversity. Instead, we pledged to step up the drive to support the efforts of disadvantaged youth to qualify for admission and preserve access to higher education. I committed $1,000,000 from private gifts, and we are seeking additional private support to fund this innovative approach.

America has come a long way since the days of Jim Crow segregation. It would be a tragedy if our nation's colleges and universities slipped backward, denying access to talented, but disadvantaged, youth and eroding the diversity that helps to prepare the leaders of the 21st century.

I find one aspect of the debate over affirmative action to be especially disturbing. There seems to be an underlying assumption that if it is eliminated, the nation will have solved the problems associated with racial division. Nothing could be further from the truth. It is critical for America to address the issue of how people from diverse backgrounds are going to study, work, and live in the same neighborhoods together in harmony, not strife.

This is the challenge in higher education. It demands the collaboration of students, faculty, staff, and alumni at universities and colleges across America. All must work together to maintain the diversity that is essential to excellence.

SERVICE REDLINING

The New Jim Crow?

By Chevon Fuller

Service redlining is the practice of refusing to offer goods or services to residents of low-income, minority neighborhoods. African Americans, Latinos, and other ethnic groups typically characterize the segregated areas. The result is disturbing and familiar: some retail establishments are creating demographic-based service policies which, like Jim Crow laws, enable them to do business only with white communities.

Delivery Services

James Robinson remembers vividly the days when African Americans were refused service in public places: in 1950, "when you went to the bus station [in the south], there was a line for blacks and a line for whites. In the restaurants, there were [separate] sections for blacks and [for] whites. White people laughed—they didn't take our anger seriously," Mr. Robinson recalls.

Almost fifty years later and despite myriad laws prohibiting such conduct, Mr. Robinson and his wife Joyce today have that same angry feeling. In November 1997, the Robinsons, who live in American Beach, Florida, sued Domino's Pizza because the company refused to deliver a pizza to them for security reasons. Although the pizza giant made residential deliveries to neighboring white communities, it had established a drop-off location for residents of American Beach. All but four residents of American Beach were African American. Domino's claimed that it had established the policy after speaking with law enforcement personnel and reviewing police crime statistics. However, the county sheriff disagreed, stating publicly that there was no additional danger in American Beach. "When my wife called Domino's last year, it took me back to the old days," Mr. Robinson recalled. "The guy [from Domino's] acted like he was happy" about refusing to serve the predominately black American Beach.

The Robinsons accused Domino's of establishing a redlining policy which violates the public accommodations provisions of the Civil Rights Act of 1964. In February 1998, the court directed Domino's to provide service to the area it had segregated. But to Mr. Robinson, the court's decision was bittersweet. "In 1998 I have to go through all this to get an $8.00 pizza? No, I'm not happy," remarked Mr. Robinson. "It's all over Jacksonville, Florida. But, if the people don't rise, nothing will be done."

In a similar case, in February 1997, Pizza Hut refused to deliver 40 pizzas to an honors program at Paseo High School in Kansas City, Missouri because it considered the school to be located in an unsafe neighborhood. Rob Doughty, vice president and spokesperson for Pizza Hut Inc., was quoted as saying, "There is hardly a town that does not have a restricted area."

Ironically, Pizza Hut regularly delivered pizzas to Paseo High School under the terms of a school lunch contract. Although the school board subsequently canceled the $170,000 contract with Pizza Hut, the impact of the company's treatment of the students weighed heavily on the minds of those involved. "If we are going to support you [through district contracts], we need you to provide services to our kids," Deputy Superintendent Phyllis Chase said.

There is no disputing that the consequences of forcing residential delivery in unsafe circumstances can be deadly. In 1995, the Bureau of Labor Statistics ranked "driver sales worker" as one of the most deadly jobs in the United States. Because of such statistics, pizza companies across the nation deny service to certain neighborhoods. Domino's spokesperson Maggie Monaghan says that crime "makes [Domino's] a victim as well."

Pizza deliverers have been beaten and killed—but such incidents do not take place exclusively in inner-city communities. In April 1997, pizza deliverers Georgia Gallara and Jeremy Giordano were killed when they answered a call which lead them to an abandoned house in suburban Sussex County, New Jersey. The Domino's and Pizza Hut disputes underscore the point that businesses often base service redlining more on stereotypes than on fact.

Businesses often base redlining more on stereotypes than facts

Retail Services

In March 1996, Dorothy Hudson called Americar to reserve a van to drive to her father's funeral. The company refused to rent to her because she "lived in a high crime, high risk area" of town. In February 1997, Delores Howard was told the same thing. Americar calls it a business decision. Ms. Howard, the mother of a slain Syracuse police officer, calls it discrimination. "It's a shame that we have to sue to be treated equally. I was in shock when this happened. I felt like nothing. Crime is everywhere. My son Walley died trying to get drugs off the streets, not for black, white, or Jewish people, but for everyone. Then, [Americar] tells me that I can't rent a car. It was a kick in the face."

To carry out its policy, Americar created a map outlining redlined areas. Rental agents refused cars to persons who lived in the red, "high risk rental" areas on the map. Rental agents used heightened scrutiny for customers who lived in the yellow, "use caution" areas on the map.

Most of the redlined areas lay at the heart of inner-city Syracuse, New York, but Americar also redlined a nearby Native American reservation. Not surprisingly, African Americans, Latinos, and Native Americans constitute a significant portion of the population that makes up the redlined areas. Chief Irving Powless of the Onondaga Indian nation near Syracuse, New York stated that, "Americar has no basis for a refusal. If you think about a group and you say that you are not going to do business with them, that is discrimination. If I walk into Americar and they say, sorry, you can't rent because you are a Native American," who resides on the reservation, that is discrimination.

In August 1997, New York's Attorney General Dennis C. Vacco sued Americar for violating State and Federal civil rights laws by maintaining a carefully crafted combination of service redlining, heightened scrutiny, and racial bias to decide who would be eligible to rent its vehicles. Although Americar claimed that its rental policies were based on crime rates in particular neighborhoods, the complaint charges that its rental policies, in reality, have more to do with the ethnic origin or skin colors of neighborhood residents than security. The large redlined zones were based on arbitrary reviews of news articles describing local crimes and encompassed only predominantly African American, Latino, and Native American communities.

In Pennsylvania, Avis Rent-A-Car, Inc. has also been accused of refusing to rent cars to local minority customers. Although the company claims it has "zero tolerance" for discrimination, in October 1997 the Pennsylvania Attorney General filed a complaint against Avis with that State's Human Relations Commission (which is still pending) to stop the alleged redlining practice. Avis has also come under close government scrutiny for alleged discrimination in New York and in Florida.

Remedies

The Domino's and Americar cases help define the sometimes blurred distinction between a legitimate non-discriminatory policy and intentional discrimination. Thorough fact investigation and analysis will make clear whether a seemingly neutral, security-prompted geographic policy is in fact driven by stereotypes or tainted with prejudice.

In 1996, the San Francisco Board of Supervisors approved the nation's first service redlining law. The ordinance followed the murder of Samuel Reyes, a 22-year-old Domino's pizza deliverer, and the pizza company's subsequent refusal to serve San Francisco's high-crime neighborhoods. The ordinance makes it unlawful for a business which regularly advertises residential delivery services to the entire city to refuse to serve any address within the city. Businesses may exclude a certain address if a customer has refused to pay or if the business has a good faith reason to believe that providing delivery service to that address would expose its employees to an unreasonable risk of harm.

Undoubtedly, the San Francisco ordinance permits some neighborhoods to be redlined to the extent that a company can demonstrate good faith reasons to refuse service. Yet, the ordinance is a first step towards making businesses accountable for redlining policies.

Linda Hall, the Executive Director of the Syracuse, New York Human Rights Commission believes that people must take action to stop such treatment. "People have to speak up about unfair treatment and give us the opportunity to fully investigate these situations" and bring lawsuits, explained Ms. Hall. "We have to network, find patterns of discrimination," and eliminate them.

Businesses with safety or property damage issues which prevent them from servicing certain neighborhoods must work with community leaders to find creative solutions, rather than turning to widespread demographic-based service redlining as the only alternative. In 1996, Domino's in San Francisco toured a redlined neighborhood and altered its policy to provide service to almost ⅔ of the area it had previously redlined. Domino's spokesperson Maggie Monaghan admitted that "in some cases, we have not evaluated the area enough. It is very important that we do." She admits

that, "there is a new, heightened awareness" because of the publicity over recent disputes.

Conclusion

Even when nondiscriminatory reasons for service redlining exist, redlining has a substantial social and economic impact on the segregated communities. As service markets expand, we can expect that service redlining will increase. In response, we must sue, enact appropriate legislation, and create innovative, community-based solutions to insure that entire communities are not left to pay for the sins of a few.

Chevon Fuller is Chief of the New York State Attorney General's Civil Rights Bureau. The opinions and analysis in the article are those of the author, and do not reflect the opinions, positions, or policies of New York State Attorney General Dennis C. Vacco, or of the New York State Department of Law.

The WAR BETWEEN MEN AND WOMEN

By Robert Sapolsky

What do you do if a lot of the struggle takes place at a molecular level and neither person knows it?

As most newlyweds quickly learn, intimate relationships, even the most blissful, can buzz with tension. Couples typically find themselves struggling over money, in-laws, ex-lovers, and how much the woman's placenta should grow when she gets pregnant. That last one is a killer. The guy wants his woman to have a fast-growing placenta, while the woman does all she can to keep it down to a reasonable size.

Of course, the fight over the placenta doesn't exactly take place out in the open. The average man, if asked what he thinks of his wife's placenta, would probably say he hasn't given it a thought. Instead the placenta conflict gets played out, unbeknownst to either person, inside the woman's body. A

strange genetic process called genomic imprinting is responsible. And its existence is only one small example of how males and females have conflicting evolutionary goals. Understanding that the struggle takes place can explain a lot of strange behavior and physiology. And it can even explain how we came to be susceptible to certain horrific diseases.

At first it might seem unlikely that men and women do have conflicting evolutionary goals. The point of life, according to evolutionary theorists, is for organisms to pass on copies of their genes to succeeding generations. Some organisms, such as cockroaches, do this by producing as many offspring as possible, hoping some will survive. Others, such as elephants and humans, have

many fewer young but shower them with care.

So yes, both mom and dad want their kid to survive. And in monogamous species, when the father can be pretty sure it really is his kid, he may well cooperate with the mother. But that's not quite the way it is in more polygamous animal species such as orangutans, nor was it that way, say many evolutionary biologists, among our own ancestors. Those males want their offspring to survive at any cost—even at the cost of the female's health and future fertility with other males. For example, if the male can figure out a way to make the female spend most of her food energy making the offspring grow big and strong, that's okay, even if she starves. That's where

Males want their offspring to survive at any cost

the struggle over the placenta comes in: men and other male mammals pass on genes to their unborn children that encourage the mother's placenta to grow big, nourishing the fetus at the mother's expense and at the expense of her future kids with other guys.

Females want their offspring to survive too, but not at the risk of their future fertility. For example, in mammals, nursing inhibits ovulation. So a mammal mom wouldn't nurse her young for the rest of her life, even if doing so greatly increased its chances of survival. Otherwise, she might never again ovulate, become pregnant, and bear more young.

This conflict is played out viciously among fruit flies. Rather than growing old in each other's arms, drosophila mate with multiple partners, none of whom stick around for a second date.

males compete against each other. After 40 generations, the evolutionary winners were males with the strongest toxic punch in their semen. Females who mated with them had a shorter life expectancy.

The same sort of coevolutionary arms race happens in humans and other mammals. As a result, we have developed a bizarre set of genes called imprinted genes, that seem to violate the basic tenets of genetics.

Think back to Gregor Mendel, high school biology, and dominant and recessive traits. That most monkish of monks taught that genetic traits are coded for by pairs of genes, one from each parent. He figured out how the pairs of genes interact to influence the organism, depending on whether the pair have identical or differing messages. According to Mendel, it doesn't matter which parent

placenta, the fetus, or the newborn. And the genes derived from the father favor greater, faster, more expensive growth, while the maternally derived genes counter that exuberance. As the evolutionist David Haig of Harvard first suggested in 1989, imprinted genes—including these genes in humans—are a case of intersexual competition, fruit fly sperm wars redux.

The first battleground is the placenta, a tissue that can seem more than a little creepy. It's only partially related to the female, but it invades (a term used in obstetrics) her body, sending tentacles toward her blood vessels to divert nutrients for the benefit of a growing fetus. The placenta is also the scene of a pitched battle, with paternally derived genes pushing it to invade more aggressively while maternally derived genes

Imprinted genes can turn the placenta into a cancer

And look at what they've come up with: male semen contains toxins that kill the sperm of other males. When a male fly mates with a female who has recently had sex with someone else, his spermicide goes to work, killing competitors' sperm. That's a great adaptation, but unfortunately the stuff is toxic to the female and gradually harms her health. This doesn't bother the male at all. It increases his evolutionary fitness, and he's never going to see her again.

William Rice, an evolutionary geneticist then at the University of California at Santa Cruz, did a wonderfully slick experiment in which he kept female fruit flies from evolving while letting the

contributed which genetic message. Whether the offspring gets the vanilla version of a gene from the mother and the chocolate version from the father or the other way around, the trait coded for by the pair of genes will look the same.

Imprinted genes violate Mendel's rules. With these genes, only the gene from one parent has input—the matching gene from the other parent is silenced, losing its influence over the trait expressed. Most experts in this new field believe that there are only a couple hundred of these genes in humans, but they can be quite influential.

About half the genes in question have something to do with growth—of the

try to hold it back. How do we know? In rare diseases, maternal or paternal genes related to placental growth are knocked out of action. Lose the paternal input and the anti-growth maternal component is left unopposed—the placenta never invades the mother's endometrium, so the fetus has no chance to grow. In contrast, remove the maternal input, leaving those paternal genes unopposed, and the placenta grows into a stupendously aggressive cancer called choriocarcinoma.

The imprinting struggle continues during fetal development. One gene, which codes for a powerful growth-stimulating hormone in mice and hu-

Stay-at-Home Dads

Conflict between males and females takes a complicated turn in the rare species with high "male parental investment." In such species, a male instinctually takes care of youngsters he thinks are his own. He mates with someone, and babies appear an appropriate

length of time later, so he protects them from predators and takes them to ice-skating lessons. A lot of bird species fit this profile. Sometimes the male does more parenting than the female. At the moment when the egg hatches, she has invested far more energy in the gestation than he

has, but afterward the tide gradually turns. In those cases, what should a heartlessly practical female do if she wants to maximize her reproductive success? She should figure out the exact moment when he's spent more cumulative energy than she has on passing on copies

of his genes via these offspring. When that moment arrives, she should abandon the youngsters. He will likely continue taking care of them, guaranteeing her reproductive success and leaving her free to start a new round of reproduction with someone else.

—R. S.

Reports of human monogamy are greatly exaggerated

mans, is expressed only by paternally derived genes. This is a classic case of dad pushing for maximal fetal development. In mice (though not in people), the mother counteracts the pro-growth tumult by expressing a gene for a cellular receptor that regulates the growth hormone's effectiveness. Thrust and parry.

Once a baby is born, imprinted genes take a particularly impressive turn. Certain paternally expressed genes help make kids active nursers. On the surface, this looks like another example of the usual picture: faster development at the cost of mom's lactational calories. But now we're talking about imprinted genes that influence behavior. Other genes influence brain development in even stranger ways (*See* Brain Genes, below).

The discovery of imprinted genes may pave the way for curing a number of unpleasant diseases involving tumors, infertility, and fetal overgrowth or underdevelopment. But philosophically, the findings are disturbing. They appear to have some deflating implications about human nature. Among fruit flies, sperm-war genes show that males care little about the females' future. What about us? "In sickness and in health," we promise, "until death do us part." We're the species that came up with Paul Newman and Joanne Woodward. For monogamous animals, the future health and fertility of the female is as much in the male's interest as hers. So what are these imprinted genes doing in a human couple pondering which appetizers to serve at their golden wedding anniversary?

Self-Conscious Scrub Jays

When biologists talk about male orangutans "realizing" that they have less to lose in mating than females, or female scrub jays "calculating" exactly when to abandon their young to a caring father, they're speaking metaphorically. Except for the most cognitively sophisticated primates, animals don't sit there with an evolution textbook and a calculator, strategizing consciously. Instead phrases like "the scrub jay wants to do this, decides that this is the right time," and so on are shorthand for the more correct but cumbersome, "Over the course of evolution, scrub jays who, at least in part through genetically influenced mechanisms, are better able to optimize the timing of their behavior leave more copies of their genes, thus making this attribute more prevalent in the population." Personifying the animals is just an expository device agreed upon to keep everyone from falling asleep during conferences.—*R. S.*

The answer is that reports of our monogamy are greatly exaggerated. Features of human anatomy and physiology argue against it. Most human cultures allow polygamy. And most studies, ranging from genetic paternity tests to *Cosmo* questionnaires, suggest that there's a lot of action going on outside the pair-bond, even in monogamous societies. We have more in common with fruit flies than commonly believed. (Mind you, we're not one of the more polygamous species around. Even the busiest patriarchs weigh in with only a few hundred kids.)

Does nature have to be so bloody in tooth and claw and gene? Must everything be based on competition? Why can't we all just get along? Here's where the evolutionary biologists, with Bogartesque weariness, pull out the great cliches of their field. Biology isn't about what should be, they explain, but what is. It's a tough evolutionary world out there. It's dog outreproduce dog. But a recent experiment by Rice and evolutionary behaviorist Brett Holland hints that intersexual competition needn't be inevitable. With careful manipulation, it can be derailed. The researchers isolated pairs of mating flies, forcing them to be monogamous. They then bred the offspring with the offspring of other such enforced monogamous pairs, continuing to maintain the monogamy. And after only 40 generations, the monogamous descendants produced less harmful seminal fluid.

They also treated their mates with unusual courtesy—normal fruit-fly courtship looks like sexual harassment. Once competition between males was no

Brain Genes

Mom wants you to be clever, but dad cares more about your metabolism. At least, that's the way the evidence of genomic imprinting points. Experiments with mice show that some maternally expressed genes favor a bigger cortex, the intellectual part of the brain. Mutations that knock out those genes cause retardation. In contrast, some paternally expressed genes favor growth of the hypothalamus, which controls many unconscious body functions.

How do these imprinted genes related to brain function fit into the scheme of intersexual warfare? Instead of the usual scenario, in which dad wants more growth while mom wants less, each parent's genes favor a different kind of growth. Does a female enhance her future health and fertility by supplying her young with a thick cortex and super SAT scores? Does a bigger hypothalamus produce a kid who is able to sap more of mom's resources? No one knows, but Eric B. Keverne of the University of Cambridge, England, who has done much of the work on brain-related imprinted genes, continues to wrestle with these intriguing findings, trying to fit them into the framework of intersexual warfare. Meanwhile, some evolutionary biologists speculate that the traits might have evolved for entirely different reasons.
—*R. S.*

Monogamous flies treat their mates with courtesy

longer a selective force, producing toxic chemicals apparently became a maladaptive waste of energy. Freed of the cost of intersexual warfare, these monogamous flies actually outbred the usual competitive flies.

Just imagine carrying out the same experiment in people. Isolate some humans and force them and their descendants into monogamy for a millennium, and we would probably begin to disarm our mammalian weapons of intersexual warfare, namely imprinted genes. They are an evolutionary burden, making possible some truly horrendous cancers. Remove their advantages by eliminating

polygamy, and natural selection should edit them out.

Having arrived at what sounds like a surreal moral—an exhortation to remember the Sixth Commandment as part of the "Let's Whip Choriocarcinoma by the Year 3000" campaign—it's time to take a step back. Understanding how intersexual competition started with flies is relatively easy. Thanks to random genetic variability, some male flies stumbled into ever so slightly toxic sperm, which the females had to detoxify or die. And from there, the competition spiraled upward. The story of imprinted genes is a bit more compli-

cated, but once paternally derived genes began pushing for the-hell-with-the-mom growth, the battle inevitably escalated. If the tribe next door shows up at the Paleolithic watering hole with clubs that seem just a wee bit on the big side for the purpose of bonking prey animals over the head, the home team will naturally respond by getting even bigger clubs, just in case. And soon we have a world with choriocarcinoma, toxic fruit-fly semen, and umpteen times the education budget buying $600 toilet seats for the military. As in so many other arenas of conflict, it's easier to ratchet up than down.

HOMOSEXUALITY ACROSS CULTURES:

SENSITIZING SOCIAL WORKERS TO HISTORICAL ISSUES FACING GAY, LESBIAN AND BISEXUAL YOUTH

BY DAVID SKIBA

Social work has a history of dealing with clients of differing backgrounds, social strata, and cultures, who require multi-dimensional services. Adolescent clients are now being recognized as having many of the same problems faced by their adult counterparts. No where is this more evident than with young clients who are members of gay, lesbian, and bisexual subgroups, as well as having diverse ethnic backgrounds. The complexities of adolescence, combined with alternative sexual orientations and cultural influences, makes working with this group extremely challenging.

The circumstances facing gay American youth are multifaceted, indicative of a range of problems stemming from issues of sexual orientation and cultural diversity. Progressive approaches in social work have already begun to target adult homosexuals. Approaches will undoubtedly need to be extended to gay, lesbian, and bisexual youth and should consider their cultural differences and related problems. The call for newly developing concepts and counseling approaches are reflected in the comments of Stephen Morin, University of California, San Francisco:

The last 20 years in the U.S. have been a time of remarkable change in thinking about lesbians and gays . . . the prevailing view of homosexual orientation moved from one of sin to one of illness, specifically mental illness. Thus, mental health professions have been critical to a reconceptualization of homosexual orientation as being natural as heterosexual orientation and equally valued as an adult outcome. This movement to remove the stigma long associated with homosexual orientation is the essence of lesbian and gay affirmative approaches to counseling (Morin, 1991, p. 245).

Approaching young, gay clientele from different racial or cultural backgrounds can be difficult. Pilkington and D'Augelli (1995) surveyed a sizable population of adolescent gay, lesbian, and bisexual youth, primarily from urban community centers across the country. Their study focused on a range of victimization experiences and fears that were an issue for this group. Of special interest was the prevalence of youths reporting that they were not comfortable disclosing their sexual orientation to professionals. In fact, people of color were more likely to feel uncomfortable disclosing to professionals than Caucasian respondents: 42 vs. 22 percent. This same cohort reported instances of victimization including verbal insults, threats of attack, completed assaults (with or without weapons), vandalism, being chased or followed, and sexual assaults. With regard to verbal, physical and sexual assaults, perpetrators consisted of members of the victim's immediate family as well as people outside the family.

The escalating prevalence of homophobia directed toward gay youth creates immeasurable damage in the lives of young people struggling with issues of sexual and cultural identity. This places adolescents at increased risk during a critically important developmental stage (Morrow, 1993). This article looks at some cultural considerations within a historical context that are associated with a youth's homosexual lifestyle. In the provision of services, social workers are not only faced with helping gay, lesbian, and bisexual youth accept their sexuality as healthy and normal (Morrow), they also must help youth who face cultural prejudice in the midst of their gay existence. Social workers need to consider the sensitive nature of ones sexual orientation as well as the cul-

From *Social Work Perspectives*, Spring 1997, pp. 27-32. © 1997 by Social Work Perspectives, School of Social Work, San Francisco State University. Reprinted with permission.

tural influences impacting the clients they work with.

A BEGINNING POINT

Kinsey, Pomeroy, and Martin (1948), were the first to bring forth scientifically based estimates of sexual orientation among the general United States population. In the 1948 publication of Sexual Behavior in the Human Male, they estimated the homosexual population to range between five to ten percent of the total American population. In 1986, the percentage of persons identified as homosexual worldwide was reported to be no more than five percent of any given country or culture (Whitam & Mathy, 1986). Even given the evidence of a worldwide existence of homosexuality, there still remains some reluctance among social scientists, politicians, and among particular groups within some cultures in acknowledging its prevalence. Although surveys by Ford and Beach (1951) show that one-third of the societies investigated disapproved of homosexual behavior, numerous journal articles, books and research endeavors have revealed that homosexuality is universal. Homosexuality has been found to exist in varying rates in nearly all societies dating back to ancient Greece and throughout history. From plato's Symposium, which makes reference to same-sex affection and actions, to Walt Whitman's use of the terms "love of comrades" and "adhesiveness" to describe his own sexual preferences, and that of a developing culture, homosexuality, or at least sexual variations have been part of world history for centuries.

PROBLEMS IN DEFINING HOMOSEXUALITY

Definitions of the gay population goes beyond simplistic references to statistics or obvious delineation of homosexuals being "like or liking the same sex." Regardless of our use of such terms as homosexual, gay, or queer, we do a disservice to those who either do not identify with these particular labels, or who have been unavoidably left out. Labeling homosexuals based solely on sexual behaviors or biological markers is too simplistic and restrictive. Our definitions should include emotional components used in defining ones sexual orientation (Crooks and Baur, 1983). An example of this is Martin and Lyon's (1972) definition of a homosexual as an individual "whose primary erotic, psychological, emotional and social interests is with a member of the same sex." We could use the term homophilia, which more accurately identifies love between same-sex persons, but still fails in comprehension (Bohan, 1996). For the sake of brevity and convenience within this text, the term gay will refer to male homosexuals, lesbians, and bisexuals. Specific reference will only be used when necessary. The reader should note that contemporary writings in the area of sexual orientation have increasingly used acronyms. Often found are references to GLBT: Gay, Lesbian, Bisexual, Transgendered People, LGBY: Lesbian, Gay, Bisexual Youth, or the more commonly used short version of GLB: Gay, Lesbian, Bisexual (Bohan, 1996).

PROMINENT THEORIES

Numerous theories of homosexuality exist. Prior to the 19th century, the prevailing argument was that there were homosexual acts but no homosexuals (Weeks, 1977). As times changed, so have proposed explanations concerning the development of homosexual orientation. This is exemplified by the removal of homosexuality as a mental disorder by the American Psychiatric Association in 1973.

In 1905, Freud proposed a psychoanalytic explanation citing childhood experiences and significant object relations as critical to the formation of the homosexual identity. This view has since received criticism for its inherent weaknesses. The critique of Magnus Hirschfeld (1944), a contemporary of Freud, identified such flaws as his predecessor's limited contact with actual homosexuals.

Other theories are used to explain homosexuality with varying degrees of empirical support. To review briefly, these alternative theories include, but are not limited to: genetics, whereby men and women were thought to possess a cross of genetic material (Richardson, 1981); hormonal causes, such as differing levels of male and female hormones (androgen and estrogen) was thought to contribute to sexual orientation (Meyer-Bahlburg, 1984 & 1995); environmental explanations, from which the nature-nurture debate is waged (Mondimore, 1996) and psychoanalytic, social learning, interactionalist, volitional and cognitive theories (Bohan, 1996).

Another important point is the prominent biological theory of homosexuality. Dr. Simon LeVay (1991), himself a self-disclosed homosexual, reports to have discovered significant differences in the measured size of the hypothalamic nucleus region of the brains of heterosexual and homosexual men. His discovery implies a correlation between sexual predetermination and proclivity. LeVay's research comes with obvious drawbacks, such as a limited sample population, approximately 30 subjects, post-mortem examinations using exclusively HIV/AIDS patients, and lack of completeness, as lesbians were not included. Greenberg and Bailey (1993) challenge LeVay's "discovery" as one of many contributing factors fueling the debate over biological underpinnings of homosexuality and to the debate which regards homosexuality as a disease or mental illness. This controversy, which is beyond the scope of this article, is paramount in understanding the gay population. It speaks of the "innateness" or "immutability" of being homosexual, as well as the need to consider environmental, social and intrapsychic influences on alternative lifestyles.

When counseling gay, lesbian or bisexual individuals, these debates are intrinsic to this population. They reflect aspects that need to be recognized as contributing to, or detracting from, therapeutic rapport between counselor and a gay client. The definition of homosexual becomes even more important, even cross-culturally, as a premise of how a client is viewed or how clients interpret being viewed by others.

Vivienne Cass (1984) provides a critical discussion of the proliferation of definitions used to describe homosexuals. This problem invades the realms of research just as much as the day to day lives of gays, lesbians and bisexuals. Cass portrays a sense of urgency for researchers to develop a well defined model of homosexuality. From a therapist's perspective, homosexual identity should include factors that are not exclusively sexual. Likewise, we should not view any one culture based exclusively on racial qualities such as skin color, facial features, or other prevailing stereotypes. A more accurate definition should include a client's personal and cultural history, lifestyle, institutions, values, world view, support systems, work, and family influences.

Beyond the contentious debates over the term homosexual, two additional issues are important to working with this population. They are defining gays as a minority as well as a subculture. For gay men or women, the argument over being a discernible member of a minority strikes at the heart of much of the social stigma they endure. At the same time, it puts gay people in an untenable position of being denied legally sanctioned rights as a minority group and adding to their identity struggles. Gonsiorek and Weinrich (1991) state that, "Homosexuals as a group are the first, second, or third most numerous minority in the U.S…depending on which variation of the estimate is used" (Gonsiorek & Weinrich, p. 12).

Finally, there is the definition of homosexuals or gays as a subculture. Apparently, attaining the status of a "culture" unto itself, is inherently problematic. Interpreted from Simmons (1988), if the dominant society (or culture) fails to recognize homosexuals as a divergent group, for all intensive purposes that "group" or subculture fails to exist. This discussion penetrates the basic level of social identity, which many gays are forced to create for themselves. Failure to develop into a gay culture, or subculture, is met with the unsavory option of assimilating into mainstream America, thus entirely robbing them of any social identity.

For this article's discourse, the existence of a gay subculture is assumed to exist. Such a subculture would exhibit specific characteristics in the realm of politics, arts, history, prospects for the future, and an individual's sense of identity to that "culture" (Bronski, 1984).

Determinants of a subculture versus a culture per se, may be irrelevant to our understanding of this social group from a social work perspective. What may be more important is that through this controversy and classification process, professionals need to recognize the unique existence of gays, lesbians and bisexuals. This recognition should serve to enrich our understanding of people, especially when contrasted against cross-cultural aspects.

A REFLECTION OF HOMOSEXUALITY ACROSS CULTURES

In Whitam and Mathy (1986), *Male Homosexuality in Four Societies,* they make the following interpretations: First, the emergence of homosexuals across cultures vary in their outward expression. Second, societies appeared to react to homosexuality for those whom emerged spontaneously suggesting that there was an already established history or subculture of homosexuals and that this was tolerated. Third, the development of a given homosexual population does not appear to be determined by societal factors like socialization. Also, cross-gender behavior such as cross-dressing, opposite sex play patterns, dance, entertainment, etc., is consistent across cultures. Unfortunately, lesbianism has received limited attention (Dynes & Donaldson, 1992). As much as men have received the majority of interest from researchers, lesbians, at least historically, have been discredited for their social feminist activism, often labeled an aberration. The recorded history of lesbianism has also suffered from systematic destruction, evidenced by missionaries in China as far back as 100–1200 A.D. (Dynes & Donaldson).

A predominant issue affecting America's own interpretation of homosexuality as a culture is based on the tendency, or unconscious process, to interpret and interact with a different culture based solely on Euro-American definitions and standards. What might be called a one-colored world view is detrimental to understanding any homosexual group. Sue & Sue (1990) state with regard to culture, we have become "culturally blind."

Not to be forgotten are aspects central to understanding homosexuality within any one particular milieu. The tendency to respond exclusively to sexual behaviors as the only descriptor of any one group, negates the proliferation of research from ethnographers and anthropologists, which talks about culture from the perspective of religion, economics, technologies and social organizations (Crooks & Baur, 1983).

HOMOSEXUALITY WITHIN CULTURES

As a means of sensitizing social workers to the different cultural backgrounds of gays whom they encounter, the following discussions will describe some of the cultural diversity that exists among homosexuals throughout the world.

A number of the same issues and problems incurred by African Americans in the general population also exist for African American homosexuals. Areas that touch upon cultural factors, social class variables, and experiences of racism are evident. Frank Browning (1993), describes how the struggles of African Americans during the years of the civil rights movements (1950's–1960's) were the beginning point of not only civil rights, social structure and legislation, but also the start of a sexual rebellion.

Dr. Alvin Poussaint (1990), Associate Professor of Psychiatry at Harvard Medical School, feels that the differences and problems of gay African Americans, from a historical perspective, are unsubstantiated. He suggests that white Europeans had little or nothing to do with the development of an African American gay culture. From a social class perspective, Dr. Poussaint states that the African American gay community is closely reflected in the historical data of Kinsey some 35 years ago. African American gays represent economic diversity and membership within a full range of social strata and include more upwardly mobile gay African Americans who are well educated and live in upscale areas. This social process is however contrary to other African American gays residing in exclusively African American impoverished urban communities.

Phil Wilson, Co-Chair of the Black, Gay and Lesbian Leadership Forum in Los Angeles, as quoted by Poussaint (1990), states that "The black community will not out-rightly reject you, but they make their love for you contingent on your being quiet about your gay orientation." Wilson goes on to say that "openly black gay demonstrations can provoke negative reactions and the black community frequently perceives gays as part of its 'problems', alongside such social ills as crime and poverty (p. 130). Social problems of racism or prejudice can be experienced differently among the African American gay population. A significant number of African American homosexuals experience racial discrimination by other members of their own gay subculture. For instance, African American gays are not welcome in all gay bars, and are typically excluded from white gay advertising. African American lesbians are also affected, having to form their

own protective identity by first referring to themselves as African American women, and only then as lesbians.

The Latino population of homosexuals has a historical precedence emanating from the early nineteenth century reforms of the French Criminal Law known as the Napoleonic Code, which included a decriminalization of homosexuality throughout Latin America. This contemporary movement represents a more open acceptance of gays within Latin America. In this sense, Latin American countries can be seen as more sophisticated and therefore more accepting of the behaviors or lifestyles of gays. This view of sexuality goes beyond the homosexual subculture, alluding to a vast social acceptance and openness toward sexuality in general and shows more tolerance than many states in the U.S. (Whitam & Mathy, 1986).

This perspective should not be generalized across all Latin American groups. Whitam and Mathy (1986) concede that not all of Latin America is accepting of homosexuality. Argentina has become notorious for outlawing such activity. Cuba has historically been restrictive to gays, although Stanford (1982), notes that Cuba is acquiring much of the same traditional Latin attitudes of sexual freedom seen in some progressive states in the United States. In a study of acculturation of young Latinos (Ford and Norris, 1993), it was noted that sexual behavior changes are consistent with the level of acculturation. Even though their research did not directly reference homosexual activity, it did focus its attention on traditional cultural values and practices and how those aspects were affected by the acculturation process in America. According to Marin, Marin and Juarez (1988), the Latin culture protects the privacy of their sexuality more so than many non-Latino cultures. Overall, the debate over acceptance of homosexuality for Latino gay youth is less defined than we would like it to be. Undoubtedly, our means of obtaining reliable data about sexual orientation across any culture is limited by

the predominant use of self-reports (Gonsiorek & Weinrich, 1991).

Native Americans reveal a rich historical experience of homosexuality to both researchers and academicians. First, reports of homosexuality in Native American societies date back to 1528, as Alvan Nunez Cabaza de Vaca observed and reported on tribes in Florida (Whitam & Mathy, 1986). Since that time, some 37 historical reports documenting gay Native American behaviors and practices have been compiled as well as later studies and analyses of those previous works (Katz, 1976).

Throughout the gay Native American culture, the term berdache has been consistently used to describe the homosexual aspect of Native American sexuality. The term was originally coined by eighteenth century French anthropologists, but has been interpreted differently by white heterosexuals throughout history. Essentially, berdache refers to Native Americans whom display exclusively homosexual, bisexual, transvestite, or effeminate characteristics, occupations or activities. Berdache was also reflective of physical abnormalities, but this hermaphrodite connotation eventually disappeared from use. This term has varied in meaning over time to include definitions of "institutionalized homosexuality" (Devaraus, 1937) and "gender mixing" (Tinker, 1986). Regardless of which definition is used, berdache is representative of a rich history of variant sexuality in the Native American culture (Whitam & Mathy, 1986).

From the literature, George Tinker (1986) synthesized five pertinent concerns for gay Native Americans: First, "some tribes have been so thoroughly Christianized . . . [therefore] no longer retain any traditional functional role or respect for the berdache," and hence have nowhere to turn for support. Second, traditionally speaking, the historical concept of the berdache does not exist in its purest sense, although some tribes have maintained cultural integrity on this matter. Third, that the urbanization of Native Americans has created third and fourth generations of city people with accultur-ated attitudes expounding American homophobia. Fourth, Native Ameri-cans have been placed in a position of "marginality" of a different sense, being positioned between traditional berdache roles and those of the con-temporary Euro-American gay experi-ences. Last, there's a vast difference in the approach of Native Americans to gay homosexuals. They reject the typical "merciless harassment or exclu-sion that one sees in the rest of American society" (Tinker, pp. 612–613).

A brief look at the Asian culture of homosexuality will include Filipi-nos, Indonesians, Koreans, Indians, Chinese, and Japanese. Homosexuality still prevails through out pacific rim countries. Researchers admit there is a paucity of information from which to derive substantive conclusions spe-cific to cultural facets of homosexual-ity (Whitam & Mathy, 1986; Ford & Beach 1951; Nanda, 1984; and Ruan & Yung, 1988). Beyond this limited data, some generalizations can still be made.

Asian beliefs generally appear to have a less tolerant view of homosexu-ality. For instance, Filipinos attach a pejorative connotation to gay youth with the use of the terms "Bayot" and "Lakin-on," which are synony-mous with "sissy" or "tomboy" (Hart, 1968). In his examination of homo-sexuality and transvestitism in the Philippines, Hart reports that public display of affection between young Filipino men and women is generally disapproved. However, beyond this dominating social disdain accorded to homosexuality, are social adjustments. Interpreted by Hart is this "release of normal emotions [by] interaction with a person of the same sex," suggesting that a degree of social tolerance, or naiveté about homosexuality does in-fact exist in the Philippine culture (Chicago, 1956, p. 432).

On the other hand, Indonesian cul-ture offers an array of theoretical ex-planations of homosexuality, but it is focused exclusively on transvestitism. Again, a scarcity of information leaves the reader without tangible

data from which to derive meaningful conclusions about gay behavior or cus-toms. Within the Indonesian culture, the concept of transvestitism is con-ceptualized in three models heavily based on a role playing scenario and strongly linked to religion and the concept of androgyny. The functional model is based on religious beliefs and practices intermingled with socie-tal structure, art, power, law, etc. The protective model involves the supersti-tious ritual of wearing clothing of the opposite sex in order to deceive pow-erful spirits. The impositional model involves ritualistic tendencies of both males and females that can be exhib-ited simultaneously (Van der Kroef, 1954, p. 257–265).

In ancient Korea, a well main-tained female cross-dressing shamanis-tic tradition existed (Kim, 1992). Today, the theater is well represented by male homosexuals divided into groups of butches and queens. Young Ja Kim's article appearing in Asian Homosexuality (Dynes & Donaldson, 1992), describes the tradition and function of corps drawn almost exclu-sively from homosexual communes. These performance groups are descen-dants of the Namsadang, a socially sanctioned performance theater dating back to 1920. The Namsadang, and latter day versions, were a means of social commentary and a voice for the common people against Confucian-ism, which viewed homosexuality as immoral (Kim, p. 81–82).

China displays a more extensive documented history of male homo-sexuality dating back to the Eastern Zhou dynasty: 722–221 B.C. (Dynes & Donaldson, 1992). The twentieth century brought drastic changes in China's social perception of homo-sexuality. China has seen scientific as well as categorical changes regarding homosexuality. The traditional erotic and romanticizing notions have been removed and replaced by a more prejudicial and pathological view of homosexuality (Dynes & Donaldson). Lesbianism is still not recognized in China, but is instead seen as an unre-lated phenomenon within the spec-

trum of human sexual expression or identity.

In Taiwan, a homosexual subcul-ture underground has developed. Simi-larly, in Japan, a less prominent acceptance of gay lifestyles exists. Ja-pan's rich cultural and literary history of homosexuality was replaced with bisexuality as the more socially ac-cepted norm. Contemporary homosex-ual lifestyles are characterized among hidden elements of private gay bars and bath houses. Historically, Japan endured vast social change after the Meiji Restoration (1868). As a result, homosexuality became a criminal act with penalties of ninety days in jail was common (Dynes & Donaldson, 1992). Today, Japanese societal views of homosexuality appear to be one of selective attention and inconspicuous denial.

CONCLUDING REMARKS AND RECOMMENDATIONS

It is fair to say that mental health problems for the subculture of homo-sexuals varies among ethnic groups. Furthermore, these rates or degrees of severity for mental health problems may be significant if not comparable to levels found in the dominate hetero-sexual population. This is especially true if we accept the notion that ho-mosexuals comprise anywhere from 10% to 15% of the population (Kin-sey, et al. 1948, 1953; Gebhard 1972).

Borrowing from the guidelines pre-sented in Counseling the Culturally Different (Sue & Sue, 1990, pp. 167–168), the following points can be eas-ily incorporated into social work practice as a means of sensitizing workers to the duality of homosexual-ity across cultures:

1. The culturally and (sexually) aware social worker is one who has moved from being cultur-ally/(sexually) unaware, to being sensitive to his/her own cultural heritage and (sexual) awareness, and to value and respect those dif-ferences.

2. The culturally/(sexually) aware social worker is aware of his/her own values and how they may affect minority clients.

3. The culturally/(sexually) aware [and] skilled social worker is comfortable with differences that exist between themselves and their clients in terms of race, culture, beliefs/and (sexual) practices.

4. The culturally/(sexually) skilled social worker is sensitive to circumstances (personal biases, stage of ethnic/sexual identity, sociopolitical influences, etc.) that may dictate referral of the minority client to a member of his/her race/culture/(sexual subculture), or to another appropriate professional.

5. The culturally/(sexually) aware social worker acknowledges and is cognizant of his/her own racist/(sexual) attitudes, beliefs, and feelings.

CONCLUSION

This article outlined prominent aspects of homosexuality across cultures from a historical perspective. Exposing social workers to many of the fundamental differences concerning alternative sexual orientations within multiple cultures, affords us the opportunity to expand our awareness and to explore the complexities of working with a diverse gay, lesbian, and bisexual population. It also serves as an impetus in developing professional skills that will ensure improved intervention outcomes and reduce the potential of homophobic or culturally biased countertransference.

REFERENCES

Bohan, J. S. (1996). *Psychology and sexual orientation: Coming to terms.* New York:, Routledge.

Bronski, M. (1984). *Culture clash: The making of gay sensibility.* Boston, MA: South End Press.

Browning, F. (1993). *The culture of desire* (1st ed.). New York: Crown Publishers.

Cass, V. C. (1984). Homosexual identity formation: Testing a theoretical model. *Journal of Sex Research, 20* (2), 143–167.

Chicago University (1956). Philippine Studies Program: Area handbook of the Philippines, human relations area files: New Haven, Conn. In W. Dynes & S. Donaldson (Eds.), *Asian Homosexuality* (p. 75). New York: Garland Publishing, Inc.

Crooks, R., & Baur, K. (1983). *Our sexuality.* Menlo Park, CA: The Benjamin/Cummings Publishing Company.

Devaraus, G. (1963). Institutionalized homosexuality of Mojave Indians. In H.M. Ruitenbeek (Ed.), *The problem of homosexuality in modern society* (pp. 183–226). New York: E.P. Dutton.

Dynes, W. R., & Donaldson, S. (1992). *Asian homosexuality.* New York: Garland Publishing Inc.

Ford, C. S., & Beach, F.A. (1951). *Patterns of sexual behavior.* New York: Harper & Row.

Ford, K., & Norris, A. (1993). Urban Hispanic adolescent and young adults: Relationship of acculturation to sexual behavior. *The Journal of Sex Research, 30,* 316–323.

Gebhard, P. H. (1972). Incidence of over homosexuality in the United States and Western Europe. In J. J. Livingood (Ed.), *NIMH task force on homosexuality: Final report and background papers* (DHEW publication No.(HSM)72–9116). Rockville, MD: National Institute of Mental Health.

Gonsiorek, J. C., & Weinrich, J.D. (1991). *Homosexuality: Research implications for public policy.* Newbury Park, CA: Sage Publications, Inc.

Greenberg, A. S., & Bailey, J. M. (1993). Do biological explanations of homosexuality have moral, legal, or policy implications? *Journal of Sex Research, 30,* 245–251.

Hart, D. V. (1968). Homosexuality and transvestitism in the Philippines: The Cuban Filipino Bayot and Lakin-on. *Behavioral Science Note, 3,* 211–248.

Hirschfeld, M. (1944). *Sexual anomalies and perversions.* New York: Emerson Books.

Katz, J. (1976). *Gay American history: Lesbian and gay men in the USA.* New York: Thomas W. Crowell.

Kim, Y. A. (1992). The Korean Namsadang. In W.R. Dynes & S. Donaldson (Eds.). *Asian homosexuality* (pp. 81–88). New York: Garland Publishing, Inc.

Kinsey, A. C., Pomeroy, W. B., & Martin, C. E. (1948). *Sexual behavior in the human male.* Philadelphia: W.B. Saunders.

Kinsey, A. C., Pomeroy, W. B., & Martin, C. E., & Gebhard, P. H. (1953). *Sexual behavior in the human female.* Philadelphia: W.B. Saunders.

LeVay, S. (1991). A difference in hypothalamic structure between heterosexual and homosexual men. *Science, 253,* 1034–1037.

Martin, D., & Lyon, P. (1972). *Lesbian women.* New York: Bantam.

Marin, B., Marin, G., & Juarez, R. (1988). *Prevention of AIDS in Latino community: Cultural issues.* Paper presented at the Annual Conference of the American Psychological Association, Atlanta, Georgia.

Meyer-Bahlburg, H. (1984). Psychoendocrine research on sexual orientation: Current status and future options. In G. J. De Vries, J. P. C. De Bruin, H. M. B. Uylings, & M. A. Corner, (Eds.), *Progress in brain research* (vol. 61, pp. 375–398). Amsterdam: Elsevier.

Meyer-Bahlburg, H. (1995). Psychoneuroendocrinology and sexual pleasure: The aspect of sexual orientation. In P.R. Abramson & S.D. Pinkerton (Eds.), *Sexual nature/sexual culture* (pp. 135–153). Chicago: University of Chicago Press.

Mondimore, F.M. (1996). *A natural history of homosexuality.* The John Hopkins Baltimore, MD: University Press.

Morin, S. (1991). Removing the stigma: Lesbian and gay affirmative counseling. *The Counseling Psychologist, 19,* 245–247.

Morrow, D. F. (1993). Social work with gay and lesbian adolescents. *Journal of the National Association of Social Workers, 38* (6), 655–660.

Nanda, S. (1984). The Hijras of India: A preliminary report. *Medicine and Law, 3,* 59–75.

Pilkington, N. W., & D'Augelli, A.R. (1995). Victimization of lesbian, gay, and bisexual youth in community settings. *Journal of Community Psychology, 3,* 34–56.

Poussaint, A. (1990). An honest look at black gays and lesbians: *Ebony, 45,* 124–131.

Richardson, D. (1981). Theoretical perspectives on homosexuality. In J. Hart & D. Richardson (Eds.). *The theory and practice of homosexuality* (pp. 5–37). London: Routledge and Kegan Paul.

Ruan, F., & Yung, T. (1988). Male homosexuality in contemporary mainland China. *Archives of Sexual Behavior, 17,* 189–199.

Simmons, J. L. (1988). The nature of deviant subcultures. In E. Rubington & M. S. Weinberg (Eds.), *Deviance: The Interactionist perspective: Text and readings in the sociology of deviance.* New York, NY: MacMillan.

Stanford, J. D. (Ed.). (1982). Spartacus International. *Gay Guide.* (12th ed.). Amsterdam: Spartacus.

Sue, D. W., &Sue, D. (1990). *Counseling the culturally different: Theory and practice.* (2nd ed.). New York: John Wiley and Sons.

Tinker, G. (1986). Review essay: American Indian Berdache and cross-cultural diversity. In W. Williams (Ed.), *The spirit and the flesh: Sexual diversity in American Indian culture,* Beacon Press.

Van der Kroef, J. M. (1954). Transvestitism and the religious hermaphrodite in Indonesia. *University of Manila Journal of East Asiatic Studies, 3* (3), 257–265.

Weeks, J. (1977). *Coming out: Homosexual politics in Britain from the nineteenth century to the present.* London: Quartet Books.

Whitam, F.L., & Mathy, R. (1986). *Male homosexuality in four societies: Brazil, Guatemala, the Philippines, and the United States.* New York, NY: Praeger.

David E. Skiba, CSW, [at this writing was] a second year Doctoral student in the Social Welfare department at State University of New York at Buffalo. His interests are in adolescent sexuality and substance abuse issues. He would like to give special thanks to his wife, Michelle, for all of her support and encouragement.

Unit Selections

Key Points to Consider

❖ Should the Social Security program be privatized? If yes, what specific changes would you support? If no, why not?

❖ In your view, does the Welfare Reform Act (the Personal Responsibility and Work Opportunity Reconciliation Act of 1996—PL104-193) contain more positive aspects than negative aspects? Take a stand and explain in detail the reasons for your position.

❖ What are the similarities and differences between poverty as experienced in rural communities in comparison to poverty as experienced in urban communities?

❖ What is your opinion about the principle of "government as the employer of last resort"?

❖ What role should the extended family (i.e., grandparents, adult children, uncles, aunts, cousins, etc.) play when someone needs help?

❖ Can every poor person eventually move from welfare to work? Defend your answer. Do some minority populations have unique needs when moving from welfare to work? If yes, cite some specific examples.

❖ What would you do with single-parent families containing school-aged children who have reached the end of their 5-year lifetime eligibility to receive TANF (Temporary Assistance to Needy Families) benefits? Be as specific as possible.

 **Links**   **www.dushkin.com/online/**

These sites are annotated on pages 4 and 5.

It is commonly accepted that the social welfare system in the United States provides benefits to its citizens in three distinct ways: (a.) *Cash.* Benefits are distributed mainly by checks, which are cashed directly by recipients; (b.) *In-Kind Benefits.* Benefits are provided in lieu of cash and have restrictions attached to them. They can be distributed either in the form of a voucher (examples are food stamps, a Medicaid card, a bus ticket), or in the form of some tangible substance (examples are a school lunch, an apartment in a public housing project, or 20 pounds of surplus flour); (c.) *Social Services.* This third form of social welfare benefit is less concrete and less visible because it comes as a provision of help by a trained professional. Examples of social services include adoption and foster care, day care, counseling, education and training, job referral and placement, and many other "soft" benefits that are neither cash nor in-kind in nature.

This unit focuses on Social Security and welfare reform, and it covers the major programs that provide both cash and in-kind benefits. The following two units will focus primarily on the various social service programs in the United States.

The largest cash benefit program in the United States is Social Security—the contributory social welfare program that provides financial support to most retirees and to some people with disabilities. The unique aspect of the Social Security program is that it is funded by automatic contributions from the participants themselves and from their employers. Because of this self-contributory factor, no stigma or embarrassment is attached to these benefits. Welfare (or income maintenance), on the other hand, is highly stigmatized because it is funded out of the general tax revenues of the federal and state governments, and a person or family must pass a "needs test" in order to be eligible for benefits. The most visible, and most criticized, part of the welfare program was called (until 1996) Aid to Families with Dependent Children (AFDC). Since that time, as President Bill Clinton works toward fulfilling his promise to "end welfare as we know it," the successor program is called Temporary Assistance to Needy Families (TANF).

This unit concentrates on the issues that have been raised about the Social Security program and

on the controversies swirling around the passage of the newer welfare reform legislation.

Social Security is discussed in the first three articles: "Missed Opportunity" by Steve Forbes, "A Critique of the Case for Privatizing Social Security" by John Williamson, and "Don't Go It Alone" by Mortimer Zuckerman. In the face of current fears about the stability of the Social Security Trust Fund, and whether it will be able to fund future retirees, these articles contain useful facts and varying perspectives on this complicated subject. The biggest challenge facing legislators is to decide whether to privatize the system, and, if so, in what form and to what extent.

The remaining articles in this section concern the current reforms within the welfare (that is, income maintenance) system. Peggy Cook and Elizabeth Dagata, in "Welfare Reform Legislation Poses Opportunities and Challenges for Rural America," provide a comprehensive summary of the Personal Responsibility and Work Opportunity Reconciliation Act of 1996, reminding us that poverty is also a rural problem with some distinct differences.

The following two articles, "Why Welfare Reform Is Working" by Daniel Casse and "Welfare to Work: What Happens When Recipient Meets Employer?" by Aaron Steelman, assume a generally positive and hopeful stance regarding the new welfare reform law.

James Payne, in "Welfare's Fatal Attraction," and Jonathan Walters, in "Beyond the Welfare Clock," are somewhat more cautious in their perspectives on this timely and controversial issue.

A most direct, frontal assault on the welfare reform legislation is launched by the authors of the concluding four articles in this section. Peter Edelman, in "Welfare and the 'Third Way,'" argues that the existing safety net for poor and vulnerable people has been destroyed with tragic consequences. The particularly devastating impact of the new policies on Hispanic women is highlighted by Alexandra Starr, in her essay "Left Behind." Jason DeParle provides a highly personalized account of one African American family trying desperately to survive in the maze of the new welfare system. Finally, Alexandra Marks, in "Now, the Hard Part of Welfare Reform," poses the critical question of whether welfare reform is really worth the human cost involved when you consider its impact on children and on the most vulnerable of the poor.

Social Security and Welfare Reform

Dropping the ball on ENTITLEMENT CONTROL

Missed Opportunity

Washington's Budget Deal Does Nothing to Fix Entitlements

By Steve Forbes

This summer's much-ballyhooed balanced-budget agreement is a disaster for entitlement reform. No improvement is made in the top-down, bureaucratic, increasingly bankrupt Medicare and Social Security programs, nor is there any serious effort to unleash the dynamism that individual choice in health care and retirement could bring. In fact, the budget agreement makes our troubling entitlements situation worse.

For instance, buried in the 1,200-page budget bill is a nasty, little-known provision, Section 4507, that begins to write socialized medicine into law. Starting January 1, 1998, American doctors will effectively be prohibited from treating elderly patients on a private basis outside of the Medicare program.

The government health care bureaucracy had already been using its regulatory powers to forbid doctors who accept Medicare patients from also treating senior citizens who choose to pay out-of-pocket. Republicans originally tried to insert into

the budget agreement a provision that would overturn this regulation, but President Clinton protested and the Republicans caved in.

Since over 90 percent of doctors accept Medicare patients, this law makes it nearly impossible for seniors to find a doctor who will also treat them on a private basis, outside Medicare's rules and regulations. Only doctors in the very wealthiest areas will be available to seniors hoping to engage in private health care between consenting adults. Astonishingly, even Britain, mother of socialized medicine, allows patients to contract privately with physicians. Senator Jon Kyl (R-Ariz.) is leading the charge to repeal Section 4507. He points out that the current law is the equivalent of forbidding everyone enrolled in Social Security from also investing his own money privately with stockbrokers: Such a law "would be met with disbelief and derision," yet it is no different from what the new Medicare law does.

The great opportunity in health care reform today is the Medical Savings Account (or MSA). Properly designed, MSAs would give seniors better coverage and

more choice at less cost, without having to take orders from an HMO. At present, the government taxes workers to pay for Medicare patients, and then forces them all into a one-size-fits-everyone health care system. This Washington-run operation has helped medical expenses skyrocket so that Medicare patients feel compelled to purchase "Medigap" insurance policies that pay for the gap between what health care actually costs and what Medicare will pay.

By contrast, seniors with MSAs would have both low-cost, high-deductible "catastrophic" health insurance plans, as well as personal savings accounts that would cover most out-of-pocket health care expenses. They could shop for their own doctors, medicine, and health care supplies with the peace of mind that (a) they know for sure what their maximum out-of-pocket costs will be; (b) they have real catastrophic insurance that won't leave them destitute; (c) they have control over their own care and are subject neither to excessive government rules nor to impersonal HMOs; and (d) if they can keep their health expenses down, the money invested in their Medical Savings Accounts will actually grow over time and so be available to them in the future.

Steve Forbes, president and CEO *of Forbes, Inc, was a candidate for president in 1996.*

We use a variation of MSAs at *Forbes*. After five years, our costs are lower than they were when we started, and not one of our people is in managed care. More than 3,000 firms use MSAs today, including the United Mine Workers, because they work. Yet rather than insist upon Medical Savings Accounts for all Medicare patients, Congress allowed only a piddling MSA "experiment" limited to fewer than one percent of all Americans, while slapping additional heavy-handed regulations on the Medicare population.

Meanwhile, Social Security, the country's other major entitlement mess, continues to be thought of by official Washington as the "third rail of American politics"—touch it and you die. So the negotiators of the budget deal drew back and did nothing to improve a system that a majority of citizens know is doomed. [See editors' sidebar.]

Younger Americans want and deserve a new retirement system that will protect them from the vagaries of Washington politics. The basics of genuine reform are breathtakingly simple and eminently feasible. First, we must preserve the current system for those already in it and those entering the system in the next 12 to 15 years. People have made real-life decisions based on the current system, and our contract with them must be honored. A promise made must be a promise kept.

Second, we should start a new Social Security system for younger people, where a substantial part—and eventually all—of their payroll taxes would go into their own Individual Retirement Accounts. Obviously, a person couldn't touch the account until a certain age, but he would receive monthly statements and be free to choose what investments to make, within bounds (mutual funds, CDs, stocks, bonds, and the like). With such an arrangement, Americans would have far more savings upon retirement than they could possibly have under the current bankrupt system. [The Jan./Feb. 1997 issue of *The American Enterprise* provided an in-depth look at this subject.]

The British are successfully changing from a government-run Social insurance system to one that permits individual choice, as a new report from the Heritage Foundation reveals. More than 73 percent of British workers have chosen to invest their payroll taxes in private stocks and equities, rather than remain completely dependent on the government-run system. The strong returns they are earning on these private investments explains their choice: From 1986 to 1995, the median private pension under this system earned 13.3 percent per year. And Britain's pension sav-

Public Supports Dramatic Entitlement Reform

Stunningly strong popular support for sharp, market-oriented reforms of the two major federal entitlement programs—Medicare and Social Security—was uncovered in a recent poll commissioned by a Democratic party organization.

Do you think that Medicare will soon face a crisis requiring us to undertake serious reform, or do you think these programs are basically sound and should not be tampered with?

Soon face crisis/undertake serious reform	73
Programs are basically sound/should not be tampered with	23

Which do you think is a bigger priority protecting Medicare from budget cuts, or reforming Medicare to ensure its long-term financial stability?

Protect from cuts	17
Reform for financial stability	80

In thinking about reforming Medicare to ensure its long-term financial stability, do you think it would be better to raise premiums and cut benefits, but essentially retain Medicare as we know it, or would it be better to make larger changes in the system, such as allowing the marketplace to determine the price and level of health care provided instead of the government setting the price and scope of Medicare coverage.

Small changes	31
Larger changes	57
Don't know	12

How much confidence do you have in the long-term financial stability of the Social Security program a great deal of confidence, some confidence, not very much confidence, or no confidence at all?

Great deal of confidence	12
Some	32
Not very much	33
None	22

Do you think that Social Security will soon face a crisis requiring us to undertake serious reform, or do you think these programs are basically sound and should not be tampered with?

Soon face crisis/undertake serious reform	72
Programs are basically sound/should not be tampered with	25

Would you support or oppose... gradually ending the existing Social Security system and instead requiring Americans to save for their retirement. This would be done by shifting the Social Security payroll tax into individually controlled personal savings accounts.

Support ending the existing system	55
Oppose	38

Source: Penn, Schoen & Berland Associates poll for the Democratic Leadership Council, July/August 1997.

ings pool now totals over $1 trillion—larger than the pension funds of all other European countries combined.

Critics say such a system of personal choice in retirement savings would be "too complicated" for average Americans. Nonsense. As the economy grows and people become more concerned about the quality of their lives upon retirement, they are investing more and more of their after-tax income in mutual funds, IRAs, and 401 (k) plans. Individual stock ownership has doubled in just the past seven years. More than four in ten Americans now own equities. Mutual funds investments have tripled in the same period. Nearly half of investors are women. More than half are under the age of 50. Even more interesting, one-half

of these investors are not college graduates, and the number of minority persons who are investing is on the rise. "People are intensely aware that they have to rely on themselves for their financial future," says Alfred R. Berkley, president of the NASDAQ stock market.

With such glittering opportunities for entitlement reform abounding, the current lack of leadership in Washington seems all the more disappointing. Thus far, Congress has adopted a bunker mentality while Bill Clinton does little more than defend the status quo.

Americans want reform. Politicos take note: If you don't provide it, the voters will look to others who will.

This article presents and then critiques arguments made by those advocating the privatization of Social Security. It refutes the argument that baby boomers will find themselves without Social Security pensions unless fundamental changes are made. It questions the claims that privatization would increase economic growth, reduce the federal deficit, make the nation more competitive in the global economy, protect workers against payroll tax increases, protect boomers against pension benefit cuts, and increase confidence in Social Security. It argues that for low-wage workers, returns on contributions would probably decrease and future benefits would become politically more vulnerable. Key Words: Policy, Pensions, Privatization, Inequity, Entitlements

A Critique of the Case for Privatizing Social Security

John B. Williamson, PhD[1]

Some changes in Social Security policy will soon be needed to deal with the burden of paying for the retirement of the baby boom generation. In the unlikely event that no changes were made in the current payroll tax levels and pension benefit levels, according to recent projections the cost of these pensions would begin to exceed payroll tax revenues in 2013, the trust fund would begin to shrink in 2019, and the trust fund balance would drop to zero in 2029 (Board of Trustees of the Federal Old-Age and Survivors Insurance and Disability Insurance Trust Funds, 1996). Some commentators in the popular press suggest that as of 2029 Social Security may go bankrupt, leaving many old people without Social Security pensions. Although this belief is not held by Social Security experts, it is widely held in the general population. In one recent national poll, only 30% of the respondents reported feeling confident that their Social Security pensions will be paid throughout their retirement (Friedland, 1994; Quadagno, 1996).

The view that the baby boomers may find themselves without Social Security pensions is wrong on several counts. Even if no policy changes were made, after 2029 payroll taxes would still be coming in that would fund pensions at approximately 77% of currently promised levels (Board of Trustees of the Federal Old-Age and Survivors Insurance and Disability Insurance Trust Funds, 1996). In addition, it is reasonable to assume that some if not most of the 23% gap that remained would be dealt with by some combination of payroll tax increase and indirect benefit cuts, such as increasing the eligibility age or means-testing benefits for high income recipients. Given the current policy of making periodic adjustments to keep the system in projected balance 75 years into the future, it is reasonable to assume that changes will be made long before 2029 to deal with the projected deficit.

Some of the changes being considered call for relatively minor adjustments, but in recent years we have also begun to hear a call for a much more fundamental change, the privatization of Social Security. Only a few years ago advocacy of privatization was confined to a few analysts, most prominently those linked to the libertarian Cato Institute (Ferrara, 1985), but today this alternative is being seriously discussed in much more mainstream venues. In 1995 Senators Robert Kerrey (D-Nebraska) and John Danforth (R-Missouri) formulated such

[1]Address correspondence to John B. Williamson, Department of Sociology, Boston College, Chestnut Hill, MA 02167. The author wishes to thank Joseph Quinn and Eric Kingson for their critical comments on an earlier draft of this article.

From *The Gerontologist,* Vol. 37, No. 5, October 1997, pp. 561-571. © 1997 by The Gerontological Society of America. Reprinted with permission.

a proposal in connection with the Bipartisan Commission on Entitlement and Tax Reform (1995). Even more important is the recent release of the report of the Advisory Council on Social Security (1997). The advisory council has offered three alternative policy proposals to the President, two of which call for the partial privatization of Social Security. The third calls for investing a substantial fraction of the Social Security trust fund in the private sector.

Although very few mainstream analysts argue that full privatization warrants serious consideration as a policy alternative for the United States, today partial privatization is being seriously considered. Were such a change made, it would represent one of the most fundamental changes in Social Security since the program was enacted in 1935. The partial privatization of Social Security might have adverse consequences for some, particularly low-wage workers (Quinn & Mitchell, 1996; U.S. Senate, 1995), but it could also become very popular, particularly among the more affluent. Even a partial privatization of Social Security would represent a fundamental shift away from the social insurance approach of the past 60 years. Advocates for privatization of Social Security seek to reduce the government's role in the provision of pension benefits to elderly persons and to increase the extent to which private sector investments are used to finance old-age security.

The debate over the privatization of Social Security has begun, and there is every reason to believe that it will become even more heated over the next few years. Much of what has been written about the topic has come from advocates of privatization, and there has been far too little systematic effort to respond to their arguments. The goals of the present article are: (a) to describe what commentators mean when they refer to the privatization of Social Security, (b) to present the major arguments that have been made by advocates of privatization, and (c) to respond to these arguments.

What Does "Privatizing" Social Security Mean?

Any assessment of the likely impact of privatization depends on what form privatization takes. Most proposals for privatizing Social Security in the United States call for some form of partial privatization, not full privatization. For some commentators, full privatization would involve doing away with the Social Security program (the suggestion is sometimes to phase it out over a period of decades), leaving it entirely up to individuals to decide whether or not to buy private insurance to provide for death, disability, or retirement (U.S. Senate, 1995).

But to most commentators, the full privatization of Social Security would involve replacing the existing set of Social Security pension programs (old-age pensions, survivors pensions, and disability pensions) with mandatory private insurance alternatives. The old-age pension component would most likely involve contributions to individual investment accounts, something along the lines of a 401(k) account. For most proposals the federal government would not manage the funds, but it would have a role with respect to the regulation of the industry

and in some cases would insure at least a portion of workers' assets in the event of a default. Something approaching the full privatization of Social Security was introduced in Chile in 1981 (Diamond, 1996; Kritzer, 1996; Myers, 1992), but no proposals for so fundamental a change are currently being seriously considered for the United States. Although some would like such a change, even the most ardent supporters of privatization recognize that it would not be politically feasible to make the shift to full privatization at this time. Most would settle for partial privatization today in the hope that it would be a first step toward full privatization at some point in the future (Porter, 1995).

The partial privatization of Social Security could take many forms. One form would be to make participation entirely voluntary (Friedland, 1996; Friedman, 1962). Poortvliet and Laine (1995) used the term "de facto privatization" to refer to a variety of policies that would produce benefit cuts such as reducing the cost-of-living adjustments, means testing benefits, and increasing the age of eligibility. Such policies would constitute a form of de facto privatization because they indirectly force workers to increase their private savings in an effort to replace the projected cut in Social Security benefits. Friedland (1996) argued that the term "privatization" can also be used to refer to a policy that would have a portion of the Social Security trust funds invested in the private sector. For example, Robert Ball's Maintenance of Benefits (MB) plan, one of the three proposals outlined by the Advisory Council on Social Security (1997), calls for investing up to 40% of the Social Security trust fund in private sector equity markets, but without the creation of individual investment accounts (Ball & Bethell, 1997). Although some commentators would classify Ball's proposal as a form of partial privatization, I would not. When I refer to privatization or partial privatization in this article, the reference is to the diversion of payroll tax contributions to individual accounts, which is not the case with Ball's MB plan.

One of the most common approaches to partial privatization would require workers to pay a portion of their Social Security contribution into 401(k)-like Individual Social Security Retirement Accounts (hereafter ISSRAs; see Appendix, Note 1). The rest of the Social Security payroll tax would be used to pay current Social Security beneficiaries. In some plans aided by a payroll tax increase and benefit cuts, this would help ease the burden associated with a gradual shift from public to private financing during a transition period that could take decades. The remainder, ranging from about 25% to 80% of the worker's contribution, depending upon the proposal, would be invested in an ISSRA (Bipartisan Commission on Entitlement and Tax Reform, 1995; Schieber, 1996).

One example of this approach is the Personal Security Account (PSA) plan backed by Sylvester Schieber (1996) and several other members of the Advisory Council on Social Security (1997). It calls for the diversion of five percentage points of the employee's portion of the payroll tax into PSA accounts that would be managed by a wide range of private firms much as is currently the case with IRA accounts. Schieber's proposal is more far reaching than most as it would eventually replace rather than merely supplement the current Social Security scheme.

Another more moderate example of this approach is the Individual Accounts (IA) plan advocated by Edward Gramlich, chairman of the Advisory Council on Social Security (1997). It calls for the creation of ISSRAs financed by a modest (1.6 percentage points) increase in the workers' share of the payroll tax that would be managed by the Social Security Administration rather than private sector money-managers. Workers would have "constrained investment choices" including equity index funds and bond index funds.

With all such proposals workers would be allowed to invest a portion of their Social Security contributions in the private sector, and in most plans they would be able to switch their holding between asset classes (stocks, bonds, money market funds) in an effort to maximize returns. Some proposals would have the federal government manage these accounts (e.g., Gramlich's IA plan), but most would have the funds managed by private sector money managers, as is the case with IRA accounts. Some proposals would allow at least a partial lump sum withdrawal of accumulated assets at retirement (Borden, 1995), but most would require that the assets be annuitized or gradually withdrawn over a period of years. Although in some variants of this approach the diversion of Social Security contributions to individual investment accounts would be optional (Ferrara, 1995), in most it would be mandatory. In some proposals the amount of the diversion would be fixed, whereas in others it would be up to the individual worker to decide, within specified limits (Ferrara, 1995).

Many of the partial privatization proposals call for the creation of what amounts to a two-tier Social Security scheme (Peterson, 1996). The first tier would in most cases be a reduced version of the pension available in connection with the existing Social Security scheme. In the PSA plan this first tier would be a flat rate monthly pension of $410 (1996 dollars) which is 65% of the poverty level for a single person living alone. The size of the second tier pension would vary as a function of the amount paid into the ISSRAs, market trends, and investment choices.

Any substantial diversion of Social Security contributions to ISSRAs runs the risk of hastening the emergence of a gap between payroll tax revenues and Social Security benefits, a gap that would begin to open up by 2013 even without partial privatization. Some advocates of privatization acknowledge this and call for increases in Social Security payroll taxes or cuts in benefits to compensate for the added costs; others ignore the issue. Schieber's PSA plan makes a serious effort to avoid increasing the gap; it even passes the test of being balanced 75 years from now. To this end it includes a 1.52 percentage point increase in the payroll tax. This would be a temporary tax scheduled to be in place for 72 years. But even with this tax the Advisory Council on Social Security (1997) projects a $1.9 trillion (1995 dollars) shortfall between 2000 and 2034 to be covered by issuing government bonds that would then be repaid using the excess of tax revenues projected for the 35 years following 2034.

Why Privatize Social Security?

Although the various proposals for the partial privatization of Social Security differ in their details, they all call for the creation of ISSRAs, and it is this component of these proposals that will be the focus here. For the purposes of the present discussion, except where specified otherwise, the alternative to privatization is assumed to be the current Social Security system with substantial increases in the payroll tax (estimates range between 2 and 3% on both the employer and the employee) as needed to pay pension benefits during the retirement of the baby boomers. The term "privatization" will typically refer to partial privatization. The 10 arguments listed below can be grouped into those dealing with: (a) national savings and economic growth (arguments 1–3), (b) protection of future generations of retirees and workers (arguments 4–7), and (c) political philosophy and confidence issues (arguments 8–10). The most crucial of these arguments are 1, 4, and 6; if they can be successfully challenged, the core of the case for the privatization of Social Security is undercut. Some of the numbered points that follow include several different but closely connected arguments; it made more sense to group them than to treat them separately.

1. Privatization Will Increase the Rate of Economic Growth.—See Poortvliet and Laine, 1995; Schieber, 1996. Essentially the argument is that the privatization of Social Security will increase the national savings rate (Ferrara, 1995). This will increase the rate of investment, which in turn will increase the rate of economic growth making for a larger national product when the boomers retire (see Appendix, Note 2). Many economists argue that the only effective way to reduce the burden of providing for the retirement of the baby boomers is to increase national savings today and therefore national product in the future (Bosworth, 1995). The larger the national product when the boomers retire, the easier it will be to provide for their consumption needs. This argument is made by all advocates of privatization, and it is also accepted by many critics who oppose privatization on other grounds.

Basically this same argument is sometimes stated in more negative terms as a criticism of Social Security today. Social Security as presently structured is criticized for having a negative impact on economic growth, productivity, international competitiveness, and job opportunities (Ferrara, 1990; Poortvliet & Laine, 1995). A closely related argument is that the current generous Social Security benefit structure undercuts the incentive for individuals to save for old age. It is argued that many workers who might otherwise put personal funds into IRA plans or other forms of retirement savings fail to do so because they believe they will be able to live adequately on their anticipated Social Security benefits.

Although many economists argue that privatization of Social Security would increase the national savings rate, which in turn would boost the rate of economic growth, this conclusion must be qualified. It is likely that the actual increase in the national savings rate would be less, possibly substantially less, than the amount invested in the ISSRAs. It is possible that some, if not much, of the increase in savings produced by contributions to the ISSRAs would be offset by reductions in personal savings (Friedland, 1996; Quadagno, 1996; Quinn & Mitchell, 1996). People who would otherwise have been making personal savings in mutual funds and corporate retirement plans might decrease such savings, particularly if the privatization plan calls for a tax increase, as many do. There is no net gain to the economy if we just substitute one source of savings for another (Bosworth, 1995; White, 1996).

Although most economists argue that an increase in the savings rate will lead to economic growth, many others agree with Robert Eisner (1994, 1995) that, depending on how it is achieved, an increase in the savings rate may or may not produce any increase in economic growth rate. To the extent that the increase in savings is achieved by cuts in public spending on infrastructure (roads, bridges) or human capital (education, training), it may produce a decrease rather than an increase in long-term economic growth. Similarly, cuts in personal consumption in response to an increase in the payroll tax called for to finance privatization may decrease rather than increase economic growth, particularly during recessionary periods.

Also important is what happens with respect to other closely related government taxation and spending decisions in response to privatization (White, 1996). Most proposals for privatization call for the diversion of some of the revenues now flowing into the Social Security trust funds into the new ISSRAs (see Appendix, Note 3). But as the federal government has been using these revenues to fund general government spending, something would have to be done to deal with the increase in the federal deficit (U.S. Senate, 1995; see Appendix, Note 4). One response might be to cut spending (see Appendix, Note 5). This could be cuts in Social Security benefits or cuts in spending on other government programs. Cutting spending is the response that most advocates of privatization support. The gap could also be filled by a tax increase, most likely an increase in the payroll tax or the federal income tax. Some have even suggested the introduction to a new consumption tax (Peterson, 1996; Schieber, 1996; U.S. Senate, 1995). A third alternative would be to borrow the difference, increasing the federal deficit and national debt.

A likely result would be some combination of spending cuts, tax increases, and increasing the deficit. The relative emphasis among these three alternatives would be very important. By far the politically easiest alternative would be to add the gap to the deficit, but to the extent that this is done any potential gains in the national savings rate would be undercut (White, 1966).

2. Privatization Will Help Protect Social Security Contributions From Being Spent to Finance Current Government Consumption.—See Borden, 1995; Porter, 1995; Stephenson, Horlacher, and Colander, 1995. This can be considered a variant of the preceding argument as decreasing government consumption is one way to increase the savings rate. Many advocates of privatization argue that the 16% or so of Social Security contributions not immediately paid out to cover pension benefits to current recipients is being used to finance government consumption, with very little of it being invested in ways that contribute to long-term economic growth. Sometimes the claim is that the money is being spent on the day-to-day cost of running the government, leaving the trust funds for all practical purposes empty as they contain nothing but IOUs.

Such claims greatly oversimplify what actually happens and do not give adequate attention to the elaborate institutional structures that are in place for the investment and management of these funds. These funds are invested in a special category of bonds that are just as secure as other U.S. Treasury bonds, with interest rates comparable to those paid on other long-term government bonds (Ross, 1997).

Sometimes the argument is that if a portion of this money were diverted to private sector investments, this would produce an increase in the level of national investment, which in turn would contribute to economic growth and a larger gross domestic product (GDP) at the time when the boomers retire.

However, this goal would probably not be achieved if much or all of the gap produced by the diversion of funds to private sector investments were filled by the government simply selling more bonds (Bosworth, 1995). Although a partial privatization of Social Security might function as an important component of a package of policy changes that would have the effect of protecting the trust fund money that is now being used to finance current government consumption, it would have to be part of a package that also included tax increases or spending cuts, or both. In addition, depending on what spending is cut and on the impact of any tax increase on personal consumption, this package of policy changes could add up to less rather than more economic growth (Eisner, 1995).

A closely related argument is that privatization will force Congress to deal more honestly with the federal budget deficit (Friedland, 1996). Many attempts have been made to build a firewall between the Social Security trust funds and the general federal budget for the purposes of calculating the size of the federal deficit, but this effort has not been successful (Quadagno, 1996). The argument is that if a portion of Social Security contributions were diverted to private sector investments, this would reduce the extent to which the Social Security trust fund assets were used to disguise the size of the federal deficit (see Appendix, Note 6).

Even some critics of privatization would agree that privatization might help Congress deal more honestly with the federal budget deficit, but this does not mean Congress would necessarily take measures to reduce the size of that deficit. Although privatization would put pressure on Congress to reduce the size of the deficit through some combination of spending cuts and tax increases, we cannot be sure that this pressure would result in substantial spending cuts or tax increases. It is often politically easier to increase the size of the deficit than to cut spending, and to the extent that this were to occur, some, if not much, of the fiscal benefit of privatization could be lost.

Another closely related argument is that privatization will decrease entitlement spending (Peterson, 1996). Many analysts have emphasized the need to control the rapidly increasing costs of entitlements as part of any effort to bring the size of the federal deficit under control (Bipartisan Commission on Entitlement and Tax Reform, 1995; Peterson, 1993; see Appendix, Note 7). The three largest of the federal entitlement programs are Social Security, Medicare, and Medicaid. Although Social Security is only one of many entitlement programs and its long-term growth appears to be less problematic than Medicare, those calling for cuts in entitlement spending do not mean to exclude Social Security. One strategy that has been proposed to reduce government spending on Social Security is to partially privatize it. In the long run this would reduce pension demands on the federal government.

Many of those who have been expressing great concern about projected long-term trends in entitlement spending have in mind trends in spending on Social Security, Medicare, and to a lesser extent Medicaid (Peterson, 1996). Most experts agree that projected spending on Medicare poses a much greater and more immediate problem than Social Security. Even the long-term problem with respect to entitlement spending is due much more to projected increases in spending on health care than on Social Security. The practice of grouping Social Security together with these other health care related programs is sometimes used as a rhetorical device for undercutting confidence in the long-term viability of Social Security based on statistical trends that are more appropriate for analyzing projected trends in health care spending. When the two categories of programs are grouped together, important differences in the magnitude of the problem are blurred. References to the "crisis in entitlement spending" often make inappropriate use of a problem the nation faces with respect to the financing of health care to attack an entirely separate program, Social Security.

3. Privatization Will Increase the Nation's Competitiveness in the Global Economy.—See Poortvliet and Laine, 1995. The high cost of pension and health benefits makes it more difficult for American corporations to compete with producers in other nations that not only pay lower wages, but also spend much less on benefits. By partially privatizing Social Security, American producers will be able to lower their prices, making them more competitive in international markets. This in turn will contribute to long-term economic growth, making it easier to support the retirement of the baby boom generation.

Critics of privatization respond by pointing out that relative to most industrial nations the United States already has a competitive advantage because it spends so little on public benefits for workers, relative to other industrial nations (International Labour Office, 1992, 1994; see Appendix, Note 8). Although cuts in Social Security spending due to privatization might well produce further gains with respect to the nation's competitiveness, these gains would have their costs. One likely cost would be increased spending on Supplemental Security Income (SSI); another would be increased pressure on adult children to provide economic support for parents. There would

most likely be higher old-age poverty rates and greater income inequality.

Another quite different response from critics is to point to the arguments made by many economists that in the end most if not all of the payroll tax is passed along to workers in the form of lower wages. If this is true, then any reduction in payroll taxes associated with privatization would in the long run translate into higher wages and would not be expected to have much impact on the cost of production or international competitiveness.

4. Privatization Will Increase the Rate of Return on Social Security Contributions.—See Beard, 1996, and Schieber, 1996. A partially privatized Social Security scheme would produce a return on contributions that corresponds more closely to a fair market rate of return (Stephenson et al., 1995). Many advocates of privatization argue that one of the most serious problems with the Social Security system today is the projected low rate of return on contributions for those retiring in the years ahead (Steuerle & Bakija, 1994; see Appendix, Note 9).

Privatization would increase the individual equity of Social Security pensions (Ferrara, 1995). Pension benefits would more closely reflect contributions over the years. There would be less redistribution and as a result many workers, particularly high-wage workers, would receive benefits that more accurately reflected the contributions they had made; they would get something closer to an actuarially fair rate of return on their contributions.

A related argument is that it is unfair to expect workers to get a rate of return on their contributions that is so much below current market rates of returns (Ferrara, 1990). The Advisory Council on Social Security (1997) estimates an average long-term real (after adjusting for inflation) return of 2.3% for investments in U.S. Government bonds, the securities Social Security contributions are currently invested in, as opposed to a real return of 7% for investments in the stock market.

Many rate of return comparisons carried out by advocates of privatization make the assumption that the 7% average real rates of return for the stock market over the past 75 years is a reasonable estimate of what the return will average over the next 75 years. A problem with this assumption is that many of these same analysts also argue that the economy's rate of growth will drop from an average of approximately 3.5% over the past 75 years to an average of 1.5% over the next 75 years. If we assume that economic growth is going to decrease this much, this assumption should be reflected in much more modest projections about future stock market returns (Baker, 1997).

Another problem with many rate of return comparisons is the tendency to compare the return for Social Security with that for the stock market (Stephenson et al., 1995; U.S. Senate, 1995). Very few workers would invest all of their ISSRA contributions in equities; it is likely that many, particularly those with lower incomes, would put much of their money in more conservative alternatives such as bonds, which have lower returns. Although the average real rate of return for contributions to Social Security may be 2.3%, in contrast to an average of 7% for stock investments, the return after administrative expenses is likely to be in the range of 3.6% (not 7%) for a balanced portfolio of stocks and bonds.

The Social Security Administration estimates administrative costs at approximately 1% of the Social Security payroll taxes collected. Diamond (1996) suggested that the cost could be double this figure, but even at 2% it is far below the comparable insurance industry average of 11.6%. Some critics of privatization point to the example of Chile, where administrative costs run approximately 20% of revenues, but this is not a fair comparison. There are many ways in which Chile is different, and many of these differences contribute to its high administrative costs. Expenses tend to be a larger share of revenues in nations with lower wages. Chile also has a large number of very small accounts further adding to administrative costs (Diamond, 1996). Relative return estimates for the proposals outlined by the Advisory Council on Social Security take into consideration differences in administrative costs, but many discussions of privatization in the popular press ignore the issue. According to estimates prepared for the Advisory Council, the increase in administrative costs would reduce the yield on accumulated assets by .005% for the MB plan, .105% for the IA plan, and 1% for the PSA plan.

David Koitz of the Congressional Research Service appropriately noted that statements about what average returns have been in the past often ignore what can and will happen to individual workers who invest unwisely or for other reasons do not experience what have been the historical returns on equity investments (U.S. Senate, 1995). The fact that historically the stock market yield has been a specified figure does not mean that everyone will be able to enjoy that yield, even if they invest exclusively in broad equity index funds.

When the argument about relative rates of return is made, many commentators neglect any mention of the portion of the Social Security contribution spent on disability and survivors insurance (U.S. Senate, 1995; Whelehan, 1996). Unless an adjustment is made, comparisons of rates of return overstate the projected increase in return associated with privatization. Those who do attempt to take into consideration the need to provide disability and survivors insurance, do not always take into consideration that Social Security insures many who might otherwise be uninsurable (Chen, 1995). The privatization plans presented by the Advisory Council on Social Security (1997) do take into consideration the need to provide for disability and survivors insurance. For the PSA plan the projected returns are very favorable even for low-wage workers if we assume a continuation of historical trends with respect to stock market appreciation. The Advisory Council's treatment does not, however, fully answer my concerns about the consequences of highly conservative investment choices, poor market timing, or the possibility that the market might fall substantially short of its historical trends for a prolonged period such as the 45% drop in real terms between 1968 and 1978 (Baker, 1997).

There are a number of other factors that may also reduce the gap between returns under Social Security as currently structured and those made possible by partial privatization. Although it is likely that this infusion of new money into the stock market would drive up equity values prior to the retire-

ment of the baby boom generation, there might well be another strong market trend in the reverse direction as the baby boomers sell these equities during their retirement. This downward movement could have an adverse impact on what had looked like substantial long-term returns, just at the time the boomers need to cash in these investments to maintain their standard of living (U.S. Senate, 1995). With privatization some workers would do better and some would do worse. One likely outcome would be an increase in the proportion of the elderly dependent upon public assistance in the form of SSI benefits. For those who do not become dependent on SSI, some of the higher investment return enjoyed as a result of privatization might be offset by an increase in tax rates linked to increased spending on SSI and other social welfare programs for the elderly poor (U.S. Senate, 1995).

Why is it problematic if the proportion of the elderly dependent on SSI increases as a result of a partial privatization of Social Security? Wouldn't it be more efficient to increase SSI benefit levels if necessary and then allow the number on SSI to increase? One advantage of such an approach that some advocates of redistribution might appreciate is that SSI is paid for by the progressive federal income tax rather than a flat payroll tax. But this line of reasoning ignores the politics of social welfare policy. It ignores the historical evidence that it is hard to get political support for programs that benefit only the poor. If we restructure Social Security in such a way that the benefits associated with the public component (or, in the case of the PSA plan, the flat rate component) offer few if any benefits to the affluent, over time we should anticipate an erosion of the standard of living provided to the low-income recipients. The redistributive structure of Social Security is not the most efficient way to provide for the low-income elderly, but it has certainly been an effective strategy.

When an argument about the superior rate of return for private sector investments is presented, it is typically made in the aggregate. It becomes an argument about the return for those who earn the average wage. However, this neglects the evidence that privatization would potentially work to the advantage of most high-wage workers, but to the detriment of low-wage workers. Although many advocates of privatization would be unwilling to accept the argument that low-wage workers would be hurt by privatization (Beard, 1996; Ferrara, 1995), there is good reason to believe that high-wage workers stand to gain more than low-wage workers as a result of privatization (American Academy of Actuaries, 1996; see Appendix, Note 10).

Due to the redistributive structure of Social Security, low-wage workers get a much better return on their contributions than do high-wage workers (Friedland, 1996). Partial privatization would most likely make the system less redistributive (American Academy of Actuaries, 1996). This would benefit many high-wage workers, but it could hurt many low-wage workers (see Appendix, Note 11). Although the reduction in the extent of redistribution is most likely one of the major reasons that privatization is getting so much attention, advocates of privatization generally frame the argument in terms of the overall rate of return rather than in terms of doing more for high-wage workers at the expense of low-wage workers. In addition, some proponents of privatization believe that higher returns on the ISSRAs will more than compensate low-wage workers for any losses as a result of the shift to a less redistributive scheme (Whelehan, 1996; see Appendix, Note 12).

For reasons outlined earlier, it is likely that partial privatization would increase the number of low-wage earners forced to depend on the SSI program for support during retirement. It is likely that a portion of the gap between what pension benefits would be under Social Security as it is presently structured and what they would be after privatization would be absorbed by the low-wage earners in the form of lower benefits. But it is also likely that it would be necessary to fill at least part of the gap with increased spending on the SSI program, which in turn could translate into higher federal income taxes. Any such trend would reduce the after-tax gap between Social Security and the privatized alternative.

5. Privatization Will Help Protect Future Generations of Workers Against Sharp Increases in Social Security Payroll Tax Rates When the Boomers Retire.—If we were to make no structural changes in Social Security and each year set the combined payroll tax to exactly the level needed to pay promised benefits, projections suggest that over the next 35 years the payroll tax needed to keep the trust funds in balance would increase from 11.6 to 17.1% (see Appendix, Note 13). By 2070 an increase to 18.8% would be needed (Board of Trustees of the Federal Old-Age and Survivors Insurance and Disability Insurance Trust Funds, 1996). It is likely that a partial privatization of Social Security would eventually help reduce the payroll tax burden on the children and grandchildren of the baby boomers.

However, many privatization proposals call for an increase in the payroll tax. Schieber's (1996) proposal calls for a 1.52% "transition" payroll tax increase scheduled to last 72 years. In some cases, for example Peterson's (1996) scheme, the increase in payroll tax (4 to 6%) called for to help finance the transition turns out to be a substantial fraction of the increase that will be called for if no structural changes are made in Social Security. Privatization alone would not do much to assure lower taxes on post boomer generations unless combined with spending cuts to make up for the Social Security revenues currently being used to finance a portion of general government spending.

6. Privatization Will Help Protect Baby Boomers Against Sharp Reductions in Their Social Security Benefits.—See Schieber, 1996. The argument is that if nothing is done now and it proves to be politically impossible to introduce substantial increases in the payroll taxes when the boomers retire, it will be necessary to make a sharp reduction in their Social Security pension benefits. The extent of such cuts would depend in part on how much it was possible to increase the payroll tax. The greater the increase, the fewer benefits would need to be cut. If steps are taken now to partially privatize Social Security, any cuts called for when the baby boomers retire would be modest. This privatization will potentially pro-

tect Social Security pensions from sharp cuts for two reasons: (a) It will contribute to a larger national product, making it easier to pay for the public portion of Social Security benefits; and (b) it will result in the creation of a privatized portion of Social Security, thus reducing dependence on public funding.

Critics argue that privatization is likely to reduce the redistributive component of Social Security to the benefit of high-wage earners and the detriment of low-wage earners (Mitchell & Zeldes, 1996; Quinn & Mitchell, 1996). It may well help to protect the Social Security benefits of the average-wage worker and it would most definitely help protect the benefits of high-wage workers, but it is not clear that it would help protect the benefits of low-wage workers. Some argue that low-wage workers would be better off with some combination of payroll tax increases and benefit cuts introduced as needed when the boomers retire.

7. Privatization Will Make Social Security Pension Benefits Less Politically Vulnerable, Particularly During the Retirement of the Baby Boom Generation.—See Mitchell and Zeldes, 1996; Schieber, 1996. As currently structured, benefits are politically vulnerable to decisions by Congress to change the formula used to calculate the worker's monthly benefit at retirement, to modify the formula used to adjust benefits for changes in the cost of living, to delay annual cost of living increments, and to make outright benefit cuts.

It is generally agreed, even by critics, that the privatized portion of the Social Security pension would be less vulnerable politically. However, to the extent that partial privatization reduces the importance of the nonprivatized portion of Social Security to middle- and upper-income wage earners, it would make that portion of the program politically vulnerable to subsequent cuts over the years (Ball & Bethell, 1997). Taxpayers are less likely to support cuts in programs (or parts of programs) from which they personally benefit.

8. Privatization Will Contribute to Greater Freedom and Autonomy for American Workers.—See Ferrara, 1985 and 1995. Senator Alan Simpson (R-Wyoming) argued that privatization of Social Security would empower Americans by giving them more control over their retirement incomes (U.S. Senate, 1995). This argument is largely based on political philosophy (see Appendix, Note 14). The reasoning here is that with most proposals for partial privatization would come choices about how at least a portion of one's Social Security contributions were invested. Depending on the specifics of the actual privatization plan selected, workers might have a very broad range of options, as do IRA investors.

Critics of privatization point out that along with this freedom of choice comes risk, and many workers, particularly low-wage workers, may end up being harmed by this freedom. The freedom to choose among investment options may do more harm than good to those who are not well informed about how to invest their money (Quinn & Mitchell, 1996). Some, possibly many, will invest very conservatively, failing to take advantage of the higher long-run returns on stock markets (see Appendix, Note 15). They may do as well as Social Security with its investment in government bonds, but not as well as advocates of privatization project. Others may end up taking too much risk during the years just prior to retirement, jeopardizing much of their retirement nest egg (Ball & Bethell, 1997). Privatization may increase autonomy and control for the primary wage earner in a family, but it may also result in increasing the risk and decrease protection for a spouse who is economically dependent upon the primary earner (Williamson, 1997). Although some would want to manage their ISSRA assets, many would not want to (Chen, 1995). More to the point, many would prefer the safety of a defined benefit plan backed by the United States government to the risks of a defined contribution plan.

9. Privatization Will Make it Possible for Those Who Die Before Retirement To Pass at Least a Portion of Their Retirement Savings on to Their Heirs.—See Ferrara, 1995, and Porter, 1995. Many privatization proposals have provisions making it possible to add the ISSRA assets to one's estate and in so doing extend the philosophical concept of property rights to Social Security benefits. Unlike Social Security, under many partial privatization plans workers would own at least a portion of their retirement assets, and these assets like any other assets could be disposed of as the deceased wished at death. Taking the Advisory Council on Social Security's (1997) PSA plan as an example, assets accumulated in the worker's PSA would at death become part of his or her estate.

Many analysts argue that the survivors benefits under Social Security are at least as valuable as the combination of death and survivor benefits available in connection with various privatization schemes. When a comparison is drawn between Social Security and a privatized alternative, it is common in popular press accounts to neglect mention of the survivor's insurance coverage that is part of Social Security. This coverage provides benefits to surviving dependent children and for an aged surviving spouse.

However, there are death-related situations in which a partially privatized scheme would have some advantages relative to Social Security as currently structured. For never-married workers with no dependents, even those with decades of contributions to Social Security, at death nothing is added to their estates based on these contributions. In contrast, with the PSA plan the assets in the PSA account would be added to the estate. These funds could be used to help provide for a domestic partner, friend, or relative not covered by Social Security. Alternatively, they could be donated to a charity of particular interest to the deceased. In short, there would be at least something to show for all of those years of contribution. Although the current provisions help target Social Security benefits to survivors most likely to be in need of support, in the context of nontraditional households this goal is not always achieved.

The flexibility of the PSA plan would represent an improvement over Social Security for some categories of survivors, but a reduction in coverage for other categories. The flexibility to designate who would get PSA assets would leave some widows worse off. Many divorced spouses would also do better with Social Security as it is; they would, for example, no

longer be able to benefit from the after-divorce earnings history of a former spouse (Williamson, 1977).

Some analysts have argued that the partial privatization of Social Security would be beneficial to African American workers because they have shorter than average life expectancies (Ferrara, 1995). Due to higher mortality rates, African Americans are less likely than Whites to live to an age at which they become eligible for Social Security old-age pension benefits, and on average they spend fewer years receiving Social Security pensions (Ferrara, 1995). Although there is some merit to this line of analysis, those making it typically do not emphasize the redistributive aspect of Social Security for those African Americans who do become eligible for pension benefits. It would seem that analysts making such a claim should also be checking for and reporting on race differences with respect to the receipt of Social Security disability and survivor benefits. After reviewing the results of a number of studies on the topic, Chen and Goss (1997) concluded that the net effect of the worker's race on the progressivity of Social Security is still in dispute.

A related argument is that workers with AIDS, cancer, and some other terminal diseases might be able to tap their ISSRA assets prior to death as a way to help ease the economic stress associated with the last few months or years of life. Depending on how the plan was structured this might be possible, and for some medical conditions it would be a major benefit. Presently it is possible to borrow against 401(k) assets under some circumstances and it is possible to withdraw IRA assets early, albeit with a stiff penalty. These programs point to what might be possible.

However, if the privatized component of Social Security were set up in such a way that it was possible to borrow against retirement savings, there would be the risk that some and possibly a substantial fraction of low-wage workers would end up outliving their retirement savings, something that cannot happen with Social Security as presently structured. Workers living close to the economic margins are more likely to be faced with economic emergencies forcing them to tap into their retirement assets. Those most likely to tap into these assets prior to retirement would also be those most dependent upon pension benefits derived from these assets during retirement. The result could be a lot of people who are worse off in old age than under the present scheme or a sharp increase in spending in connection with the SSI program, or both (American Academy of Actuaries, 1996).

10. Privatization Will Increase Confidence That Current Contributions Will Become the Source of Eventual Social Security Pension Benefits.—See Beard, 1996; Ferrara, 1995; and Schieber, 1996. There have been a number of public opinion polls suggesting that in recent years only 30 to 40% of adult Americans feel confident about the integrity of the Social Security system (Quinn, 1996; Reno & Friedland, 1997). Workers will have more confidence that they will eventually receive a Social Security pension if they have individual accounts and receive periodic statements providing current account balances. The parallel to personal IRA and 401(k) accounts would be obvious. The freedom to shift between various investment options would further contribute to that confidence.

Currently the Social Security Administration sends out statements to those requesting them, providing estimates of eventual pension benefits, but they do not report individual account balances. Soon these statements will be automatically sent to all covered workers once a year. This may increase confidence that Social Security pension benefits will eventually be forthcoming. Would workers have more confidence in the integrity of Social Security if they received actual account balances for their PSA accounts as many do on a quarterly basis for their 401(k) plans? It is not obvious that they would.

Partial privatization and the associated quarterly or annual reports would probably increase confidence in Social Security if the stock market were to continue to perform as it did for most of the period between 1982 and 1996, but what will happen to confidence when workers are faced with a prolonged bear market—such as the 48% decline between 1973 and 1974, which was followed by a recovery that took nearly 10 years? After the Crash of 1929, the stock market did not return to its 1929 high until 1954. Given that we have not experienced a prolonged bear market in recent years, it is reasonable to ask questions about how much confidence people are likely to have in a partially privatized variant of Social Security in the event of a prolonged market decline. Even if we assume that in the long run the stock market will recover from any correction or bear market, and that workers can attempt to delay retirement for a few years in the event of a major market drop, it is possible that for many workers the resulting delay of retirement may be longer than health permits.

Conclusion

In recent years the idea of partially privatizing Social Security has come to be viewed as an innovative strategy for dealing with the impending retirement of the baby boom generation. This approach is consistent with a more general shift in social welfare policy that the nation has experienced in recent decades, a shift away from policies based on the values of social adequacy and shared risk embodied in the concept of social insurance to alternative policies emphasizing self-reliance and individualism. This shift can be traced back to the taxpayers' revolt that began in California in the late 1970s with Proposition 13 and the emergence of the generational equity debate during the 1980s (Kingson, 1988). It was also strongly reflected in the Contract With America that received so much support from Congressional Republicans during the mid-1990s. Although advocates for downsizing the American welfare state have typically not had increasing the level of economic inequality in American society as a goal, they have not hesitated to push for policies that many analysts believe will have this effect.

The privatization of Social Security, if done in such a way as not to add to the federal deficit, could help ease the burden of providing for the retirement of baby boomers. However, there is a risk that privatization, by itself, would do little or nothing to ease the burden of providing for the retirement of the boomers, and it could make the experience a lot worse for the most vulnerable of the boomers, particularly low-wage workers. Even if a privatization scheme is designed so as to give a substantial boost to the American economy and to ensure that the average worker would be better off than under the current Social Security scheme, it is possible that many workers, particularly low-wage workers, would end up worse off. Many would invest in bonds with yields similar to those in the Social Security trust funds, but due to the higher administrative costs associated with privatized accounts would end up with lower returns. Some, due either to lack of access to good investing advice or bad judgment, would make poor market timing decisions, leaving them with long-term returns substantially below those for the stock market as a whole. But the greatest risk to the low-wage worker would be the potential loss of political support for the redistributive aspects of Social Security as currently structured. In this era of individualism and free market solutions, it is possible that in the long-run, concern for the retirement income needs of low-wage workers would atrophy.

References

Advisory Council on Social Security. (1997). *Report of the 1994–1996 Advisory Council on Social Security. Volume 1: Findings and Recommendations.* Washington, DC: U.S. Government Printing Office.

American Academy of Actuaries. (1996). Social Security privatization: Individual accounts. *Issue Brief,* Spring, 1–4.

Baker, D. (1997). The privateers' free lunch. *American Prospect,* May/June, 81–84.

Ball, R. M., & Bethell, T. N. (1997). Bridging the centuries: The case for traditional Social Security. In E. R. Kingson & J. H. Schulz (Eds.), *Social Security in the 21st century* (pp. 259–294). New York: Oxford University Press.

Beard, S. (1996). *Restoring hope in America: The Social Security solution.* San Francisco: ICS Press.

Bipartison Commission on Entitlement and Tax Reform. (1995). *Bipartison Commission on Entitlement and Tax Reform: Final report.* Washington DC: U.S. Government Printing Office.

Borden, K. (1995). *Dismantling the pyramid: The why and how of privatizing Social Security.* (The Cato Project on Social Security Privatization SSP. No. 1.) Washington, DC: Cato Institute.

Board of Trustees of the Federal Old-Age and Survivors Insurance and Disability Insurance Trust Funds. (1996). *1996 annual report.* Washington DC: U.S. Government Printing Office.

Bosworth, B. (1995). Putting Social Security to work: How to restore the balance between generations. *Brookings Review, 13*(4), 36–39.

Burkhauser, R., & Warlick, J. (1981). Disentangling the annuity from the redistributive aspects of Social Security. *Review of Income and Wealth, 27,* 401–421.

Chen, Y. P. (1995). The key issues in the privatization debate. In K. Stephenson (Ed.), *Social Security: Time for a change* (pp. 193–203). Greenwich, CT: JAI Press.

Chen, Y. P., & Goss, S. C. (1997). Are returns on payroll taxes fair? In E. R. Kingson & J. H. Schulz (Eds.), *Social Security in the 21st century* (pp. 76–90). New York: Oxford University Press.

Council of Economic Advisors. (1996). *Economic report of the President.* Washington DC: U.S. Government Printing Office.

Diamond, P. A. (1996). Proposals to restructure Social Security. *Journal of Economic Perspectives, 10*(3), 67–88.

Eisner, R. (1994). *The misunderstood economy: What counts and how to count it.* Boston: Harvard Business School Press.

Eisner, R. (1995). Savings, economic growth, and the arrow of causality. *Challenge, 38*(3), 10–14.

Ferrara, P. J. (1985). Social Security and the super IRA: A populist proposal. In P. Ferrara (Ed.), *Social Security: Prospects for real reform* (pp. 193–220). Washington, DC: Cato Institute.

Ferrara, P. J. (1990) Social Security and the private sector. *National Forum,* 70(1), 32–33.

Ferrara, P. J. (1995). A private option for Social Security. In K. Stephenson (Ed.), *Social Security: Time for a change* (pp. 205–213). Greenwich, CT: JAI Press.

Friedland, R. B. (1994). *When support and confidence are at odds: The public's understanding of the Social Security program.* Washington, DC: National Academy of Social Insurance.

Friedland, R. B.(1996). Privatizing social insurance. *Public Policy and Aging Report, 7* (June), 11–15.

Friedman, M. (1962). *Capitalism and freedom.* Chicago: University of Chicago Press.

International Labour Office. (1992). *The cost of social security: Thirteenth international inquiry, 1984–1986.* Geneva: International Labour Office.

International Labour Office. (1994). *World labour report 1994.* Geneva: International Labour Office.

Kingson, E. R. (1988). Generational equity: An unexpected opportunity to broaden the politics of aging. *The Gerontologist, 28,* 765–772.

Kritzer, B. E. (1996). Privatizing Social Security: The Chilean experience. *Social Security Bulletin, 59*(3), 45–55.

Mitchell, O. S., & Zeldes, S. P. (1996, January) *Social Security privatization: A structure for analysis.* Paper presented at the Annual Meeting of the American Economic Association, San Francisco, CA.

Munnell, A., & Ernsberger, N. (1990). Foreign experience with public pension surpluses and national savings. In C. L. Weaver (Ed.), *Social Security's looming surpluses, prospects and implications* (pp. 85–118). Washington, DC: The American Enterprise Institute.

Myers, R. J. (1992). Chile's social security reform, after ten years. *Benefits Quarterly, 8*(3), 41–55.

Perez, R. C. (1995). No way to run a railroad: Social Security funds should invest in common stocks! In K. Stephenson (Ed.), *Social Security: Time for a change* (pp. 177–190). Greenwich, CT: JAI Press.

Peterson, P. G. (1993). *Facing up: How to rescue the economy from crushing debt and restore the American dream.* New York: Simon & Schuster.

Peterson, P. G. (1996). Will America grow up before it grows old? *The Atlantic Monthly,* May, 55–86.

Poortvliet, W. G., & Laine, T. P. (1995). A global trend: Privatization and reform of social security pension plans. *Benefits Quarterly, 11*(3) 63–84.

Porter, J. E. (1995). Individual Social Security retirement accounts. In K. Stephenson (Ed.), *Social Security: Time for a change* (pp. 197–203). Greenwich, CT: JAI Press.

Quadagno, J. (1996). Social Security and the myth of the entitlement "crisis." *The Gerontologist, 36,* 391–399.

Quinn, J. F. (1996). *Entitlements and the federal budget: Securing our future.* Washington, DC: National Academy on Aging.

Quinn, J. F., & Mitchell, O. S. (1996). Social Security on the table. *American Prospect,* May/June, 76–81.

Reno, V. P., & Friedland, R. B. (1997). Strong support but low confidence: What explains the contradiction? In E. R. Kingson & J. H. Schulz (Eds.), *Social Security in the 21st century* (pp. 178–194). New York: Oxford University Press.

Ross, S. G. (1997). Institutional and administrative issues. In E. R. Kingson and J. H. Schulz (Eds.), *Social Security in the 21st century* (pp. 231–238). New York: Oxford University Press.

Schieber, S. (1996). A new vision for Social Security. *Public Policy and Aging Report, 7*(June), 1, 6–7, 9.

Stephenson, K., Horlacher, D., & Colander, D. (1995). An overview of the U.S. Social Security system: Problems and options. In K. Stephenson (Ed.), *Social Security: Time for a change* (pp. 3–23). Greenwich, CT: JAI Press.

Steuerle, C. E., & Bakija, J. M. (1994). *Retooling Social Security for the 21st century: Right and wrong approaches to reform.* Washington, DC: Urban Institute Press.

U.S. Senate. (1995). *Privatization of the Social Security Old Age and Survivors Insurance Program* (Hearing before the Subcommittee on Social Security and Family Protection of the Committee on Finance, 104th Congress, 1st session on S. 824, August 2nd). Washington DC: U.S. Government Printing Office.

Whelehan, B. M. (1996). Taking stock of Social Security. *Mutual Funds,* May, 27–29.

White, L. J. (1996). Investing the assets of the Social Security trust funds in equity securities: An analysis. *Perspective, 2*(4), 1–20. Washington, DC: Investment Company Institute.

Williamson, J. B. (1997). Should women support the privatization of Social Security? *Challenge, 40*(4), 97–108.

Received September 30, 1996
Accepted April 4, 1997

Appendix

1. There is no agreement as to what to call these accounts. Among the other names that have been suggested are super IRAs, personal retirement accounts, personal investment plans, personal security accounts, and individual retirement savings accounts.

2. Most economists agree that sustained productivity growth requires investment, but there is some disagreement as to how dependent the United States is on domestic investment as there are foreign investors willing to put up investment capital for projects in this country (Perez, 1995). Some take the position that the globalization of capital markets decreases our dependence on domestic savings. However, the view that the nation's long-term growth prospects are not highly dependent upon domestic savings rates is currently a minority position.

3. Social Security is made up of four separate trust funds. Two relate to pensions and two relate to Medicare. The two pension-related trust funds are Old Age and Survivors Insurance (OASI) and Disability Insurance (DI). Together they are often referred to as OASDI.

4. Some federal spending, such as on roads, bridges, education, and the like, is a form of investment and does contribute to economic growth (Munnell & Ernsberger, 1990; Stephenson et al., 1995), but most government spending is not in this category.

5. If Social Security contributions were to flow into the stock market and not directly into government bonds, this would increase the cost of government borrowing, which in turn might reduce the government's willingness to borrow. In this context, privatization advocates ask why those who contribute to Social Security should continue to subsidize government borrowing.

6. There are two ways to measure the federal deficit, with and without including Social Security. Not all economists would agree with my assessment that emphasis on the version that includes Social Security contributions is evidence of disguising the size of the deficit.

7. The federal deficit peaked in 1983 at 6.3% of GDP. Since then it has declined considerably and was at 2.3% in 1995 (Council of Economic Advisors, 1996). Between the early 1970s and 1995 there was not much of an increase in the size of the federal budget relative to GDP. What did change dramatically was the composition of the budget, with an increase in the share of spending on entitlement programs such as Social Security, Medicare, and Medicaid and a decrease in the share on spending on other categories, particularly defense (Quinn, 1996).

8. In 1991 the average Social Security pension benefit in the United States was $6,539, which was higher than the

$4,450 average for the United Kingdom, but below average relative to other industrial nations such as Germany ($13,333) and the Netherlands ($8,299; International Labour Office, 1994).

9. Steuerle and Bakija (1994) did some projections suggesting that as of 1995, OASDI contributions exceeded expected lifetime benefits for high-wage single men, but not other categories of workers. However, between 1995 and 2005 the situation will change and contributions will exceed expected benefits for several other categories of workers, including average-wage single men, high-wage single women, and high-wage two-earner couples. Schieber (1996) pointed out that for the average wage worker born in 1960 who is single or married to a spouse who is also an average wage worker, expected lifetime benefits are projected to be between 75 and 90% of the value of contributions made. For quite some time analysts have warned that when younger and more affluent workers come to realize that they would not get the generous benefits received by earlier generations, the near-universal support for the program would weaken (Burkhauser & Warlick, 1981).

10. It is possible but unlikely, that pension benefits in connection with a partially privatized scheme would exceed current Social Security levels even for low-wage workers (American Academy of Actuaries, 1996).

11. The Advisory Council on Social Security (1997, p. 200) presented projections suggesting that under the PSA plan low-wage workers would get a better return on their contributions than they would under present law or with the MB plan. This conclusion is based on models making a number of assumptions that I do not accept. I do not accept the assumption that we can infer how low-wage workers would allocate assets between stocks and bonds based on the behavior of those currently enrolled in 401(k) plans, a group that tends to have more education and higher incomes than minimum-wage workers. I also do not accept the assumption that the equity portion of these portfolios will over the long run yield the average rate of return since the turn of the century, despite the evidence that in recent years the rate of growth in real GDP and labor productivity is down. Carolyn Weaver made a persuasive case that these projections must be interpreted with a great deal of caution as the models greatly oversimplify—small changes in some of the model parameters produce big differences in projected outcomes (Advisory Council on Social Security, 1997, pp. 160–162).

12. Whelehan (1996) projected a monthly pension benefit of $2,490 for low-wage earners under a privatized scheme, as opposed to $631 under Social Security as currently structured for those born in 1950 and retiring at age 65. This projection is based on the (optimistic) assumption that low-wage workers would earn average yearly returns of 10% on their contributions.

13. The 11.6% figure is the rate that would be needed to finance current benefits without any surplus.

14. Friedman (1962) is sometimes mentioned in this context given the emphasis he placed on individual freedom. However, Friedman's book advocates doing away with mandatory retirement savings of all sorts; this includes Social Security as it stands and would also include partially privatized alternatives.

15. Studies have been done comparing the investment returns for pension plans where the employer made the investment decisions with the returns when the employee made the investment decisions. On average, plans where the employer made the investment decisions (and bore the investment risk) had yields that were greater by 1.5 to 2.5%. Investment yield may be higher in connection with a partially privatized scheme than with Social Security as it is presently structured, but it is not reasonable to assume that the average returns in connection with a privatized scheme would be as high as that for pension plans in which the employer makes the investment decisions or as high as for the stock market as a whole (American Academy of Actuaries, 1996).

BY MORTIMER B. ZUCKERMAN

Don't go it alone

Social Security was designed to avoid the risks of free markets

It's time to look carefully and skeptically at the proposals for saving Social Security from bankruptcy. The Clinton approach would deliver 62 percent of federal surpluses to support the program. Another plan, the brainchild of Martin Feldstein, chairman of the Council of Economic Advisers under President Reagan, promises to cure the fund's insolvency without cutting a dime in future benefits or raising a nickel in taxes—if only we could divert our FICA taxes into our own mini-IRAS and ride the stock market boom of the future.

Let's give it a hard look.

First, history may be a misleading indicator. The economy has been growing at about 3.5 percent a year for the past 75 years, and stocks have earned close to 7 percent compounded, about twice the yield on treasuries. However, the Social Security trustees estimate that over the next 75 years the economy will grow at only 1.4 percent annually. If they're right, the yields from stocks are unlikely to continue at 7 percent.

I argued last week that the trustees may well be too pessimistic. If the economy does grow at its historic rate, government revenues should cover the program's remaining needs after the allocation of the federal surplus funds.

Financial illiteracy. Beyond assessing the proposals, we have to consider whether individual investors are sophisticated enough to match the hypothetical returns. At least 10 studies analyzed by the Securities and Exchange Commission indicate a disturbing level of financial illiteracy. Only 12 percent of investors can distinguish between a load and a no-load mutual fund; only 14 percent understood the difference between a growth stock and an income stock; only 38 percent knew that when interest rates go up, bond prices go down; almost half said that diversification guarantees that their portfolio won't suffer if the market drops; and 40 percent thought that a fund's operating costs are not deducted from their returns.

In short, just because people have money in the markets does not mean they have the investment savvy to handle their retirement funds. Most people are shrewd enough to know this, which is why they invest in mutual funds. The 60 percent of Americans who aren't in the market presumably have even less knowledge and experience. Historical averages of stock market returns are hardly a guide to future performance. Much depends on what individuals buy and sell and when. Too many people drown walking across a river where the average depth is 4 feet; chances are that it's 10 feet deep in the middle.

The timing of retirement is also important. If you retire just after the market dives, you could lose a good chunk of your retirement account. The market fell by 45 percent in real terms between 1968 and 1978. Those who retired at the beginning enjoyed slightly higher income than they earned while working, but those retiring at the bottom of the market were stuck with only about 40 percent of their working income.

> "If you retire just after the market dives, you could lose a good chunk of your retirement account."

Privatizing all or part of our retirement funds for investment purposes has another catch. Individuals would be glad to pocket gains, but what would happen if millions of retirees suffered dramatic losses? The government would come under enormous political pressure to come to the rescue. Thus we would very likely end up privatizing the gains and socializing the losses. If Social Security funds are to be put into the stock market, it is better to invest them through the government. That would avoid the high administrative costs of individual accounts and spread the risks of downturns to the overall work force.

The go-it-alone solution is misconceived. Social Security was not meant to re-create the free market. On the contrary, it was designed as insurance against the vagaries and cruelties of the markets. The trust fund provides the ultimate risk pool in which good and bad outcomes can be spread over tens of millions of people.

Stock market investments do not provide a pain-free way to make Social Security solvent. There is no free lunch. Our bedrock protections against destitution in old age should not be subject to market gyrations or the poor judgments of individual investors. We should not risk Social Security to save it.

From *U.S. News & World Report*, March 15, 1999, p. 76. © 1999 by U.S. News & World Report. Reprinted by permission.

Welfare Reform Legislation Poses Opportunities and Challenges for Rural America

Welfare reform legislation enacted in 1996 devolves responsibility for providing assistance to needy families and children from Federal to State governments through Federal block grants. It shifts the fundamental intent of public welfare away from providing cash assistance to moving families from welfare to work. The new legislation may foster more productive communities as families leave welfare for work. It also presents some rural States and communities with formidable challenges.

The Personal Responsibility and Work Opportunity Reconciliation Act (PL104-193), signed into law in August 1996, dramatically overhauls the national system of public welfare in operation since the 1930's. Enactment of the new law follows years of national debate and many past welfare reform efforts; recent actions, according to the Institute for Research on Poverty, include 6 major House bills, 11 major Senate bills, 13 minor bills, 2 Presidential vetoes, and 43 State waivers.

With welfare reform, responsibility for providing assistance to needy families and children devolves from Federal to State governments through a system of individually tailored State programs funded by Federal block grants. At the same time, the new law shifts the fundamental intent of public aid away from providing cash assistance to helping families transition from welfare to work. How different States and local communities respond to the challenges and opportunities presented by the welfare reform law depends on many factors, including past programmatic experiences, the characteristics of their low-income populations, and prevailing economic conditions in the State and Nation. For example, States dominated by rural areas and large rural populations or com-

Reprinted from *Rural Conditions and Trends,* a United States Department of Agriculture (USDA) publication, Vol. 8, No. 1, June 1997, pp. 38-47.

Figure 1

Federal spending for social welfare programs, 1996

Programs mainly affected by PL104-193 accounted for about one-tenth of Federal social welfare spending

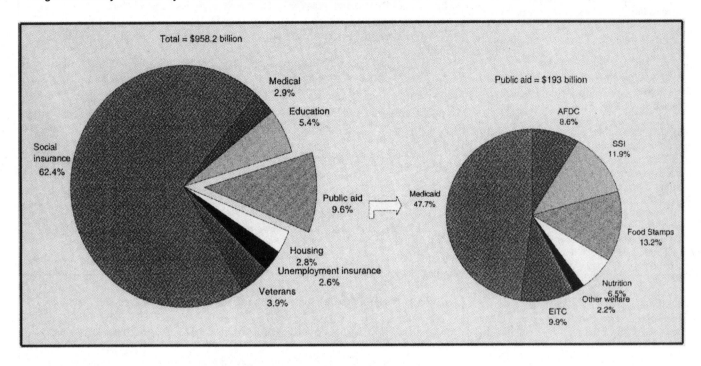

Source: Calculated by ERS using data from the Budget of the United State Government, fiscal year 1998.

munities face different challenges than States dominated by large urban centers.

Provisions Affect Several Low-Income Programs

PL104-193 makes important changes in several major low-income programs and lesser changes in other programs. Programs affected most by the law accounted for over $190 billion of Federal outlays in 1996—about one-tenth of Federal welfare expenditures (fig. 1).

One of the most important of the act's many complex provisions replaces the 61-year-old Federal welfare program, Aid to Families with Dependent Children (AFDC), with Temporary Assistance for Needy Families (TANF), a system of State-controlled low-income assistance programs funded by Federal block grants capped at mid-1994 funding levels through 2002 (see box on next page). While giving States considerable flexibility and autonomy for designing and operating their own State plans, TANF provisions limit the total lifetime maximum for receiving Federal welfare benefits to 60 months, with hardship exemptions, and specify parental work requirements. State plans must indi-

cate how States intend to meet the requirement that able-bodied parents must engage in work activities after receiving benefits for a maximum of 24 months. To avoid reductions in their Federal block grants, States must act to increase the percentage of their family caseloads participating in approved work activities from minimum rates of 25 percent for all families and 75 percent for two-parent families in 1997, rising to 50 percent (all families) and 90 percent (two-parent families) by 2002. Other provisions provide additional funds for child care and health insurance and call for State actions to reduce teen and out-of-wedlock births.

The act also substantially reforms other low-income programs. Provisions tightening eligibility criteria for the Supplemental Security Income (SSI) disability program restrict many formerly eligible children under age 18 from receiving benefits. Provisions affecting the Food Stamp Program limit benefits for childless able-bodied adults unless they are working. Other changes altering the criteria for determining Food Stamp benefits will result in an overall reduction in benefits in the future. Provisions involving aliens restrict most legal aliens (with a few special exceptions) from receiving SSI and Food Stamp benefits until they have either worked for 10

years or become citizens. States have the option whether or not to provide TANF and Medicaid benefits to legal aliens already in the country. New legal aliens are ineligible for TANF and Medicaid Federal benefits until they have been in the country for 5 years, although States may use State funds to provide such benefits. Additional provisions pertain to child nutrition programs, Medicaid, foster care, social support services, earned income tax credit (EITC), and Social Security benefits for prison inmates.

Beginning in 1997, States must maintain State spending levels for TANF benefits and administration, emergency assistance, JOBS, and selected child care programs at 80 percent of their 1994 levels or risk dollar-for-dollar shortfall reductions in the following year. States with high unemployment rates and/or large increases in Food Stamp caseloads may qualify for supplemental payments worth up to 20 percent of their block grant allocations. Beginning in 1998, more modest Federal supplements will be available to qualifying States with rapid population growth and a history of low AFDC spending levels, States with high-performing TANF programs, and the top five States with the largest declines in out-of-wedlock births.

SSI and Food Assistance Programs Account for More Than 80 Percent of Federal Public Welfare Spending Reductions

Estimated budgetary impacts of the new law on Federal public welfare spending indicate a decline of about $54 billion over the 6-year period, 1997–2002 (table 1). Because the core Federal funding for TANF is a sum fixed at mid-1994 funding levels through fiscal year 2002 (about $16.5 billion annually), projected overall Federal savings realized from the new cash assistance programs are negligible. According to a recently released report by the Urban Institute, annual projected spending on non-Medicaid public welfare between 1998 and 2002 amounts to less than 2 percent of Gross Domestic Product (GDP). New child-care block grants, coupled with additional spending for child support enforcement, total $13.2 billion, a $3.9-billion increase over the amount that would have been spent under the old law. The bulk (over 80 percent) of the spending reductions derives from reductions in SSI ($22.7 billion) and Food Stamp programs ($23.3 billion). Of these reductions, restrictions involving alien benefits make up $13.2 billion and $3.7 billion of SSI and Food Stamps savings, respectively, plus an additional $4.1-billion savings in projected Medicaid benefits.

It is too soon to tell how much of the projected Federal savings will actually materialize. As of this writing, media sources report that 40 States have requested or received 1-year exemptions from the provision scheduled to begin this spring that cuts off Food Stamp benefits to unemployed able-bodied childless adults who live in high-unemployment areas. If many such exemptions are granted, the projected savings from the Food Stamp program will be less than estimated.

Recent Drops in Caseloads Create Favorable Funding Picture in Some States

The immediate goal facing all States is the development and submission of a State TANF plan for certification from the Department of Health and Human Services by no later than July 1, 1997. Certification triggers the release of Federal funds under the new block grant program. Until then, States will continue to operate under the old AFDC funding rules. As of February 24, 1997, 41 States had submitted TANF proposals, of which 38 had been certified by HHS and 3 were pending certification.

The number of States that have already submitted plans clearly suggests that many States and communities are hopeful that

Key Provisions: The Personal Responsibility and Work Opportunity Reconciliation Act

Establishes Temporary Assistance for Needy Families (TANF) that:

—Replaces former entitlement programs with federal block grants

—Devolves authority and responsibility for welfare programs from Federal to State government

—Emphasizes moving from welfare to work through time limits and work requirements

Changes eligibility standards for Supplemental Security Income (SSI) child disability benefits

—Restricts certain formerly eligible children from receiving benefits

—Changes eligibility rules for new applicants and eligibility redetermination

Requires States to enforce a strong child support program for collection of child support payments

Restricts aliens' eligibility for welfare and other public benefits

—Denies illegal aliens most public benefits, except emergency medical services

—Restricts most legal aliens from receiving Food Stamps and SSI benefits until they become citizens or work for at least 10 years

—Allows States the option of providing Federal cash assistance to legal aliens already in the country

—Restricts most new legal aliens from receiving Federal cash assistance for 5 years

—Allows States the option of using State funds to provide cash assistance to non-qualifying aliens

Provides resources for foster care data systems and national child welfare study

Establishes a block grant to States to provide child care for working parents

Alters eligibility criteria and benefits for child nutrition programs

—Modifies reimbursement rates

—Makes families (including aliens) that are eligible for free public education also eligible for school meal benefits

Tightens national standards for Food Stamps and Commodity Distribution

—Institutes an across-the-board reduction in benefits

—Caps standard deduction at fiscal year 1995 level

—Limits receipt of benefits to 3 months in every 3 years by childless able-bodied adults age 18–50 unless working or in training welfare reform, along with a possible increase in funds, will help speed up the transition from welfare to work and result in more productive communities with rising tax bases, better public services, and industrial growth. While this may prove to be the case in traditionally high welfare-benefit States, where the welfare population is distributed among communities with stable economies, strong local tax bases, and well-developed social service delivery systems, it may prove to be less true for many predominantly rural States and rural areas in other States.

According to HHS, estimated block grants for fiscal year 1997 will vary from $3.7 billion in California to $21.8 million in Wyoming. Under the previous AFDC law, a State's Federal funds were determined by a matching formula based on State spending. State funds were matched 50 cents on the dollar for more affluent States, while less affluent States received an even higher match. Under TANF, Federal block grants to States are tied to the Federal share of State funding levels in either 1994, 1995, or the 1992–94 average (whichever is higher). Furthermore, States choosing to divert State funds toward benefits to groups not covered by the law, such as nonqualifying aliens, will receive no additional Federal funds.

The upside for States is that recipient caseloads have undergone a substantial decline in the last 3 years, partly influenced by the operation of State waiver demonstration projects in many States and a strong national economy. Since 1994, national welfare rolls have dropped by 3 million people. All States, except Hawaii, experienced at least a 5-

percent drop in welfare recipients from 1994 to 1996, and 20 States realized a 25- to 41-percent decline (fig. 2). Thus, former high-benefit States, including some with well-developed waiver demonstrations already in place, will reap large windfalls because they have to cover fewer recipients with their block grants. These gains, coupled with a potential 25-percent savings on State funds, give States the option of using the surplus resources to fund other programs or to provide tax relief.

The downside to block grants is that some traditionally low-benefit States with disproportionately large rural and/or minority populations and historically high poverty rates will receive fewer Federal dollars than other States to deal with unusually high welfare dependency rates. As of 1993, 18 mostly Southern States paying average monthly benefits of less than $300 per family accounted for 50 percent of the rural population and 60 percent of the rural poor. Fortunately, some of these States may qualify eventually for supplemental funds under the new law.

Rural counties with high rates of family welfare dependency often have high concentrations of minorities (Native Americans, Hispanics, African Americans) and/or historically high-poverty populations (fig. 3). These counties are disproportionately located in Southern States, including the Carolinas, Georgia, the northern Florida panhandle, parts of Alabama, Mississippi, Louisiana, and Arkansas, much of Appalachia, and areas of the Missouri Ozarks as well as in the Southwest, Northwest, the Dakotas, New England and the Great Lakes region. Of the

775 counties classified as high dependency in 1994, 586 are nonmetro (rural) counties. Nearly 60 percent of these rural high-dependency counties have had poverty rates in excess of 20 percent spanning several decades, and 56 percent are remote counties located away from urban centers.

Rural Leaders Face Unique Challenges in Moving Families From Welfare to Work

A review of State plans for 16 predominantly rural States indicates that several will require welfare parents to enter the labor market sooner than required by Federal guidelines (see box "State Plans Have Been Submitted. . ."). In a few States, parents will be required to work in community service jobs after 2 months of receiving benefits. Yet, rural county jurisdictions within these States have disproportionately high rates of welfare dependency, poverty, and unemployment, and are remotely located from urban centers (table 2).

Rural State and local leaders face many challenges in implementing State TANF plans that will effectively move families from welfare to work in their States. These challenges (elaborated below) include (1) creating enough new full-time jobs in the local labor market to absorb new unemployed and involuntary part-time welfare entrants without displacing nonwelfare workers; (2) providing job training and education that rural welfare parents need to obtain and retain jobs; (3) helping welfare families find jobs that provide a livable income; and (4) providing transportation to

Table 1

Estimated Federal budget effects of PL 104-193, 1997-2002

Food Stamp Program and SSI account for over 80 percent of savings over 6 years

Program	Pre-law projected spending	Post-law projected spending	Change	Percent change
		Billion dollars		Percent
Family support	112.5	112.4	–0.1	–0.1
Child care	9.3	13.2	+3.9	+41.9
Food Stamps	190.5	167.2	–23.3[1]	–12.2
SSI	203.5	180.8	–22.7[1]	–11.2
Medicaid	803.0	798.9	–4.1[1]	–.5
Child nutrition[2]	61.9	59.0	–2.9	–4.7
OASDI	2,484.4	2,484.3	–.1	–0.0
Other[3]	182.6	177.7	–4.9	–2.7
Total	4,047.7	3,993.5	–54.2	–1.3

[1]Includes $23.7 billion of projected savings from restricting benefits to aliens.
[2]Child nutrition includes programs authorized under National School Lunch and Child Nutrition Acts.
[3]Other includes social services, foster care, maternal and child care, and Earned Income Tax Credit.
Source: Compiled by ERS from Congressional Budget Office report to OMB, August 9, 1996.

jobs in places that lack public transportation and sufficient access to safe and affordable child care.

Finding available jobs for increasing proportions of a State's welfare parents in the next few years without displacing nonwelfare workers may be the greatest challenge that rural States face, because of the limited capacity of rural labor markets to absorb large numbers of new workers into entry-level jobs commensurate with the education and work experience of many welfare parents. This is especially true for rural communities with high welfare dependency, and

unemployment and poverty rates. In 1994, 60 percent of the 586 rural counties that were classified as highly welfare-dependent were also high-unemployment counties (fig. 4). Many of these same highly welfare-dependent counties have had poverty rates in excess of 20 percent over several decades. Thus, welfare job seekers will often have to compete with unemployed workers not on welfare for available jobs. However, some rural States with unusually high unemployment rates may apply for supplemental funds up to 20 percent of their annual block grants. Furthermore,

some States providing cash subsidies to employers who hire welfare recipients have built safeguards in their State plans to ensure that welfare workers will not displace workers already on the job.

Even if rural States find innovative ways to create more jobs, these jobs may not be accessible to many welfare parents with low education levels and little work experience without remedial education and training. In 1996, 35 percent of rural welfare parents lacked a high school education. Furthermore, preparing many welfare parents to enter and remain in

Figure 2

Change in AFDC recipiency by State, 1994–96

Number of recipients declined by at least 5 percent in every State but Hawaii

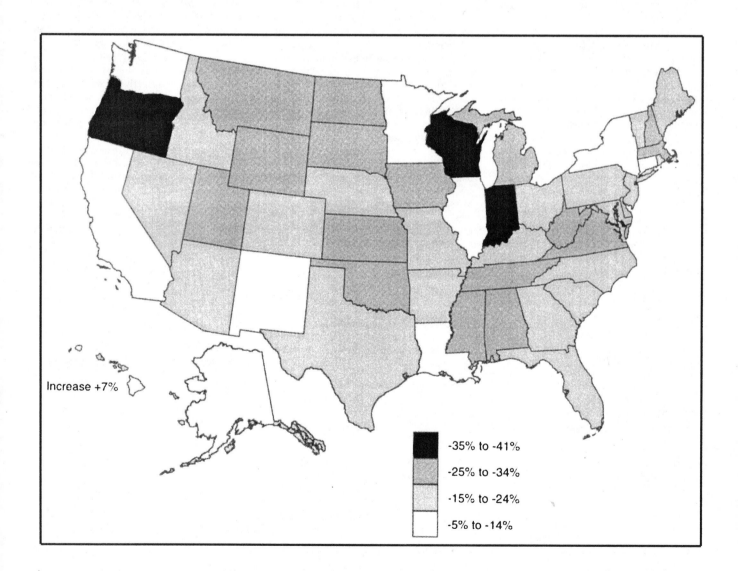

Increase +7%

-35% to -41%
-25% to -34%
-15% to -24%
-5% to -14%

Source: Prepared by ERS using data from the Department of Health and Human Services.

Figure 3

Family dependency on AFDC for rural counties, 1994*

Three out of every five high welfare-dependency counties are persistent-poverty counties

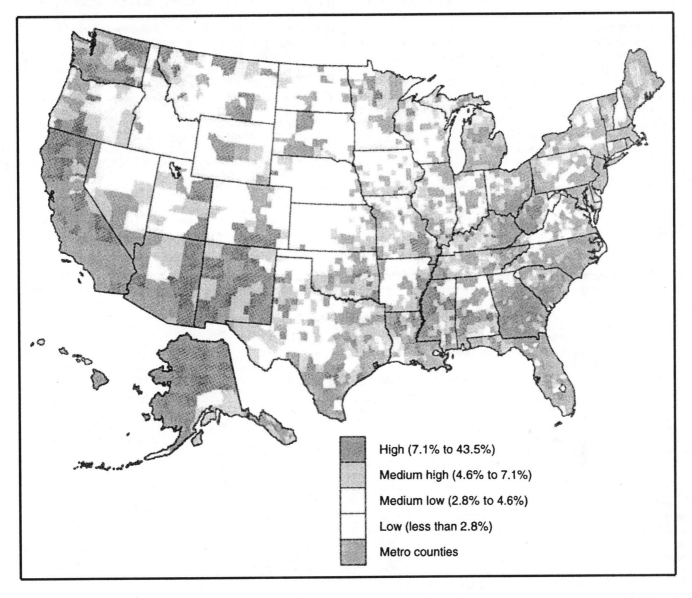

High (7.1% to 43.5%)

Medium high (4.6% to 7.1%)

Medium low (2.8% to 4.6%)

Low (less than 2.8%)

Metro counties

*Percent of families receiving AFDC benefits.
Source: Estimated by ERS using data from 1990 Census, Bureau of Economic Analysis, and Social Security Administration.

the work world requires developing the appropriate life skills and workplace habits needed to sustain employment. Such training is expensive and time-consuming, and may not be available in many rural communities. Most welfare recipients face another hurdle. Well over 80 percent of welfare parents are single mothers who will have to cope simultaneously with the demands of being a parent and a breadwinner.

The gains of promoting work among welfare recipients will be best realized if work lifts families out of poverty. Declining real wages over the past 15 years have left many rural families poor or nearly poor. In 1995, nearly 60 percent of rural poor families had either a head or spouse that worked some during the year, and 24 percent of rural poor families had either a head or spouse that worked full-time year-round. Although the metro/nonmetro poverty gap has narrowed greatly in recent years, 39 percent of rural families had near-poverty incomes (under 200 percent of the poverty line) in 1995, compared with 29 percent of urban families. The end goal of achieving self-sufficiency requires helping welfare parents find and re-

tain jobs that pay decent wages as well as increasing the share of children who live in two-parent worker families.

Community leaders must also find ways to overcome the lack of public transportation from home to work in most rural communities. Public transportation is important because rural welfare families do not generally own cars and often live in remote locations far from work opportunities. (Some States have prohibited welfare recipients from owning cars in the past.)

Another major rural concern is helping parents gain access to adequate

State Plans Have Been Submitted by 16 to 22 Predominantly Rural States

To date, TANF State plans have been submitted and certified for 16 of 22 predominantly rural States. These States either have large rural populations and/or have a considerable share of county jurisdictions that are classified as rural nonadjacent (see table 2 for list and definition). Proposals have not been submitted by the remaining six States. The estimated amounts of Federal TANF block grants for fiscal year 1997 vary from $775.4 million in Michigan to $21.8 million in Wyoming. This translates to annual amounts per 1994 family ranging from a high of $5,000 in Alaska to a low of $1,559 in Mississippi (table 2).

Eleven of the 16 State plans indicate that they will continue to work under waiver demonstration projects already in effect, and 2 will require welfare parents to work in community service activities after 2 months of receiving benefits. All but one of the States will offer eligible interstate migrants the same benefits as instate recipients. Three States will use State funds to provide benefits for nonqualifying aliens. The maximum lifetime limits for receiving cash assistance fall below the Federal guideline of 60 months in seven States; three of these will provide benefits for only 24 months out of every 60 months. Five States have set work requirements more stringent than the Federal guidelines. Only two States plan to implement TANF uniformly across all jurisdictions.

Table 2

Selected characteristics of predominantly rural States[1]

All but three States have more than one-half of their counties located in remote areas

| State | AFDC monthly benefit, 1993[2] | Estimated 1997 block grant in millions | Annual 1994 family benefit, 1997 | Rural counties | | | |
				Mean welfare dependency rate, 1994	Mean unemployment rate, 1994	Persistent poverty, 1990[3]	Nonadjacent counties, 1994
	Dollars			Percent			
Alaska	High	63.6	5,000	12.91	9.51	23.0	91.7
Arkansas	Low	56.7	2,205	4.38	6.36	48.4	54.7
Idaho	Medium	31.9	3,635	2.76	6.65	2.4	79.5
Iowa*	Medium	130.1	3,292	3.85	4.00	0.0	54.5
Kansas*	Medium	101.9	3,418	2.87	4.44	0.0	73.3
Kentucky*	Low	181.3	2,291	8.96	6.84	55.1	52.5
Maine*	High	78.1	3,447	6.66	8.37	0.0	31.3
Michigan*	High	775.4	3,525	5.93	9.18	1.7	50.6
Minnesota	High	266.4	4,323	3.61	5.70	2.9	50.6
Missippi*	Low	86.8	1,559	9.31	8.29	82.7	68.3
Missouri*	Low	214.6	2,329	5.91	6.03	30.0	51.3
Montana*	Medium	45.5	3,840	4.27	5.10	5.6	78.6
Nebraska*	Medium	58.0	3,704	1.70	2.84	2.3	80.6
New Hampshire*	High	38.5	3,359	3.86	4.17	0.0	30.0
New Mexico	Medium	126.1	3,696	8.94	8.47	48.2	57.6
North Carolina*	Low	302.2	2,314	7.80	6.26	29.2	26.0
North Dakota	Medium	25.9	4,551	2.65	4.29	14.3	71.7
Oregon*	Medium	167.9	4,036	4.35	7.45	0.0	52.8
South Dakota*	Low	21.9	3,223	4.71	4.39	27.0	88.3
Vermont*	High	21.9	4,799	6.69	5.53	0.0	50.0
West Virginia*	Low	110.2	2,728	8.51	11.34	25.6	52.7
Wyoming*	Medium	21.8	3,855	3.54	5.15	0.0	87.0
U.S. total	------	16,389.0	3,256	5.62	6.54	23.5	56.8

[1]Predominantly rural States have less than 45 percent of 1995 population residing inurban portions of metro areas and/or other States (nonurban) with at least one-half of counties classified as nonmetro counties (see appendix A). States indicated with an * have TANF State Plans certified as of February 24, 1997.

[2]Low-benefit States have benefits less than $300, medium-benefits between $300 and $400, and high-benefit States have benefits over $400.

[3]See appendix A.

Sources: Calculated by ERS using data from the Bureau of Economic Analysis, Bureau of the Census, Bureau of Labor Statistics, Social Security Administration, and Department of Health and Human Services.

Figure 4

Overlap of rural counties by AFDC dependency and unemployment rates, 1994

Over 60 percent of high welfare-dependent counties have high unemployment rates

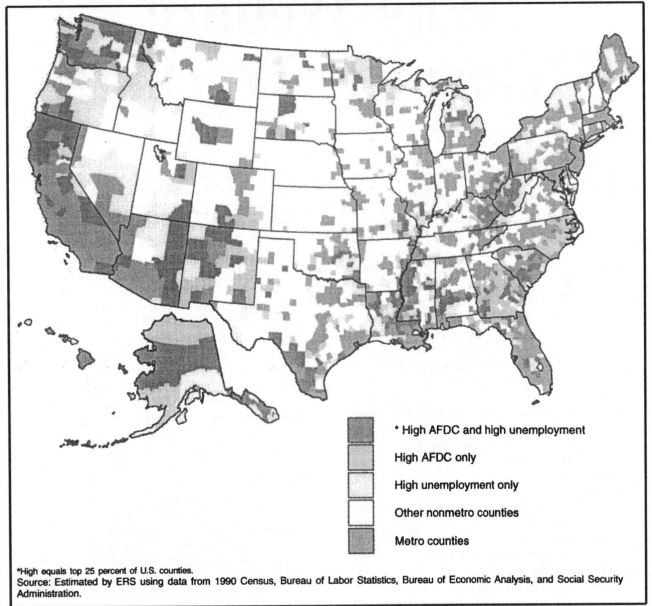

* High AFDC and high unemployment

High AFDC only

High unemployment only

Other nonmetro counties

Metro counties

*High equals top 25 percent of U.S. counties.
Source: Estimated by ERS using data from 1990 Census, Bureau of Labor Statistics, Bureau of Economic Analysis, and Social Security Administration.

child care. Almost two-thirds of rural welfare families had at least one child under age 6 in 1996. Yet, the availability of day-care centers in many small rural communities is limited, or nonexistent, causing welfare parents to rely on families, friends, and neighbors for child care.

A final challenge for all States is to incorporate ways to address the unique needs of rural areas and rural people (especially in very remote locations) into their State plans. If State plans do not reflect rural concerns, there is a real chance that rural areas will be overlooked, especially in States that do not

intend to implement all aspects of welfare reform uniformly across jurisdictions.

[Peggy J. Cook, pross@econ.ag.gov, and Elizabeth M. Dagata, edagata@econ. ag. gov]

Why Welfare Reform Is Working

Daniel Casse

ON JULY 1, the "end of welfare as we know it" began in earnest. On that day, the federal legislation that President Clinton had signed nearly a year earlier went into effect, terminating a 62-year-old federal entitlement and creating, for the first time, a limit on how long one can receive federal welfare assistance.

In Washington, however, it seems impossible to leave well enough alone. Clinton himself had promised last year to "fix" troublesome portions of the welfare law, and by the end of July, as Congress passed a balanced-budget plan, it became apparent that the law's implementation was still susceptible of political manipulation. In the final days of negotiation over the budget, a passive Republican Congress and a politically alert White House began diluting the potent formula conceived and signed a year earlier and in effect for all of three weeks.

These eleventh-hour changes are not insignificant. But they should not obscure the larger achievement. The welfare-reform legislation that went into effect on July 1 is the most far-reaching policy move of the Clinton presidency—and also, to date, the most successful. Not surprisingly, the President used his July 4 national radio address to crow about it. Since he took office in January 1993, he announced, three million fewer people were on the welfare rolls. Even more impressive was the fact that an astonishing 1.2 million had come off the rolls in the first nine months since the welfare-reform legislation passed Congress and before it formally went into effect. Using rhetoric that was once the

preserve of conservative polemicists, the President told the nation on July 4 that "we have begun to put an end to the culture of dependency, and to elevate our values of family, work, and responsibility."

In truth, the legislation itself deserves only part of the credit. Earlier this year, the President's own Council of Economic Advisers concluded that the drop in the number of people on welfare was due in some measure to the healthy economy and also to the wide variety of initiatives that had emerged over the last few years at the state level. We have, indeed, never witnessed such a fertile period of experimentation, with dozens of state legislatures trying new ways to move people off government assistance and onto a path of self-sufficiency. Most of these former recipients have gone successfully into full- or part-time jobs, while others, recognizing the new demands the local welfare office will soon place on them, have voluntarily dropped out of the system. With the more comprehensive measures of the federal law now taking effect—and notwithstanding the deleterious changes introduced in the balanced-budget negotiations—we have every reason to expect that these trends will continue.

Not everyone is rejoicing, to be sure. The hand-wringing among some conservatives over the last-minute changes smuggled in by the White House in late July is one thing; but it pales in comparison to the deep distress which the legislation, amended or unamended, has brought to liberal policy circles, not to mention the real rifts which the President's support for welfare reform has caused within his own party. For those who have not wanted to hear that the era of big government is over, the welfare-reform bill has been, indeed, a bitter pill to swallow.

DANIEL CASSE *is a senior director of the White House Writers Group, a public-policy communications firm. His article, "Clinton and the Democrats: A Party of One," appeared in our July 1996 issue.*

Reprinted from *Commentary,* September 1997, pp. 36-42, by permission. © 1997 by *Commentary* and Daniel Casse.

That may explain why, from the beginning, those opposed to the plan repeatedly resorted to a kind of demagoguery that was shameless even by Washington standards. Thus, when the first round of legislation began moving through the Republican-controlled Congress in 1994, Senator Daniel Patrick Moynihan boldly predicted that the result would be "scenes of social trauma such as we haven't known since the cholera epidemics." Not to be outdone, Senator Edward M. Kennedy called an early version of the reform bill "legislative child-abuse."

By the summer of 1996, when it was clear that a bipartisan coalition existed for replacing the federal welfare entitlement with state block grants, time limits, and work requirements, still more alarms were set off. The Urban Institute warned that one million children would fall into poverty, the *New York Times* condemned the bill as "atrocious," and Moynihan pronounced it "an obscene act of social regression." Finally, days after the President signed the legislation, two of his top policy appointees at the Department of Health and Human Services resigned in protest. One of them, Peter Edelman, waited less than six months before publishing an article in the *Atlantic* calling the welfare-reform plan "the worst thing Bill Clinton has done." As Edelman saw it, the new legislation offered a grim future for America's poor:

> [T]here will be suffering.... There will be more malnutrition and more crime, increased infant mortality and increased drug and alcohol abuse. There will be increased family violence and abuse against children and women, and a consequent spillover of the problem into the already overloaded child-welfare system and battered-women's shelters.

Today, a year after the legislation was signed, there is scant evidence of a looming crisis, yet the predictions of gloom, albeit somewhat less hysterical in tone, have continued to pour in. In the *American Prospect*, the eminent social scientist Christopher Jencks has forecast that without a well-funded system of public employment, "states will either have to fudge their time limits or let a lot of destitute families break up." Writing in response to Jencks, Kimberly Christensen has suggested that he is too optimistic. "Many abused women," she charges, "will eventually lose their benefits for nonattendance at workfare placements, or reach the [time] limit, with

disastrous results for themselves and their children." To the *Washington Post* columnist E.J. Dionne, echoing what has become a conventional liberal criticism, "the danger of the reforms is not that they will force people to work but that people will be forced off the rolls without work to go to." And in the August 4 *New Republic*, a pair of articles warns that the new law, for all its early success, is unlikely to help the most disadvantaged among us.

Quite obviously, no one knows at this early stage what the ultimate effect of welfare reform will be. But the critics, having lost the legislative battle, now seem determined to convince us that without a massive infusion of new federal funds, the nation's poor are headed pell-mell toward cruel deprivation and suffering. Fortunately for the country, the facts suggest otherwise.

THE PERSONAL Responsibility and Work Opportunity Reconciliation Act of 1996 passed both Houses of Congress with considerable bipartisan support. Like all such sweeping pieces of legislation, it makes changes to numerous federal laws and regulations. But the bulk of the legislation is directed at Aid to Families with Dependent Children (AFDC), the Roosevelt-era assistance program that was the target of most of the growing public dissatisfaction with welfare. The new law effectively repeals AFDC and replaces it with a new program known as Temporary Assistance for Needy Families (TANF). In addition, the law introduces four fundamental changes that distinguish it from every attempt at welfare reform that has come before.

First, it ends the federal entitlement to cash assistance. In the past, eligibility for this assistance was means-tested: anyone meeting the income requirements was automatically qualified. Under the new law, each state determines eligibility. Second, the new law gives a block grant to each of the 50 states, permitting it to design a cash-assistance program as it sees fit. Third, the law establishes a five-year lifetime limit on cash assistance and a two-year limit on receiving assistance without working, thus ensuring that welfare cannot become a way of life. Finally, the law requires each state to craft work requirements as part of its welfare program. By the year 2002, states will need to show that at least 50 percent of those receiving welfare are involved in some form of work or training in exchange for benefits.

These changes all come with a catalogue of exemptions, qualifications, and alternative requirements in special cases—a flexibility that guarantees that the actual programs will vary considerably from state to state. The law will not, for example, "throw a million children into poverty." States can exempt 20 percent of their caseload from the time limit, and also convert block-grant money into vouchers for children after their families have reached the limit. Even when the federal limits are triggered, states can continue to spend their own money helping poor families (as they do now). And states may exempt parents of infants from all work requirements, while single parents with children under six will be asked to work only part-time.

Although one would never know it from the critics, left untouched by this reform are a host of poverty-assistance programs. Medicaid, a program still in need of reform, continues to provide health coverage to all poor families under the new welfare law. Public-housing programs remain in effect, as do child-nutrition programs and the Earned Income Tax Credit. The food-stamp program will continue to grow, if at a slower rate. Again contrary to what has been charged, children with serious long-term medical conditions and disabilities will *not* lose their Supplemental Security Income aid; the new law merely narrows the definition of "disability" to exclude some purely behavioral problems.

Most of the bill's critics have also misunderstood the financing behind it. According to the *Washington Post*, the new law "hands the problem to the states and fails to equip them with the resources to solve" it. In fact, the bill represents a giant windfall for state welfare spending. The block grants replacing the old, formula-driven AFDC payments have been fixed at 1994 spending levels—but in the meantime, as the President reminded us in his July 4 radio address, the welfare caseload across the nation has been dropping dramatically. (In Maryland, Oregon, Massachusetts, Oklahoma, and Michigan, the AFDC caseload has shrunk by 20 to 30 percent in the past two years alone.) For many states, then, the new block grants, financed on the basis of the more crowded welfare rolls of two years ago, represent a significant hike in funding—hardly the outcome one would anticipate from a Republican Congress routinely described as mean-spirited, heartless, and insensitive to the needs of the poor.

BUT MOST confounding of all to critics of the bill, and most heartening to its supporters, is the fact that welfare reform, in its embryonic stages, has wildly surpassed expectations. In April of this year, eleven million people were on welfare, the lowest share of the U.S. population since 1970. Nor have any of the widely predicted nightmare scenarios materialized. Even in cities like Milwaukee, where thousands of welfare recipients have dropped off the rolls in the last two years, local shelters and food banks have reported no new surges in demand for their services.

What accounts for these early signs of success? Following the lead of the Council of Economic Advisers, some have suggested that the drop in caseloads is traceable entirely to the current strength of the economy. But this cannot be right. The economy has indeed been strong; yet previous cycles of prosperity have failed to produce anything close to the reductions we see today.

What is different, clearly, is that the *rules* governing welfare dependence have started to change. Indeed, they started to change well before the federal law was passed last year. Impatient with Washington's habitual inaction, both Democratic and Republican governors began introducing time limits, work requirements, and rules designed to promote responsibility in their own state systems. The burgeoning economy has made their work easier, but there is no denying that in states where the rules have changed, the lives and behavior of welfare recipients have also changed, and for the better.

Wisconsin's much-touted reforms are a case in point. In a detailed study published in *Policy Review*, Robert Rector has shown how two new programs in that state, Self-Sufficiency First and Pay for Performance, fundamentally altered the relationship between welfare recipients and government. Implemented in April 1996, the programs required recipients to work in the private sector or perform community service, attend remedial-education classes, or participate in a supervised job search in exchange for AFDC payments or food stamps. Those who did not want to work, take classes, or look for a job were no longer eligible for payments. Seven months after the programs began, the AFDC caseload had dropped 33 percent.

Recent experience in Tennessee, though less widely reported, is no less impressive. As it happens, Tennessee is not subject to the provisions of the new federal law, having won prior approval for an equally comprehensive program of its own. Like the federal law, the Tennessee plan, known as Families First, replaces AFDC with a cash-assistance program that requires recipients to work, go to school, or train while working part-time. Tennessee exempts almost a third of its welfare recipients from the time limits (and from some of the work requirements), and in that respect its plan is even more flexible than the federal law. On the other hand, Tennessee imposes a tighter restriction on the number of consecutive months welfare recipients can receive cash benefits. Finally, everyone eligible for benefits, even if exempt from the work requirements and the time limits, must sign a "personal-responsibility contract" outlining the steps to be taken toward self-sufficiency.

In the first six months of the program, 19,000 Tennesseans left the welfare rolls—a 21-percent drop, unprecedented in the state's history. What makes this reduction more remarkable still is that during these early months no one was being forcibly removed from the rolls by an arbitrary cut-off date. Instead, social-service officials in Tennessee discovered that the mere requirement to show up at a welfare office, sign a statement of personal responsibility, and participate in a work or educational program had a dramatic impact on the lives of people accustomed to receiving a government check without anything being asked of them at all.

Tennessee officials broke down the declining caseload to understand what was taking place. The results are revealing: 5,800 recipients asked that their cases be closed within the first month ("I don't want to be bothered," was a common response). Another 5,500 found work and earned enough money to make them ineligible. Almost a third either refused to sign the personal-responsibility contract, or failed to comply with its terms, or refused to attend classes or begin a job search. The rest moved out of the state. As for those still receiving cash assistance, many appear to be enthusiastically pursuing a route to independence. In the first six months of Families First, 18 percent of this group had found full-time employment; 22 percent were in training or were looking for a job; 19 percent were pursuing adult education; 6 percent had gotten some form of employment mixed with training.

Tennessee's record so far vividly contradicts the most prevalent and longstanding liberal criticism of a decentralized welfare system: that it will spur a "race to the bottom" among the states. Harvard's David Ellwood, who served as an assistant secretary of Health and Human Services and was a point man for the administration's welfare-reform plans before quitting in frustration, has made this criticism most explicitly:

> History is filled with examples of states choosing to ignore poor families or ignoring racial minorities, regions, or types of families. Moreover, if one state's rules differ markedly from those of another, there will be an incentive for migration. It is a lot easier to move poor people from welfare to the state border than from welfare to work. Needs and resources also differ widely across states. The states with the smallest tax base are usually the states with the greatest proportion of poor children and families. Fearful of becoming "welfare magnets," some states may cut benefits and impose more punitive measures than they would otherwise prefer.

On almost every point, the Tennessee example has disproved Ellwood and those who repeat his arguments. Tennessee, a relatively poor Southern state, is also no stranger to racial tensions. With no state income tax, a lean state budget, a recent history of political corruption, and a strong Republican tilt in recent elections, it would hardly seem an ideal candidate for meaningful welfare reform. Yet Tennessee's program *has* promoted work and independence without suddenly snatching away the safety net. Moreover, as part of its reform initiative, the state legislature has actually increased spending on welfare by 22 percent since 1994. Nor is Tennessee unique in this respect. The *New York Times* recently reported that, to the surprise of antipoverty advocates, state legislatures, flush with federal dollars from the welfare-reform bill, have been spending money on day-care services, emergency loans for car repairs, and free subway passes, all designed to make it easier for welfare recipients to find work.

NONE OF this is to say that the bill initially passed by Congress and signed by the President last year was without significant flaws or risks. Undoubtedly, the most egregious and widely publicized clause was the one denying benefits to poor, elderly immigrants who were already legally residing in the country. At a cost of $12 billion, July's budget agreement has repaired this defect by applying restrictions to future immigrants only, thereby retaining the legitimate purpose of discouraging future welfare-seekers from coming to the U.S. without penalizing new, legal residents.

As for the risks, no one knows how states will manage if regional economies start to fizzle, depriving former welfare recipients of their jobs. Nor can we be sure state programs will discourage *new* entrants to the welfare system as successfully as they have been moving people off. There is also reason to question whether work requirements will deter out-of-wedlock births, which is bound to be a major criterion in judging their success.

Still, the early stages of state reform have already told us volumes about the American welfare population itself, and this will be of inestimable value in addressing the dilemmas of the future. Over the decades, as the evidence of a crisis mounted, it had become customary to speak of this population as if it were a single class of people exhibiting a uniform set of behaviors, motivations, and responses to public policy. If the last few months have taught us anything, it is that welfare recipients are a varied lot.

At one end of the spectrum are those who are unlikely ever to find or hold a job, or to lead a life free of government support. They are the disabled, the chronically ill, and those with severe learning problems or long-term histories of drug and alcohol abuse. They have often been on AFDC without interruption for many years, even decades; their families may have been on AFDC for generations. No mix of carrots and sticks is likely to move such people from welfare to independence. In virtually every state they will be exempt from welfare requirements—quite sensibly so—and continue to depend on government support.

Then there is the opposite end of the spectrum: the considerable portion of the welfare population, perhaps as many as 30 percent, who are easily moved off the rolls at the slightest prompting. Many may have already been in the workforce at some point or other (or may have been defrauding the system by working and collecting welfare simultaneously); when compelled to comply with tighter rules, they simply stop showing up for their check. Others move readily into the

workforce when they need to. Still others, as we have seen in Tennessee, would rather drop out of the system than be held accountable for their daily activities. Although some of these welfare recipients may find themselves falling back onto government assistance after a short period of time, they are among those best-equipped to move off welfare permanently, and a well-designed program may be all the motivation they need for long-term self-reliance.

BETWEEN THESE two groups are those who are neither highly motivated nor completely incapable of self-sufficiency. Almost all the major efforts in the months ahead will be focused on this group. But consider how much more doable the task has become. To critics, most of the success so far is attributable to "cherry picking." As the *New Republic* put it dramatically on the cover of its August 4 issue: "Welfare Reform Has Moved More Than a Million People Off the Rolls. But Those Were the Easy Cases." This, however, is wide of the mark; the fact that the states have a significantly smaller caseload to work with means they can devote more money to each family struggling to get off welfare. Policymakers have never enjoyed this luxury before.

How should the money be spent? There is, unfortunately, no proven formula. Many states will no doubt invest millions of dollars in job training and preparedness programs. But the evidence that these can lead to success is, at best, mixed. Thus, the Job Training Partnership Act, one of the largest government-funded training programs, has led to some improvement in women's earnings but very little in men's. Similarly unencouraging is a recent study of New Chance, a program operating in twelve U.S. cities and designed to help teenage mothers gain self-sufficiency. Although New Chance spent approximately $9,000 per mother on education, training, child care, parenting skills, and health care, the study (conducted by the same corporation that designed the program) found that these young mothers were no more likely than before to find a job, leave welfare, or delay future pregnancies.

More hopeful are initiatives to replace training and counseling with real work, or at least rigorous preparation for work. In a recent book, *It Takes a Nation*, Rebecca Blank, an intelligent critic of the legislation passed by Congress, concedes that for welfare recipients with minimal job experience, some time at work often proves far more effective than months of training or classroom education. The work environment introduces into their lives a higher level of accountability and stimulates them to acquire more training if they want to move up the ladder. Most important, job placement and work programs shift the relationship between welfare recipients and their local social-service agency. Putting someone in a job is an entirely different mandate from merely certifying his eligibility for cash benefits, and the change is beneficial to both sides.

The most frequent question raised by skeptics is how welfare recipients will find employment. Following the lead of critics like Christopher Jencks, liberals now propose the creation of thousands of public-sector jobs as the only way to absorb the welfare population into the workforce. States that heed their advice, however, will quickly discover that these programs are expensive and extraordinarily difficult to manage. The history of similar efforts at the federal level—most notoriously, the Comprehensive Employment and Training Act (CETA)—confirms the folly of replacing one welfare system with another that goes by a different name.

Nevertheless, there may be a virtue in putting people in some form of *temporary* public-sector workfare or community service. As Robert Rector has pointed out, Wisconsin has created thousands of such jobs, not for make-work but to establish the principle of pay for performance. The same model is now to be seen in other states and cities, including New York, where more than half of the public-park workers are welfare recipients earning their benefits. Ironically, though, this quintessential New Deal-style program has also enraged liberals. In July, a coalition of New York churches, synagogues, and nonprofit groups, evidently oblivious to the social destruction the city's *existing* welfare system has wrought, announced that its members would not offer workfare positions to welfare recipients, on the grounds that the program is tantamount to slavery.

Such moral posturing aside, it is true that mandatory public-work programs are not always ideal: under them, many older, laid-off skilled workers may be forced to do menial labor in order to gain temporary cash assistance while seeking a new job. But the vast majority of welfare recipients do not have the skills or wherewithal to enter the job market

on their own—they are predominantly young women who have never held a full- *or* part-time job—and for them, programs that demand work in exchange for cash harbor a twofold benefit. First, they habituate a welfare recipient to the norms of the workplace: arriving on time, following instructions, working with others, and so on. Second, by transforming welfare itself, they make it a far less attractive option for a young woman who might once have seen AFDC as a way out of the world of adult responsibility.

I T CANNOT be stressed enough that the current round of welfare reform is different from all that have preceded it. In the past, reform initiatives simply added a labyrinth of incentives to what remained, at heart, a system of entitlements. Work programs, counseling, job searches, child care, and transportation subsidies are surely limited tools if the recipient knows that at the end of the day, there will be no penalty for failing to respond to the rules and incentives. And the most able welfare recipients *always* knew how to "game" the system.

That is why a legal work requirement and a clear time limit for cash assistance are so crucial. Without the certainty of a fixed cutoff date, workfare programs of the past invariably devolved into another form of open-ended government job training that did little to move the trainee into a real job. The key to the current reform is that it promotes self-sufficiency by *removing* welfare as a long-term alternative.

And that, regrettably, is also where the changes introduced in this July's budget agreement are likely to do the most damage. A number of state governors have reacted to these changes by charging that the President has effectively undermined the whole thrust of the legislation. "Even Democratic governors are screaming he's all but killed it," wrote the columnist Paul Gigot in the *Wall Street Journal*.

There is much justice in the governors' complaints. The administration's $3-billion Welfare-to-Work program, for example, was stuffed into the July budget agreement as a payoff to big-city mayors who had been left out of the welfare-reform process. Federal funding for yet another unproven job-preparedness initiative like this one runs counter to the main intent of welfare reform, which is (again) to require work, not training, in exchange for a government check. By permitting such alternatives to thrive, the administration has succeeded in creating yet more loopholes for welfare recipients—the very thing that has repeatedly undone past efforts at reform.

But the administration's attempt to roll back or qualify the progress that has been made has taken on an even more disturbing aspect. Both the President and his Department of Labor have begun to insist that all work performed by welfare recipients, even those in community-service jobs, must be treated as "employment" and therefore subject to the panoply of federal labor regulations. Such an interpretation not only runs contrary to 30 years of sensible precedent, but, by asserting a new and intrusive federal role, it has the very real potential to prevent every new state workfare program from getting off the ground. If the administration has its way, more than two dozen federal requirements would be placed on any workfare position, including the payment of minimum wages (and prevailing wages in construction jobs), payroll taxes for employers, workers'-compensation programs, and so on. It would be hard to conceive a greater obstacle in the path of programs that were intended, after all, to help those most unlikely to find work in the private sector.

As the Republican Congress was notably unenthusiastic about fighting off these rearguard actions against a bill it spent two years struggling to pass, it will now be up to state governments to challenge ongoing efforts to exert federal control over workfare. Still, these legal and technical issues, and others like them, are *all* that remains of the welfare discussion. Which means that the larger debate that began in the early 1980's is finally over. That debate has been decisively lost by those who wanted to cling to a system with a guaranteed federal entitlement for the poor. Still to be seen is the extent to which the new state policies will succeed; but whatever the final consequences, it is unlikely we will ever return to the old model.

Indeed, together with the defeat of national health-care legislation in 1994, the passage of welfare reform represents the second major body blow to big-government liberalism during the Clinton presidency. Interestingly, some liberals who have chosen to make their peace with welfare reform have taken to arguing that by ending the country's old and highly unpopular policy, President Clinton has actually set the stage for a *revival* of liberalism. Mickey Kaus, for example, one of the most persuasive liberal advocates of the new reforms, is now trying to cast them as a defeat for conservative governance. "Liberals," he wrote in the *New York Times* last year, "can now rebuild an active government on a more defensible foundation"—because the states, having gained control of the pursestrings, are outdoing even Washington in spending money to help the poor.

But quite apart from the question of whether levels of spending are the right criterion by which to judge the prospects of liberalism, Kaus's argument misses the essential point. It is a mistake to believe that the welfare debate was ever about the amount of money the country was spending. If, over the last 30 years, billions of dollars had gone into a poverty-assistance program that had actually helped to foster stable families, safe and clean public housing, higher achievement in education, and a reduction in illegitimate births, no one would ever have complained about a welfare "crisis" in the first place. Money alone was never the problem.

Instead, what distinguishes the current reform is that it has forced both federal and state governments to take seriously the idea that welfare policy can deter, or encourage, behavior. The fact that Tennessee will increase welfare spending this year tells us nothing in itself. But the fact that Tennessee now holds parents accountable for their children's immunizations and school attendance; that it forces teen parents to stay in school and live at home or with a guardian; and that it provides no additional benefits for single mothers who have additional children while on welfare, means that government is no longer indifferent to the way welfare recipients live and raise their children. All this represents a stark departure from the liberalism that has dominated government policy toward the poor for the last three decades.

Changing the way the poor behave may not make them prosperous, and there will always be critics to insist that until poverty is eradicated, no program can claim success. But by eliminating the certainty that one will be paid whether or not one works or seeks work, we have already taken the most important step on the road toward the end of welfare—and of liberalism—as we have known them.

Welfare to Work

WHAT HAPPENS WHEN RECIPIENT MEETS EMPLOYER?

BY AARON STEELMAN

IN 1996, CONGRESS CONVERTED FOUR FEDERAL welfare entitlements into Temporary Assistance for Needy Families, a program that will limit recipients to a lifetime eligibility of five years. The significance of this change has been widely debated.

While the Left calls the reform cruel and inhumane, critics on the right maintain it is but a Band-Aid on a hemorrhaging wound. For example, the new rules allow states to excuse up to 20 percent of their recipients from the five-year limit. Michael Tanner, director of health and welfare studies at the Cato Institute, argues that "by allowing states to exempt a fifth of their welfare population from the five-year lifetime limit, the act may actually motivate relatively few welfare recipients to go to work. After all, most welfare recipients already leave the program in less than five years. The group the one-fifth exemption is likeliest to shelter is the minority who are long-term recipients—precisely the people Americans are most unhappy to see on welfare."

Nevertheless, Tanner concedes that because it ends the federal entitlement to aid, "the act represents an important first step on the road to welfare reform." And if states decide *not* to exempt substantial numbers of recipients from the lifetime limit, then whole generations of people who have never worked will be forced to find jobs.

Preparing for that possibility, the Clinton White House has set up the Welfare to Work Partnership, an organization that tries to persuade companies to hire welfare recipients. So far, more than 2,100 companies have joined the Partnership and vowed to start hiring former recipients. Citing a Coopers and Lybrand survey, Partnership director Eli Segal claims that more than one-quarter of the country's 400 fastest-growing firms

Aaron Steelman is the staff writer at The Cato Institute.

have hired workers from the welfare rolls, and that another 4 percent plan to do so soon.

The evidence, however, suggests that most companies aren't interested in welfare-to-work programs. According to the Associated Press, only eight of the country's 100 largest corporations have welfare-to-work programs at present. A poll by Wirthlin Worldwide found that just one percent of senior executives are "extremely interested" in such undertakings, and that 57 percent fear most former welfare recipients will be poor employees.

If welfare rolls are to be scaled down, individuals now getting checks must become productive workers. To find out how this can happen, *The American Enterprise* recently spoke with managers at several companies that have hired former welfare dependents, and asked them how success can be had in this undertaking.

PHILADELPHIA-BASED ARAMARK is one of the world's largest service companies. The firm's employees distribute magazines and books, serve food, supply uniforms, provide child care, and clean buildings for hundreds of companies, schools, and government agencies. More than 350 colleges and universities have contracted with ARAMARK to run their cafeterias and concession stands, as have major league teams like the Boston Red Sox, Philadelphia Flyers, and New York Mets. Perhaps more than any other U.S. company, ARAMARK has benefited from and contributed to the recent trend toward corporate outsourcing.

ARAMARK's chairman and CEO, Joseph Neubauer, joined the company in 1979. The business skills that previously helped him to become the youngest treasurer of a *Fortune* 500 company (PepsiCo), and the senior vice president of Wilson Sporting Goods, also helped him in his quick rise to the top position at ARAMARK. And for Neubauer, playing a role in the welfare-to-work movement is very much a business decision, not charity.

"We come at this from a perspective of what I like to call 'enlightened self-interest,' Neubauer states. "We can't afford to let our partners down. We have to deliver on our commitments. And most of our commitments involve people-intensive jobs. Companies like ARAMARK that provide services are constantly looking for people."

ARAMARK's total employment has been growing at eight to ten percent a year in a tight labor market, and some of the company's recent hires have been people just off of welfare. But according to vice president of human resources Brian Mulvaney, ARAMARK will continue to absorb welfare recipients even if the economy slumps. "In previous economic downturns, while they have affected the growth rates of some of our businesses, we continue to grow. I think the corporate outsourcing phenomenon is so powerful and makes so much economic sense that it is going to continue if we hit an economic downturn. ARAMARK is still going to have a need for entry-level employees."

In order to turn welfare recipients into service workers, Neubauer observes, you sometimes have to go the extra mile— at least in the beginning. "The soft skills in life are very important if you want to be successful with your job. And a lot of these people don't come to us with the soft skills that you and I learn as a child," he notes. "Many of them don't understand that if you're in line, for example, you wait your turn— you simply can't push your way to the front. In the environment in which many welfare recipients grow up, standing in line is not an accepted skill—pushing, or whatever it takes to get in front, is. That said, once you teach them the soft skills and reward them for practicing them, you see that they respond positively."

Indeed, if they can get past the first 90 days on the job, Neubauer thinks that welfare recipients frequently make better—or at least more enthusiastic—ARAMARK employees than the typical hire off the street. People who have held steady jobs before can become complacent, but for welfare recipients, "having a full-time job, belonging to an established group, being recognized as a team member, and receiving recognition and praise are enormously important and gratifying."

Other employers make this same point. Jack Donohue, who supervises Borg-Warner security guards in New York, New Jersey, and Connecticut, says that while he "didn't hold out much hope in the beginning," he has found that former welfare recipients often become very reliable employees. "When times weren't very good a couple of years ago, I saw lots of people interviewing here with master's degrees and very good work experience," says Donohue. "They did a good job but their attitude was, 'As soon as I find another job, I'm outta here. I've had enough with working security at all hours of the night.' The people that we've gotten off welfare, however, generally look at it much more as a career opportunity. Their ex-

If they can get past the first 90 days on the job, Neubauer thinks welfare recipients frequently make more enthusiastic employees than the typical hire off the street.

pectation, their immediate horizon, is a little lower, and so they are much more apt to look at this as a big step. And you find that they stay with it and therefore begin getting supervisory jobs."

At ARAMARK, the key to successfully training and keeping employees in entry-level jobs has been decentralization. "What works in Baton Rouge won't necessarily work in Boston," says Neubauer. With more than 6,000 different "profit-centers" around the country, ARAMARK has hundreds of front-line managers who act, in effect, as the CEOs of their units. For example, while ARAMARK has no company-wide transportation subsidy program, units in areas with low unemployment rates have set up their own, as a way of attracting new employees.

Each new ARAMARK employee becomes part of a small, tight-knit group, where everyone depends on each other and where a slip-up can be very costly to everybody. In such a setting, co-workers have an incentive to make sure that new employees are properly trained and ready for the job, and newly hired welfare recipients, seeking the approval and praise that is so crucial to boosting their self-images, have an incentive to be responsible workers.

Alan Leo, 41, has taken advantage of ARAMARK's "if you do, you get" management approach. He began working for ARAMARK as a chef at age 17, having gained experience at his immigrant father's Chinese restaurant, and now heads the company's food services branch at Boston University. He says that "ARAMARK really allows us—the front-line managers—to run our businesses and make decisions about what's best at our locations. So we are able to respond to our employees. And there are lots of people on the management staff like me who have been here for several years and know what it's like to start at the bottom."

Leo says that whether a welfare recipient will be successful is largely dependent on the training he gets before coming to ARAMARK. "We work with a lot of agencies—particularly, a lot of private, ethnic groups and community groups—who work with people who are marginally employable. We don't ask them to do the technical training of running a cash register and things of that sort—we do that ourselves—but we do ask them to weed out those people who aren't ready for customer service and who are going to fail. They really do our pre-screening."

And when Leo finds an agency that can deliver suitable employees, he sticks with it. About ten years ago, one agency sent him "twenty Chinese women who were displaced garment workers. The agency trained them for about a month. And even though none of them could speak much English, I had worked with this organization before and I knew I could trust them. At least a dozen of those folks are still with us."

WHEN THE NATIONAL auto parts chain Pep Boys decided to hire welfare recipients to staff a distribution center in Indiana, reports manager Lori Milburn, it also looked for an outside agency to help screen candidates. The company eventually turned to Goodwill Industries. Of the 27 people Pep Boys hired last May (starting them at $8 an hour), 15 are still with the company, a ratio Milburn is quite happy with. "Our overall annual turnover rate is near 80 percent," she notes, and "the people who have stayed have proven to be very good employees." When hiring in Southern California, Pep Boys used the National Urban League to perform similar screenings for hiring ex-welfare recipients.

The Marriott Corporation has likewise relied on private and public agencies to screen welfare recipients. Janet Tully, director of Pathways to Independence, Marriott's welfare-to-work program, says that about 25 percent of applicants are accepted into the Pathways program. Frequently, she says, welfare recipients come to Marriott with the wrong attitude. "Many of the people entering the program have a victim mentality—it's always someone else's fault. We start off right away by telling them that they are the ones who need to be in control of the situation."

Marriott's program has had moderate success. About 90 percent of the people who enter the Pathways program—which provides 60 hours of classroom training and 120 hours of on-the-job training—eventually graduate. And 78 percent of Pathways graduates are still with Marriott after two years, compared to approximately 50 percent of Marriott employees as a whole. The program still is not profitable, however, because Marriott spends more than $5,000 training each Pathways graduate. "Let's not use the word 'profitable,' " says Tully. " 'Possible' is the word. Our big dream is to get to be revenue neutral and offset our training costs. And if we didn't share the costs of training with other groups, this wouldn't even be possible at all, even though our retention rates are high."

So why does Marriott continue the Pathways to Independence program? Because, Tully says, "We think it has value. You have to realize we started this program eight years before welfare-to-work was popular. We are committed to it and that commitment comes from the top down. Mr. Marriott himself is strongly in favor of this program."

Among the biggest rewards of working with Pathways graduates, says Tully, is seeing how they progress professionally and personally: "After our six-week training session we have a graduation ceremony. In many cases, these are people who, when they first come into the program, you can't even get eye contact out of them—they're practically under the tables hiding. Six weeks later, they are up on a stage, behind a podium and microphone, some of them singing and praying. To me, the things they say are so eloquent in their simplicity. I still get goose bumps when I think of this one woman who came up and said, 'I'm so happy. My daughter went to school today and told her friends that her mommy went to work today. That makes me so proud. Christmas is coming, and I'm going to buy her presents with money I made myself.' There is never a dry eye in the house after one of those graduation ceremo-

"I've seen the way that working has changed my children's opinions about me and themselves."

nies. And that's when we see the tremendous impact that our program is having." ERIC BROWN, 33, GRADuated from the Pathways program in April and is now a painter's helper at an Arlington, Virginia, Marriott. He had been receiving food stamps for about four months before entering the program and was living at a government-run homeless shelter in Washington, D.C., where he was in treatment for drug abuse. He now lives in a recovery house with seven other former addicts and says he has gotten his life on the right track for the first time in many years.

"To be honest, the money was important to me, but not as important as the self-esteem," says Brown. "I had been doing drugs for a long period of time, and I really needed to establish some things and get some accomplishments under my belt. I needed to feel like I was part of society again. Now, I have a lot of plans running around in my head about what I would like to do with my life and what my long-term goals should be. Before, I had no long-term goals and actually very few short-term goals."

Although he kicked his drug habit before coming to Marriott, Brown argues that "the work atmosphere helped me to stay clean. It reinforced the type of things I learned in treatment."

All 12 students in Eric Brown's class graduated, and 11 are still with Marriott—including Katrina Glover, a mother of two who had been on public assistance for two years before being admitted to the Pathways program. Glover now works in a Marriott kitchen. When asked how long she intends to stay at Marriott, she responds, "Oh, until about retirement time. I work with the chefs in the kitchen, and I tell them to watch out because I'm looking to take their jobs." Glover says that child care was a serious concern for her when she started the Pathways program, but she has worked out a suitable arrangement with a cousin.

Glover has relatives who are still on welfare. "I tell my sister that getting a job is something that you need to do for yourself and your children. Because I've seen the way that working has changed my children's opinions about me and themselves. My sister's told me that there are no jobs out there. But there are—you just have to want to do it. You have to want to do something and take control of your life. There's nothing free in this world."

Boscart Construction, located in Washington, D.C., began hiring welfare recipients for two reasons, says owner Barbara Turner. She needed unskilled workers. And, "as an African-American woman in a non-traditional industry, and as someone who was poor growing up, I've always felt that there's a real need for all of us to give back and help others." Five of Boscart's 22 employees are former welfare recipients, including her superintendent.

But Turner has also encountered some problems recently. "We're finding that a lot of people are not ready for the workforce. It's almost like the people who came to us early on were really the cream of the crop. And I think now we're reaching into that bottom two-thirds and Lord knows what we're going to find when we reach the very bottom. The bottom two-thirds realize that they're going to have to work, but I'm not sure that they understand what it really means to work." Turner says that earlier this fall her company interviewed a father of two who had been on welfare and was excited about the prospects of returning to the workplace. She hired him. "But the day before he was supposed to start, he paged my foreman and said that he couldn't make it for his first day of work. So my foreman told him, 'Well, I don't think you need to bother showing up any other day either.'"

Turner's sentiment is echoed by others. Janet Tully of Marriott argues that "the top 25 percent are employable, have been in and out of the system before, and will find jobs. Then there's the next 25 percent who have more difficulties. With effort, they can be employed. But, no question, there's that bottom 50 percent, and I don't know what's going to happen to them. They scare me. They are people who, under no circumstances, is any employer going to work with. You couldn't pay me enough to make me deal with those people." Several observers suggest that eventually there will have to be a second stage of welfare reform that deals with recipients with extreme problems.

One of the most important long-term solutions will be to change people's attitudes about being on the dole. Shirley Riley, who along with her husband and several of her children owns and runs the Nursery Hut, a day-care center in Washington, D.C., recalls that her mother received welfare payments for a short time after her father developed a drinking problem. But "she didn't stay on it for long. I respected what my mom was able to do, and I learned a lot from it. I never wanted my life to be run by the government. Even after my first husband was stabbed to death I never thought about going on public assistance."

"Helping people to find jobs is not going to be good enough," Riley argues. "We're going to have to change the attitudes of people, particularly young people. Because you have to understand that a lot of young people—kids 15 or 16 years old—who are getting ready to enter the workplace have never really been around people who have worked. A lot of times they haven't been around their fathers—or don't even know who they are—and their mothers have always been on welfare."

Riley has hired several former welfare recipients, provides free day care to people who are trying to leave the welfare rolls, and has set up her own non-profit group to run adult literacy and job-training classes and provide counseling to teenage parents and victims of child abuse. She has also recruited more than 50 Washington-area businesses into the Welfare to Work Partnership. "I have dreams for bigger and better things. You know, when you get to be almost 60, you start having dreams. I'm committed. I believe in this cause."

IF THE WELFARE-TO-WORK movement is successful, it will be due largely to the work of companies like ARAMARK, who have gotten involved because of tight labor markets and "enlightened self-interest." But it will also take the efforts of people like Shirley Riley—who want to work against the destruction the welfare state has wreaked on America's inner cities. "We need to teach people that life's possibilities are endless," says Riley, "that they need to do things for themselves. And they will be happier if they do."

Welfare's fatal attraction

JAMES L. PAYNE

W HEN President Clinton signed legislation ending "welfare as we know it," neither he nor the nation seemed to realize that this was business as usual. For nearly two centuries, policy makers have tried to reform unsound welfare systems. In 1834, the English undertook a sweeping reform of the old Elizabethan Poor Law System, an arrangement that taxed working people to give generous welfare benefits to the idle. The 1834 reform cut the welfare rolls, but not permanently. By the 1850s, benefits were re-liberalized, and dependency climbed back to previous levels. Reformers tightened requirements again; by 1890, caseloads were down, only to be followed by a new wave of welfare programs.

In New York City in the 1860s, a generous public dole gave rise, as newspaperman Horace Greeley complained, to a "very numerous and remarkably impudent" class of "thriftless vagabonds." Policy makers, concerned about the way the handouts were "pauperizing" the lower classes, abolished general assistance. Their efforts were only temporarily successful, however. At the turn of the century, New York added new assistance programs—fast becoming the welfare capital of America.

In 1981, Congress and the Reagan administration made an effort to contain a soaring Food Stamp program.

When originally proposed in 1963, the program was intended to serve four million beneficiaries. By the early 1980s, it had grown to 21 million. The 1981 reforms helped trim the rolls, to 19 million in 1988, but the effect was temporary. New legislation dropped restrictions and added new benefits, so that by 1995 the number of beneficiaries had climbed to 27 million.

It seems that however serious the effort at reform, welfare with all its flaws keeps coming back. If reformers are to have any real success curtailing welfare, they must understand what lies behind this futile cycle; and they will need to develop ways to break it.

Good kings and good fairies

Let's look first at the state of mind that keeps bringing welfare programs back. From a distance, the problems of the poor appear transparently simple. Give them what they lack—food, housing, money, clothing—and you have solved their difficulty. Storytellers have made this point for centuries: Good kings and good fairies transform the lives of poor people by giving them wealth. When we first come upon it, a government welfare system looks rather like a morality play performed on a

Reprinted with permission of the author from *The Public Interest*, No. 130, Winter 1998, pp. 126-133. © 1998 by National Affairs, Inc.

distant stage. A simple question is posed for the audience: Should the king—or senators and representatives—give to the poor? The audience knows nothing about the poor, and it assumes that the funds to be given to them are merely stage money supplied from an inexhaustible source. Naturally, therefore, the first impulse is to shout, "Give, give!" Sometimes, an actor—conventionally dressed in black—enters the scene and says, "Don't give." He must be evil, the audience reasons, to refuse to give the poor what they want and need.

For many liberals, this is all the welfare debate involves. They reacted to the 1996 welfare reform legislation, which cuts some benefits for some recipients, as if it were a simple morality play. "Where is the sense of decency," asked Democratic congressman John Lewis. "This bill is mean. It is base. It is downright lowdown." Conservatives think this rhetoric is demagogic, a hypocritical ploy to get media attention. Actually, it is mainly sincere. Many on the left never get beyond that first impulse to suppose that giving things to the poor is the right thing to do.

A longer, more sophisticated view, one that includes the indirect consequences of welfare programs, reveals why giving things to the poor is unfair and, in many cases, harmful.

1. The incapacitation effect. Need is a powerful stimulus to industry, one that government largess inevitably undermines. Payments for unemployment can slacken the desire for work; payments for disability can weaken the motivation to overcome the disability; food stamps can keep people from learning how to feed themselves. Welfare renders the recipient idle, leading to low self-esteem, depression, and self-destructive vices. In other words, though welfare ameliorates physical need, it breeds social and moral pathology.

2. The aggravation effect. Giving material aid to compensate for dysfunctional behavior will encourage more individuals to engage in that behavior, with the result that the need for assistance continues to mount. The aggravation effect explains why the $5.4 trillion war on poverty did not solve the problems of the poor, as it was expected to, but actually triggered an increase in the social dysfunctions of poverty.

3. The exploitation effect. Any tax-funded welfare system involves unfairness. It will force many needy people who are taxpayers to give funds to less needy recipients; and it will force responsible taxpayers to give benefits to many irresponsible claimants. Much of the unfairness is the result of the fraud and misrepresentation that are so widespread in government welfare programs. But much of it is perfectly legal, the inevitable consequence of programs that relieve needs without asking about deserts. Thus a hardworking single mother is forced to pay benefits to a non-working single mother on welfare.

We are all welfare spenders

These arguments against welfare are not unknown. They are in the back of most people's minds when they express skepticism about welfare. But people are also affected by that first, primitive impulse to suppose that giving things to needy people is the way to help them. The result is a schizophrenic public opinion. In 1994, the National Opinion Research Center asked a national sample whether we were "spending too much, too little, or about the right amount on welfare." Sixty percent said "too much" and only 16 percent said "too little." Then the same respondents were asked the same question, except that the phrase "assistance for the poor" was substituted for "welfare." The percentages reversed: only 15 percent said "too much" and 57 percent said "too little."

The upshot: Specific assistance programs will tend to have popular support. Americans may be "against welfare" in general, but, when it comes to job training for the poor, or medical care for those who can't afford it, or rehabilitation for addicts and alcoholics, or training for disadvantaged youths, or day care for single moms, they adopt the morality-play perspective. And they hiss at any black-coated congressman who recommends cutting aid to the poor.

In this context, attempting to check the growth of welfare spending becomes a thankless political task—as Republicans have found out on more than one occasion. Their effort in 1995 to hold down the rate of increase in spending for the school-lunch program to only 4.5 percent illustrates the pattern. The welfare lobby accused them of "punishing children," and President Clinton made electoral hay declaring, "We have to give our children more support so they can make the most of their own lives."

In any case, Republicans are not, in their heart of hearts, welfare cutters. They are somewhat more aware of the harmful effects of welfare than liberals, but like everyone, they have succumbed to the idea that giving things to the poor is the nice thing to do. Their aim in reforming welfare programs is simply to curtail the worst abuses. When accused of making cuts, Republicans don't proudly defend the idea of eliminating welfare programs, citing the incapacitation, aggravation, and exploitation effects. To the contrary, they take credit for expanding welfare programs.

This pattern was evident throughout the Reagan administration. When, in 1988, Edward Kennedy and other liberals accused the administration of "unconscionable budget cuts" in federal food assistance, the administrator of the Food and Nutrition Service accepted his premise—that nice people spend more on food programs—and simply disputed the senator's facts. "Readers should know," she wrote in a letter to the *New York Times*, "that our annual $20.5 billion food assistance budget is the highest ever, $6.2 billion higher than in 1980." When *Time* magazine claimed that "subsidized housing has been slashed 77 percent," Reagan's housing secretary said, "Wrong; it has been doubled." He never suggested that this was bad: He assumed, with everyone else, that virtue lay in spending the greatest possible amount of money on housing for the poor.

The 1996 welfare reform did not change the pattern. When Republican leaders met the press after the measure was passed, they did not emphasize cuts but the assistance they were providing. Newt Gingrich hailed the measure as a bill that would "dramatically help young Americans to have a chance to rise and to do better." And he took credit for boosting spending: "I also believe the additional money that was put in for child care is very, very important, and the fact is I think we have about a billion dollars more in child care than the President asked for."

In that same press conference, Congressman John Kasich, chairman of the Budget Committee and a principal architect of the reform, expressed the approach to welfare that has dominated policy for the past century, a view shared by the Left and the Right. "The American people feel fundamentally that if somebody's disabled, we're going to help him. But if somebody's able-bodied and can work, then they need to go to work." This position, that government should help those who need help but not those who don't need it, seems at first glance sensible and balanced. But it is without foundation, for there is no clear distinction between those who need help and those who don't. We all face some kind of limitation, some kind of physical, mental, social, or environmental deficit. There is no place you can draw the line. Since pressure groups and bureaucracies have a vested interest in seeking out and dramatizing our bad breaks, lacks, and needs, there will never be a shortage of proposed programs to meet these needs. If you start out saying government is going to take care of people with some kind of disability or disadvantage, you end up with a perpetually growing welfare state.

Three alternatives

The mistake, then, is the premise that government should help people who need help. No welfare reform can succeed in the long run unless this assumption is rejected. It will not be rejected, however, unless alternatives to government aid are clearly visible. It's no good proving that government programs are wasteful, unfair, and harmful, and then cutting them. On the very next day, the morality play starts all over again, and the crowd clamors for more aid to the poor.

But we may be closer to a change in perspectives than is generally realized. The frustration with existing welfare programs has reached unprecedented levels. Even officials who built and directed the existing system are now saying, "I hate welfare." The disappointment is causing much serious rethinking, especially among pol-

icy makers who are exploring plausible alternatives to government aid. The first one is the idea that the needy should help themselves. Many are now saying that, until the poor have seriously tried to find jobs on their own, government aid isn't merited. The idea of including work requirements in welfare legislation goes back many decades, but for a long time it was little more than window dressing. In recent years, however, lawmakers have taken this idea more seriously, and it is now a key point in many federal, state, and local welfare plans. As of December 1996, over 8,000 recipients in 14 states had been removed from AFDC rolls because they had failed to comply with state work requirements.

A second alternative to government aid is the idea that private charitable groups can help the poor. The public was made aware of this possibility in 1994 when Gingrich popularized Marvin Olasky's book, *The Tragedy of American Compassion*. Olasky showed how a vast array of private organizations helped the poor in the nineteenth century; Gingrich and other leaders pointed out that they could play this role again. Though strongly resisted by the Left, the idea continues to gain popularity, as evidenced by the April 1997 Presidents' Summit that focused on how private voluntary organizations can help America's youth.

A third alternative to government action is one that has received less attention, but it is probably the most persuasive of all. This is the idea that family members should be responsible for helping the needy. In the past, the American welfare system has ignored family responsibilities. In program after program, the applicant is assumed to be alone. Policy doesn't have to work this way. In Japan, where the proportion of citizens on welfare is less than one-tenth of the U.S. figure, welfare applicants are obliged to seek help from their families before turning to government aid.

Such a "family first" approach to welfare would not make taxpayers help someone unless family members are already doing their utmost. Of course, it is possible in a particular case that no suitable sources of family aid exist, and then there is a role for public or private charity. Today, in contrast, the welfare office takes care of you when your sister throws you out for getting drunk. Such well-intentioned government intervention undermines the efforts of family members to improve the behavior of their relatives. It should be the other way around. Instead of saying, "Here's free food and a free apartment," the social worker should say, "Go back and apologize to your sister."

Recent welfare reforms have started to include the role of family members, but we have not stressed the philosophical reason for doing so. In chasing deadbeat dads, for example, the main justification given is to extract money to ease the state's welfare budget. The aim should be much larger: to make it clear that the proper source of support for a mother with a newborn child is the father and other family members. Similarly, in denying aid to aliens, the state should emphasize that new arrivals have family members whose responsibility it is to support them. Today, reporters blame Congress for not giving aid to immigrants. Under a family-first policy, they would interview immigrants' relatives, and ask them why they were not doing more to help out.

Winning the argument

Star Parker is a black former welfare recipient who now speaks out for family values and against welfare. She went on the Oprah Winfrey show in April 1995 to confront two welfare recipients, an episode she describes in her book *Pimps, Whores, and Welfare Brats*. She won the support of the audience at first by pointing to the unfairness of expecting taxpayers to support the irresponsible behavior of welfare recipients. But then Oprah weighed in. Pointing to Linda, one of the welfare moms, she asked, "Why must we have to see her in the street?"

"I felt a surge from the audience," reports Parker. "I sensed they were now getting behind Oprah. There was sympathy building up for these women." Parker had walked right into the welfare morality play and was about to be cast in the role of villain. But she changed the terms of the debate by bringing up family. "We don't have to see anyone in the streets," she said. Turning to Linda, she asked, "Linda, where's your mama?" The audience cheered. Linda replied in subdued tones, "My mother feels the same way you do." Then Star drove the point home. "Where are your cousins? Where's your auntie? Where are your brothers? They're comfortable with the system taking care of you?"

The American people don't like welfare, but they are going to keep coming back to it unless reformers present alternative ways of helping those in need. The most natural and compelling alternative to government assistance is help from family members. Only when the family is put at the center of the welfare drama will there be a real chance of "ending welfare as we know it."

Beyond the Welfare Clock

Time limits get a lot of attention, but it is sanctions for failing to live up to work requirements that are cutting the welfare rolls in a big way.

BY JONATHAN WALTERS

THE U.S. SENATORS who debated welfare reform two years ago didn't agree on the merits of the bill before them, but they were unanimous about one thing: It was an attempt at shock therapy. "A system that has failed in every single respect will now be thrown away," said New Mexico Republican Pete V. Domenici, "and we will start over." New York Democrat Daniel Patrick Moynihan didn't disagree about that. But the proposed law, he said, would be "the most brutal act of social policy we have known since Reconstruction."

Moynihan was referring specifically to the new time limits: 60 months of welfare payments—that was it for the recipient's life. But as he spoke, many states were writing their own provisions even tougher than the congressional ones. Florida went for a 24-month limit over any four-year period. Tennessee passed a law forcing recipients off the rolls anytime they had been there 18 months. The specifics varied from state to state, but the projected impact was the same everywhere: a drastic reduction or outright elimination of benefits long before the 60-month federal cutoff had ever been reached.

Three years later, the deadlines are here. In Tennessee, the first ones arrived a year ago. In the period since then, some 5,000 families there have run out of time. But the result hasn't exactly been what was predicted. "About 2,800 were exempt from the time limit, either because they are disabled or for other reasons," says Mike O'Hara, assistant commissioner for family assistance in

the Tennessee Human Services Division. "Of the remaining 2,200 cases, 1,400 have been extended for good cause, like illness or because they were cooperating in trying to find work." Which left 800, less than a fifth of those who had exhausted their benefits, who were actually cut off.

In Florida, where 1,000 families were on schedule to bump up against that state's 24-month limit on benefits on October 1, 1998, only 100 were actually dropped from the rolls. The others applied for and received benefit extensions, either due to hardship exemptions or the fact that they were cooperating in trying to find work but simply hadn't yet landed a job. On top of that, Florida had an even longer time limit—36 months—for long-term welfare recipients with poor job skills and little work experience.

Roughly the same scenario has unfolded in Connecticut, where welfare recipients started hitting that state's 21-month lifetime limit last fall. Of the roughly 23,000 who have used up their 21 months of benefits since time limits came into force in Connecticut, only around 500 have been dropped from the rolls, and those cases immediately become eligible for a state safety-net program that offers vouchers in lieu of cash payments.

Even staunch opponents of time limits such as Randy Albelda, a University of Massachusetts-Boston economics professor who has been tracking the impact of welfare reform, seem a little amazed by the Nutmeg

State's performance. "Connecticut just turned to mush," says Albelda.

So it would seem that the verdict is in: While time limits had the hard ring of tough love when states adopted them, hard-liners are becoming social softies when time runs out on recipients. Across the country, states are turning to a host of exemptions and extensions that are allowing thousands of cases to continue, a policy approach that would seem to render the threat of time limits almost meaningless.

That would be an easy conclusion to come to if it weren't for the indisputable fact that caseloads have been plummeting. Because of time limits, caseworkers and clients alike are getting the message that welfare is no longer forever. "Time limits take a very complicated message about new programs and new expectations and make it simple for both the client and the caseworker," says Toby Herr, executive director of Project Match, the ground-breaking welfare-to-work program first established to work with clients from Chicago's hard-case Cabrini-Green housing project in the early 1980s: " 'The clock is ticking, and you have X amount of time until you lose your grant' "

Some, like Jack Tweedie, who has been monitoring welfare reform for the National Conference of State Legislatures, believe that states aren't using time limits as a vehicle to close cases because the message is getting through. "Most of these time limits were adopted to enforce cooperation," says Tweedie. "So if a client is working or is

From *Governing*, April 1999, pp. 21-26. © 1999 by Jonathan Walters. Reprinted by permission.

looking for work, in most places they get an extension."

Tweedie's last point is central to the real reason why time limits have not been a huge issue so far: It's not so much that states haven't been tough about sticking with them; it's that, given the tremendous emphasis on work that is now central to almost every state welfare-reform program, most people are simply gone from the rolls long before they ever reach their limit, either because they've found jobs or because they have been sanctioned off welfare for failing to comply with work requirements.

"Time limits don't seem to be where the action's at, or to be the immediate cause of why people lose benefits," says Mark Greenberg, senior staff attorney for the Center on Law and Social Policy, a liberal think tank that has been critical of the 1996 welfare-reform measure. Where states have been tough is in enforcing work requirements, and in sanctioning those who fail to live up to them. "That's where we see lots of people losing benefits," says Greenberg.

Florida is a prime case in point. When the time-limit clock started ticking in October 1996, the state was carrying 150,000 cases, raising the specter of time-limit carnage come October 1998. But when the state's 24-month limit on benefits rolled around, an astounding 120,000 cases had already been closed: At a time when jobs are plentiful, Florida, like most states, has been insistent and consistent in signaling that welfare is now a two-way street and that to receive benefits, clients must look for and accept work. Such pacts are typically formalized through "personal responsibility agreements." Failure to live up to the conditions in those agreements invariably means an escalating series of sanctions, with 100 percent loss of benefits, known as a "full family sanction," for repeated non-compliance in most states.

And so Florida's version of work-first— its "Work and Gain Economic Self-sufficiency" (WAGES) program—has had the same impact as other similar state programs: huge numbers of clients off the rolls. Some found work, but some just never returned to the welfare office once the terms of the new deal had been explained to them.

It is through such immediate work requirements and sanction policies—as opposed to the somewhat distant threat of exhausted benefits due to time limits—that states have really sent the message that this time around, welfare reform is serious business. "This is a landmark shift in signalling, and the threat of sanctions has really gotten through to people, says Richard P. Nathan, director of the Rockefeller Institute of Government, which is studying the administrative response to welfare in 20 states.

While there is broad consensus that states and localities have indeed been fairly flex-

Off the Rolls

Change in welfare caseloads since enactment of the 1996 federal welfare reform law

Percent change in number of recipients of Temporary Aid to Needy Families benefits, August 1996 to September 1998

▨ Decrease of 50% or more	20% to 29% decrease
40% to 49% decrease	Decrease of less than 20%
30% to 39% decrease	

Source: U.S. Department of Health and Human Services

ible when it comes to time limits, state and local policy on sanctions is another story. Client advocates charge that in some places sanctions are being used in an overly aggressive and punitive fashion. There is also anecdotal evidence that in many local welfare offices, caseworkers aren't doing a very good job of "signalling" to clients the bottom-line consequences of not living up to the new welfare-for-work equation or helping them get ready for and find work.

In Colorado, for example, a class-action suit filed against Denver and Adams counties charges that local officials have been unlawfully sanctioning clients in an overly aggressive effort to cut welfare rolls. New York City was recently slapped with a court order putting a hold on reorganization of its welfare system because judges ruled that city officials were actively discouraging applicants from signing up for any benefits—food stamps, Medicaid or cash assistance—as part of its conversion of "income support centers" into "job centers." In Arizona, which has been using sanctions to close a hefty 500 cases a month, field researchers with the Rockefeller Institute say caseworkers aren't doing a good job of communicating to clients the new expectations of welfare for work, perhaps in part because in Arizona there has been an old-style emphasis on tightening up error rates on food stamp eligibility rather than a new-style emphasis on

helping clients find jobs. "In some states, it's just the same old bureaucracy with new rules," says Tom Gais, who is heading up the Rockefeller Institute study, "and that can be a bad combination."

It was inevitable, of course, that some states and localities would use the newfound flexibility handed to them under federal welfare reform to cut rolls more aggressively than might have been intended by reformers. It was also inevitable that in some states and localities, government's performance in implementing the new regimen would be uneven.

But clearly, sanctions have become a centerpiece of welfare reform in most places, regardless of how judiciously they are administered or how well they are explained to clients by caseworkers. According to an Urban Institute analysis of state welfare policy in the wake of federal reform, 36 states have adopted full family sanctions for repeated failure to comply with work requirements. Under a full sanction, families lose 100 percent of their cash benefit, rather than just the amount apportioned to adults. In most states, families that come back into compliance are once again eligible for benefits. Seven states, however, have lifetime bans for repeat offenders, according to the Urban Institute study.

Welfare People

Percentage of U.S. population on welfare, 1960-98

6.0%
5.5
5.0
4.5
4.0
3.5
3.0
2.5
2.0
1.5
1.0
0.5
0.0

'60 '61 '62 '63 '64 '65 '66 '67 '68 '69 '70 '71 '72 '73 '74 '75 '76 '77 '78 '79 '80 '81 '82 '83 '84 '85 '86 '87 '88 '89 '90 '91 '92 '93 '94 '95 '96 '97 '98

Note: figures are for average monthly caseload; 1998 figure is as of September   Source: U.S. Department of Health and Human Services

Even as some states have been tough about sanctions, though, others have gone out of their way not to be. Rhode Island, which ranks 49th in closing cases, is emphasizing incentives rather than sanctions in its welfare-reform program. And in some states, caseworkers are concerned enough about the lifetime cutoff that they recommend to clients that they voluntarily leave welfare rather than suffer a lifetime sanction for noncompliance with work requirements. "Georgia has a lifetime ban on assistance once you've received a full set of sanctions," says LaDonna Pavetti, a senior researcher at Mathematica Policy Research Inc. who is studying state sanction policies. "The way some caseworkers handle that is they will call a client and ask them to either come in and comply with work requirements or voluntarily close their case."

But it isn't sanctions on active cases that have been the dramatic driver of tumbling welfare rolls. As was amply demonstrated in Florida—and in dozens of other states—it has been the closing of those cases where clients showed up for their initial post-welfare-reform interview and then just never came back. What nobody anticipated, say Pavetti and others on the welfare-reform front, was the huge number of people who would simply walk away from welfare upon learning about the new quid pro quo of work for benefits.

Since Durham County, North Carolina, started getting serious about workfare—which it did about 20 months ago—caseloads have tumbled 42 percent, says Dan Hudgins, the county's director of social services. Of the 3,500 cases that have been closed, Hudgins says 2,000 found jobs, but 1,500 simply took their entitlements—food stamps and Medicaid—and walked away from the $238 a month of cash assistance that now comes only with work.

What happens to people who just disappear like that? That's one of the major mysteries looming over sanctioning policies. Did they drop out because they decided "the juice wasn't worth the squeeze?" asks Linda Wolf, deputy director of the American Public Human Services Association (formerly the American Public Welfare Association). Or, she asks, "are they

the hard-to-serve, multi-problem, more-than-one-barrier-to-employment clients," individuals who are so disorganized or have such poor social and work skills that they simply gave up in the face of the new requirements? It's a mystery that many in the social services world aren't comfortable with. "Now that we've achieved the numbers that make us look good," says Dan Hudgins, "I want to know what we've really accomplished."

While dozens of states and localities are in the process of studying what happened to families that left welfare, so far only a handful have done any research that is considered statistically reliable. Indiana, South Carolina and Washington state found that more than 60 percent of those who left welfare voluntarily found work; in Maryland, it was 55 percent. Montgomery County, Ohio, reports that virtually all the 10,000 clients who have left the rolls since 1996 left to take jobs; the county knows this because it placed them all in jobs.

There are also states that have tried to track clients who were dropped from welfare because of time limits. A study done by the Massachusetts Department of Transitional Assistance of those who left welfare because they had exhausted their 24 months of benefits—more than 2,000 families—found that 75 percent were working an average of 28 hours a week at $7 an hour.

A similar study in Florida suggests, likewise, that most of those who use up their benefits are coping. "Things for this group in general are tough, but not catastrophic," says Don Winstead, head of welfare reform for Florida's Children and Families Department. "Lots of people had some other safeguard to fall back on, either extended family or they had kids receiving SSI or they had some other income." What was difficult to tell, though, says Winstead, "was whether

the people had other means and so decided to reach the end of their time limits or whether they reached the end of their time limit and then found other means."

Somewhat more troubling are the results of studies of those who were sanctioned off of welfare for failing to comply with or complete personal responsibility agreements. A New Jersey study found that only 30 percent had found jobs; in Tennessee it was 39 percent. A study of those sanctioned for non-compliance under Delaware's "Better Chance Program," done by Abt Associates Inc. for the Delaware Health and Social Services Department suggests that sanction rates do tend to be higher for clients who either don't understand the new work requirements or who can't comply due to other circumstances. The study also notes that "caseworkers may be varyingly effective in communicating program requirements and helping clients meet those requirements." The report noted substantial differences in

There is awareness that sanction policies need to be pursued with the same care as states have shown toward time limits.

local office sanction rates, even controlling for caseload composition. That would seem to support Rockefeller Institute field research findings that caseworkers do indeed have significant influence over how individual cases and overall sanction rates play out.

Given the preliminary nature of all such studies, it might be tempting to defer conclusions about the effectiveness of welfare time limits and sanctions pending further study. But more than two years into the welfare-reform experiment, there is actually quite a bit that officials do know.

Most fundamental is that the end of the cash assistance entitlement under the old federal Aid to Families with Dependent Children program, combined with the work requirements under the new federal program, Temporary Assistance for Needy Families, are at least having the intended effect of pushing people into work. In Connecticut, a Manpower Demonstration Research Corp. study comparing welfare recipients who continue to collect benefits under AFDC (part of continuing research under a waiver granted to Connecticut prior to passage of federal welfare reform) with those enrolled in Connecticut's new Temporary Family Assistance program found that 16 percent of those on AFDC find work compared with 50 percent for those enrolled in TFA.

While it is generally agreed that the new law deserves credit for inspiring unprecedented numbers of welfare recipients to go to work, there also seems to be a growing awareness that the sanction policies underpinning the work requirements need to be pursued with the same care that states have shown toward time limits. Few states seem interested in "turning to mush" on work requirements, but in the wake of such studies as that done in Delaware, more states have recently been opting for some intense intervention before slapping families with full sanctions for work-requirement non-compliance. In January, Tennessee announced a program that requires a thorough review of cases that are about to be closed for non-cooperation with work requirements. Montana has already instituted an internal review of cases about to receive a full family sanction. Arizona's Department of Economic Security is backing a legislative request for $3 million

to fund a program that would, likewise, provide for a formal review of cases about to suffer full sanction.

It is programs like those in Tennessee, Montana and Arizona that highlight the fundamental dilemma that is now being distilled out of welfare reform, a dilemma that grows increasingly pronounced as states and localities dig down into tougher-to-serve cases: how to work with a more entrenched and problem-plagued welfare population in a way that continues to signal that states and localities mean business when it comes to work requirements and time limits. "It's a difficult balance," says Project Match's Toby Herr. "Being tough while making exceptions."

In that regard, both the shorter state time limits on benefits and states' track record on sanctions have provided some valuable early lessons. And while states and localities have been working through those lessons, they also bear directly on future federal policy, which ultimately dictates time-limit and sanction policies for everybody.

Just as most states have taken less than a hard line on enforcing their own time limits, so might Congress choose to if cases start hitting the 60-month federal lifetime limit, especially if enough states appear to be struggling in meeting the more stringent federal work-participation requirements that arrive in 2002. Furthermore, Congress might have to consider adjusting what activities

meet the definition of "work" for the purposes of continuing eligibility. Currently, so-called "family-building" activities—those focused on adults doing things for their kids, such as enrolling them in special programs or after-school activities—don't count. Yet for very dysfunctional families or problem-plagued adults, that may be as much as government can reasonably expect. "We may have to create a modest package of activities for clients who might not be able to work but who are willing to help their kids," says Herr. "Maybe it's enrolling their kids in an asthma education course, or taking them to the Scouts, or enrolling them in Special Olympics." Montana has already adopted such alternatives for work requirements, which the state has been allowed to do based on a waiver granted pre-federal reform.

Looming over the whole experiment, of course, are the intertwined issues of the U.S. economy's health and its ability to spawn living-wage jobs. Any economic downturn—or widespread evidence that there aren't enough living-wage jobs to sustain families off of assistance—could also quickly put serious pressure on Washington to reconsider its trickle-down time-limit and sanction policies. And the lesson that Washington can take from states and localities as it considers any potential policy adjustments is straightforward: There has been merit in being firm, but also wisdom in being flexible.

Peter Edelman

Welfare and the "Third Way"

ROBERT KENNEDY was fond of this quote from Camus: "Perhaps we cannot make this a world in which children are no longer tortured. But at least we can reduce the number of children who are tortured."

In both the United States and Europe in the 1990s, we are told that the answer to such problems as the suffering of some of our children is a new politics that has been given the name of the Third Way. Championed by Bill Clinton and Tony Blair, it claims to be situated somewhere between old-style social democracy and neoliberalism.

The Third Way, we are told, involves the superiority of neither the government nor the corporate sector, but the partnership of both with a third force, civil society. The Third Way, we are told further, combines a belief in the dynamism of the free market with a commitment to social justice. A hallmark of that combination is said to be the end of entitlement politics, the end of people getting something for nothing, the end of the era in which rights exist without corresponding responsibilities.

Those are not the exact words I would use to express my views, but they are not inconsistent with the social policies that I support for children and other vulnerable groups. I believe in the market economy, combined with whatever regulation is necessary to control its excesses. I believe in social justice and in an important role for civic institutions. In fact, I believe very strongly in the importance of a civic commitment in every community to work to cut off poverty at its roots. And I believe in personal responsibility, although I believe also that the idea of "no rights without responsibility" ought to apply to everyone in society and not just the poor.

The problem is that, for many proponents of the Third Way in the United States, the words do not mean what I have just interpreted them to mean. The Third Way turns out to mean not a genuine three-way partnership and division of responsibility, but abdication of governmental responsibility to an amorphous group of people and institutions in the private sector. The social justice envisaged by Third Way proponents turns out to be a matter of the largesse of private actors. The personal responsibility that the Third Way calls for turns out to be the responsibility of the poor to behave themselves better, not a responsibility that extends across all the institutions of society. Corporations and wealthy individuals are still entitled to lobby the government for subsidies that seem startlingly like something for nothing, and nobody appears to have a responsibility to help the poor except the poor themselves. Third Way adherents in the United States might quote Camus approvingly, but their policy prescriptions seem more reminiscent of Anatole France's famous remark that the rich and poor have an equal right to sleep under a bridge.

America has never had a welfare state in the European sense. It has never offered a safety net that provides a baseline of income support, health coverage, and other assistance for everyone. America's safety net has always been a patchwork, providing benefits based on society's judgments about who is deserving and who is not. Even so, the radical right in the United States has been joined by a new constellation calling itself various names—the Third Way, the Democratic Leadership Council, the "blue dogs"—which has built a rather successful politics by attacking an American welfare state that never was.

This debate is hardly new. Conservatives have always attacked efforts to expand help for the poor and for the vulnerable by saying these were matters for which government had no responsibility. President Herbert Hoover said exactly that when the bonus marchers converged on Washington during the Great Depression. He was personally sympathetic, he said. The Red Cross should do everything it could to help, he said. But not the government. The New Deal ended the acceptability of that kind of thinking. At least we thought

Originally appeared in *Dissent* magazine, Winter 1999, pp. 14-16. © 1999 by Dissent. Reprinted by permission.

so. In the prosperity of post–World War II America we thought it was just a matter of time before we would succeed in filling in the holes in our safety net. We would have national health insurance, seek full employment, and have truly comprehensive unemployment insurance for those who needed it. We would also have income support for everyone who needed it, especially children. Unfortunately, none of this came to pass.

W E DID make progress. The elderly, our most favored group, achieved national health insurance coverage in 1965, and their Social Security benefits were indexed to inflation in 1972. Once the poorest Americans, the elderly became less poor than the rest of America by 1982. The disabled received income protection in stages, together with legislative protection against discrimination in employment and accessibility to public accommodations. The working poor have come into vogue in recent years with a major expansion of a federal tax provision that adds to their income. The poor received an across-the-board income floor in the form of food stamps in the 1970s, and the welfare-poor and the disabled received health coverage in the 1960s, a program that in its total cost has become more expensive than any piece of the safety net except for Social Security. Low-income housing, assistance to the poor to help with the cost of heat and air-conditioning, extra educational help for poor children, grants for low-income people to go to college, and other programs fill out the picture.

The most controversial group over the past thirty years has been nondisabled people of working age, and especially those with children. Those without children were never eligible for federal benefits other than food stamps. Those with children—mainly unmarried women—had since 1935 been eligible for the program traditionally called welfare. It was never generous. Benefit levels were set by the states, and the federal government paid for a portion of the cost. In Mississippi the benefits have for years been 11 percent of the poverty line—with food stamps added in, 40 percent of the poverty line. The cost of the program to the federal government has always been well under 1 percent of the federal budget.

Before the 1960s, the states, especially in the South, generally gave welfare benefits to people they liked and not to people they didn't like. In the 1960s a combination of newly subsidized lawyers for the poor, Supreme Court decisions, and a militant movement of welfare recipients converted the program into the entitlement that federal law had always said it was but that everyone in authority had always ignored. A backlash began, with racial overtones. The program always helped African Americans disproportionately because the poor in America are disproportionately African American. But the myth developed that it was a majority-black program, and that welfare recipients were lazy and unwilling to work.

In fact, nobody liked welfare. Beneficiaries hated the way they were treated by the bureaucrats. Most of them would have preferred to work. The system didn't help people to become self-sufficient, there wasn't enough assistance to prevent people from having to go on welfare in the first place, and the benefits didn't get anybody out of poverty. And the right wing hated welfare for reasons I already have indicated.

Over the years there were bipartisan efforts to change the system. Richard Nixon actually proposed a guaranteed annual income. In the 1980s the states tried a number of experiments to make welfare more work oriented, and there was a modest federal reform in that direction in 1988. A genuinely good policy or a radically terrible policy would have required a massive change in the distribution of political power in Congress, and there was a deadlock in Congress—until the elections of 1994. Still, the radical conservative change represented by the 1996 so-called welfare reform would not have happened if America had not had a president who advocated a Third Way but engaged in a politics of personal political survival at any price. (Ironically, three of Clinton's most senior political advisers told him he would benefit politically by vetoing the legislation, but he was unwilling to chance even a relatively low political risk.)

I S THE 1996 law really that bad? Haven't over five million people left the welfare rolls since the peak caseload of 14.3 million adults and children combined was reached in 1993, over three million since the law was signed in 1996?

It is that bad. The numbers are correct, but they are also misleading. Real welfare reform would make sure people receive the help they need to get and keep jobs, and would provide a safety net for children. This law literally removed any obligation for any state to assist anyone, and installed a lifetime limit of five years for federally financed assistance to a family, regardless of whether there is a recession. A few states have pursued good policies, and a number are pursuing policies that are extremely punitive. If, at first glance, the picture doesn't look too bad, that is mainly because this is a time of prosperity. Even so, only 60 percent of those leaving the rolls are getting jobs, at best. Most of the rest have been forced off the rolls by punitive policies that sanction them for failure to comply with work rules and for other misbehavior, such as failure to show up for an appointment at the welfare office. We literally don't know what has happened to them. None of this is publicized by politicians taking credit for a great reform. When the time limits hit or a recession comes or if both occur together, we will be beset by very serious problems. The Third Way has ended "rights without responsibilities" by presenting the poor with a slogan in place of assistance: "Find a job."

Despite all this, welfare reform also creates new opportunities if our civic institutions, especially at the community level, can mobilize in response. This means business, labor unions, philanthropies, religious institutions, universities, nonprofit organizations—in short, everyone. Federal policies remain vital, but by themselves they are insufficient. And an activated civil society must be animated by a politics of economics. Over half the American people have lost economic ground during the past twenty-five years, while the top 20 percent have done very well and the top 1 percent extraordinarily well. We need a politics that addresses this inequality, that talks about a living wage for all (not just the poor), that makes issues of the widely shared health coverage, child care, housing, and educational needs of so many millions of people. And while we must still struggle against discrimination of all kinds, we need also to pare down the rough edges of identity politics so as to accentuate the unaddressed common interests that taken together could build a new majority.

America has always had strong civic institutions in its communities. Whatever the rhetoric of the "Third Way," liberals and progressives have been struggling for a long time to find the right balance between government and the private sector, between national policy and local initiative and control. What we need now is still the right balance; not just a clever repackaging.

PETER EDELMAN is former assistant secretary for health and human services in the Clinton administration. He now teaches at Georgetown University Law Center. This talk was given to the international seminar on the welfare state cosponsored by *Dissent* and its Italian sibling publication, *Reset*, in Abano Terme, Italy, in October 1998.

Left Behind

Everybody's leaving the welfare rolls—except Latinas

BY ALEXANDRA STARR

MARIA IS A SLIGHT, DIFFIDENT WOMAN WHO HAS floated on and off of welfare for the better part of a decade. A native of Guatemala, she has raised six children, survived an abusive marriage, and suffered from medical conditions ranging from hypertension to diabetes. For the past six months, she and her two elementary school-aged children have slept on the living room floor of her eldest daughter's one-bedroom apartment as Maria has conducted a disheartening job search. "There are two things I can do," Maria explains in Spanish as she fingers her wispy black hair. "Take care of kids or work as a housecleaner." She has papered local motels with applications, but the only position she could find was a babysitting job on Saturday mornings. "It doesn't cover anything," she says quietly.

Over the past five years, the nation's welfare rolls have plunged by about 40 percent. But the decline mostly reflects an exodus of white women from public assistance. Minorities have lagged behind, and Latinas like Maria are leaving at the slowest pace of all. While Hispanics are 11 percent of the population, they now account for 22 percent of welfare recipients. That's nearly double the level of a decade ago. And in areas with a heavy concentration of Hispanics, the numbers are much higher: In New York City, for example, Latinas outnumber white welfare mothers almost twelve to one.

These women are subject to much more stringent regulations than they were just a few years ago. The Personal Responsibility and Work Opportunity Act of 1996 did away with the federal entitlement to assistance. Now states parcel out welfare checks with strict work requirements attached. There is a five year lifetime limit on cash assistance, and with few exceptions, recipients must work after two years on the dole. States were required to reduce their caseloads by 25 percent last year, and another 25 percent in 2000. In order to meet those goals, caseworkers have put enormous pressure on their clients to find jobs. There are loopholes in the legislation, however, that could allow some recipients to stay on the rolls beyond the time limits. States can exempt 20 percent of their caseload from the five year cap. In addition, the welfare bill's restrictions apply only to the funds states receive from the federal government; once the five years

are up, welfare clients could continue to receive state money. In other words, the current restrictions allow for a residue of long-term public aid recipients.

Latinas will probably be disproportionately represented in this category. On virtually every predictor of gaining self-sufficiency, they are at the very bottom of the scale. According to a 1994 Census Bureau report, 64 percent of Hispanic welfare recipients did not finish high school, almost double the rate for white women on public assistance. In addition, nearly half of Latinas living in the United States are immigrants, and the vast majority speak poor English, disqualifying them from all but a handful of jobs. These women are also concentrated in inner cities, where employment is hard to come by. According to a report in *The New York Times*, competition is so fierce in some poor urban areas that supermarket managers can insist that even employees who bag groceries speak English.

Obviously, with their low levels of education and poor language skills, many Latinas would profit from employment training or literacy classes. But they are the women most likely to be shut out of existing programs. According to Community Voices Heard, a welfare advocacy group based in New York City, only 25 percent of Latinas on the dole have access to job placement and training services, compared with 40 percent of African American women. That's not just because most of those services aren't offered in Spanish. In many cases, Latinas can't even communicate with their caseworkers, who would refer them to programs.

Poor English proficiency isn't the only obstacle first generation Hispanics trip over in their effort to become self-sufficient. Hispanic culture is deeply conservative, and many Latinas cling to traditional views of motherhood. They are hesitant to leave their children, and voice doubts about their ability to measure up on the job. For now, many of these women have maintained their welfare eligibility by participating in state-sponsored workfare programs or providing constant proof they are job hunting. And as long as these women make a "good faith" effort to find work, most states probably will not cut them from public assistance.

That fact that Latinas are having trouble leaving the rolls isn't a good sign. Hispanics are the fastest growing minority in the United States, and they show indications of developing an underclass. Teenage Latinas have a high pregnancy rate and the highest high school drop-out rate of all major ethnic groups, which translates into a high likelihood of becoming welfare mothers themselves. Latinas earn the lowest salaries of all women workers. And as they labor in low skill jobs, or struggle to find employment, it seems increasingly unlikely they will pull their families into the economic mainstream. "Latinos already have the highest rate of poverty in the United States," says Ramona Hernandez of the University of Massachusetts at Boston. "I think that number is just going to keep going up."

apartments without speaking a word of English. And Adams Morgan is by no means an abnormality—swaths of cities across the country resemble transplanted slices of Latin America. Many Latinos ensconce themselves in the

> With their low levels of education and poor language skills, many Latinas would profit from employment training or literacy classes. But they are the women most likely to be shut out of existing programs.

Spanning Generations

Latinas on welfare are not a uniform group. They include teenagers and aging grandmothers; some are third generation Americans, others came to this country just a few years ago. "More recent immigrants have to deal with the language issue," says Minerva Delgado of the Puerto Rican Legal Defense Fund. "Second and third generation Latinas have their own set of problems. They have low levels of education and literacy, and bigger families. Finding work is challenging for them, too."

Diana Perez, a third generation Mexican American living in Chicago, can testify to some of those challenges. Perez is among the 30 percent of Latinas on welfare who have less than a ninth grade education. As the single mother of six children, child care is expensive and difficult to find. And like many Latinas, she has a spotty work history; after 25 years on the dole, her resume only lists a brief stint on an assembly line.

Perez is not a woman of immodest ambitions. "I want to work in an office," she says. "A place that is clean." But after two years of job hunting, she hasn't even been able to find work in a factory or on a cleaning crew. "It makes you feel like putting your head in a bucket," she says of her unsuccessful job search. "You feel like you are nothing." But despite the frustrations she's grappling with, Perez possesses an enormous advantage over many first generation Latinas: She speaks English. Women who can only chat in Spanish have trouble landing jobs at McDonald's. "It's the biggest barrier for women trying to leave public assistance," says Ramona Hernandez.

It's not just Central Americans fresh off of the boat whose English proficiency is limited to a handful of phrases. Many first generation Hispanics never become bilingual. Walk through the streets of Adams Morgan, in Washington, D.C., where wizened men hawk green plantains and salsa music pulses at full volume, and the reason becomes readily apparent. In this Havana-like environment, women can buy their groceries and rent

small radius of these barrios. That doesn't do much for their English skills. And most of these neighborhoods are located in inner cities, where jobs are difficult to find. These residents are also sealed off from networks that could inform them about work opportunities in surrounding areas.

Many immigrants are undocumented, a status that can lead to some unusual welfare cases. Women who enter the United States illegally can't go on the dole. But their children born in the United States are eligible for benefits. There are roughly 100,000 "child-only" immigrant cases in the United States, according to a spokesman for the Department of Health and Human Services. Many more families are eligible for government largesse, but shy away from applying for aid because they fear being deported. Those who do receive a welfare check through their children end up playing by different rules than direct recipients. Most significantly, they are exempt from the five year time restriction. By the same token, they can't enroll in job training or English classes. Without work papers or access to social services, these women are doubly dependent on public assistance. Freed from short time restrictions, many will rely on government charity until their children are no longer eligible.

Take a 24-year-old Salvadoran woman we'll call Lourdes. Lourdes immigrated to the United States eight years ago, and all three of her U.S.-born children are on the rolls. She briefly scrubbed toilets in an office building and found her salary barely covered her babysitting bills. Now she shares a one-bedroom apartment with six other people, putting out feelers to find work as a maid. Even if she did have a green card, it's hard to see what other jobs she's qualified for—her seven-year-old son has more formal education than she does. And because of her illegal status, she can't attend state-sponsored English classes or enroll in job training workshops. "The only way I could get papers is through a lawyer," she says almost inaudibly over the phone. "I can't pay for that."

Madres First

Scanty education, language barriers, and not-quite-above-board residency papers aren't the only stumbling blocks Latinas encounter as they attempt to move from welfare into work. Latin American culture is scarcely progressive, and many Hispanic women see their primary role as caretakers to their children. "The biggest issue in these women's lives is raising their children," says Tim Bell, coordinator of the adult education program at Erie Neighborhood House in Chicago. "They're being forced to take on an entirely new identity."

One of the thorniest issues all working parents have to confront is child care. For women raised to consider themselves *madres* first, spending time away from their kids can be particularly difficult. Latinas tend to have more children than white women, and they harbor a deep distrust of day care. A 1991 New York state study of female welfare recipients found that 75 percent of Hispanic mothers feared their children would be mistreated in day care, compared with 45 percent of non-Hispanic mothers. It's worth noting that most Latinas can only afford unlicensed day care, facilities that often run the gamut from terrible to mediocre. And in conversations with several women I got the impression they had all seen the same horror stories about deviant care givers on television. In any case, when they work, Hispanics generally have family members watch over their kids—an arrangement that may ease their consciences, but is far more unreliable.

Perhaps because so many Hispanic women primarily identify themselves as wives and mothers, they are less confident about what they can accomplish on the job. According to the New York study of public aid recipients, 45 percent of Hispanics on the dole feared they could not perform as well as others at work, compared with 26 percent of non-Hispanic women. That makes sense in the context of Latin culture. From a young age, women are barraged with the message that they must be deferential and self-sacrificing. Sociologist Evelyn Stevens dubbed the Hispanic image of the ideal woman *marianismo*—she postulates that the ultimate role model for Latinas is none other than the Virgin Mary herself. As psychologists Rosa Maria Gil and Carmen Inoa Vaszquez point out, the tenets of marianismo may make for accommodating housewives, but they don't mesh with the dictates of the workplace. "Can you imagine a list of attributes [like abnegation and submissiveness] in a resume, job description, or want ad?" they ask in *The Maria Paradox*.

Getting off of public assistance will require many Latinas to shake some of the most deeply held creeds of their culture. For that reason, public policy analysts say, it's important for social workers and teachers in job training programs to have a sense of the world Hispanics are coming from. But most social services not only flunk the "culturally sensitive test"—they are literally conducted in a different language. Fifty-seven percent of Spanish-speaking welfare recipients in Brooklyn and Queens cannot communicate with their case worker, according to Andrew Friedman of the welfare advocacy group Make the Road by Walking. Few states offer bilingual training

programs. There are private and community-based organizations across the country that provide training in Spanish. But since the national zeitgeist became "work first" with the overhaul of the welfare system, many women have been barred from these programs, too.

Shunted

Until a year ago, there was no limit on the length of time welfare mothers could take classes at the Chicago Commons Employment Training Center, which serves a predominately Latina clientele. Because women encounter different obstacles as they prepare for work, it didn't make sense to impose an arbitrary "one-size-fits-all" deadline, explains program director Jenny Wittner. "A lot of these women need an enormous amount of help to have a shot at a decent job," she says. A whopping 82 percent of the women have been in abusive relationships. Some students can't decipher the help wanted ads or balance a checkbook. And Hispanics who are illiterate in both Spanish and English often need months of language classes before they can function in even low-paying jobs, says Wittner. In part because the program was open-ended, Chicago Commons has posted a solid success rate: Four years after leaving the program, 63 percent of the women are still working.

When the welfare reform bill was passed in 1996, however, caseworkers began pulling their clients out of the Commons. It wasn't the caseworkers' fault, Wittner hastens to add. The legislation's strict requirements for caseload reduction have placed enormous pressure on social workers to shove women into jobs or short-term training programs. While Wittner cut the Commons' program down to six months, 12 of her students were forced to drop out in January alone. Wittner says service providers across the country are running into the same problem. "States are only allowing for two to three weeks of training," she says. "That just doesn't encompass enough time for learning."

Cristina di Meo of the Federation of Protestant Welfare Agencies says Latinas in New York City have seen their educational opportunities fall, too. Community based literacy classes in the City were once stuffed with welfare mothers trying to learn English, she says. That changed in 1997, when New York City instituted a "workfare" program which requires able bodied public aid recipients to work 35 hours a week in exchange for cash assistance. "Students have dropped out of English courses in droves in order to meet the workfare requirement," says di Meo. The only program open to Spanish-speakers now is a workfare arrangement providing English classes two days a week over six months. "It's inadequate," she says. "The students hardly learn any English at all."

Second generation Latinas seem to have more opportunities to get ahead in workfare programs. Bronx native Sandra Agront has been on the dole her entire life: Her mother raised seven children on public assistance, and Agront opened her own account when she had the first of her three kids at 18. Nine years later, the second-generation Puerto Rican is working and preparing to take the GED high-school equivalency test. In order to fulfill her workfare requirement, she watches over kids at a shelter. She enjoys spending time with children; her goal now is to become a teacher's assistant. Even if it were an option, she wouldn't want to go back to collecting a welfare check and spending long days watching soap operas. "I like what I'm doing," she says.

Agront is an example of what workfare can be under the best of circumstances. Enrolling in GED classes was the first step to realizing her aspiration of attending college, and her internship is at least linked to her career goals. But Agront's arrangement wasn't the product of considered state planning—instead, she seems to have chanced upon it. Her first workfare job was sweeping floors in a tenement. The job training program she attends in the Bronx generally requires students to enroll full-time; the directors have made exceptions for some workfare participants. She's also fortunate to have two family members who can watch her young kids. With her support network and some lucky placements, she has a good chance of becoming self-supporting over the long term.

That's not the case for many monolingual and poorly educated Hispanics. Without English and basic literacy classes, these women will have trouble finding even low-skill jobs. And if they are hired, not all of these positions will lead to long-term employment. Take Maria, the mother of six who is currently unemployed. The primary reason she's been on the dole four times is because most of her work experience consists of cleaning motel rooms: When tourist seasons draw to a close, a round of layoffs generally ensues, and she goes back on welfare. In addition, few "pink collar" jobs provide benefits. If workers or their children fall sick, many will go on public assistance to qualify for Medicaid. They will, of course, lose this safety net if states begin to strictly enforce time limits.

A Two-Way Street

That's why we should stop giving short shrift to training programs. Providing instruction need not rule out requiring women to work or perform community service. If programs were time-flexible and provided on-site child care, many women would find ways to juggle jobs and classes. And in order to steer women away from the revolving door of work to welfare, it makes sense to prepare them for skilled jobs that pay above the minimum

wage and provide benefits. "We've found that women who undergo vocational training have higher rates of job retention and more opportunities for advancement," says Wittner. "They have careers, not temporary jobs."

It's a challenge to persuade Latinas raised on a steady diet of *marianismo* to aspire to become electricians or weld-

---

"The biggest issue in these women's lives is raising their children," says Tim Bell. "They're being forced to take on an entirely new identity."

---

ers. Aside from their own cultural biases, these women face pressure from boyfriends, husbands, and parents to keep out of traditionally *macho* professions. As one woman put it, "[y]ou can bust your knees scrubbing floors, and they think that's much better than being a foreman at a construction job earning $20 an hour." But single Latina mothers have to put food on the table, and they want to do meaningful work. When they realize how much heftier the paychecks are for fixing cars rather than flipping burgers, many will abandon the values in which they were raised and train for traditionally male crafts.

These women will also have to accept the fact they cannot be stay-at-home parents. Many Latinas already understand this. "I can count on one hand the women who have told me they don't want to work," says Andrew Friedman. "These women want jobs." If Hispanics feel more comfortable leaving their kids with family members, we should respect that choice. But caseworkers and employers should also insist these mothers have back up plans for the days aunts and grandmothers do not come through. And we should assure the child care available is safe and affordable.

If we met these women half way, and provided them with the training they need to become self-sufficient, the vast majority of Latinas would rise to the challenge. Like most welfare recipients, they want to make their own decisions and provide their children with decent upbringings. But we are not meeting these women half way. Quite the opposite; we are actually cutting them off from the few comprehensive training programs that are open to them. And with the rules rigged this way, most service providers are pessimistic about the prospects for indigent Hispanics. "These women are going to end up in low-paying, low skill jobs," warns Tim Bell, director of adult education at Erie House. "Their kids will grow up on the street. And believe me, we will pay a price for it."

Three years ago, Mary Ann Moore was on the cover of
this magazine—as a welfare-reform heroine. Her life since then
is a cautionary tale for those who think that simply
cutting the rolls will transform lives in the big-city ghettos.

Welfare to Work: A Sequel

By Jason DeParle

AT 7:30 ON A NOVEMBER SCHOOL MORNING, THE TWINS FINALLY STIR.
They tumble off the couch in the kindergarten outfits they
have worn for 24 hours and pad down the hall, all whis-
pers and giggles. They turn the bathroom sink into a balance beam and dangle themselves from the shower rod.
They paint luncheon meat with stripes of mayonnaise to
make breadless breakfast sandwiches. What they cannot
do is rouse their mother, who remains slumped on the
couch with a worrisome case of depression and a lapsed
prescription for Prozac.

"Fifteen minutes, skinny little girl," she says to a tap
on her shoulder. "I ain't ready to get up." The tap continues, and her voice sharpens: "Girl! Would you stop!"

The apartment looks like a thrift shop hit by a cyclone.
A month of dirty laundry sits stuffed in plastic bags and
a week's dishes are scattered around the kitchen. The
blinds are drawn, the room is dark and when Mary Ann
Moore opens her eyes, she peers out with a cracked gaze.

By 8:15, she pulls herself up to brush her daughters'
hair. By 8:30, she orders them into their coats and points
them toward the door. "Bye, you little smookers—I love
you," she says, on her feet for a goodbye kiss. She watches
from the window until they reach the Chicago schoolyard
and returns for a day on the couch.

Jason DeParle is a staff writer for the Magazine.

Three years ago, she was beating the sunlight to the
streets. She was up at 3:30 A.M. the first time I visited
her, snapping on lights and bundling up children. She was
out the door at 5 and on the job, as a cook, by 6. Her
car scarcely worked; the twins' father felt neglected, and
the routine left her bone-tired. But after 14 years of public
aid, she had kept the job for nearly a year and talked of
escaping to the suburbs.

Now even she has a hard time explaining her tailspin
into homelessness and addiction. Perhaps the depression
keyed her drug relapse; certainly the relapse deepened
her depression. Three years after starring as a welfare-to-
work heroine, Moore is back among the 2,000 welfare
families living in and around the public-housing high-rises
of Cabrini-Green.

Impressed by the recent caseload declines, much of the
country has already declared last Washington's monumen-
tal welfare overhaul a success. But the new system has
barely begun to grapple with the Mary Ann Moores—the
one or two million long-term recipients who pose the
greatest challenge. For all the drama of last year's debate,
welfare is mostly a proxy for a far larger problem: the
condition of the central cities. There are more people on
welfare in Chicago alone than there are among the combined populations of Alaska, Delaware, Idaho, Kansas,
Montana, Nebraska, Nevada, New Hampshire, North Dakota, South Dakota, Utah, Vermont and Wyoming. There

are nearly as many welfare families in Cabrini-Green as there are in all of Wyoming.

Last year's debate brought extravagant claims on all sides about what time limits and work requirements would mean in these neighborhoods. Bemoaning the "stereotypes," one side argued that long-term welfare recipients were basically like everyone else—just less lucky. Then it argued that new restrictions might cause children to starve. The other side warned of a welfare underclass so dysfunctional it posed a threat to civilization. Then it supposed that a legal finger snap would prompt the poor to stand up and prosper.

After spending a week with Moore, and piecing together her fall, it seems safe to say three things: She and many people around her very much need help. The old system wasn't providing it. To do better, the country will have to do far more than celebrate caseload declines.

"IT'S LIKE I WENT THROUGH A DEPRESSIVE STAGE," MOORE SAYS, HER face puffy with fatigue. She is picking at a diner omelet and trying to explain what went wrong. Depression, drugs, a tangled life with an unemployed man—Moore is talking about herself. But she is also describing the troubled landscape in which the new welfare programs will try to take root. She is mapping an ecosystem of inner-city defeat. What's missing is the spirited, self-mocking humor that used to abound despite the unhappy basics of her life: a childhood in Cabrini without a father; no high-school degree; four children by three men; dozens of jobs, and eventually an addiction to crack. Her mood swings could be biological, of course. Or they could be rooted in the violence that has saturated her life. (She saw her first neighborhood shooting when she was 8.) A doctor recommended an antidepressant a decade ago, but Moore, who is now 36, says, "I thought it was for crazy people or something."

Examined in psychological terms, her staccato bursts of work seem less a plan for self-support than an expression of underlying mania—the mirror image of her current, depleted self. In the fall of 1994, Moore worked her kitchen job for stretches of two weeks at a time. She never went to bed; she had no bed. Then as now, she catnapped through the night on a living-room couch. "I'm depressed when I'm not doing something," she says.

At times, her mood swung around Michael, the father of the young twins. When I first visited in 1994 his place in her life was unclear. He was a handsome, articulate man in his mid-40's who had worked in a steel mill before he developed a cocaine habit. They met at a party where Moore had gotten high, and they conceived the twins that night. They reunited two years later, after Moore had finished a drug treatment program, when they happened to be staying at the same shelter. Outwardly, she rolled her eyes at his love poems and his roses. But she also kept him around.

The role of the men is one of the great missing elements of the welfare debate. Like many women leaving welfare

for work, Moore had to contend with a man who felt left behind. Michael beseeched her to work less, and told her that her emotional neglect had pushed him to a relapse. When a relative of Moore's moved in with a crack problem of his own, the household was poised for a fall. Mary Anne was home one afternoon with a stomach virus when she awoke to a familiar smell. The pipe passed into her hands, and in just a few weeks, her job was gone, food was scarce and dealers were banging on the door to collect. "It got bad," she says. "It got real bad." It took her teen-age son, Marchello, to summon a posse of relatives to put the addicted men out. Moore says she later found powders, leaves and "something like an eyeball in a little, bitty medicine jar" that convinced her Michael had harmed her with voodoo. "Every time I tell somebody that, they think I'm crazy," she says.

Whether by black magic or bad judgment, Moore virtually collapsed. Marchello, who is now 17, escaped on a scholarship to a boarding school in Colorado. She sent her other son, Omotunde, now 8, to live with his father. And for most of the next two years, Moore and the girls, Roshea and Roshaun, became inner-city nomads. They slept on a couch in the overcrowded apartment that belongs to Moore's mother, and sublet rooms from Cabrini addicts for $100 a month.

Amazingly enough, throughout this time Moore mostly stayed employed. Her mother is a tenant manager in Cabrini, and when all else fails Moore signs on as a security guard. (In that job and others, she has rarely earned enough to leave welfare; over the last 10 years, she has received some cash aid in all but eight months.) Some theorists argue that work is a reforming force in itself: a bond to a larger community that brings meaning and purpose to life. Moore accepts this idea—she feels better about herself when she works. But a job alone has never been enough to rescue her. "We'd get our paychecks, buy food, go off on a binge and go back to work two days later," she said.

WHEN HELP FINALLY CAME, IT DID NOT COME FROM THE WELFARE DE- partment, which simply mailed a monthly check. Years earlier, Moore had joined a Salvation Army program for homeless women and children, and the social workers there went to extraordinary efforts to stay in touch. Often unable to reach her by phone, they would show up at Cabrini with baskets of food; they once talked their way in to see her in the middle of a gang shooting. Their files reveal a sustained, personal relationship almost unheard of in the public realm: "She was supposed to work yesterday but the depression came over her. . . . There has been gang fighting going on all morning and it is getting on her nerves. . . . She had a lot of clothes over at L.'s house. . . . She left there because he was starting to want sex from her. . . . They are not eating well since MA did not get paid this week."

By contrast, Moore's welfare file looks like a work sheet at H&R Block: it is choked with the arithmetic of grant calculation and devoid of any other insight. The Salvation Army workers have college degrees and six to eight clients at a time. Half of the welfare workers are high-school graduates and they carry caseloads of 180. They are the ones, as Illinois phases in the new welfare rules, who are expected to take charge of the nation's toughest social problems.

In the end, the Salvation Army all but dragged Moore back into drug treatment. Arriving there with the recidivist's shame, she wrote angry diatribes at herself. ("A supit fool. Thinking I alright because I have a job. when in fact I was working for the dope.") She also wrote apologetic letters to her family and friends, many of which lie unmailed at the bottom of her closet.

One is addressed to Toby Herr. At 54, Herr is a nervous, talky, leaf-thin woman whose prominence in the welfare world has surprised no one more than herself. Unlike her clients, she was raised in material security, but she describes her childhood as an 18-year panic attack. "When they called attendance in grammar school, I'd practice saying 'Here,' because I couldn't stand to hear my voice," she says. In 1968, Herr landed a job teaching grade school in Cabrini—hardly a haven for the emotionally fragile. But she felt as though she had found a home. "I could identify with low self-esteem," she says.

Three decades later, Herr may know as much as anyone of the dynamics between inner-city women and work. In 1985, she converted a dozen years of Cabrini experience, teaching and evaluating social services into a shoestring employment program called Project Match. At first it seemed remarkably easy: her first eight clients got hired. But most quickly quit or got fired. "The job loss was staggering," she says. Or as she put it, in what has become a maxim of the field, "Leaving welfare is a process, not an event."

Few people cover the pitfalls as encyclopedically as Moore, who joined Project Match in 1989 and raced through eight jobs in the first three years. She drove a delivery truck; peddled nuts; fried eggs, and guarded a parking lot. She quit because her car died and her baby sitter fell through; because her boyfriends were jealous and she wanted to get high. Because "I was young-minded." Because "I just got tired." Because "I just got depressed."

The job losses posed a question to Herr that the country now has to face: how to design an effective program when failure is so frequent? Herr tries to reduce the time spent between jobs. She tries to get clients to learn from mistakes, while celebrating the "incremental progress" that

even a short-lived job can represent. And she emphasizes a long-term relationship with clients that can unmask the underlying problems; Project Match helped Moore find her first treatment program.

The results look as good as any, but still the numbers are cautionary. Herr (with a research associate, Suzanne Wagner) has found that about 36 percent of her clients settle into stable employment within two years. Another 13 percent do so after a much longer period of spinning their wheels. That still means half either do no formal work (23 percent) or, like Moore, work intermittently but never stabilize (28 percent). "The question is, What do you do with this large group of moms who really don't function very well?" Herr says.

Last year, a Republican Congress and a Democratic President settled on an answer: time limits and work requirements. While most of her profession reacted with dismay, Herr has more complicated feelings. Thirty years in one of the nation's most blighted neighborhoods has convinced her that everyone can do something, even if it's just volunteering at a school. At the same time, she does not believe most Cabrini women can do what the law envisions: work full time while raising children.

> **The role of the men is one of the great missing elements of the welfare debate. Like many women leaving for work, Moore had to contend with the jealousies of an unemployed man who felt left behind.**

The law restricts most recipients to five years of Federal support in a lifetime. While states can grant extensions to 20 percent of their caseload, Herr thinks that won't be nearly enough. Her hope is that the law will serve as a sorting mechanism "to figure out who can do what"—who can work full time; who can work part time; who needs to mix volunteer work with drug or mental-health treatment. It is revealing that her mission statement says nothing of "self-sufficiency," the buzzword of the moment. It aims at "economic and social stability," a more important goal. "We're trying to get people's lives together, not just get them off of welfare," she says.

One question is whether her notion of flexible-but-rising expectations can find any political support. (Herr says it might if recipients seem to progress—a big if.) Another is whether caseworkers have the competence to formulate and enforce such individualized plans. And the country will still be left with a group—"and it's not a small group," Herr says—that cannot or will not comply. What to do then? It's easy to talk about orphanages. But as Herr notes, "Mary Ann, for all her shortcomings, has a very strong bond with her children." She may seem inadequate. She's also irreplaceable.

"We have no reason to believe a lot of pressure will push her forward, because it hasn't. But she *can* work.

She *does* work. She needs to be in a system where she's closely monitored.

"I'm furious at her and I'm crazy about her," Herr says. "She is everyone's concern."

AND SHE IS LYING ON THE COUCH IN THE EARLY EVENING WHEN JEAN knocks on the door. A thin, neatly dressed woman with watery eyes, Jean comes in, sits on the floor, smokes cigarettes and says that she has been through drug treatment six times. She has ostensibly come to help with the chores, since Moore's grandmother has just died. It also appears that she has no place else to spend the night. Moore never fully committed to the drug treatment program and left it in February without much of a plan. She moved to a shelter with the twins and mixed welfare with unemployment benefits. Her big break came in June when she landed a subsidized apartment in a private, well-guarded building a few blocks from Cabrini. It is her first home in nearly three years.

When I leave one morning last month, Moore is on the couch and Jean is in the kitchen, smoking. When I return in midafternoon, Moore smells like wine, and she volunteers that they've been drinking. When I pick her up for dinner, she meets me outside, and by now she is exploding with anger.

"I'm not stupid!" she says. "She's using me!"

She says the talk of chores was just a cover for an addict needing a place to stay. Moore's welfare payment had just arrived, and in her view, Jean borrowed the money and bought the bottle in the hope of igniting a binge. "She thought I'd have some wine and trigger off"— get high—"and just go spending money!"

"I'm vulnerable right now!" she says. "I'm grieving!"

In three years I've never seen her so upset. I'd known she was hurting when I came to Chicago, but I hadn't gauged the fullness of her pain and defeat. As we sit in the car, she rails at Jean and then she rails at herself: for her deficiencies as a worker, as a woman in recovery and as a parent. Then, oddly, she begins to apologize for a more obscure sin: her failure, three years ago, to thank the readers of the Magazine article who sent her money. She chooses this, of all times, to worry that she is not teaching her children to say thanks. "I didn't send a card or nothing!" she says. "It's hard to tell your kids things when you don't practice it."

Sitting beside this grief-stricken woman, the welfare debate seems far removed. Time limits, work requirements, bonuses to reduce out-of-wedlock births—the welfare bill is 250 pages of small print rooted in theories of cause and effect. Do this and the poor will do that. But Moore's life is guided by different physics: the constant collisions between the decency of her intentions and the depth of her wounds.

The discomforting truth about situations like this is that no one really knows what to do. Even in her crisis, Moore seems to suggest as much with a flash of self-awareness. "I said, 'Jean, I cannot help you, 'cause what I'm going through, I can't even help myself.'"

After I left there were a few more developments. Throughout our visit, I had noticed that Moore was talking about Michael in surprisingly nostalgic tones. ("He cared about me, but the way he cared—it was dangerous.") After a separation of three years, he began writing and calling again, and he was now disabled with kidney disease. His first visit came a week after I left. Moore played it down, but the reunion continued over subsequent days. About the same time, Herr spent half an hour waiting outside Moore's apartment. They were supposed to go get the Prozac refilled, but Moore never appeared. And with Michael disabled, it turns out that the twins now qualify for Social Security payments. Since the $594 total exceeds Moore's $485 welfare grant, her case has just closed. For her, at least, the great national welfare debate has just become a moot point. She is off the rolls, an addition to the celebrated statistics, and as much in need as ever.

TOUGHEST CASES

Now, the hard part of welfare reform

Rolls are falling, but now states must find a way to get the chronically dependent into jobs.

By Alexandra Marks
Staff writer of The Christian Science Monitor

NEW YORK — Douglas McWilliams is homeless and on welfare. He hasn't had a job for "eight or 10 years." He's been in and out of jail, his scarred hands have a slight shake, and he says he can't work right now because he broke two ribs during a fight.

"But I would like to work, if they get me a job," he says.

Mr. McWilliams, whose cash benefits have been cut back for failure to work, is one of hundreds of thousands of people caught up in New York City's controversial welfare-reform experiment. Conservatives praise it as one of the bolder efforts to transform a culture of dependency into one of self-reliance. To critics, the program here is a destructive bureaucratic exercise designed to cut welfare rolls — even at the expense of the most vulnerable poor people.

But both sides agree on one thing: The success or failure of New York City's program could help determine the direction welfare reform will take around the country.

"We've come a long distance, but we still have a long distance to go," says Barbara Blum of the Research Forum on Children, Families, and the New Federalism at Columbia University here. "We really haven't tackled the tougher cases, and that's when it's going to get complicated," she adds, referring to chronically dependent people like McWilliams.

So far, reform efforts have helped cut welfare rolls by almost 40 percent nationally during the past three years. Yet demand for emergency food services is up—dramatically in some cities—along with the need for shelters.

The national statistics also hide a wide variation in success rates among the states, according to a study by the Heritage Foundation, a conservative think tank in Washington. Wisconsin, with some of the toughest sanctions and work requirements, has seen its rolls plummet more than 80 percent. Alaska, with one of the most liberal work policies, has culled its rolls by less than 10 percent. Such disparities are fueling an ideological battle about the next step welfare reform must take, or whether in some cases, as critics say in New York, it has already gone too far.

At the heart of the dispute is whether the discomfort some people are experiencing is acceptable. Conservatives see it as a necessary short-term adjustment as the old culture of dependency is transformed into one of self-reliance. To liberals, it is the first step toward the creation of a permanent underclass.

New York City falls in the middle of the debate in several ways. Its rolls have dropped 35 percent in the past three years, and it has one of the toughest work requirements in the country. But it also has fairly weak sanctions for people who fail to fulfill work and job-hunting requirements.

Mayor Rudolph Giuliani is hoping to emulate Wisconsin's success, so much so that last year he made Jason Turner, architect of the Wisconsin Works program, his chief of the Human Resources Administration. "You have to say there are two options: One is to work for the government in a public job [in return for temporary assistance], or work for yourself in a private job and make more money," says Mr. Turner.

In Wisconsin, this "must work" theory helped reduce the rolls dramatically.

But the disputed question is whether people who left are now better off. A recent study there found that 62 percent of former welfare recipients had jobs. But two-thirds of them had incomes below the poverty level. And most say they are now worse off financially.

Then there are Wisconsin's 38 percent who are simply unemployed. "What's happened to those people who've left and are still not working? We still don't know," says Sheila Zedlewski of the Income Benefits Policy Center at the Urban Institute, a liberal think tank in Washington.

"We haven't tackled the tougher cases. That's when it's going to get complicated.

—Barbara Blum, welfare analyst

But many former welfare recipients are also proud they're working and don't want to go back to public assistance. Robert Rector of the Heritage Foundation says the issue isn't whether someone suffers from material poverty. He's more concerned about what he calls "behavioral poverty," which he defines as "an eroded worth ethic, welfare dependence, marital disintegration, and a whole host of problems that go along with that."

He adds: "What we need to combat is out-of-wedlock births, weak relationships between men and women, and dependency."

Many advocates of the poor question such assumptions, and they're also more worried about the immediate health and welfare of vulnerable people, particularly children. "Anyone can have a lower caseload, it's not very hard. All you do is a variation on locking the front door, pulling down the shades, and not an-swering the phone," says Liz Krueger of the Community Food Resource Center in New York. "That's what we're doing here in New York."

The city has been criticized for making it difficult for people to qualify for benefits. Besides enduring a rigorous application process, people must meet several times with a financial planner and go through a 30-day job search, during which they must show up on time every day.

Advocates for the poor say this puts many applicants in an impossible situation. For the month-long job search, they receive no benefits yet have to pay for child care. They also say applicants are routinely given wrong information, penalized unfairly, and turned away without cause. The Legal Aid Society and others have challenged the new system in court, and a federal judge has issued a temporary restraining order prohibiting the city from turning any more of its welfare offices into "job centers."

McWilliams in many ways represents the program's successes and drawbacks. He's eager to work. But he has not found a job, and he missed an appointment with a social worker to start his job search. As a result, his benefits check has been reduced.

But it won't be taken away all together. The state decided that was too punitive. Yet in Wisconsin, people who fail to meet the work requirements can lose their checks completely. And that, says the Heritage Foundation's Mr. Rector, is one of the keys to Wisconsin's success.

But for many people who work with the poor, including those who supported welfare reform such as former New York Human Resources Commissioner Lilliam Barrios-Paoli, that's pushing reform too far.

"There clearly were abuses, but now we've gone to the other extreme," says Ms. Barrios-Paoli. "Most people get into welfare because they don't see any other way."

That's true of New Yorker James Ham. With only a 10-hour-a-month job to support his family, he has applied for temporary aid. "If I didn't need the short-term help, I wouldn't be asking for it," says Mr. Ham, who was told he probably won't qualify. "If things don't get better, I might have to go into a shelter and allow the system take care of my wife and the kids."

Getting off the dole

The welfare rolls are at a 30-year low, thanks in part to the strong economy and in part to tough new rules. States are now allowed to cut benefits from people who do not cooperate, but they are using that power very differently.

A closer look at reasons some states dropped welfare cases:

Florida - - - - - - - -

Sanctions and non-cooperation 27% · 49% — Other reasons

24% — Found work

New Hampshire - - - - - - -

Found work · 28% · 66% Unexplained

4% Got married

2% Increased income or no longer eligible

Iowa - - - - - - - -

Increased income 30% — Non-cooperation

12% Left voluntarily · 47%

6% No children at home · 4% Moved out of state · 1% Other reasons

Kentucky - - - - - - - -

5% Couldn't be located · 32% — Failed to recertify

8% Moved out of state · 28% · 29% — Other reasons

Noncooperation

Nebraska - - - - - - - -

Did not fulfill work requirements · 85% Found work

10%

5% Moved out of state

AP

Unit Selections

Key Points to Consider

❖ Do you believe that many of our current social problems are due to the fact that we have so many single-parent families? Defend your answer.

❖ What are the main social welfare needs that children have today? Adolescents? Families?

❖ What can be done, specifically, to involve fathers more actively in family life? Do you agree that more can be done in this area? How?

❖ What solutions do you propose for the national phenomenon of youth violence, particularly in school environments? Do you believe that there is just as much national concern expressed when violence occurs among minority youth in urban schools? Explain.

❖ What can we learn by viewing children's needs in an international perspective?

❖ Why is it essential to view all of the social welfare programs that interact with the child welfare system?

 **Links** **www.dushkin.com/online/**

These sites are annotated on pages 4 and 5.

The majority of articles in this section relate to social services that are provided through the social welfare system to children, adolescents, and their families. As noted in the introduction to Unit 3, social services are those "soft" benefits that are neither in the form of cash nor in-kind resources and are widely distributed in some manner to many individuals and families throughout the United States. Social workers make up one of the leading professions that provide these social services, either directly to recipients or indirectly through their roles as super- visors, administrators, policy analysts, or researchers.

The first two articles in this unit address several aspects of the issue of single parenthood. Patrick Fagan answers his own rhetorical question positively in his article, "Q: Are Single-Parent Families a Major Cause of Social Dysfunction?" Using a different approach, Elaine Stuart, in "Father's Day Every Day" provides a concise national overview of programs designed to encourage fathers, whether married or not, to stabilize their families.

In "Youth at Risk: Saving the World's Most Precious Resource," Gene Stephens compiles a list of all the problems facing children and youth today. As such, it serves as a helpful introduction to a discussion of what specific social services are needed if those children and youth are to survive and develop into responsible adults.

The final three articles in unit 4 cover many of the issues that arise in a field of practice within the social work profession that is called child welfare.

The report "Weapon-Carrying and Youth Violence," by Randy Page and Jon Hammermeister, demonstrates the urgent need to respond to the presence of guns and adolescent violence, particularly within school environments. Next, Arlene

Bowers Andrews and Asher Ben-Arieh provide an international perspective on the health, welfare, and safety of children. Finally, you can see clearly the interrelationship between the problems of poverty, substance abuse, mental illness, and violence as they affect families in "Beyond the Boundaries of Child Welfare: Connecting with Welfare, Juvenile Justice, Family Violence and Mental Health Systems," which is produced by the Child Welfare League of America.

Social Services in Family and Child welfare

Q: Are single-parent families a major cause of social dysfunction?

Yes: Broken families strongly correlate with a range of social pathologies.

BY PATRICK FAGAN

Fagan, a resident scholar in family and culture at the Heritage Foundation, served as deputy assistant secretary of health and human services in the Bush administration.

Is the single-parent family a symptom or a cause of social disintegration in the United States? Paradoxical as it may sound, it is both. Obviously, people living in single-parent families do not have bad intentions, but they are trapped by their own or their parents' actions in a form of community that harms children. The evidence is all around us: dangerous, failing schools in America's inner cities, crime-plagued neighborhoods, crowded prisons and high rates of drug addiction.

Different family forms are the end result of two major kinds of rejection among adult parents: either out-of-wedlock birth or divorce. In 1950, for every 100 children born, 12 children entered a broken family. In 1992, for every 100 children born, 58 entered a broken family. With proportions this high it is more difficult for the nation to have a consensus on family life. But, even as the consensus decreases, the case for the intact married family becomes more compelling, as does the evidence that the single-parent family is a much riskier place for a child. Of course

some single-parent families do a better—sometimes a much better—job of raising their children than some married parents do. But, all other things being equal, the intact married family beats the single-parent family in every measurable dimension.

That does not mean that single-parent families are to be blamed in any way—quite the opposite. Because of the difficulty of raising children, of forming the next nation, single parents need all the help they can get. But neither the nation nor single parents need to hear that their family form is just as good for their children as any other one. This will shortchange their grandchildren, doubly so, because behind every single-parent family is a serious and hurtful rejection between the adults. The rejection between the adults has myriad consequences for the physical, intellectual, emotional, economic and social development of the child and of society. No one can be indifferent to this rejection or say it does not have serious consequences. Claiming that all family forms should be equally esteemed is to insist—against all evidence—that there is no difference between the love of father and mother and the love of only one parent. We cannot afford to hide the truth just to be nice. Much more than feelings are at stake as the following summary of the broad directions of the social-science research data show.

Right from birth the health of the newborn is at risk. Controlling for education, income and health of the mother, being born out of wedlock increases the risk of infant mortality and of ill health in early infancy, according to the National Health Interview survey of 1989. Nicholas Eberstadt, a visiting scholar at Harvard University's Center for Population Studies, has written that the health of a child born to a college-educated single mother is at greater risk than the health of a child born to married grade-school dropouts.

The verbal IQ of children in single-parent families also is at risk. As Hillary Rodham Clinton has made popularly known, the verbal IQ of the child is intimately linked to the amount of verbal stimulation the child gets. The single parent has a hard time giving the same amount of stimulation as two married parents can give, all other things being equal. That is common sense.

The verbal IQ is the building block of education, and at all levels of family income the child from a single-parent family will perform at lower levels all through grade school, high school and college. This translates into lower job attainment and salary upon joining the workforce. This means that, overall, children of single-parent families are less productive in the marketplace as a group, produce less and therefore contribute less to the common tax base. At the other end of the job spectrum—welfare dependence—the risk is much higher for children from single-parent families.

Consider the correlation of personal psychological problems—the ability of children of broken families to control their impulses, particularly sex and aggression—and single-parent families. They will have more out-of-wedlock births and contract more sexually transmitted diseases. Crime rates also will be higher. Crime rates are low for children of married intact families, black or white, and high for children of broken families, regardless of race.

Alcohol and drug-addiction problems similarly are different for married and single-parent families, when all other things are equal. The same holds for teenage suicide and child abuse, where the rates of abuse are dramatically different across family structures. A recent British study found that the rate of child abuse is lowest in intact families, six times higher in blended families, 13 times higher in single-mother families and 20 times higher in single-father families. By far the most dangerous place for a mother or her child is in a family structure where the mother's boyfriend is cohabiting. Ample scientific data show that as a group children in broken families will not reach the same level of human capacity as children from intact married families. One of their parents will have shortchanged them despite the subsequent best efforts of the other parent or even of both parents.

The effects on parents themselves are different but similarly disruptive. David Larson, a psychiatrist and president of the National Institute for Healthcare Research in Rockville, Md., has noted that the emotional stress of divorce has the same effects on a husband's health as if he smoked two packs of cigarettes a day for the rest of his life; for the wife the effect compares to the impact of her smoking one pack a day for the same period.

The likely impact on the family life of the next generation is not a happy story either. A Princeton University study has found that compared to young women growing up in two-parent families, girls who are in single-parent families at age 16 are 72 percent more likely to become single mothers, too. While many children of broken families are determined and succeed in having a better marriage than their parents, all other things being equal, children from intact married families will be more likely to pull it off. Children of divorced parents are more likely to be anxious about marriage and more tentative in their commitment. Though understandable, this is not best for the marriages they enter.

Love between married parents is the greatest nourishment for a child, and with it . . . poverty, lack of education and ill health can be overcome.

These changes are having dramatic effects at the community level. Among our very poor families, those with incomes less than $15,000 per year, marriage has all but disappeared, and among working-class families with incomes between $15,000 to $30,000 a year, married parents don't exist for 45 percent of the children. As social scientist Charles Murray has observed, when the rate of single-parent families reaches 30 percent in a neighborhood, the quality of life dramatically collapses. Adolescent boys run wild and form gangs; crime rates soar and drug abuse increases.

In all likelihood many of these children will not marry as adults because they have not experienced marriage in their families or seen it around them. As time goes on, these communities have more and more second-, third- and even fourth-generation single-parent families. Judging from statistics released in the federal National Longitudinal Survey of Youth, this appears to be happening: The second generation is affected even more than the first. One may conclude from the survey that, as family ties progressively are frayed with each succeeding generation of single parenthood, the fabric of neighborhood communities unravels and, rather than being a source of support for families, the community becomes a hindrance to parents' ability to raise their children well. Increasingly, America's lower-income communities are becoming dangerous anticommunities—where social cooperation is less and less possible.

This is most apparent in the public schools in poverty-stricken areas. But the same drift exists in middle-class neighborhoods.

It may be argued that the fundamental cause of our changing family forms is the change in relationships between men and women. Sexual mores have changed radically in the last three generations, and adult men and women find it less and less within their abilities to select, commit and follow through on lifelong marriage. The capacity to move from sexual attraction to emotional attraction to courtship to marriage to lifelong fidelity has diminished immensely. The ability of the sexes to love each other has been seriously eroded, and their children suffer, for if there is one thing that a child needs more than anything else from his parents it is their love for each other. Because love between the parents is the greatest nourishment for a child, with it the effects of poverty, lack of education and ill health all can be overcome. Without it the child spends much of life trying to make up for it,

frequently being drawn down blind alleys of experimentation with sex, drugs and alcohol as substitutes for what he or she wants: the love that lasts through all the challenges and disappointments of life.

Alienation between men and women explains more about America's troubles than anything else. While those who have suffered this type of pain need the support and love of all the rest of us—and need it more than those of us blessed with married, loving parents—it does not help them to say that this pain is nothing and makes no difference. To do that is to deny the human heart finding its need and capacity for love, the biggest task of our existence. That this debate be flushed out is good and also critical for the nation. If we do not correct course on this one the United States will crumble and disintegrate. It already is well on the way there. The question is: Can we turn around in time to prevent national disintegration, and can we discover how the single parents of today can live to see their grandchildren with happily married parents?

No: Social problems correlate more closely with poverty than family background.

BY STEPHANIE COONTZ

Coontz is a family historian at The Evergreen State College in Olympia, Wash., and author of The Way We Really Are: Coming to Terms With America's Changing Families.

"Family breakdown is behind all our problems."

"Marriage is the solution to poverty and social alienation."

Political pundits love one-ingredient recipes, whether for disasters or success. That may be understandable for people who live in 13-second sound bites, but it's hard on everyday Americans trying to sort through the complex challenges facing their families.

The idea that single-parent families are a major cause of the social dysfunctions in contemporary America glosses over the stresses facing two-parent families while telling one-parent families they essentially are out of luck. This isn't helpful to either family type. Worse, it leads to bad social policy, such as attempts to abolish no-fault divorce or pressure single mothers into getting married.

Let's start with a reality check. Three-fourths of married mothers with children work outside the home, earning on average 41 percent of family income. In 23 percent of couples, the wife makes more than the husband. Increasingly, women have the option to leave a bad marriage or refuse a shotgun one. At the same time, marriage organizes a smaller part of our lives than ever. The age of marriage for women is at a historic high, while for men it has tied its previous high in 1890. At the other end of life, the average 60-year-old has another 20 years to live. For both young and old, there are more opportunities for a satisfying life outside of marriage than ever before. Combined with women's new economic independence, this limits how many people feel compelled to get or stay married. Even if states repeal no-fault divorce, the partner with the most resources and least scruples simply can desert, fabricate evidence or move to a more permissive state.

Divorce, then, is probably here to stay. How big a cause of social dysfunction is that? It is true that children of divorced parents are more likely to have problems than children of always-married parents. But the average differences are not large and often stem from factors other than single parenthood per se.

Sometimes the "increased risk" associated with divorce, for example, sounds dramatic when expressed in percentages, but still remains quite small. A parental divorce, for instance, triples the chance that a woman will have a premarital birth—but this raises the probability of such a birth from .05 percent to .17 percent. As Princeton University researcher Sara McLanahan points out: "Outlawing divorce would raise the national high-school graduation rate from about 86 percent to 88 percent.... It would reduce the risk of a premarital birth among young black women from about 45 percent to 39 percent."

What about the psychological effects of divorce? Obviously, kids raised by two involved, cooperating parents have a big advantage. But involved, cooperating parents are not always what kids get. It often is a bad marriage, rather than subsequent divorce, that accounts for children's problems.

About 20 percent of children of divorced parents have emotional and behavioral problems, compared with about 10 percent of children in married families. This finding certainly should concern us. But the difference is not always a result of divorce itself. Researchers studying children who do poorly after divorce have found that behavior problems often already were evident 8 to 12 years before the divorce took place, suggesting that both the child's maladjustment and the divorce were symptoms of more deep-rooted family and parenting dysfunctions.

Certainly, divorce can trigger new difficulties connected with loss of income, school relocation and constriction of extended-family ties. While some divorces improve the situation for kids by decreasing conflict, others lead to escalating hostility about custody and finances. Intense conflict after a divorce can be especially damaging to children. But rolling back divorce rights will not reverse the effects of bad marriages and may exacerbate the parental hostility associated with the worst outcomes for kids.

Individuals should know the risks of single parenthood, and parents who simply are bored with their marriages certainly should consider sticking it out. But life is too complicated to let some local judge veto whatever decision people end up making. A man who is discontented with his wife, for example, often treats his daughter with contempt, threatening the girl's self-confidence and academic achievement. An unhappy married woman may have trouble dealing with a teenage son's behavior that reminds her of her spouse. One recent study of teens found no overall difference in self-image by family form. But the lowest self-esteem of all was found in adolescents in intact families where the father, though not hostile, showed little interest in the youth.

Never-married single parenthood often is more problematic than divorce because it so frequently occurs in the context of income deprivation. But nonmarriage is not the major cause of poverty in America and, since most

low-income mothers were impregnated by low-income men, marriage is seldom the answer.

Correlations, contrary to sound-bite specialists, are not causes. Yes, kids in one-parent families are more likely to be poor, but there's a chicken-and-egg question here. Poor parents are twice as likely to divorce, unemployed men are three to four times less likely to marry in the first place and girls with poor life prospects are five to seven times more likely to become unwed teen mothers than more fortunate girls. According to Census Bureau figures, even if you reunited every single child in America with both biological parents, two-thirds of the kids who are poor today still would be poor. For never-married mothers who are not poor, factors such as maternal education and parenting skills have more effect on their children's outcomes than their marital status.

Marriage is not a psychological cure-all any more than it is an economic one. One study of teens who had a nonmarital birth found that the reading scores of their children were higher when the mothers remained single than when they married the father of their child, probably because such marriages tended to be especially conflict-prone. Similarly, single African-American teens have a lower infant mortality rate than those who marry. This is likely due to the fact that marriage to a man with poor job prospects or low wages provides less social support than maternal kin networks.

Parental conflict, in or out of marriage, is the worst psychological risk for kids. Poverty, income loss, residential insecurity and the social alienation caused by widening income disparities and mean-spirited finger-pointing are the worst social risks.

Poverty during the first five years of life leads to an average IQ deficit of 9 points, regardless of family form. Kids with elevated levels of lead in their bloodstreams or bones—a frequent outcome of living in run-down neighborhoods where the pipes and paint haven't been changed since 1975—are six times more likely to engage in violence and seven times more likely to drop out of school than other kids, again regardless of family form. Poverty also frequently produces bad parenting. Low-income mothers, whether single or married, are 60 percent more likely than other moms to inflict severe violence on their children.

It is true that our prisons contain disproportionate numbers of people who were raised in single-parent families. That's partly because most crimes occur in neighborhoods where desperation breeds both broken families and youthful violence, as well as depriving children of mentors beyond the family. It's partly because kids of single parents are more likely to have been exposed to adult conflict during the course of a marriage or a series of transitory relationships. The Rand Corp. reports that parental conflict has a stronger relation with youth delinquency and aggression than parental absence, per se.

When researchers have asked young people themselves how much delinquency they engage in, "family structure was unrelated to the seriousness of the offense." But school officials, juvenile authorities and police are more likely to record and penalize behaviors committed by children from single-parent families. Such children are more likely to be prosecuted, less likely to get probation and more likely to spend time in jail than kids of two-parent families who've committed similar offenses. Walter Bien, head of the preeminent German family research institute, reports he has found exactly the same pattern in Germany.

All this is not to deny that there are serious problems associated with many divorces and single-parent situations. Putting them in perspective, however, helps us avoid panic responses that create bad social policy and blind us to the many other forces that threaten effective parenting and child well-being.

Every family needs help raising children in today's fast-paced culture. Working parents, married or unmarried, need quality child care, medical insurance and livable-wage jobs. We must adjust our attitudes toward marriage, our work policies and our school hours to the reality that women are in the workforce to stay. We should provide marital and parental counseling before and during marriage, teaching individuals how to manage personal conflict. But we must pay equal attention to helping people minimize the acrimony of divorce when it cannot healthfully be headed off. Child-support enforcement should be strengthened and, if a spouse sacrificed earnings potential during the marriage to raise the children, the other spouse should provide a maintenance allowance for some period after the divorce.

Finally, we should tell the truth about the fact that almost any family that is not overwhelmed with other risks can learn to function effectively. For married parents, the key to successful parenting is mutual respect and good problem-solving. Divorced parents should minimize conflict, establish economic security for the custodial parent and keep the noncustodial parent acting like a parent rather than a rival or indulgent grandparent. Single parents must resist being seduced by the special intimacy such parents have with their children; they need clear limits and rules to deal with the inevitable separation issues of the teenage years. Stepfamilies require flexibility about gender roles and household boundaries, because there are four parents and four sets of grandparents involved in their kids' lives.

Every family is at risk when we pretend we can go it alone; we're almost all resilient when we get social support. The search for easy answers and quick-fix solutions deprives families of the support and information we all need.

Father's day every day

There's a movement to encourage fathers —married and not— to help raise and support their children.

BY ELAINE STUART

For South Carolina Gov. David M. Beasley, the message that too many fathers are absent from their children's lives hit home during a visit to a juvenile justice facility. Many of the youth had committed violent crimes. The governor, whose parents divorced when he was young, asked the young offenders, "How many of you had a dad at home?"

No one said a word. Yet the so-called tough kids nearly cried when Beasley asked them if having a dad or mom at home would have made a difference in their lives. Beasley related his experience to fellow governors at the winter meeting of the National Governors' Association in a session on initiatives promoting responsible fatherhood.

States and communities are moving to encourage fathers, married and unmarried, to support their children financially and emotionally. Governors formed a Task Force on Fatherhood Promotion that will work with the National Fatherhood Initiative, a nonpartisan civic organization based in Gaithersburg, Md.

Wade F. Horn, NFI president, said, "The trend toward fatherless families is not just one of many problems. It is the core problem of our time."

Horn said the absence of fathers directly correlates to many of society's worst problems, including teen pregnancy, teen suicide, crime and educational decline. "The evidence suggests unless we reverse the trend toward fatherlessness, we will be a nation in decline," Horn said. "We still have time because the majority of kids still live with their fathers."

Pennsylvania Gov. Tom Ridge and Delaware Gov. Tom Carper are heading the NGA task force. Ridge cited sobering statistics about the absence of fathers: 24.7 million children each night sleep in homes without their biological father present, representing four of every 10 children in America. Fatherless children, according to a 1993 report of the U.S. Department of Health and Human Services, are five times more likely to live in poverty compared to children who live with two parents. Such children are three times more likely to fail at school or drop out. About 70 percent of violent offenders grew up without fathers.

Horn said the NGA task force and other efforts show the issue is getting attention. In addition, many fathers are more involved in rearing their children. Despite this attention, there's no proof that the number of absent fathers is dwindling. Horn said most states are just now raising public awareness. Few states, he said, have taken action beyond beefing up child support enforcement. Even though financial support is vital, it is not everything, Horn said. He said it is disconcerting to say that involved, responsible fathers are important and then to say, "if you don't pay child support, we'll put you in jail."

Virginia funds local efforts

Horn called Virginia a leader in addressing the issue. A commission appointed by former Gov. George Allen found the breakup of families caused many people to go on welfare and that remarriage resulted in many leaving welfare. This led to the state launching the Virginia Fatherhood Campaign in 1996. Since then, the Fatherhood Campaign has conducted a public education effort, trained community leaders and funded local programs.

Virginia's mass media campaign on t.v., radio and in print resulted in more than 100,000 people calling the Fatherhood Campaign's toll-free number for more information. A survey showed nearly 40 percent of the state's adult population recalled the

From *State Government News*, August 1998, pp. 22-25. © 1998 by The Council of State Governments. Reprinted by permission.

campaign's message that dads make a difference in children's lives. The survey also showed that people changed their attitude toward fatherhood as a result, said Ron Clark, director of the Virginia Fatherhood Campaign, located in the state Department of Health.

The Fatherhood Campaign has held 12 regional forums, which have each trained 150 community leaders to implement fatherhood programs. Most importantly, the state has given seed grants totaling $300,000 over the past two fiscal years to fund 50 community programs assisting fathers. Demand for the grants was so high that funding was increased to $200,000 for fiscal 1999. To help local groups and agencies jointly apply for grants, the state is encouraging communities and agencies to join in fatherhood coalitions. Clark said that the most successful local programs collaborate with other agencies, which results in more resources to help fathers.

Because the campaign is partially funded by child-support enforcement funds, it encourages programs aimed at fathers providing financial support, including job development and placement efforts. Programs also encourage fathers to spend time with their children and become better parents. Existing programs to deal with domestic violence or substance abuse, for example, added fatherhood components. Parenting programs also added services to appeal to fathers. Other local programs work with fa-

thers who are in prison. Some programs encourage young boys and men to delay fatherhood until they are older.

The state doesn't dictate the type of program, but lets the community assess its own needs, Clark said. The state, which is home to many military bases, also held a program attended by 200 fathers who are in the military. Clark said many youth get in trouble when their dads are away on duty.

Clark said the goal is to reduce social ills, such as teen pregnancy and criminal behavior, linked to father absence. To see if the programs are working, the state is having an independent evaluation made. "If we haven't changed fathers' behavior, we've failed," Clark said.

Across the nation, states are trying to change fathers' behavior with public awareness campaigns, child-support enforcement and job services, parenting training, funding for local programs and pregnancy prevention efforts.

Pennsylvania jobs and mentors

Like many other states, Pennsylvania focuses on child support and

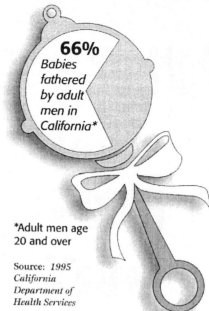

Births to teen mothers

66% *Babies fathered by adult men in California**

*Adult men age 20 and over

Source: *1995 California Department of Health Services*

works with community groups on mentoring programs. Pennsylvania will use welfare funds to provide noncustodial parents, most of whom are fathers, with job training and education so they can pay child support. "We want to try to get unemployed fathers to work," Ridge said. He added that more is at stake. "Being a good father is not a matter of dollars, but love. There's no substitute for a father in the household."

Beyond financial support, Ridge said the state wants to help dads spend time with their kids. The welfare agency will award grants to public and private groups in Pennsylvania to help provide noncustodial parents with innovative child visitation programs. Already, local programs educate and counsel absent fathers to form relationships with their children. "Father to Father" in Erie County links teenage dads with older, responsible adult fathers to guide them. A Pittsburgh program helps out-of-work fathers ages 18 to 21 with job training, counseling, parenting education and mentoring.

At North Philadelphia's William Penn High School, a teen-parenting program helps keep teen parents in school and prepares them for work

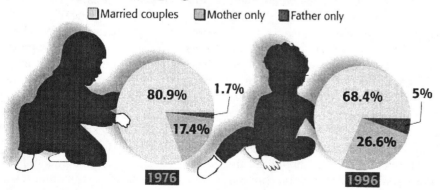

U.S. changing families, 1976-1996

Married couples ☐ Mother only ☐ Father only ■

80.9% 1.7% 17.4% **1976**

68.4% 5% 26.6% **1996**

Source: *NCCP analysis of data from the U.S. Bureau of Census, March current population surveys.*

or college. The program is one of eight in the Philadelphia schools.

If more fathers get involved in their children's lives, Ridge said he thinks the call on government for help with economic, social and criminal problems should decrease.

California educates and intervenes

California Gov. Pete Wilson said a sign of changing times is that one of every three births is out-of-wedlock. Wilson said, "The most destructive thing welfare did was to

Poverty facts

• Nearly half of all children in mother-only families live in poverty.

• Close to half of all children with absent parents lack child support orders.

• Many absent parents are poor.

• Nearly half of all children have a high school education or less.

Source: National Center on Children in Poverty, 1997

Father facts

• An estimated 24.7 million U.S. children live absent their biological father.

• Almost 17 million children live with their single mothers.

• 1.25 million or nearly one-third of all births in 1995 were out-of-wedlock.

• One out of every six children is a stepchild.

• About 40 percent of children have not seen their absent father in at least a year.

• Children living without their biological fathers on average are more likely to be poor, have educational, health, emotional and psychological problems, be victims of child abuse and engage in criminal behavior than children who live with their married parents (biological or adoptive).

Source: The National Fatherhood Inititiatve, 1998

States active

At least 30 governors submitted descriptions of fatherhood initiatives in their states to the National Governors' Association. Seven states reported they help low-income, noncustodial fathers find jobs to pay child support. Many states reported on projects that build parenting skills of fathers. Public awareness campaigns are widespread. Descriptions of state programs are available from the NGA Center for Best Practices, 444 N. Capitol St., Washington, D.C. 20001-1512 www.nga.org.

All states, the District of Columbia and Puerto Rico, promote responsible fatherhood in some way, the National Center for Children in Poverty reported in 1997. The center said state activities seek to increase public awareness about responsible fatherhood, prevent too-early or unwanted fatherhood, promote fathers as caregivers and build community and state leadership around a fatherhood agenda. Contact the National Center on Children in Poverty, Columbia University School of Public Health, 154 Haven Ave., N.Y., N.Y. 10032, (212) 304-7119, e-mail nccp@columbia.edu.

encourage 15 year-old girls that they could be viable economic units by getting pregnant."

Society, he said, pays the cost. "I shudder every year when I look at budget spending to remedy the absence of fathers," he said. "We build prisons instead of libraries."

Wilson held the first California Focus on Fathers' Summit in 1995 and has held summits annually since. The governor established the Partnership for Responsible Parenting in 1996.

The state provides grants to community programs to decrease teen pregnancy. The partnership also promotes mentoring programs to link adults with at-risk youth, seeks stronger enforcement of statutory rape laws, and has a media campaign to educate the public on teen and unwed pregnancy and responsible fatherhood.

The "truth about sex" media campaign stresses that preventing pregnancy is the male's responsibility as well as the female's, said Terry Hodges of the campaign. When the ads air on radio or t.v., calls increase to the toll-free telephone line that refers people to local programs. One print ad reads, "Children need fathers in their lives to provide love, support and guidance. If you are not ready to be a responsible father, don't make a baby now."

The media campaign also spreads the word that "sex with a minor is

a major crime." Because two-thirds of the men who impregnate and then desert teen moms are adults, Wilson initiated the Statutory Rape Vertical Prosecution program. The state provided grants to local district attorneys to enforce statutory rape provisions. While the crime of an adult having sex with a minor was ignored for years, since the effort began in 1995, local prosecutors have filed 2,617 statutory rape cases and 56 percent resulted in convictions and sentences.

The male responsibility component of the partnership seeks to educate high-risk young males about violence, drugs and sex and link them with mentors. The state is one quarter of the way toward its goal of recruiting 250,000 mentors to work with children and youth one-on-one. Wilson and his wife also mentor a young boy.

California provides $2 million to 23 local agencies for various male involvement programs and $20 million in grants to 112 local agencies for pregnancy prevention and the like. Hodges said, "This message is still needed and always will be needed to make sure kids have the information they need to have control of their future."

Michigan's team approach

Michigan's statewide public awareness campaign features the National

Football League's Detroit Lions. The campaign kicked off its third year last September at a news conference with Gov. John Engler and members of the team.

The program grew out of the state's effort to have fathers accept paternity when they visit their newborns at the hospital. Engler said the Lions' promotion "works wonders" because big, tough football players demonstrate that it is okay to love and cuddle your kids. The campaign features Lions' players with their children in billboard ads, public service announcements on television and radio, newspaper advertisements and calendars. The message is: "Whether you're married, divorced or single, fatherhood is forever."

The team also devotes one game day to recognizing child support efforts, said Margaret Gravina, assistant director of the communications office in the Family Independence Agency. The Lions' campaign emphasizes the importance of fathers supporting their children financially and emotionally. "It points out that

Resources

The National Fatherhood Initiative operates a clearinghouse and resource center. It works with state and local governments, civic organizations and others. NFI, One Bank St., Suite 160, Gaithersburg, Md. 20878, (301) 948–0599, Web:www.register.com/father.

Pregnancy prevention programs aimed at males are reported in the Spring 1998 *State Trends*, published by CSG. Becca Hamrin, a CSG research associate, writes at least 40 states report having specific strategies to prevent unwanted or too early fatherhood. Call CSG's publication sales department, (800) 800–1910 or www.csg.org.

it is critical for a father to have a continuing role," Gravina said.

Since Michigan launched its media campaign at least 17 other states have joined with professional teams in similar campaigns. States, however, might pick carefully among professional sports teams. The cover story for the May

4 *Sports Illustrated* reports that out-of-wedlock births are epidemic among professional athletes. The article, "Paternity Ward," focuses on NBA players, but points out that other athletes have been subjects of paternity suits for children born out of wedlock. With 32 percent of all U.S. children born to unmarried mothers in 1995, some say it is a societal problem. The article's reports of millionaire athletes who ignore their children, even if they pay child support, show that the plague of absent fathers goes beyond teenage pregnancies, welfare or poverty.

Beasley of South Carolina said he benefited because his father continued to spend time with him after his parents divorced. As governor, Beasley has his staff block out family time for him. He said governors need to bring that message to everyone. "If a governor can set aside time for his children, then every mom and dad can," he said.

Youth at Risk:

Saving the World's Most Precious Resource

More and more children are given no hope for the future. A criminal-justice expert outlines the problems, analyzes promising solutions, and proposes an eight-point plan to save youth at risk.

By Gene Stephens

Growing numbers of children are being neglected, abused, and ignored. Without change, the dark specter of generational warfare could become all too real.

After two decades of study, however, I conclude that we can stop this negative trend and do a better job of nourishing this most important resource. To do otherwise would surely be a violation of our obligation to future generations.

Child care advocates claim that up to 15% of 16- to 19-year-olds are at risk of never reaching their potential and simply becoming lost in society. Others would add to this category children of any age if they are at risk of not becoming self-supporting adults, headed for a life in institutions for delinquency, crime, mental illness, addiction, and dependency. We could also describe as "at risk" those teens and preteens who take on child rearing themselves and drop out of school.

The task of saving these children has become increasingly formidable. Compounding the problem are the expanding gap between the rich and poor, the increasing number of sin-

gle-parent households, the rise of homes where both parents work, the growing gun culture, and the recent increase in negative attitudes about children, such as courts that treat younger and younger children as adult criminals.

As a result, children lose hope for the future. They turn to peers for attention; they turn to guns for protection, security and status; and they turn to sex and drugs for comfort and relief of boredom. The gang too often becomes their "family"—the only place where they receive attention and approval.

Criminologist James Fox of Northeastern University predicts that the murders committed by teenagers (4,000 in the United States in 1995) will skyrocket as the 39 million children now under age 10 swell the ranks of teenagers by 20% in the first decade of the twenty-first century. The result could be a juvenile crime wave such as the United States has never seen.

Yet, such a catastrophe is not inevitable. There are some signs of hope: a slightly decreased birth rate among teenagers in the mid-1990s, a

rising bipartisan concern about "saving the children," burgeoning community-based experiments for meeting the needs of youth, and a movement to regard poor prenatal care, poor parenting skills, child abuse, and child neglect as public-health problems.

Beyond this, a striking change in the rearing of children in many families has been observed. Countering the trend toward ignoring or even abusing children is a trend toward cherishing and nurturing them. Thousands or even millions of young parents are taking turns working while the other stays at home and makes child care almost a full-time vocation. There is an unrecognized renaissance in parenting progressing quietly in neighborhoods across the nation and possibly the world.

Of course, having youth at risk is not a problem unique to the United States. Wars, social upheaval, rapidly changing economic systems, political instability, and cultural animosity have placed millions of children at risk around the world. Children die of starvation while oth-

From *The Futurist*, March/April 1997, pp. 1-7. © 1997 by the World Future Society, Bethesda, MD; http://www.wfs.org/wfs. Reprinted with permission.

ers wander aimlessly in search of home and family.

PROBLEMS

Singling out specific problems is difficult, for most are interrelated. For example, children left alone without adult attention are more likely to experiment with sex and drugs. Teenagers who try drugs are more likely to be involved in delinquent behavior. Children who experiment with sex increase their likelihood of becoming unmarried teenage parents. Youngsters who are physically and sexually abused are more likely to adopt abusive behavior toward others. Clearly, however, the following are major factors in the dilemma.

Teenage Pregnancy

Many child advocates see teenage pregnancy as the main problem. Children having children puts both generations at risk and often leads to poverty, poor health care, truancy, and underemployment. The dimensions of the issue—as reported by the National Commission on Children, the United States Census Bureau, and others—are staggering:

• Every year, one in 10 teenage females becomes pregnant—more than 3,000 a day.

• One of four teenage mothers will have a second child within one year of her first child's birth.

• Most teenage mothers are single and receive no support from the father.

• Eight of 10 teenage mothers do not finish high school.

About one-fourth of the families in America are headed by a single parent—usually the mother. In the Hispanic community, it is one-third; among black families, it is one-half. Most of the children in these families were born to teenagers.

According to the Centers for Disease Control (CDC), 85% of all children exhibiting behavioral disorders come from fatherless homes. Other statistical findings indicate that children from fatherless homes are: 32 times more likely to run away; nine times more likely to drop out of high school; 14 times more likely to commit rape; 10 times more likely to be substance abusers; and 20 times more likely to end up in prison.

Poverty

Whereas 75% of single-female-headed households are in poverty at least some of the time, and 33% are chronically poor, poverty is also endemic to a majority of young households. Already, one in three children under 6 lives below the poverty line.

About half of the homeless are families with children. A million divorces each year create new female-headed households below the poverty line.

Poor Health Care

CDC and other agencies have found that at least 25 million children in the United States have no health care. This means that they are taken to the hospital emergency room or to nonprofessionals for health problems. Without change in health provider arrangements, half of the nation's children could be without health care by the year 2000. Already, most unwed mothers receive no prenatal care.

Lack of health care too often equals stunted ability to learn, life-altering

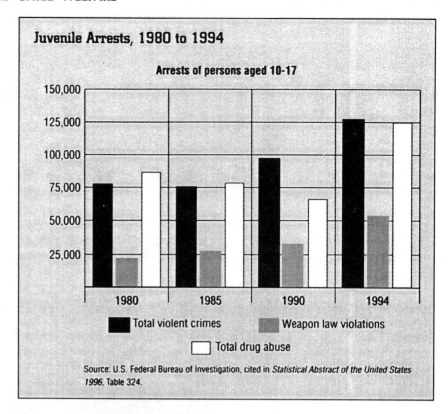

Juvenile Arrests, 1980 to 1994

Arrests of persons aged 10-17

Legend: Total violent crimes — Weapon law violations — Total drug abuse

Source: U.S. Federal Bureau of Investigation, cited in *Statistical Abstract of the United States 1996*, Table 324.

Victimization Rates, 1994 (rate per 1,000 persons)

Age of Victim	All Crime	All Crimes of Violence	Total Assault	Rape, Sexual Assault
12-15	117.4	114.8	99.7	3.1
16-19	125.9	121.7	104.8	5.1
All	53.1	50.8	42.7	2.0

Source: U.S. Bureau of Justice Statistics, cited in *Statistical Abstract of the United States 1996*, Table 320.

health problems, lowered ability to cope in a free-market system, and, as a result, greater likelihood of drug abuse, delinquency, and crime.

Child Abuse

There is substantial evidence of child abuse or neglect in the background of every known serial killer. In most cases, the abuse was physically or sexually severe.

Beyond blatant abuse, neglect itself—ignoring the child's physical and emotional needs—is a form of abuse that scars the child as much or more than beatings.

Child abuse and neglect are often called the "silent epidemic" in the United States. Alleged abuse more than quadrupled between the mid-1970s and the mid-1990s to more than 3 million cases a year reported (and 1 million substantiated). A Gallup Poll reported that physical abuse cases were 16 times greater than reported rates, and sexual abuse was 10 times greater.

The U.S. Department of Justice reports that abused or neglected children are 40% more likely to be arrested as juvenile delinquents and adult criminals; three times as likely to use drugs and alcohol, get into fights, and deliberately damage property; and four times as likely to steal and be arrested. It is also reported that one in eight neglected children was later arrested for a violent offense.

Chronic Truancy and School Dropout

On the average school day, as many as 15% of junior and senior high school students are not in school. For too many, this is a pattern that leads to dropout.

Truants represent a large portion of those arrested for daytime break-ins and thefts, and dropouts are over-represented in jails and prisons.

The Census Bureau reports that earnings of students without a high school diploma average far below the poverty line.

Alcohol and Drug Abuse

Polls of youth indicate that nine out of 10 teenagers drink alcohol to some extent by the time they finish high school, and a majority have used illegal drugs. A study of 1,200 school dropouts in California found their weekly alcohol-use rates were twice as high as in-school counterparts, and their use of hard drugs was two to five times as high. Dropout drug users were much more likely to be involved in violent and criminal activities. One-third said they had sold drugs in the past year, and twice as many dropouts as in-school students said they belonged to a gang.

Lack of Faith in Tomorrow

The Gallup Poll reported that 70% of 16- to 24-year-olds believe that the world was a better place when their parents were their age, and 56% said it will be worse for their own children. A joint *Washington Post*, Kaiser, and Harvard survey reported that the belief that "most people can be trusted" fell from 54% to 35%, and trust in government dropped from 76% to 25% over a three-decade period ending in 1995. At-risk youth, in particular, say they "live for today" and see no hope for their future.

Crime and Homicide

In 1996, the Justice Department reported that the juvenile homicide rate had almost doubled in over a decade, and blacks and males were by far the most likely to be killed.

The major correlating factor was an increase in the use of firearms. Guns were also found to be the single factor that could account for tripling the number of juvenile homicide offenders over the decade. Justice predicts another doubling of crime by juveniles by 2010 if current trends continue.

Tragically, most victims of juvenile violence are other juveniles, often children who are not even involved in the dispute.

PROMISES

Numerous programs have been developed to cope with the at-risk youth population. Here are some of the best approaches.

Positive Reinforcement

Children crave attention more than anything else, especially positive attention. A baby who is cuddled, talked to, and stimulated in the first six weeks of life is much more likely to be intelligent and well adjusted than a baby ignored and simply fed and cleaned up in silence. Later, the child who is rewarded with praise for accomplishments is much more likely than others to become optimistic and achievement oriented.

So how does one extinguish unacceptable behavior? By ignoring it and eliminating the child's ability to gain attention. The simplest examples are having the child sit in a corner or placing the child in a closed room for a short "time out."

For older children, pats on the back, awards, and ceremonies to celebrate accomplishments are particularly effective in fostering prosocial behavior and giving at-risk youth a stake in society, helping them overcome lack of hope and lack of faith in the future. The bottom line: Using positive reinforcement must become a way of life for parents, teachers, and others.

Parent Education

Teaching positive reinforcement to prospective parents has been effective in reducing the at-risk population. Parent education can provide information and skills to assist the parent-to-be with incentives to learn and use good child-rearing practices.

To be effective in reducing teenage parenting, these classes must reach children early—sixth grade or shortly thereafter. In programs that force them to carry a computerized crying and wetting doll around for a couple of weeks, many teenagers decide to postpone parenthood.

Healthy Start

The Justice Department and Health and Human Services each have Healthy Start programs. Justice's program was designed to reduce neglect and abuse, while the Health and Human Services program was designed to reduce infant mortality by strengthening the maternal and infant care systems at the community level.

A similar program, Healthy Families America, was launched in 1992 by the National Committee to Prevent Child Abuse to help establish home visitation programs, service networks, and funding opportunities so all new parents can receive the necessary education and support.

Mentoring

To help provide positive adult role models for at-risk youths, leaders in Kansas City are on a quest to recruit, train, and assign 30,000 mentors—one for every at-risk child in the city. Other communities have greatly expanded existing mentoring programs, such as Big Brothers and Big Sisters.

Nonviolent Conflict Resolution

Programs are now appearing in schools and community centers to provide attitudes and skills necessary to resolve conflict nonviolently. Models have been developed by the American Bar Association and the Justice Department, as well as by educators. One of the best models involves training school staff— teachers, administrators, custodians, bus drivers, and cafeteria workers— in creative non-violent conflict-resolution methods. Older students are also taught these techniques, and they in turn teach younger students, turning peer pressure into a positive rather than negative force.

Community Schools Programs

All communities have schools, but all communities do not use those schools effectively in breaking the cycle of violence and frustration among at-risk youth. A federal initiative—the Community Schools Program—has been effective in rallying the community around the school.

Other examples of successful partnerships include:

- In Missouri, 6,000 volunteers keep 675 schools open for extra hours.
- Boys' and Girls' Clubs offer mentoring in New Jersey schools.
- In New York City, Safe Haven programs provide safe environments and positive after-school tutoring and enrichment programs.
- Year-round schools in many communities facilitate better learning—since students no longer have the long summer to forget what they learned—and foster more opportunities for extracurricular programs, from tutoring and mentoring to family activities and counseling.

Character Education

Character education in schools generally revolves around universally accepted values (e.g., love, truthfulness, fairness, tolerance, responsibility) that find little opposition based on differing political, social, and religious beliefs. Schools with large numbers of at-risk children have reported pregnancy and dropout rates cut in half, along with reduced fights and suspensions, after character education took hold.

Youth Initiatives

Surveys by Gallup Poll, Wirthlin Group, and others consistently find that 95% of teenagers believe it is important for adults and teens "to get involved in local civic, charitable, cultural, environmental, and political activities." More than three-fourths of teens say they are already participating in some volunteer work, such as working at soup kitchens for the poor, nursing homes for the elderly, or shelters for the homeless.

Programs such as Americorps, Job Corps, Peace Corps, and others provide young people a chance to learn the joy of giving to others; at the same time, it gives them a stake in society by developing skills, discipline, and a chance to go to trade school or college through grants and loans. Many communities and even some states (Georgia, for example) are developing youth-oriented community service programs of their own.

Community Policing

Law enforcement programs are increasingly working in partnership with the community to identify crime-breeding problems and implement solutions. Many of the at-risk youths' problems thus become community problems and lend themselves to community solutions. Homelessness, poverty, lack of positive adult role models, and poor health care may lead to safe shelters, community assistance, mentors, and in-school or community clinics.

One of the best examples of this approach took place in Milton Keynes, England, which faced a rash of shoplifting, burglary, and a few store robberies. Rather than seek out, arrest, and prosecute the young offenders, Police Commander Caroline Nicholl instituted a series of conferences in which police, merchants, and neighbors met with offenders and suspects to identify reasons for the offenses. As a result, Nicholl says, "We learned about child abuse, bullying, alcoholism, and many other problems, and the community set to work on these."

Restorative Justice

Most at-risk youth encounter the justice system early in life. Where juvenile justice once focused on the *needs* of the child, it now focuses on the *deeds* of the child and a belief that someone, adult or child, has to pay for the offense.

Countering this trend is a restorative justice movement, which holds that the purpose of justice is to bring peace and harmony back to the community by restoring victim, community, and offender to a symbiotic relationship. Often, restoring includes restitution, service, and reclamation.

In the case of juvenile offenders, the child usually makes restitution to the victim either by his or her own earnings or through closely monitored personal service (cutting the lawn, raking leaves, chopping wood, or making home repairs), several hours of service to the community, an apology to the victim, counseling, and essays and/or school talks on the harm the offense does to society. Once the restitution is completed, the child's record is purged.

There are literally hundreds of programs being tried in small and large communities across the nation and, indeed, worldwide.

A PLAN

The plan that follows represents a consensus from groups to whom I've given the same assignment over the past decade: "Develop a program to turn your community's youth into productive, happy, law-abiding adults." These groups have included students from high school to graduate school, practitioners from police to social service workers, and community leaders, all participating in brainstorming and planning sessions to alleviate the youth-at-risk problem.

Here is a comprehensive plan based on my 10-plus years' experience with these exercises.

1. **Commit to positive reinforcement** through community and school-based parenting classes (mandatory in schools), ongoing media campaigns, positive attention, and recognition in all schools (preschool through high school) and community-based programs.

2. **Promote nonviolent conflict resolution** among peers through man-

To Help Youth, Should Easy Divorce Be Stopped?

If society were truly interested in looking out for children's futures, it would put an end to easy divorces, claims William A. Galston, former assistant to President Clinton for domestic policy.

"Since the 1960s, the number of children directly touched by divorce has jumped from 485,000 to one million a year" in the United States, writes Galston in *The American Enterprise*.

Except in households where parents are abusive, most children fare better when marriages are maintained.

"Divorces in nonabusive cases have a negative effect on children in a number of key areas: school performance; psychological illness; crime; suicide; out-of-wedlock births; adult work performance; and the propensity to become divorced," Galston argues. "There is also evidence that the experience of divorce diminishes trust in people and institutions, and impedes the capacity of individuals to form stable, lasting relationships."

Galston blames these problems on the ease with which divorces have become attainable through no-fault laws and other policies. Marriage—and its dissolution—has become focused on the personal happiness of adults rather than on the nurturing and development of children.

To turn the focus back toward the well-being of children, Galston recommends increasing pre-marriage education (perhaps taking the place of sex education in schools), reorienting economic and social policies to create a "marriage-friendly environment," and rescinding no-fault divorce laws for couples with minor children.

Source: "Braking Divorce for the Sake of Children" by William A. Galston, *The American Enterprise* (May/June 1996).

Future Possibilities For Controlling Risk

Technology is beginning to offer several other possibilities to reduce the problems of at-risk youth, though some of these possibilities may offend many people's concept of justice and humanity.

For example, new birth-control devices could be implanted in all youth or all at-risk youth. Already, courts have ordered women to either have five-year birth-control implants or face prison for child abuse.

Another possibility is to implant body-functioning monitors and control devices, which may be developed as early as the first decade of the twenty-first century. These very small computer-controlled machines would be implanted in the body to monitor all systems and add or subtract chemicals and hormones, slow down or speed up electrical synapses, and correct genetic abnormalities. The monitor could thus control behavior and eliminate most delinquent and criminal actions.

The question raised for society is whether these controls would be used only on criminals, or also on at-risk youth (potential criminals), or on anyone at all.

—*Gene Stephens*

datory educational programs for students, parents, teachers, counselors, administrators, media, and community campaigns.

3. **Encourage mentoring** for all children. Civic, business, and community campaigns should recruit and train mentors, matching them by needs and temperament. Programs such as Big Brothers and Big Sisters should be expanded.

4. **Establish community-school partnerships** to offer before- and after-school tutoring. Enlist youth to

The Youth Corps Solution

A wide variety of programs and proposals seek to improve the futures of youth at risk.

In Washington, D.C., the U.S. Corporation for National Service coordinates 120 youth corps programs in 37 states. These programs, now involving 22,000 young people, combine work experience and education within the context of community service. The programs are funded by federal, state, and local governments, foundations, and corporations. In addition, the programs are compensated under fee-for-service contracts.

Besides teaching skills and providing a benefit to the public, the programs try to instill a work ethic in participants and help them to understand the meaning of working with others toward a common goal.

The youth corps program is a cost effective way to help young people earn more, work more, and steer away from trouble, according to a recent study by Abt Associates for the Corporation for National Service. Among other results, the study found that participation in the corps reduced incidence of unwanted pregnancies among African-American women and increased the likelihood of Hispanic women to work and express a desire to obtain a college degree.

Youth corps' impacts were found to be especially positive for young black men, who obtained more work and higher earnings and increased both their educational aspirations and civil participation.

"Given the widespread perception that 'nothing works' to positively influence the life chances of disadvantaged youth, it is especially important to be able to document the benefits of programs like youth corps," says JoAnn Jastrzab, director of the study.

Sources: The Corporation for National Service, 1201 New York Avenue, N.W., Washington, D.C. 20525. Telephone 202/606-5000.
Abt Associates, Inc., 55 Wheeler Street, Cambridge, Massachusetts 02138. Telephone 617/492-7100; fax 617/492-5219.

---

perform services to the community to enhance their stake in society.

5. Develop community-oriented proactive policing programs that begin with a philosophy of prevention. Examples of prevention programs include midnight basketball leagues, police-youth athletic leagues, neighborhood housing project substations, and foot patrols. These all involve partnerships of police, parents, church, business, civic, and community organizations.

6. Initiate ethical and cultural awareness programs that build on partnerships among family, church, school, media, civic, business, and other community groups. These programs would emphasize finding common ground on basic values, such as respect, responsibility, and restraint.

7. Design youth opportunity programs to provide all children the chance to reach their potential, regardless of circumstances. Such programs could be run through school, business, and community partnerships that provide in-school jobs and child care, career counseling and training, opportunity scholarships, and recognition for achievement.

8. Set up peer counseling hotlines to help youth help each other through the trying times of adolescence.

To this basic plan we may also consider in the future adding more dramatic (though often controversial) measures, such as birth-control implants, health monitoring and treatment implants, behavioral control implants in extreme cases, computer-assisted brain implants, and educational implants. But these measures should only be considered after reaching consensus concerning ethical issues.

In addition, we must focus on justice where delinquency and crime occur. Youth offenders must recognize the consequences of their actions on the victim, the victim's family, and the community. The harm must be ameliorated and restored through mediation and arbitration, restitution, service to the victim and community, reclamation, and reconciliation.

Final Thoughts

Every community can develop programs guided by this model. But all plans must adopt certain guiding principles that permeate the approach.

Children want attention above everything. Thus, giving attention reinforces behavior and denying attention extinguishes behavior. Both praise and punishment are attention, and both will reinforce behavior that gets that attention.

It is important to instill optimism and faith in the future in all children, as they are the key to success. The very nature of adolescence is to challenge authority, but most children drift through this troubled period and become law-abiding adults unless they become labeled as delinquents, criminals, or losers.

Surely we can see the need to reach out and lend a hand to the world's most precious resource.

About the Author

Gene Stephens is a professor in the College of Criminal Justice, University of South Carolina, Columbia, South Carolina 29208. Telephone 803/777-7315; fax 803/777-9600. He is the criminal-justice editor of THE FUTURIST; his last article, "Crime in Cyberspace: The Digital Underworld," appeared in the September-October 1995 issue.

WEAPON-CARRYING AND YOUTH VIOLENCE

Randy M. Page and Jon Hammermeister

ABSTRACT

Weapons, and firearms in particular, are widely available in the United States and are at the heart of youth violence. Many schools and communities throughout the nation have identified weapon-carrying among youth as a substantial health, educational, and social problem. In fact, one of the national health objectives for the year 2000 is to substantially reduce the incidence of weapon-carrying among adolescents. This paper reviews the prevalence of weapon-carrying by youth, reasons they carry weapons, ways that firearms are obtained, firearms and violence (especially youth violence), and the controlling of weapons in schools.

PREVALENCE OF WEAPON-CARRYING BY YOUTH

A higher incidence of weapon-carrying, and guns in particular, among youths has been identified as a key factor in the recent increase in youth violence. Weapon-carrying increases risk of death and serious injury to both the carrier and others. In recent years a number of studies have investigated the accessibility of weapons and the extent to which youth carry them.

According to the 1990 Youth Risk Behavior Survey, 1 in 20 senior high school students carried a firearm, usually a handgun, and 1 in 5 carried a weapon of some type during the 30 days preceding the survey (Centers for Disease Control, 1991). A survey of 10 inner-city high schools in four states found that 35% of male and 11% of female students reported carrying a gun (Sheley, McGee, & Wright, 1992). A study of rural school students in southeast Texas found that 6% of male students had taken guns to school, and almost 2% reported that they did so almost

Jon Hammermeister, Ph.D., Instructor, Department of Health and Human Performance, Central Oregon Community College, Bend, Oregon.

Reprint requests to Randy M. Page, Ph.D., Professor, Division of Health, Physical Education, Recreation, and Dance, PEB 103, University of Idaho, Moscow, Idaho 83844.

From *Adolescence*, Vol. 32, Fall 1997, pp. 505-513. © 1997 by Libra Publishers, Inc. Reprinted with permission.

every day. In addition, 42.3% of those surveyed said they could get a gun if they wanted one (Kissell, 1993). More than one-third (34%) of urban high school students in Seattle reported having easy access to handguns, while 11.4% of males and 1.5% of females reported owning a handgun. One-third of those who owned handguns reported that they had fired at someone. Further, almost 10% of female students reported a firearm homicide or suicide among family members or close friends (Callahan & Rivara, 1992). Another study from the southeast U.S. found that 9% of urban and suburban youth owned a handgun (Larson, 1994).

A poll of students in grades six through twelve conducted by Louis Harris for the Harvard School of Public Health in 1993 found that 59% said they could get a handgun if they wanted one, and 21% said they could get one within the hour. More than 60% of urban youth reported that they could get a handgun, and 58% of suburban youth also claimed that they could (Larson, 1994). Fifteen percent of students reported carrying a handgun in the past month, 11% said that they had been shot at, 9% said that they had fired a gun at someone, and 4% said they had carried a gun to school in the past year (Drevitch, 1994; Hull, 1993).

In a study of two public inner-city junior high schools in Washington, D.C., 47% of males reported having ever carried knives, and 25% reported having ever carried guns for protection or to use in case they got into a fight; 37% of females reported having carried a knife for these purposes. Both schools are located in high-crime areas (Webster, Gainer, & Champion, 1993).

WHY DO YOUNG PEOPLE CARRY WEAPONS?

A common reason given by young people for carrying weapons is for protection against being "jumped" (Price, Desmond, & Smith, 1991). However, research has shown that weapon-carrying among youth appears to be more closely associated with criminal activity, delinquency, and aggressiveness than to purely defensive behavior (Sheley, McGee, & Wright, 1992; Webster, Gainer, & Champion, 1993). Handgun ownership by inner-city high school youth has been associated with gang membership, selling drugs, interpersonal violence, being convicted of crimes, and either suspension or expulsion from school (Callahan & Rivara, 1992). Gun-carrying among junior high students is also strongly linked with indicators of serious delinquency, such as having been arrested (Webster, Gainer, & Champion, 1993). These studies have the following implications for the prevention of gun-carrying among youth (Webster, Gainer, & Champion, 1993):

If gun carrying stems largely from antisocial attitudes and behaviors rather than from purely defensive motives of otherwise nonviolent youths, interventions designed to prevent delinquency may be more effective than those that focus only on educating youths about the risks associated with carrying a gun. The latter may, however, be able to deter less hardened youths from carrying weapons in the future. Intensive and comprehensive interventions directed at high-risk children could possibly "inoculate" children against the many social factors that foster criminal deviance and the most violent behavior patterns. (p. 1608)

HOW ARE FIREARMS OBTAINED?

Adult criminals and youth involved in illegal activities have reported that guns are not difficult to obtain. Illegal or unregulated transactions are the primary sources of guns used in violent acts; stealing, borrowing from friends or acquaintances, and illegal purchasing of guns are the most common. Less than 1 in 5 guns used for illegal activities were purchased from licensed dealers. The most commonly cited reason for acquiring a gun is "self-defense" (Roth, 1994).

FIREARMS AND VIOLENCE

Every day in the United States there are 733 shootings (Cotton, 1992). It is estimated that 66.7 million handguns and 200 million firearms of all kinds are in circulation (Larson, 1994). About one-half of all households own at least one firearm and one-quarter own a handgun (Reiss & Roth, 1993). Experts assert that greater availability of guns increases the rates of murder and felony gun use. However, the greater availability of guns does not appear to affect levels of violence in general (Roth, 1994).

Firearm-Related Deaths

Gun-related homicides, suicides, and accidental shootings account for approximately 38,000 deaths a year in the United States (Buchsbaum, 1994); approximately 60% of all homicide victims in the United States are killed with firearms. Handguns account for 80% of homicides committed with firearms, although they comprise only about one-third of all firearms owned (Roth, 1994). For the first time in many decades, the number of firearm-related deaths surpassed that of motor-vehicle-related deaths in seven states (California, Louisiana, Maryland, Nevada, New York, Texas, and Virginia) and the District of Columbia (Centers for Disease Control, 1994). If recent trends continue, firearms will displace motor vehicle crashes as the leading cause of injury death nationally within a few years (Fingerhut, Jones, & Makuc, 1994). Firearm injuries primarily affect young people, resulting in greater loss of potential life years than cancer and heart disease combined.

Larson (1994) noted:

Over the last two years firearms killed almost 70,000 Americans, more than the total of U.S. soldiers killed in the entire Vietnam War. Every year handguns alone account for 22,000 deaths. In Los Angeles County, 8,050 people were killed or wounded in 1991, according to a report in the *Los Angeles Times*—thirteen times the number of U.S. forces killed in the Persian Gulf war. Every day, the handguns of America kill sixty-four people: twenty-five of the dead are victims of homicide; most of the rest shoot themselves. Handguns are used to terrorize countless others; over the next twenty-four hours, handgun-wielding assailants will rape 33 women, rob 575 people, and assault another 1,116. (p. 17)

Firearms and Health Care Costs

Each year, firearm attacks injure 70,000 victims in the United States, some of whom are left permanently disabled. The cost of firearm shootings, through violent attacks, accidents, or intentional self-infliction, is estimated at $19 billion nationwide for medical care, long-term disability, and premature death (New York Academy of Medicine, 1994). The average cost per firearm fatality is $373,000, and 40% of spinal injuries in inner-city areas are the result of gunshot injuries (Cotton, 1992). A study of one urban area hospital revealed that 86% of the costs of firearm injuries are paid by taxes (Cotton, 1992).

Firearm Violence and Youth

Among teenagers 15–19 years of age and young adults 20–24 years of age, 1 of every 4 deaths is by a firearm. One of every 8 deaths in children 10–14 is by a firearm. For those 15–19 there are substantial variations by race and sex in the percentage of deaths due to firearms. Among African-American teenage males, 60% of deaths result from firearm injury compared with 23% of white teenage males. Among African-American teenage females it is 22% compared with 10% of white female teenagers (Fingerhut, 1993). The number of African-American males aged 15–19 who died from gunshot wounds in 1990 was nearly five times higher than the number who died from AIDS, sickle-cell disease, and all other natural causes combined (Fingerhut, 1993; Kellerman, 1994).

In 1990, 82% of all homicide victims aged 15–19 (91% and 77% African-American and white males, respectively) and 76% of victims aged 20–24 (87% and 71% among African-American and white males, respectively) were killed with guns. Firearm homicide for African-American males 15–19 years of age was 11 times the rate among white males, 105.3 compared with 9.7 per 100,000 population. The rate for African-

American females was five times the rate for white females, 10.4 compared with 2.0 per 100,000 population (Fingerhut, 1993).

In 1990, 67.3% of all suicides among teenagers aged 15–19 were the result of firearms. Since 1985 the overall rate of suicide for teenagers by firearms increased from 6.0 to 7.5 per 100,000. The group of teenagers with the largest percent increase was African-American males; however, white male teenagers (13.5 per 100,000) had a higher firearm suicide rate in 1990 compared with African-American males (8.8 per 100,000). During this same time period, the rate of suicide not involving firearms decreased for both African-American and white males and females (Fingerhut, 1993).

CONTROLLING THE CARRYING OF WEAPONS IN SCHOOLS

Schools are grappling with the problem of protecting children and school staff from the violence surrounding them. Episodes of violence, particularly gun violence, are increasing in schools (Nordland, 1992) and violent attacks involving even elementary school children appear to be on the increase. Thus, gun violence has become a major concern for schools across the nation—a concern that is no longer limited to large cities, but extends to smaller cities and rural areas (Morganthau, 1992).

School security and law enforcement officials estimate that four of every five firearms that are carried into schools come from the students' homes; they bring one of their parents' firearms for "show and tell" with friends. Law enforcement officials also note that firearms are easily accessible by other means. They are readily borrowed from friends, bought by proxy, stolen, or even rented. On the street, guns can be purchased for as little as $25.

The following position paper of the National Association of Secondary School Principals Board on Weapons in Schools outlines the need to control weapons and offers several ways in which educators can work toward that end (Kressly, 1994):

Whereas, students have a right to attend school without a fear of weapons' violence to themselves or others;
Whereas, safe schools enhance the learning environment, necessary to quality schools, which are essential to a successful democracy;
Whereas, the causes of violence are multiple: chronic poverty, the lack of jobs and role models, the disintegration of families, the loss of moral values, and a popular culture that seems to glorify violence at every turn;
Whereas, a major 1993 Louis Harris poll about guns among American youth reports that 1 in 25 students takes a handgun to school in a single month, and 59% know where to get a handgun if they need one;
Whereas, violence is exacerbated with the increase of weapons in our schools, resulting in some 31 deaths from guns during the 1992–93 school year; be it therefore known that The National Association of Secondary School Principals:

• supports passage of the Brady Bill, which requires a waiting period and background check before legal purchase of a handgun;
• urges full enforcement of the Gun-Free School Zones Act of 1990;
• calls on Congress to pass the Safe Schools Act of 1993, with an amendment that will ban the purchase of a handgun and semi-automatic guns for any person under the age of 21;
• urges schools to provide staff training for weapons situations arising in school, and to implement student awareness programs which challenge youths' falsely held beliefs that they are invincible;
• challenges schools to implement apprehension, prevention, intervention, and counseling programs to combat possession of weapons and violent acts;
• encourages school-based parent involvement programs to include violence prevention strategies that emphasize the issue of easy access to handguns;
• exhorts school districts to establish violence prevention curriculum, grades K–12, and promote articulation among levels to ensure continuity in policies and practices;
• challenges Schools of Education to add conflict resolution and violence coping skills to their teacher preparation programs.

Weapon-Security Measures

When weapons are carried into schools, especially guns, the potential for a violent episode is heightened and, in recent years, there have been far too many violent episodes involving weapons on school campuses that have led to tragedy (Morganthau, 1992). Preventing violence calls for school policies that provide for school environments that are free from violence for students, staff, and others on school premises (Friedlander, 1993). For some school systems this may mean providing such controls as locker searches, weapons searches, hiring police to patrol school premises, allowing students to wear only see-through backpacks, and possibly providing metal detectors upon entry. Some school systems have even created separate alternative schools for young people with a history of violent and abusive behavior. While this option is attracting attention, it is also controversial (Harrington-Lueker, 1992).

A study by the American School Board revealed that 50% of school districts conduct locker searches, 36% conduct search and seizure activities, 36% maintain security personnel in schools, 31% have gunfree school zones, and 15% have metal detectors (Natale, 1994). Approximately one-fourth of large urban school districts in the United States use metal detectors to help reduce weapon-carrying in schools (Centers for Disease Control, 1993). According to the Centers for Disease Control, these detectors may help reduce, but do not eliminate, weapon-carrying in schools and to and from schools. Students who attended schools with metal detector programs were as likely as those attending schools without metal detectors to carry weapons elsewhere, but were less likely to have carried a weapon inside the school building (7.8% versus 13.6%) or going to and from school (7.7% versus 15.2%). Decreases in school-related weapon-carrying were due to decreases in the carrying of both knives and handguns. The presence of metal detectors had no apparent effect on the prevalence of threats and physical fights inside the school, to and from school, or anywhere else (Centers for Disease Control, 1993).

Security measures and equipment are expensive; walk-through metal detectors can cost up to $10,000 each and X-ray equipment designed to detect weapons in book bags can cost as much as $17,000. Hiring security personnel is also expensive. Despite these measures, students are known to have successfully carried weapons into schools, usually by sneaking them through windows or unguarded entrances, much to the frustration of many school administrators. Some school districts are reluctant to implement new security measures, particularly metal detectors, because they fear it may open them up to lawsuits (Glazer, 1992).

The Need for Cooperative Action

It is obvious that schools alone cannot be totally effective in controlling availability of weapons. Controlling access will require the cooperation of many individuals and institutions. The New York Academy of Medicine (1994) has proposed the following:

1. Implementing a national licensure system for firearm possession;
2. Limiting the manufacture, sale, and distribution of military-style assault weapons;
3. Increasing the tax on firearms and ammunition;
4. Tightening federal licensing requirements for gun dealers;
5. Limiting the number of guns an individual can buy;
6. Implementing a gun return program;
7. Implementing a firearm fatality and injury reporting system; and
8. Educating the public to the dangers of guns and the need for national regulation.

References

Buchsbaum, H. (1994). Guns r us. *Scholastic Update,* February 11, 18–19.

Callahan, C. M., & Rivara, F. P. (1992). Urban high school youth and handguns: A school-based survey. *Journal of the American Medical Association,* 267, 3038–3042.

Centers for Disease Control. (1991). Weapon-carrying among high school students—United States, 1990. *Morbidity and Mortality Weekly Report,* 40, 681–684.

Centers for Disease Control. (1993). Violence-related attitudes and behaviors of high school students—New York City, 1992. *Morbidity and Mortality Weekly Report,* 42, 773–777.

Centers for Disease Control. (1994). Deaths resulting from firearm- and motor-vehicle-related injuries—United States, 1968–1991. *Morbidity and Mortality Weekly Report,* 43, 37–42.

Cotton, P. (1992). Gun-associated violence increasingly viewed as public health challenge. *Journal of the American Medical Association,* 267, 1171–1173.

Drevitch, G. (1994). River of blood, river of tears. *Scholastic Update,* February 11, 4–5.

Fingerhut, L. A. (1993). Firearm mortality among children, youth, and young adults 1–34 years of age, trends and current status: United States, 1985–90. *Advance Data from Vital and Health Statistics* (No. 231). Hyattsville, MD: National Center for Health Statistics.

Fingerhut, L. A., Jones, C., & Makuc, D. M. (1994). Firearm and motor vehicle injury mortality—Variations by state, race, and ethnicity: United States, 1990–1991. *Advance Data from Vital and Health Statistics* (No. 242). Hyattsville, MD: National Center for Health Statistics.

Friedlander, B. Z. (1993). We can fight violence in the schools. *Educational Digest,* May, 11–14.

Glazer, S. (1992). Violence in schools. *CQ Researcher,* September 11, 787–803.

Harrington-Lueker, D. (1992). Blown away by school violence. *American School Board Journal,* 179, 20–26.

Hull, J. D. (1993). A boy and a gun: Even in a town like Omaha, Nebraska, the young are packing weapons in a deadly battle against fear and boredom. *Time,* August 2, 21–27.

Kellerman, A. L. (1994). Annotation: Firearm-related violence—What we don't know is killing us. *American Journal of Public Health,* 84, 541–542.

Kissell, K. P. (1993). Guns on rise in rural schools. *The Morning Call,* March 21.

Kressly, J. C. (1994). Targeting potential violence before tragedy strikes. *Schools in the Middle,* February, 27–30.

Larson, E. (1994). *Lethal passage: How the travels of a single handgun expose the roots of America's gun crisis.* New York: Crown.

Morganthau, T. (1992). It's not just New York . . . Big cities, small towns: More and more guns in younger hands. *Newsweek,* March 9, 25–29.

Natale, J. A. (1994). Roots of violence. *American School Board Journal,* March, 33–40.

New York Academy of Medicine. (1994). Firearm violence and public health: Limiting the availability of guns. *Journal of the American Medical Association,* 271, 1281–1283.

Nordland, R. (1992). Deadly lessons. *Newsweek,* March 9, 22–24.

Price, J. H., Desmond, S. M., & Smith, D. (1991). Inner city adolescents' perceptions of guns—A preliminary investigation. *Journal of School Health,* 61, 255–259.

Reiss, A. J., & Roth, J. A. (1993). *Understanding and preventing violence: Panel on the understanding and control of violent behavior.* Washington, D.C.: National Academy Press.

Roth, J. A. (1994). Firearms and violence. *National Institute of Justice: Research in Brief,* February, 1–7.

Sheley, J. F., McGee, Z. T., & Wright, J. D. (1992). Gun-related violence in and around inner-city schools. *American Journal of Diseases in Children,* 146, 677–682.

Webster, D. W., Gainer, P. S., & Champion, H. R. (1993). Weapon carrying among inner-city junior high school students: Defensive behavior vs. aggressive delinquency. *American Journal of Public Health,* 83, 1604–1608.

Measuring and Monitoring Children's Well-Being across the World

Arlene Bowers Andrews and Asher Ben-Arieh

An international initiative to measure and monitor the status of children beyond survival is an effort to use tools of the information age to promote understanding of children's life perspectives and an action to improve their condition. An interdisciplinary group proposes widespread consensus on the selection and monitoring of cross-cultural indicators to cover the following children's life domains: social connectedness, civil life skills, personal life skills that enable children to contribute to their own well-being, safety and physical status, and children's subculture. Social workers can contribute substantially to the design, collection, interpretation, and use of indicators in various arenas ranging from local to global levels.

Key words: *children, cross-cultural indicators, well-being*

As an undergraduate psychology student, I was required to sit for an hour each week watching a preschool child at the university lab school, writing copious notes about every move she made, every word she said, everything she did. The exercise was intended to develop our budding observational skills as behavioral scientists. It accomplished more than that. As I watched and wrote, an empathic awareness grew within me about how this child saw and felt her world. By collecting and analyzing child behavioral data, I changed. I began to cast away the socialization that led me to exclude and trivialize children in my life. I tried to understand the child and what the child was contributing to my world.

—A. B. Andrews

What would the earth be like if, for the first time in human history, adults collectively focused attention on the lives of the youngest members of the race? Granted, most adults

generally try to act in the best interests of children, although they do so from their own adult-centric perspectives as nurturers and protectors. For adults to listen to children or view the world through the eyes of children departs radically from the dominant paradigm. This article describes an evolving international effort to use tools of the information age to help people, young and old, understand children and their environments. The effort, driven by a moral imperative to honor the dignity of young humans and a practical compulsion to improve the overall human condition, promotes cross-cultural measurement and monitoring of the state of children beyond survival.

The social work profession can contribute substantially to this effort. Social workers, trained to value information as power recognize how information shapes public policy and social services. The policy arena is full of

From *Social Work*, March 1999, pp. 105-115. © 1999 by the National Association of Social Workers, Inc. Reprinted by permission.

facts, opinions, and beliefs with varying degrees of accuracy. Increasingly, policymakers and managers expect reliable, valid information. People with access to data and options about how to use it (or not) wield considerable influence in the policy process. Those without information remain frustratingly powerless.

Children are among the groups in society who have rarely been encouraged to speak for themselves in the public policy arena. They are invisible and their voices are relatively silent, although caring adults do attempt to represent their interests. Throughout the history of democracy, information about children has been offered in the policy process to promote and evaluate policies and programs that affect children's lives. The information is meager compared with that produced in the interest of economic wealth (for example, hourly and daily market reports), military security (for example, immediate status reports on all systems), or the physical environment (for example, moment-by-moment weather and pollution reports). Sophisticated data systems permit monitoring of trends and forecasts of needs for everything from pork bellies to airline tickets, but the capacity to portray children's needs and resources is limited. The combination of silent voices and insufficient information in their interests has contributed to the relatively powerless position of children in society.

Debate continues about whether children should have political power, stature, or human rights, even though revolutionary action has been taken by almost all nations of the world through their adoption of the United Nations' *Convention on the Rights of the Child*. (As of this writing, the United States is one of the few countries that has not ratified the treaty. Even without weight of law, it is useful as a set of principles to guide policy and programs.) The convention establishes children's rights to survive, develop, be protected, and participate in matters affecting them while acknowledging respect for the rights and duties of family, community (as provided for by local custom), legal guardians, or others responsible for the children. Nations are working to transform children's rights from rhetoric to reality at varying paces depending on political will and resources. Even if children's rights were never to be realized, gathering information about children's lives and well-being has value simply because the knowledge would

contribute to understanding human potential throughout the life span.

This article summarizes a current international initiative that is an effort to measure and monitor child well-being with emphasis on the child's perspective and reality (Ben-Arieh & Wintersberger, 1997). The initiative builds on current trends within and across nations to gather and report statistical and qualitative data about children's lives. Current knowledge tends to be deficit-based, emphasizing children's problems rather than strengths. The initiative proposes new ways to present existing data and gather information that portrays the lives of children more holistically. Availability of such information should have significant implications for social policy development and social work practice.

The Call for Information about Children's Lives

The movement to monitor children's lives internationally emerges from several convergent trends: increased political attention to the human ecology, global interdependence, progress in human rights, emphasis by human services professionals on the strengths perspective, social scientific technology, the call for improved government and community accountability, and the need and obligation of society to advance children's well-being.

Human Ecology

Social workers are well versed in the ecology of human development throughout the life span (Bronfenbrenner, 1979; Germain, 1987; Lyons, Wodarski, & Feit, 1997). Growing public awareness of this perspective is demonstrated by international popularity of the African proverb, "It takes a village to raise a child," and political emphasis on improving the family and neighborhood environments in which children are raised (Andrews, 1997). Thus far political emphasis has been on promoting positive processes and resource transfers into the lives of children. Relatively little attention has been given to the contributions children make to the world, although ecological science informs us that humans are interdependent across generations, implying that adults need children. Danish sociologist Jens Qvortrup called for a shift beyond the conventional preoccupation with children as the so-called "next generation" (Qvortrup, 1991). He argued that the tendency to regard children as human "becomings" rather than human beings denies their worth and dignity. Children profoundly influence their immediate and distant environments, yet remarkably little is known about the transfer of resources from them to others and how they influence the social processes of which they are a part. Clearly more knowledge is needed about how children influence their own and others' lives.

Global Interdependence

As understanding of human ecology advances, knowledge about the increasing global interdependence among nations and people grows. National economies are inextricably linked, communication and transportation allow frequent contact and connectedness across political and geographic boundaries, and human migration patterns create increasingly diverse populations. Meanwhile, notions about what conditions are adequate and necessary for child development vary across nations and habitats and within societal groups. Although standards for child development may vary across jurisdictions, children would benefit from international efforts to discover standards that promote equitable living conditions for all children. This process would require social scientific research and political discourse about child well-being.

Notions about what conditions are adequate and necessary for child development vary across nations and habitats and within societal groups.

Human Rights

The international human rights movement, girded by various declarations and conventions of the United Nations, brings attention to the conditions of excluded and marginalized people around the world. In 1989 the UN *Convention on the Rights of the Child* recognized each child as fully human and designated children as a group in need of special care and protection. The convention stipulates numerous child rights, including the child's right to living conditions adequate for physical, mental, spiritual, moral, and social development. The convention requires the participation of children in decisions that affect their lives, given their evolving capacity, thus stipulating that children's voices be heard. It requires state parties to report measures taken to secure the various rights in their countries and creates a UN committee to monitor international progress on children's rights attainment. The monitoring of children's rights throughout the world will generate valuable information about the potential lives of children, but monitoring human rights is a legal process that differs substantially from monitoring the status of children. As with the experience of civil rights monitoring in the United States, the existence of a right does not automatically lead to its realization in the lives of all people. To know the condition of a child, a measure of the child's status must be taken.

Strengths Perspective

Another trend is the search for positive indicators of human status and development beyond survival. With regard to children, social indicator research has essentially included social "problem" indicators. The body of knowledge about children's problems and threats to their survival and development far exceeds what is known about children's strengths, satisfaction, and realization of opportunities. Even measuring the absence of risk factors or negative behaviors differs form measuring the presence of protective factors or positive behaviors (Aber & Jones, 1995).

Technology

The information age has brought sufficient technology to allow accurate monitoring of children's lives using quantifiable and qualitative measures. Social indicators research has evolved for several decades, although considerably more progress has been made with regard to health, education, and economic indicators. Economic indicators often are used to connote social conditions, although the reliance on money as the key indicator falls short as a direct measure of quality of life. Zill (1995) called the origin of social indicators a "protest against the economic world view" (p. 18), noting that affluence or economic growth often are equated with the good society and that family income is regarded as the central measure of children's well-being. This view ignores research demonstrating that rampant social problems can and do increase as an economy grows and that family dynamics, regardless of family resources, powerfully predict child developmental outcomes. Economically, the United States can produce precise measures such as the gross domestic product (GDP), stock market reports, and consumer price index and can describe patterns such as expansion, inflation, recession, and cycle (Miringoff, 1995), but it cannot accurately report how many young children are unsupervised for part of the day or how many teenagers perform community service. International studies have shown that people in poor economic conditions as measured by income (which excludes other resources) may have high quality of life (Morris, 1979), reinforcing the need to develop indices that measure nonmonetary aspects of life.

The capacity for information processing is emerging in all but the most destitute countries. Measurement science and tools exist, and procedures have been used to develop reliable measures of social conditions across cultures, as focused studies have demonstrated (King, Wold, Tudor-Smith, & Harel, 1996; National Research Council, 1994–95; Smith, 1995). As developed nations blend the expertise of statisticians, human services professionals, policy analysts, computer scientists, and others to develop social indicators, special attention must be given to countries with inadequate capacity for information production so that their children can benefit from discoveries that are made elsewhere about children's lives.

Accountability

The call for improved government and community accountability has intensified as democracy has spread throughout the world. Accountability-based public policy requires accurate data about the outcomes of programs and policies. Also, there are macro forces other than government that affect children's lives. For example, children interact with the free market, mass media, natural environment, and other factors in their communities. Information about the effects of these factors on children's lives can inform social action as well as political action. Specific data about children are critical for needs and resource assessment, planning and monitoring, and results evaluation.

Civil Society

Finally, with relevant data, a society can examine itself and question whether its value system includes a commitment to its children, and if so, how that commitment is met. Collecting data on and monitoring the status of

child well-being is the only way society can answer such questions.

The State of the World's Children: What We Know

Monitoring the status of children is not new. UNICEF has published its *State of the World's Children* report since 1979. In recent years some developed countries have produced national reports, such as the U.S. Federal Interagency Forum on Child and Family Statistics' report, *America's Children: Key National Indicators of Well-Being* (1997), and *The State of the Child in Israel* (Ben-Arieh, 1992–96). In the United States, many states produce their own reports, such as those stimulated by the Annie E. Casey Foundation's Kids Count project (1997). A review of more than 20 "state of the child" reports from various nations reveals that the material is organized primarily by services system or resources that are available within the child's living conditions. For example, common domains are economic status (emphasis on poverty), health and nutrition (emphasis on mortality and morbidity, immunizations, low birthweight, teenage pregnancy), family structure, housing, educational achievement and failure, victimization, and negative social behavior (Ben-Arieh, 1997). Such indicators reveal more about how sick children are rather than how well they are.

Current efforts to monitor the status of children tend to emphasize children at extremes—those in the depths of despair and those who have attained remarkable levels of development or achievement. Compassion and moral responsibility compel nations to address the needs of those who suffer. Beyond identifying relative suffering and deprivation, the reliance on measures of central tendency may fail to serve the interests of children. Disaggregated data and measures that reflect the range and diversity of life situations among children would provide a more accurate and enriched perspective of what childhood is like (Miringoff & Miringoff, 1995).

Current studies verify that childhood living conditions vary dramatically across and within nations. Resources and opportunities have never been equitably distributed among children. Disparities between those who "have" and those who "have not" can be vast. A child's well-being is determined substantially by circumstances of birth: national origin; familial, social, racial, or ethnic identity and socioeconomic status; geographic location; gender; physical and mental ability; or other factors. Across the world, children of particular ethnic groups are excluded, marginalized, and exploited. Circumstances often change during a child's development, but many confront persistent deprivation, while others are indulged by privilege.

Two studies illustrate the discrepancy in living conditions. Using data from the annual UNICEF report on the condition of the world's children, Jordan (1993) estimated the quality of life for children in 122 countries on the basis of selected variables: mortality rate for children under age five, intake of daily caloric requirements, secondary school enrollment, life expectancy, percentage of females in the workforce, literacy rate, and GNP per capita. The differences between the top and bottom deciles (12 countries in each group) are extensive. For example, the mean under-five mortality rate (deaths per 1,000) was 10.33 for the top decile, 231.33 for the bottom. Mean female secondary school enrollment was 97.45 percent for the top decile, 6.27 percent for the bottom. Similarly, vast differences can exist within a nation. The Luxembourg Income Study examined wealth and poverty in 18 Western industrialized nations (Aber, 1997). The study demonstrated that the wealthiest U.S. children (those in the highest 10 percent by family after-tax income) were the richest of the nations studied. The poorest U.S. children (those in the bottom 10 percent) were poorer than children in 15 of 18 countries. The gap between affluent and poor U.S. children was the largest among the nations. The gap has been growing wider for more than 25 years, such that by 1994 the richest 20 percent of all Americans had 49.3 percent of the nation's income, whereas the poorest 20 percent had only 3.6 percent of the income (Haggarty & Johnson, 1996). One can only surmise what these discrepancies mean for children without more specific information about their lives and perceptions.

Existing data indicate how and where children's survival is threatened and has stimulated action (often insufficient) to save their lives. Current information reveals little about the lives of children beyond survival in various cultural contexts. Existing indicators often signify achievement, such as how much the child has grown or performed on a math test, but say little about how the child has been nourished physically and emotionally or how the child learns. With adults, quality of life

indices typically are composed of multiple measures that take into account life satisfaction and perceptions of needs, priorities, and aspirations (Baster, 1985). The qualitative data can validate the adequacy and relevance of more objective measures about living conditions.

Two critical factors must be considered in developing quality of life indicators about children: (1) focus on the child as the unit of observation and (2) the child's perspective. Often, indicators of child well-being are based on data that do not directly assess the child at all; rather, the unit of analysis is the family or the mother. For example, household composition—people with whom the child primarily resides—is often used to indicate family structure; from the child's point of view, the family may include the noncustodial parent, grandparent, or others with whom he or she stays for extended periods. Such information is lost in traditional measures. Children are thus invisible in statistical reports about social indicators in various countries (Jensen & Saporti, 1992). As Macer (1995) noted, "If analysts are interested in whether children are well fed, well housed, and provided sufficient medical care, they must measure these directly" (p. 6). Sen (1987) has argued for measures that reflect the life a person is actually living rather than the resources and means a person has for living conditions. Applying Sen's approach to assessment of a child's living conditions requires focus on the child rather than the household or community as the unit of observation.

Traditional measures of childhood living conditions and threats to well-being also fail to reflect the "subjective" perceptions and experiences of children (Prout, 1997). Social scientists historically have been reluctant to accept the reliability of children's self-reported information or their competence (Cases, 1997). That perception is changing, inspired in part by child advocates who maintain that the real problem is that adults have been unwilling or incompetent to understand children's expressions, perceptions, language, and culture. Adult-centric views exclude children, ignoring their truths and realities. Social scientists must accept the challenge of continuing to find ways to elicit information directly from children by using methods that are interesting, relevant, understandable, and developmentally appropriate (Aber & Jones, 1995).

Measures that have been widely available reflect former dominant theoretical perspec-

Table 1

Variables Associated with Positive Child Development

- adequate nourishment
- good health and access to health services when needed
- dependable attachments to parents or other adult caregivers
- more than one consistently involved adult who provides economic resources, interaction, support, regulation, and positive role modeling to the child
- firm, consistent, flexible discipline strategies
- social support and guidance when faced with adversity
- protection from physical and psychological harm
- cognitively stimulating physical and social environments
- play activities and opportunities to explore
- meaningful participation in community life appropriate for age and ability
- access to resources for special needs

tives that emphasize ranking, competition, and dualism. In essence, the changing political, social, economic, and technological forces across the world now permit focus on the diversity and qualitative differences in children's lives, so the time has come to adapt measurement and monitoring processes accordingly.

The State of the World's Children: What Could We Know?

The search for more thorough and accurate indicators of children's lives is underway. A group of 40 experts representing diverse disciplines (statistics, demography, social work, political science, international law, developmental psychology, economics, and community development) from 20 countries has convened twice to discuss development of more appropriate indicators to measure the well-being of children beyond survival (Ben-Arieh & Wintersberger, 1997). Thus far the group has reviewed previous and current efforts to measure and monitor the status of children within and across countries and has formulated a preliminary conceptual framework and principles for developing indicators. Their work parallels interorganizational efforts in the United States reported by the Institute for Research on Poverty (Hauser, Brown, & Prosser, 1997; University of Wisconsin-Madison, 1995).

Substantial primary research exists to support the selection of standards for adequate childhood levels of living in many areas. For example, studies of U.S. children indicate that positive child development, as evidenced by academic achievement, social adjustment, and

physical health, are associated with factors such as those listed on Table 1 (Amato, 1995; Bronfenbrenner, 1979; Hamburg, 1996; McDonald & Moyle, 1997). Material resources such as nutritious food, safe water, clothing, and housing are necessary but insufficient for holistic development. Stable, nurturing social relationships and safe, stimulating environments are also essential (Hutton, 1991). Indicators can be developed to reflect such knowledge.

The international study group has considered hundreds of discrete indicators within a variety of frameworks for organizing a view of children's lives. Consensus is emerging that indicators should cover the following life domains:

- social connectedness: The child's social networks include family, peer, and community groups and can be measured according to density and quality. Such factors include children's participation in and perceptions of developmentally relevant activities such as school, informal education, recreation, and information networks and the relative organization they and their caregivers give to their lives.
- civil life skills: Children can develop social and civic responsibilities even in the early years, learning cooperation and participation in their small environments and gradually expanding their contributions as citizens as their environments expand with their evolving capacities. The nature and extent of their opportunities to express themselves, to learn respect for others and honor diversity, or to practice skills for civic life can be assessed.

- personal life skills: Children must learn skills to contribute to their own well-being, including self-esteem and assertiveness and the capacity to learn and work. These areas can be assessed through culturally relevant measures of education, developmental resources for special needs, personal traits, work, and protection from work or educational exploitation. Also, measures can be developed to understand the economy of childhood, including children's capacity to contribute to their own economic situations.
- safety and physical status: Millions of children are in threatening circumstances because of family violence; community violence; sexual exploitation; war and civil conflict; drought and famine; or their own institutionalization, homelessness, or refugee status. Even more are threatened because of inadequate health or mental health care. Measures can determine the nature and extent of such threats and conditions under which children feel safe. Children also can tell us about how they promote their own safety. From a strengths perspective, much more needs to be known about children's avenues to wellness through exercise, nutrition, and the health behaviors of themselves and those who care for them.
- children's subculture: Across political jurisdictions and cultures, children engage in work, play, creativity, consumption, social interactions, and other activities that are analogous to adult activities yet qualitatively different. To understand better the lives of children from a child-centric perspective and to enable their empowerment and life satisfaction, measures must be developed to assess their activities. Remarkably little is known on a broad scale about how children's subcultures survive and thrive within the dominant culture.

An array of existing measures can serve as the foundation for selecting key indicators of children's well-being (Ben-Arieh & Wintersberger, 1997). Many have methodological problems that affect cross-cultural and jurisdictional comparability, requiring further work to adapt the measures for international monitoring. Administrative data, such as school reports, birth certificates, and child protection reports, are relatively inexpensive to gather. Census or survey data exist in all but the poorest countries and can provide rich detail about the contexts in which children live. Primary research has addressed critical questions about specific aspects in children's lives, such as the causal linkages and mediating factors among life conditions and child status. Qualitative research methods are increasingly applied to studies of children's lives.

The selection of core indicators to measure the various domains of child life can draw from existing data but also will require development of new tools and processes. The selection must be guided by principles that address the purpose and scope of the measuring and monitoring process as well as the measurement accuracy. The indicators are intended to promote child well-being beyond survival to influence social and political change processes. Thus, they must raise the child's stature in the policy process by emphasizing the child as unit of observation, reflecting the child's voice and perceptions and enabling the child's rights. To meet this purpose the indicators should cover positive as well as negative aspects of child life and offer qualitative information to promote understanding of the context of living conditions. Politically, the emphasis on negative indicators—"bad news" without contextual information—has led to speculation about causal factors and the tendency to search for blame and punishment, contributing to political polarization that has failed to serve the interests of children. If the indicators are to serve an international monitoring function, they must have enduring importance across various cultures and include short- and long-term measures.

To be comprehensive the set of indicators should balance measures across various domains of children's lives and be constructed carefully to include current and historically excluded subpopulations of children (for example, those with disabilities; those in indigenous, ethnic minority, very poor, or isolated populations; those separated from families; or who are homeless, migrants, refugees, or immigrants). The measures should adequately portray the range, instability, and diversity of children's experiences by examining disaggregated data and central tendencies. Quantifiable and qualitative measures should address children's behaviors and processes and the structures of which they are a part. They should be grounded in theory and research that meets the tests of valid and reliable measurement (Moore, 1995).

Knowing the state of children, and even planning the best policy and interventions for children, is not enough. Monitoring the implementation of policies and programs is no less important. A society can see its achievements, its rate of progress, and its failures and barriers. The capacity for international data to affect local action for children is illustrated by the global response to UNICEF's "State of the World's Children" project (Adamson, 1996). As a result of the report, many countries, including the United States, have improved their immunization and school enrollment rates remarkably.

In short, the selection of indicators must be grounded in a vision that informed political and social action can support childhood as a phase of human life that is unique and inherently valuable to the child and all society.

Implications for Social Policy and Social Work Practice

Clearly, measuring and monitoring the status of children beyond survival has implications for advocacy, planning, and evaluation. Through local, national, and global organizations, social workers have long been actively engaged in collecting and using data about children. As efforts evolve to broaden the scope and perspectives of these processes, social workers can contribute substantially to the design, data collection, interpretation, and use of measures.

In particular the wisdom of direct practitioners can inform how to frame research questions and data collection procedures. For example, efforts to address teenage pregnancy often have relied on indicator research that asks youths about their sexual activity and contraceptive behavior. Alternative indicators based in practice and social research information would ask teenagers questions about the existence and nature of their steady, meaningful relationships with peers and adults and their productive activities. Increases in the presence and diversity of youth relationships and productive experiences would predictably be associated with decreasing sexual activity and unintended conception rates. Social workers can help frame such alternative questions and link researchers with child and youth populations for study.

Social workers have expertise to apply to data interpretation. Knowledge about the needs or assets of children suggests numerous potential interventions to improve or maintain their condition. Choosing among alternative courses of action requires additional information about effective policies, programs, and other responses that are empirically or theoretically linked to the indicators. Social workers can ensure that children, youths, and those who care for them are included in the decision-making process. As an applied profession, social work's role is critical at this stage of the measuring and monitoring process. Social scientists tend to observe changes; social workers make change happen.

Social workers also must contribute to mobilizing the potential users of information about children. In this information age, vast amounts of data are generated, analyzed, reported, and stored. Huge amounts of information are held in concrete or virtual data banks. Unleashing the power of the information requires careful packaging and audience preparation. Advocacy can grasp the attention of people who can influence children's lives and promote their use of international indicators of child well-being beyond survival.

Conclusion

The call for more information about the state of the world's children beyond survival reflects an ideological shift with regard to children that reinforces social work's ethical commitment to social justice and inclusiveness. The movement honors the significance of the child's voice and perspective, values childhood for its own sake as well as its place in human ecology, and acknowledges that children can teach and contribute as well as learn and receive.

References

Aber, J. L. (1997). Measuring child poverty for use in comparative policy analysis. In A. Ben-Arieh & H. Wintersberger (Eds.), *Monitoring and measuring the state of children—Beyond survival* (Eurosocial Report No. 62, pp. 193–207). Vienna: European Centre for Social Welfare Policy and Research.

Aber, J. L., & Jones, S. (1995). Indicators of positive development in early childhood: Improving concepts and measures. In *Indicators of children's well-being* (Conference Papers, Vol. III). Madison: University of Wisconsin-Madison, Institute for Research on Poverty (Special Report Series, 60c).

Adamson, P. (1996). *The state of the world's children 1995*. New York: UNICEF.

Amato, P. R. (1995). Single-parent households as settings for children's development, well-being, and attainment: A social network/resources perspective. *Sociological Studies of Children, 7,* 19–47.

Andrews, A. B. (1997). Assessing neighbourhood and community factors that influence children's well-being. In A. Ben-Arieh & H. Wintersberger (Eds.), *Monitoring and measuring the state of children—Beyond survival* (Eurosocial Report No. 62, pp. 127–141). Vienna: European Centre for Social Welfare Policy and Research.

Annie E. Casey Foundation. (1997). *Kids count data book: State profiles of child well-being—1996.* Baltimore: Author.

Baster, N. (1985). Social indicator research: Some issues and debates. In J. G. M. Hilhorst & M. Klatter (Eds.), *Social development in the third world: Level of living indicators and social planning* (pp. 23–46). London: Croom Helm.

Ben-Arieh, A. (1992–96). *The state of the child in Israel* (Hebrew). Jerusalem: The National Council for the Child.

Ben-Arieh, A. (1997). Measuring and monitoring the state of children (Introduction). In A. Ben-Arieh & H. Wintersberger (Eds.), *Monitoring and measuring the state of children—Beyond survival* (Eurosocial Report No. 62, pp. 9–26). Vienna: European Centre for Social Welfare Policy and Research.

Ben-Arieh, A., & Wintersberger, H. (Eds.). (1997). *Monitoring and measuring the state of children—Beyond survival* (Eurosocial Report No. 62). Vienna: Europoean Centre for Social Welfare Policy and Research.

Bronfenbrenner, U. (1979). *The ecology of human development: Experiments by nature and design.* Cambridge, MA: Harvard University Press.

Cases, F. (1997). Children's rights and children's quality of life: Conceptual and practical issues. *Social Indicators Research, 6,* 1–16.

Germain, C. B. (1987). Human development in contemporary environments. *Social Service Review, 61,* 565–580.

Haggarty, M., & Johnson, C. (1996). The social construction of the distribution of income and health. *Journal of Economic Issues, 30,* 525–532.

Hamburg, D. (1996). *A developmental strategy to prevent lifelong damage.* New York: Carnegie Corporation of New York.

Hauser, R., Brown, B. V., & Prosser, W. (Eds.). (1997). *Indicators of children's well-being.* New York: Russell Sage Foundation.

Hutton, S. (1991). Measuring living standards using existing national data sets. *Journal of Social Policy, 20,* 237–257.

Jensen, A. M., & Saporti, A. (1992). *Do children count?* Vienna: European Centre for Social Welfare Policy and Research.

Jordan, T. E. (1993). Estimating the quality of life for children around the world: NICQL '92. *Social Indicators Research, 30,* 17–38.

King, A., Wold, B., Tudor-Smith, C., & Harel, Y. (1996). *The health of youth: A cross-national survey.* New York: World Health Organization.

Lyons, P., Wodarski, J. S., & Feit, M. D. (1997). Human behavior theory: Emerging trends and issues. *Journal of Human Behavior in the Social Environment, 1*(1), 1–21.

Macer, S. E. (1995). Measuring income, employment, and the support of children. *Focus, 3,* 6. (University of Wisconsin-Madison, Institute for Research on Poverty).

McDonald, P., & Moyle, H. (1997). Self-fulfillment of children. In A. Ben-Arieh & H. Wintersberger (Eds.), *Monitoring and measuring the state of children—Beyond survival* (Eurosocial Report No. 62, pp. 229–237). Vienna: European Centre for Social Welfare Policy and Research.

Miringoff, M. L. (1995). Toward a national standard of social health: The need for progress in social indicators. *American Journal of Orthopsychiatry, 65,* 462–467.

Miringoff, M. L. & Miringoff, M. (1995). *Context and connection in social indicators: Enhancing what we measure and monitor.* Paper presented at Indicators of Child Well-Being Conference, Bethesda, MD, November 1994, sponsored by the University of Wisconsin-Madison, Institute for Research on Poverty.

Moore, K. (1995). Criteria for indicators of child well-being. *Focus, 3,* 8. (University of Wisconsin-Madison, Institute for Research on Poverty).

Morris, M. D. (1979). *Measuring the condition of the world's poor: The Physical Quality of Life Index.* New York: Pergamon.

National Research Council. (1994–95, Winter). *International comparative studies in education: Descriptions of selected large-scale assessments and case studies.* Washington, DC: National Research Council, Commission on Behavioral and Social Sciences and Education.

Prout, A. (1997). Objective vs. subjective indicators or both? Whose perspective counts? In a Ben-Arieh & H. Wintersberger (Eds.), *Monitoring and measuring the state of children—Beyond survival* (Eurosocial Report No. 62, pp. 89–100). Vienna: European Centre for Social Welfare Policy and Research.

Qvortrup, J. (1991). *Childhood as a social phenomenon: An introduction to a series of national reports* (2nd ed., Eurosocial Reports, Vol. 36). Vienna: European Centre for Social Welfare Policy and Research.

Sen, A. (1987). *The standard of living: The Tanner lectures, Clare Hall, Cambridge, 1985.* Cambridge, England: Cambridge University Press.

Smith, T. (1995). The international social survey program. *ICPSR Bulletin, 16*(1).

University of Wisconsin-Madison, Institute for Research on Poverty. (1995). Special issue on indicators of children's well being: A conference. *Focus, 3,* 1–32.

U.S. Federal Interagency Forum on Child and Family Statistics. (1997). *America's children: Key national indicators of well-being.* Washington, DC: U.S. Government Printing Office.

Zill, N. (1995). Back to the future: Improving child indicators by remembering their origins. *Focus, 3,* 17–24. (University of Wisconsin-Madison, Institute for Research on Poverty).

Arlene Bowers Andrews, PhD, LISW, is associate professor of social work and director, Division of Family Policy, Institute for Families in Society, University of South Carolina, Columbia, SC 29208; email: aandrews@ss1.csd.sc.edu. Asher Ben-Arieh, MSW, is director, Center for Research and Public Education, National Council for the Child, Jerusalem, Israel. The authors, part of an interdisciplinary international group, appreciate the ideas and information shared by the group members for this article.

Beyond the Boundaries of Child Welfare: Connecting with Welfare, Juvenile Justice, Family Violence and Mental Health Systems

A common thread linking child welfare systems, the juvenile justice system and domestic-violence incidents is substance abuse. This chapter excerpted from the Child Welfare League of America's report Responding to Alcohol and Other Drug Problems in Child Welfare, *examines the role of drug dependency in child welfare and explores the role of drug treatment in combating child abuse and child poverty.*

Several service systems outside the parameters of child welfare affect and are affected by alcohol and other drug (AOD) problems among children and families. Agencies in the domains of welfare reform, juvenile justice, family violence, and mental health are, at various stages, participants in the identification, assessment and prevention/treatment of problems among children and families affected by substance abuse. Child welfare services (CWS) practitioners have also emphasized the importance of school systems, primary health agencies, law enforcement and housing agencies in meeting the needs of CWS families with AOD problems. Child-welfare officials must acknowledge that these other systems are essential players in addressing AOD problems faced by children and families. This section describes the existing overlap of cases among these systems, highlighting the interrelated nature of these problems and their solutions, which often require services from systems other than AOD and child welfare.

The Link to TANF

The overlap of AOD problems with welfare caseloads underscores the importance of addressing poverty as well as the other underlying factors in child welfare caseloads. A recent work that has masterfully woven together the three policy arenas of human services reform, community organizing and community economic development is *Building Community*, by Bruner and Parachini (1997). Many practitioners would add a greater emphasis upon community or neighborhood development to efforts to build community partnerships for CWS, following the conclusions of a massive study of community prevention programs commissioned by the Office of Justice programs in the U.S. Department of Justice:

> ...community prevention programs address none of [the] causes of community composition and structure, which in turn influence community culture and the availability of criminogenic substances like guns and drugs.

From *Spectrum: The Journal of State Government*, Winter 1999, pp. 14-18. © 1999 by The Council of State Governments. Reprinted by permission.

Predictions in some states that welfare cuts will affect CWS caseloads have led to efforts to look more closely at the effects of the 1996 welfare-reform legislation on children. A series of federally and foundation-funded efforts based in a select group of states are monitoring the impact of welfare changes on the children of TANF recipients, including assessments of child-welfare impact. With the recently announced decline of welfare caseloads to below the level of 10,000,000 for the first time since 1970, information on the effects of these reductions on CWS caseloads becomes critical, especially those for child neglect. Judith Gueron of the Manpower Demonstration Research Corporation, which is conducting studies in Minnesota and Florida, stated in January 1998 that "about half of the people leaving welfare are employed, and half are not." The second group is the portion in which monitoring child neglect would seem critically important, since neglect is already making up a majority of Child Protective Services cases in most states.

A possible problem arises from the traditional separation between income support and child-welfare programs. Though often placed within the same agency, the two systems have tended to seek different goals: the welfare system seeks the removal of parents from welfare and the child-welfare system focuses upon children who may be endangered. With different eligibility rules, and now with different ideas of entitlement and time limits, the two systems will only work together effectively if these barriers can be overcome in family-centered approaches that take a wider view of clients' needs and strengths.

The Juvenile Justice Connection

The problems of substance-abusing parents of children are not confined to the domains of child welfare and welfare systems for some families—they extend further to impact the juvenile justice system. As the Child Welfare League of America notes: "The courts, like the child-welfare system, are in crisis—overwhelmed by . . . increasing numbers of cases involving alcohol and other drug abuse." Yet, there exists a major disconnect between the child welfare and juvenile justice systems. Recognizing the need for stronger linkages, participants at a recent Office of Juvenile Justice and Delinquency Prevention (OJJDP) conference concluded that "one large system"

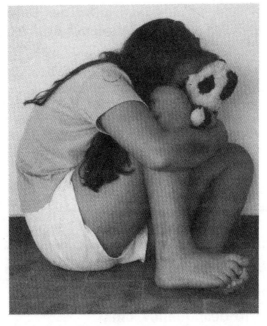

Drug and alcohol abuse are the biggest threats to child well-being, a Child Welfare League of America report says.

tice to work in tandem. Findings from the Rochester Youth Development Study, for instance, indicated that children who were abused or neglected were significantly more likely to engage in serious and violent delinquency. Forty-five percent of maltreated youth, compared to less than one-third (32 percent) of maltreated youth, had official records of delinquency. Maltreated children were also at increased risk of other interrelated problems in adolescence including drug use, poor academic performance, teen pregnancy, emotional and mental health disorders.

Family Violence, AOD Problems, and Child Welfare

The family violence problem overlaps child protec-

was needed to meet these families' complex needs. The conference summary captures the essence of the problem: Because abuse and dependency have root causes in dysfunctional families and unfavorable environments, and because being abused engenders the mental and emotional turmoil likely to lead to delinquency, child welfare and juvenile justice professionals end up working with many of the same kids.

Why the Juvenile Justice Connection Is Critical

Research on the relationship between childhood maltreatment and subsequent adolescent problem behaviors provides clear evidence of the need for child-welfare services and juvenile jus-

Fast Facts . . .

Forty-five percent of maltreated youth, compared to less than one-third (32 percent) of nonmaltreated youth, had official records of delinquency.

In a study of domestic assault incidents in Tennessee, 94 percent of the assailants and 43 percent of the victims had used alcohol and/or other drugs in the six hours prior to the assault.

Maltreated children were also at increased risk of other interrelated problems in adolescence including drug use, poor academic performance, teen pregnancy and emotional and mental health disorders.

tive services caseloads in many of the same ways that AOD problems do. There are important differences between the two problems, but first we need to understand how family violence and AOD issues are similar:

> Many professionals traditionally viewed the presence of adult-on-adult family violence as a problem that was irrelevant to their goal of protecting the children, and therefore did not ask about it during screening, investigation or assessment. As a result, effective child-abuse interventions were often sabotaged by the ongoing occurrence and escalation of domestic violence over time, and the children remained in danger.

Because abuse and dependency have root causes in dysfunctional families and unfavorable environments, and because being abused engenders the mental and emotional turmoil likely to lead to delinquency, child welfare and juvenile justice professionals end up working with many of the same kids.

If the words "domestic violence" and "family violence" were replaced with the words "AOD problems" in this selection, this quote would remain just as accurate. That underscores the extent to which both problems affect CWS caseloads and require changes in CWS practice to reduce the harm to children. Both problems are underemphasized in the typical CWS assessment, reflecting the limited training provided to CWS staff on the nature of the problems. Both problems undermine the effectiveness of child-abuse interventions. For example, parent-education courses may ignore the two problems in their curricula. Family-preservation programs undermine efforts to address family violence and AOD problems if they screen out these parents.

In addition to families in the CWS system, family violence and substance abuse also coexist in a significant number of other families. Both battered women and batterers are significantly affected by AOD use; several studies have found that more than 40 percent of homeless, lower income women report both physical and AOD abuse. In a study of domestic assault incidents in Tennessee, 94 percent of the assailants and 43 percent of the victims had used alcohol and/or other drugs in the six hours prior to the assault. A 1997 Treatment Improvement Protocol issued by the Center for Substance Abuse Treatment, titled *Substance Abuse Treatment and Domestic Violence*, included persuasive evidence that linked these two problems, and concluded that "failure to address domestic-violence issues interferes with treatment effectiveness and contributes to relapse."

Similarities Between Responses to Family Violence and AOD Problems

In response to these problems, similar proposals for reform have been developed by providers and advocates in both areas. These include strengthened training, revised assessment and screening protocols, access to experts in the specific fields of family violence and AOD, collaborative links to other agencies addressing problems of families in the CWS system, stronger links to community-based organizations and informal supports and changes in court procedures and legal requirements.

As is the case for AOD problems, the issue of assessment has special significance in addressing family violence, since routine assessment practices do not seek information on family violence in sufficient depth to ensure that this condition is tracked over time to determine its impact on the family. Several articles on family violence and its impact on families have recommended more thorough assessment practices, but without taking into account the "layering" effect discussed previously, in which each problem is the focus of another, entirely separate assessment. This problem of layered assessments also complicates making separate AOD assessments on top of current risk-assessment procedures. An issue of added importance in assessing family-violence problems is the need to conduct separate interviews with the victims of family violence, apart from the perpetrators of violence and their children.

Training is also an area of reform addressed by advocates for more attention to both AOD and family violence with the models for AOD-CWS training described above as prime examples. Within the family-violence field, training curricula have been developed by the Family Violence Prevention Fund and the University of Iowa for use in training CWS staff, as well as other human service intake workers, in several states and communities.

In both areas, community norms are an important factor. On the one hand, there is still acceptance of family violence and substance abuse as "normal" behavior that is often viewed by law-enforcement staff as a private matter within the family. However, the community can also serve as an important source of pressure on parents whose behavior endangers their children, as well as a source of support for parents who want help. Reforms aimed at law-enforcement personnel and court staff have been undertaken as a means of improving the responses of both sets of critical agencies.

Specific language in the welfare-reform legislation refers to family violence, and with the substantial overlap between AOD use and family violence, policy-makers should carefully review the extent to which these two problems affect an overlapping group of both TANF and CWS clients.

Differences Between Responses to Family Violence and AOD Problems

In family-violence situations, there are usually a clear perpetrator and a clear victim, as opposed to AOD problems in the CWS system, where the parents are abusing alcohol and/or other drugs or are chemically dependent in a way that affects their parenting. This difference in perspective regarding the target of intervention leads to a different focus for treatment and prevention. In the family-violence situation, the batterer is the focus of treatment efforts and the victim is the focus for supportive services and advocacy. In the CWS system, the effects on children are the focus, but in the AOD system, the focus is on the AOD user.

Abuse is the typical problem for family-violence victims in the CWS system, while neglect is a much more common problem for families affected by AOD (although some studies have found that alcohol abuse is correlated with physical abuse and illicit drug use is correlated with neglect).

Sanctions are viewed differently in the two systems, with family-violence agencies seeking heavier sanctions against perpetrators and AOD systems using sanctions to reinforce the behavior sought in improved parenting. Family-violence personnel typically favor noncoercive intervention for victims and sanctions applied to perpetrators, with some important exceptions when children are endangered. AOD systems use both coercive and noncoercive treatment, since research shows little difference in the ultimate outcomes.

Working with Family Violence Prevention and Treatment Agencies

Unfortunately, these differences and the traditional tendency of the human-service systems to take a categorical approach to all problems have meant that the majority of literature and training materials addressing AOD or family violence has almost completely ignored the other issue. As a 1994 review of child abuse and substance abuse stated: Experts have been identified in chemical dependency, child abuse, and violence, but cross-fertilization in these highly correlated fields seldom occurs.

There are important recent exceptions, however. Discussions sponsored by the Clark Foundation, both under the auspices of its Community Partnerships initiative and in an earlier Executive Session on the future of the CWS system convened by the John F. Kennedy School of Government at Harvard University from 1994 to 1997, have begun to frame the issues of the overlap more ex-

plicitly. Materials developed by Susan Schechter of the University of Iowa have proposed treatment programs that address both family violence and AOD problems of batterers. But much remains to be done in this area.

Important organizational issues are also raised by the attempt to create new units that address family violence and AOD problems in the CWS system. Establishing a unit specifically to deal with family-violence issues is an appropriate recommendation, although establishing a similar unit for AOD issues—and for child sexual abuse, mental health, and TANF liaison—is also appropriate. But a significant problem with forming a new unit is that it sometimes enables an organization to isolate an innovation and keep it away from the mainstream of the organization. The larger challenge may be infusing the concepts of sensitivity to both family violence and AOD problems throughout the organization. Recently, San Diego County, California, reorganized its health and human services agency to include an AOD focus in each of the new operating units, rather than in a separate, more isolated AOD unit. Massachusetts has used a separate unit to pilot interdisciplinary teams that include family-violence expertise as well as other disciplines relevant to CWS. Service providers may not always welcome the infusion approach, as opposed to having their own identifiable unit. But at the very least, the trade-off between a new entity and the infusion approach should be addressed explicitly. It is critical that efforts to improve the child welfare system's handling of both AOD problems and family violence devote adequate attention to documenting that such efforts will succeed in improving outcomes for children and families. As Aron and Olson note:

> It may be worthwhile to develop methods to justify these resources, such as documenting the number of families in need, tracking these families over time, and observing if they are more likely to re-enter the child welfare system or use more expensive services because of unaddressed domestic-violence concerns.

The same questions apply to AOD-targeted reforms, in which changes in clients, workers and systems should all be the focus of serious evaluation designed to make the case for such reforms based on results, not just good intentions. These discussions about outcomes will get to the heart of some of the important philosophical differences in perspectives, including the issue of whether removal of children (and parents) from the home is an indicator of success or failure. In serious discussion of outcomes across the boundaries of the fields of AOD, CWS and family violence, the measures of success must be defined in ways that are clear to all three groups, while allowing flexibility for different perspectives on the needs of children and families. For a copy of the full report, contact the Child Welfare League of America (202) 638—2952.

Unit 5

Key Points to Consider

❖ Is universal health care for all a realistic and affordable goal for the United States? Why or why not?

❖ How would you react to the statement, "In any mixed group discussion on abortion, all the men present should remain quiet and listen for the first 30 minutes, since abortion can never personally affect them"? Defend your answer.

❖ What are your thoughts on managed care within both health and mental health environments?

❖ Do you agree that religion and spirituality have a legitimate place within the social welfare system in the United States? Why or why not?

❖ Why are cultural sensitivities so important in mental health treatment situations? Can you think of any examples from your own cultural, ethnic, or racial heritage? Explain.

❖ Should poor defendants be expected to pay for their legal fees when they have been arrested? What about in civil cases? What if their sole source of income is public assistance? Discuss.

❖ React to the statement, "Private, for-profit prisons, operating under the rules of the competitive marketplace, will be more effective in their outcomes and more efficient in their operations as compared to publicly funded prisons." Defend your answer.

 **Links** **www.dushkin.com/online/**

These sites are annotated on pages 4 and 5.

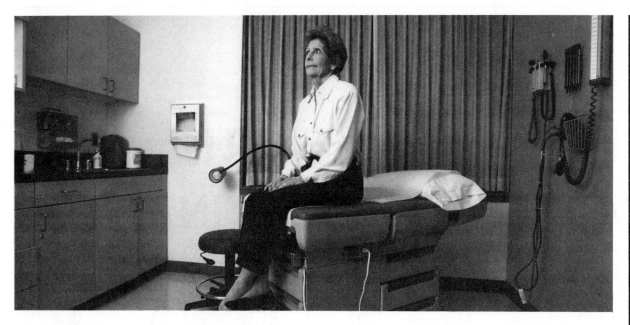

As discussed in unit 3, social services are those "soft" benefits that are neither in the form of cash nor in-kind resources and are widely distributed in some manner to many individuals and families throughout the United States. Social workers are one of the leading group of professionals who provide these social services, either directly to recipients or indirectly through their roles as supervisors, administrators, policy analysts, or researchers.

As the title of this final section indicates, the articles are grouped in subsections that provide information about social services in areas of health, mental health and mental retardation, and corrections.

The first four articles in this section relate to issues of concern to social workers within a medical care environment. Stephen Gorin outlines the parameters of a national health policy that would guarantee comprehensive health care protection for all Americans in his article, "Universal Health Care Coverage in the United States: Barriers, Prospects, and Implications." This provides a framework to understand what an "ideal" health care system would look like to most social workers.

Helen Edelman's article, "Safe to Talk: Abortion Narratives as a Rite of Return," takes no stand either pro-choice or pro-life. Instead, Edelman gives voice to women who have had abortions and who now wish to express their feelings about the extremely personal decision they have made. In "The Chasm in Care," Josie Glausiusz discusses the latest information regarding the spread of HIV and the availability of drug treatments in international contexts. "Religion/Spirituality and Health among Elderly African Americans and Hispanics" introduces the somewhat controversial issue of spirituality and health care. Drawing on distinct minority cultural experiences, Jacqueline Stolley and Harold Koenig encourage all human service workers to incorporate the religious beliefs and spiritual yearnings of their clients in their professional interventions in health care settings.

The next three articles delve into issues within the mental health realm of professional practice. In "The Managed Care Experience: The Social Worker's Perspective," Holly Riffe explores the rapid increase of managed care within the mental health field and identifies a series of ethical concerns that have been raised by social workers. Frank Vertosick Jr. reminds us of the return of an old scourge within the mental health community in his article, "Lobotomy's Back." Though not as horrific as its former version, when parts of the brain were severed, the current version of lobotomy (now known as "psychosurgery") still raises some of the original ethical issues. Then, Kathleen Earle, in "Cultural Diversity and Mental Health: The Haudenosaunee of New York State," examines some of the cultural differences between white and Native American clients that should be addressed in mental health treatment settings.

Social workers also provide social services within juvenile justice programs and adult correction institutions. The final three articles address many of the issues confronting this area, which is generally referred to simply as Corrections within the larger social welfare system. The first article, "Pay per Plea: Public Defenders Come at a Price," is an admittedly provocative piece by Erin Middlewood that exposes a practice gaining in popularity throughout the United States: poor defendents are being charged legal fees by public defenders.

Fred Pelka then focuses our attention on the unique plight of the mentally retarded individual who is thrust into the corrections system. Basically abandoned by the mental health/mental retardation system, many mentally challenged individuals are not caught by the "safety net" that is supposedly in place throughout the social welfare system. Finally, in "Private Prisons" by Eric Bates, the controversial issue of for-profit prisons is introduced. This article asks the question: Is the profit motive appropriate within the juvenile and adult corrections system?

UNIVERSAL HEALTH CARE COVERAGE IN THE UNITED STATES:

Barriers, Prospects, and Implications

Stephen Gorin

Universal health care coverage has long been a concern for social workers. This article examines barriers to and prospects for universal coverage in the United States. The article identifies major obstacles to universal coverage, addresses current problems with the U.S. health care system, discusses the debate over Medicare and Medicaid, and considers possible routes to universal coverage. The article also discusses implications for NASW and other supporters of a single-payer system.

Key words

access
health care
Health Security Act
single-payer system
universal coverage

On September 22, 1993, President Bill Clinton, in a televised address, introduced the Health Security Act (HSA) (H.R. 3600, 1993), which would have provided universal health care coverage, or as Clinton (1993) put it, "comprehensive health benefits that can never be taken away" (p. vi). Clinton's speech received wide acclaim, and polls showed broad support for health care reform (Skocpol, 1995). A year later the HSA was dead without having ever come to a vote. In November 1994, in what many viewed as a repudiation of the HSA, voters swept Democrats from Congress and handed control to the Republicans. Universal coverage has disappeared from national debate, and many believe it will not surface again for many years (Aaron & Reischauer, 1995).

Universal coverage has long been a concern for social workers. During the 1930s the committee on Economic Health Security, led by Secretary of Labor Frances Perkins, proposed national health insurance (Wencour & Reisch, 1989). Later Wilbur Cohen, assistant secretary of health, education, and welfare under President John F. Kennedy, and other social workers played leading roles in the development

From *Health & Social Work,* August 1997, pp. 223-230. © 1997 by the National Association of Social Workers. Reprinted with permission.

of Medicare. In recent years, NASW has identified universal coverage as a priority for the profession. In 1993 Sen. Daniel Inouye (D-HI) introduced the National Health Care Act (S. 684, 1993), NASW's proposal for a Canadian-style single-payer system (Mizrahi, 1995).

This article examines barriers to and prospects for universal coverage in the United States. The article identifies major obstacles and possible routes to universal coverage, addresses current problems with the U.S. health care system, and discusses the debate over Medicare and Medicaid. The article also discusses implications for NASW and other supporters of a single-payer system.

BARRIERS TO UNIVERSAL COVERAGE

The history of the HSA provides insight into barriers to universal coverage in the United States. Perhaps the chief obstacle is the lack of political support for health care reformers. In 1992, despite polls showing widespread support for universal coverage. Bill Clinton, the only presidential candidate who advocated this goal, received only 43 percent of the vote. From the beginning Clinton faced serious opposition. His effort to enact a modest economic stimulus package failed, and his budget passed by only one vote. He became bogged down by controversy over gay men and lesbians in the military, the Whitewater scandal, and other issues, which prevented him from waging an all-out battle for health care reform.

Clinton could not even count on support within his own party. Although the congressional Democrats had enough votes to enact the HSA, they did not do so. Liberals believed the HSA did not go far enough, and many supported the McDermott single-payer bill—American Health Security Act (H.R. 3940, 1994) (McClure, 1994). Conservatives thought the HSA went too far and supported the Cooper bill—Managed Competition Act of 1993 (H.R. 3222), which did not provide universal coverage. Two influential Senators, Bob Kerry (D-NE) and Daniel Moynihan (D-NY), publicly attacked the HSA (Starr, 1995).

Health care advocates, particularly supporters of a single-payer system, were also divided (McClure, 1994; McKenzie & Bilofsky, 1993; Rasell & Lillie-Blanton, 1994). The administration had in part designed the HSA to appeal to advocates (Zelman, 1994). The act included universal cover-

age, comprehensive benefits, and a range of supportive services and allowed the states to create single-payer systems of their own (NASW, 1993a). Despite this, single-payer backers were ambivalent. Although some viewed the HSA as a path to universal coverage and perhaps a single-payer system, others dismissed it as a sell-out to the insurance industry (McClure, 1994). Advocates continually pressured Clinton to change the act, threatening to withhold support if he refused. These demands usually had merit, but many advocates spent more time criticizing or ignoring the act than supporting it. In California single-payer supporters focused on the state's single-payer ballot initiative and failed to respond when Sen. Dianne Feinstein (D-CA) withdrew support for universal coverage. Feinstein's switch "fatally wounded" Sen. George Mitchell's (D-ME) attempt "to build a majority for a revised version of Clinton's plan" (Rothstein, 1995, p. 36).

Social workers also had mixed feelings about the act (Mizrahi, 1995). In October 1993 NASW (1993a) stated that "the Clinton health care plan goes a long way toward meeting" (p. 1) the association's basic principles. NASW's Board of Directors commended Clinton for his efforts and expressed support for this goal of universal coverage (NASW, 1993b). NASW noted that the HSA embraced "many of the principles of the single-payer approach" (p. 1). Yet NASW did not urge enactment of the HSA or try to mobilize social workers to support it. Instead, the association restated its belief that a single-payer system offered the best approach to universal access. While acknowledging that the HSA lay at the center of debate, NASW seemed to hold out hope that a single-payer system might yet emerge. Although individual social workers and NASW staff members worked to pass the HSA, the profession as a whole remained largely uninvolved.

Another obstacle to universal coverage is opposition from powerful interest groups. When Clinton introduced the HSA, he believed that moderate Republicans, such as Sen. Bob Packwood (R-OR) and perhaps even Sen. Bob Dole (R-KS), would work toward a compromise (Johnson & Broder, 1996). However, conservatives, fearing that compromise would strengthen the Democrats, resolved to defeat the act (Johnson & Broder, 1996). Using the media, lobbying groups, and think tanks, they distorted the act and intimidated moderates (Pellett, 1994; Reinhardt, 1995; Skocpol,

1995). Small insurers and others with an economic stake fueled the opposition, but ideology played a key role (Judis, 1995). Although small businesses would have benefited from the act, many small business groups, such as the National Federation of Independent Business, opposed it on philosophical grounds. According to Altman (1995), business, insurance, and other "monied interests" employed the "tools of political campaigns . . . on a scale . . . never seen before." Members of Congress "heard constantly . . . from anti-reform groups, but almost never from advocates of reform" (p. 25).

A final obstacle was the lack of a crisis that would motivate people to change the health care system. In 1993 and 1994 anxiety about health care did not grip the nation. Despite concern about the system, most people had insurance and expressed satisfaction with their own health care (Yankelovich, 1995). This complacency enabled HSA's opponents to persuade the public that it had more to fear from change than from the status quo. Before long, public opinion turned against the HSA. In the months after Clinton's speech, the number of people claiming to understand the act fell. By August 1994 less than 20 percent of the population felt "very well informed about the debate" (Yankelovich, 1995, p. 15). This knowledge deficit was due in part to the complexity of the HSA, but it seems unlikely that any proposal for universal coverage could have survived the onslaught of opposition. Ironically, although the public rejected the HSA, the key components of the act, namely, universal coverage, employers' contributions, and cost controls, enjoyed wide support (Starr, 1995).

From a broader perspective, the public's confusion reflected ambivalence about government itself. Although people believe in universal coverage, they question the ability of government to achieve it (Yankelovich, 1995). This skepticism is rooted in a profound distrust of government and dissatisfaction with growing inequality and a regressive tax structure (Bartlett & Steele, 1994; Krugman, 1994).

CURRENT HEALTH CARE SYSTEM

The U.S. health care system continues to have serious problems, particularly in the area of coverage. First, 40.3 million people lack health insurance, and 29 million people have inadequate coverage. Twenty-eight million people have inadequate insurance that does not fully protect them (Donelan et al., 1996). The fraction of the population insured by employers has fallen in recent years, and many companies have shifted some or all costs of coverage to their workers (Fronstin, 1996; Holahan, Winterbottom, & Rajan, 1995; Thorpe, Shields, Gold, Altman, & Shactman, 1995). Hospital emergency rooms, long providers of last resort, face overcrowding, and many patients leave without having seen a physician (Grumbach, Keane, & Bindman, 1993; Preston, 1996). In some inner-city areas, hospitals charge for services they once delivered free (Rosenthal, 1995).

Second, health care costs remain a problem. The United States spends more on health care than any nation, yet in many instances, has no better outcome (Knox, 1994; Reinhardt, 1996). Although the rate of inflation in health care has slowed in recent years, this may be a result of one-time savings from managed care (Ginzberg & Ostow, 1997). The slowdown also may be short lived. Some observers believe that sagging profits in the insurance industry may soon impel premiums (Levit, Lazenby, & Sivarajan, 1996). If health care inflation accelerates, it would likely lead to an increase in the uninsured population.

Third, the United States faces the "corporatization of health care" and the subjection of medicine to the "morality of the marketplace" (Eckholm, 1994; Kassirer, 1995). These trends include a rapid growth in for-profit health care, the takeover by large corporations of previously independent hospitals and institutions, and the emergence of corporate networks and systems (Etheredge, Jones, & Lewin, 1996; Iglehart, 1994). These developments have been accompanied by the dramatic growth of managed care organizations. Two-thirds of insured workers belong to managed care plans, and three-fourths of all physicians belong to managed care networks (Eckholm, 1994).

The spread of managed care has raised concern that capitated systems induce providers to undertreat patients (Angell & Kassirer, 1996; Blumenthal, 1996; Ellwood & Lundberg, 1996; Mark & Mueller, 1996; Ware, Bayliss, Rogers, Kosinski, & Tarlov, 1996; Zwanziger & Melnick, 1996). In response managed care organizations have been forced to eliminate many practices that "reward" providers "for limiting care" (Freudenheim, 1996). The states also have begun regulating managed care organizations (Families USA, 1996a). In March President Clinton appointed an Advisory Commission on Consumer Protection and Quality in the Health Care Industry (White House, 1997).

MEDICAID AND MEDICARE

A discussion of universal coverage would be incomplete without addressing the battle between Clinton and the congressional Republicans over Medicare and Medicaid (Knox, 1996). In a sense, the battle over Medicare dates back to April 1995, when the Medicare trustees, in their annual report, warned that Medicare's Hospital Insurance (HI) Trust Fund faced exhaustion in 2002 (Social Security and Medicare Boards of Trustees, 1996). This was hardly a surprise. Since 1970 the trustees had issued numerous warnings about the HI Trust Fund, and the Republicans ignored a similar report in 1994 (Johnson & Broder, 1996). Despite this, the Republicans welcomed the 1995 report as "manna from heaven," hoping it would justify the $270 billion they needed to cut from Medicare to balance the budget and reduce taxes (Maraniss & Weisskopf, 1996).

In addition to this spending reduction, the Republicans proposed structural changes in Medicare. Perhaps the most controversial of these were medical savings accounts, which would allow beneficiaries to buy inexpensive, high-deductible insurance policies and use tax-free dollars to meet their health care costs. The Republicans also wanted to change Medicare from its current system, in which beneficiaries are guaranteed a defined benefit package, to one in which beneficiaries would be entitled to a voucher that they would use to buy insurance of their own (Aaron & Reischauer, 1995; Ball, 1995; Moon, 1996). These and other proposals were eventually incorporated into the Seven-Year Balanced Budget Reconciliation Act of 1995 (H. R. 2491), which President Clinton vetoed on December 6, 1995 ("Bill Summary," 1996; Moon, 1996).

Medicaid, the federal health care program for low-income people and people with disabilities, has also generated controversy. H.R. 2491 would have reduced spending for Medicaid by $163 billion over seven years (Families USA, 1996b). More important, the bill would have turned Medicaid into a block grant, removing the current guarantee of coverage to anyone who meets the program's eligibility requirements.

H.R. 2491 could have exacerbated the problem of declining coverage (Thorpe et al., 1995). Reduced funding and coverage for Medicaid would likely increase the uninsured population, particularly among children (U.S. General Accounting Office, 1996). Structural changes in Medicare could undermine the risk pool and place more of the risk and burdens on beneficiaries (Moon, 1996; Thorpe, 1995). In addition, because Medicare subsidizes "safety-net" and teaching hospitals, reduced funding could force these facilities to close and leave beneficiaries and uninsured people without access to health care (Davis & Burner, 1995).

The future of these programs remains unclear. During the spring of 1996, Clinton and the Republicans narrowed their differences on spending for Medicare and Medicaid; however, they continued to disagree on the structure of the programs (Friedman, 1996; Kogan, 1996; personal communication with C. Jennings, special assistant to the president for health policy, July 1996). In the wake of the 1996 elections, both sides stressed their commitment to compromise, but it is difficult to imagine what such an agreement might look like (Starr, 1996). In any event, both sides support reductions in spending for Medicare and Medicaid, and in the absence of universal coverage these cuts could increase the uninsured population. Although Congress and the president will likely prevent the exhaustion of Medicare's HI Trust Fund, they still face the more difficult problem of covering the baby boom generation, which begins turning 65 in 2011.

PATHS TO UNIVERSAL COVERAGE

How might universal coverage come to the United States? Feder and Levitt (1995) proposed an incremental approach that would limit disruption while clearly improving the status quo. They identified possible steps to universal coverage that included reforming the insurance market, covering all children, and supporting home and community-based care. This strategy could result in legislation that decreases rather than expands health care coverage; for example, without universal coverage or cost controls, insurance reform could increase the cost of premiums and cause low-income people to drop their insurance. Yet with the defeat of the HSA, Feder and Levitt believed that reform proponents had no choice but to move a step at a time.

The debate over the Health Insurance Portability and Accountability Act of 1996 (P.L. 104–191) (known as the Kassebaum-Kennedy act) illustrates the difficulty of incremental reform (Skocpol, 1997). This act bans pre-existing-condition exclusions in group health insurance and makes it easier for employees to change jobs without losing coverage. The act's congressional backers included single-payer supporters such as Senators Daniel Inoyue (D-HI) and Paul Wellstone (D-MI). Because the act does not address the cost of insurance and will likely expand the insurance pool only minimally, NASW and other single-payer groups initially refused to support it (Hoechstetter, 1996). When the Senate amended the bill to require parity between mental and physical health coverage, NASW quickly endorsed it ("Therapy Parity," 1996). Mental health parity was eventually dropped from the final version of the act. However, a "scaled-back" version was included in Title 7 of the Fiscal Year 1997 Appropriations Bill for the Departments of Veterans Affairs and Housing and Urban Development, which President Clinton signed on September 16, 1996 (NASW, 1996). The history of the Kassebaum-Kennedy act suggests that reformers will have a difficult time agreeing on specific steps to universal coverage.

In contrast with Deder and Levitt (1995), Aaron (1996) developed a crisis theory of universal coverage. He believed that although the possibility of national health insurance ended with the HSA, discontent with decreasing coverage and managed care will continue to grow, eventually forcing the government to treat health care as a "public utility" by regulating the system and providing coverage for uninsured people. "Through this circuitous route, all Americans will achieve access to health care." Single-payer advocates also believe that discontent will grow, but they hope it will lead to a single-payer plan (Nichols, 1996).

Achieving universal coverage will likely require both incremental reforms and a crisis. On one hand, struggle for incremental reforms is needed to raise awareness of the problems of the health care system and the need for universal coverage. (In addition, as the battle over the Kassebaum-Kennedy act demonstrated, the struggle for incremental changes also isolates opponents of reform.) A strategy based solely on waiting for a crisis ignores day-to-day realities and issues and amounts to a strategy of inaction. On the other hand, as the history of the HSA suggests, without a crisis atmosphere, demand for fundamental change is unlikely.

NASW AND UNIVERSAL COVERAGE

NASW has advocated a Canadian-style single-payer system as the best approach to universal coverage. The association might wish to re-evaluate, although not necessarily abandon, this position. In hindsight, single-payer supporters, including NASW, may have been too rigid in 1993 and 1994. If single-payer groups had energetically supported the HSA, they might have succeeded in isolating opponents of universal coverage. The HSA did embody elements of a single-payer system and might have served as a point of transition to a single-payer system (Rachlis & Kushner, 1994). In reality, single-payer advocates and supporters of the HSA often worked at cross-purposes, playing into the hands of their mutual opponents. Ironically, NASW's commitment to a single-payer system may have undermined its commitment to universal coverage.

NASW also might take into account new thinking in the United States and Canada. In their influential work *Reinventing Government*, Osborne and Gaebler (1993) argued that the role of government should be to establish goals and parameters and evaluate outcomes, not deliver services. Applying this to health care, they advocated an "entrepreneurial" system in which the government would "set the rules"—organize the market to promote competition, empower consumers, and discourage hierarchy. The government would also require everyone to have health insurance (with employers and worker sharing the cost) and subsidize those who could not afford it.

Recently, Rachlis and Kushner (1994), two leading Canadian health policy analysts and strong defenders of Canada's single-payer system, considered the implications for Canada of Osborne and Gaebler's (1993) analysis. According to Rachlis and Kusher (1994), Canada's health care delivery system is plagued by "poor planning, a lack of standards, an inefficient use of existing resources, and poor communications" (p. 6). To address these problems, they proposed incorporating managed, or "publicly financed," competition into the Canadian system of government insurance and universal coverage. The heart of this new system would be a network of government-regulated community health centers that would compete on the basis of quality of care and service.

For NASW the lesson is that the end—in this case, universal coverage—is more important than the means—a single-payer system—of achieving it. NASW has already acknowledged this point, at least implicitly. The 1996 Delegate Assembly endorsed principles for health care reform, including universal coverage, comprehensive benefits, integrated services, consumer empowerment, and progressive financing (NASW, 1997). NASW has long identified a single-payer system as the best way of implementing these principles, but it is not the only way. Despite its limitations, the HSA met most of NASW's criteria. The scenario described by Aaron (1996) also represents a step in the right direction. In short, NASW's commitment to a single-payer system should not prevent the association from supporting other, more politically viable approaches to universal coverage.

Finally, NASW might reconsider the relationship between incremental change and fundamental reform. In 1993 and 1994 NASW and other groups argued plausibly that incremental changes, such as insurance market reform, would derail efforts of universal coverage and hurt more people than they help. With universal coverage now off the immediate policy agenda, advocacy groups have focused on defending Medicare and Medicaid. In this context, limited reforms, such as the Kassebaum-Kennedy act, which even critics acknowledge would aid some people, may have more merit than they did a few years ago (Hoechstetter, 1996). Interestingly, the *Wall Street Journal*, the leading conservative newspaper in the United States, recognizes the potency and, from its perspective, the danger of incremental change. In an editorial, the *Journal* warned that "Kennedy-Kassebaum" could "fuel calls for still more government intervention to 'solve' the health care crisis" (Hillary's New Strategy," 1996, p. A19). Again, the central issue is supporting reforms that can lead to universal coverage. These might include coverage for children and premium assistance to unemployed workers (Feder & Levitt, 1995; Worker Transition Initiative, 1996).

CONCLUSION

In the long run, universal coverage and a single-payer system seem inevitable. The U.S. health care system faces a contradiction between its increasing technological sophistication and its decreasing ability to provide coverage to its citizens (Bennefield, 1996; Knox, 1994; Schwartz, 1994). The only long-term solution is a universal system in which individuals are covered as a right of citizenship (Quadagno, 1994). Anything less—linking health care coverage with employment—raises the possibility of a two-tiered system and less than universal coverage.

Yet in the absence of a national crisis, universal coverage with a single-payer system will probably emerge only in stages. For years many advocates have assumed that universal coverage would (and should) come through a single-payer system. It may work out the other way, however. Movement toward universal coverage (insurance reform, premium assistance for unemployed workers, coverage for children, and so forth) may precede and provide a path to a single-payer system. For the time being, it makes sense for NASW to focus on steps toward universal coverage. Such a strategy is both consistent with NASW's traditional commitment to social justice and congruent with the political realities of our time.

REFERENCES

Aaron, H. J. (1996, January 15). Newest public utility? Health care. *Newsday*. Available http://www.brook.edu/es/oped/aaron/newsday.htm.

Aaron, H. J., & Reischauer, R. D. (1995). The Medicare reform debate: What is the next step? *Health Affairs, 14*(4), 8–30.

Altman, D. E. (1995). The realities behind the polls. *Health Affairs, 14*(1), 24–26.

Angell, M., & Kassirer, J. P. (1996, September 19). Quality and the medical marketplace—Following elephants [Editorial]. *New England Journal of Medicine, 335*, 883–886.

Ball, R. M. (1995). What Medicare's architects had in mind. *Health Affairs, 14*(4), 62–72.

Bartlett, D. L., & Steele, J. B. (1994). *America: Who really pays the taxes?* New York: Simon & Schuster.

Bennefield, R. L. (1996, May). Who loses coverage and for how long? In *Household economic studies, Dynamics of economic well-being: Health insurance, 1992 to 1993* (Current population reports). Washington, DC: U.S. Government Printing Office.

Bill summary and status for the 104th Congress. (1996). H.R. 2491. *Thomas: Legislative information on the Internet*. Available http://thomas.loc.gov/cgi-bin/bdquery/z?d104:HR02491:@@@L.

Blumenthal, D. (1996). Effects of market reforms on doctors and their patients. *Health Affairs, 15*(2), 170–184.

Clinton, B. (1993). *Health security: The President's Report to the American People.* Washington, DC: White House Domestic Policy Council.

Davis, M. H., & Burner, S. T. (1995). Three decades of Medicare: What the numbers tell us. *Health Affairs, 14*(4), 230–243.

Donelan, K., Blendon, R. J., Hill, C. A., Hoffman, C., Rowland, D., Frankel, M., & Altman, D. (1996). Whatever happened to the health insurance crisis in the United States? *JAMA, 276,* 1346–1350.

Eckholm, E. (1994), December 18). While Congress remains silent, health care transforms itself. *New York Times,* p. A1.

Ellwood, P. M., & Lundberg, G. D. (1996). Managed care: A work in progress [Editorial]. *JAMA, 276,* 1083–1087.

Etheredge, L., Jones, S. B., & Lewin, L. (1996). What is driving health system change? *Health Affairs 15*(4), 93–104.

Families USA. (1996a, July). *HMO consumers at risk: States to the rescue.* Washington, DC: Author.

Families USA. (1996b, June). *The new Republican Medicaid bill: A chip off the old block grant.* Washington, DC: Author.

Feder, J., & Levitt, L. (1995). Steps toward universal coverage. *Health Affairs, 14*(1), 140–149.

Freudenheim, M. (1996, April 2). Managed care empires in the making. *New York Times,* p. D1.

Friedman, B. (1996, October 31). There they go again. *New York Review of Books, 43,* 27–33.

Fronstin, P. (1996). The decline in health insurance and labor market trends. *Statistical Bulletin, 77*(3), 28–36.

Ginzberg, E., & Ostow, M. (1997). Managed care—A look back and a look ahead. *New England Journal of Medicine, 14,* 1018–1020.

Grumbach, K., Keane, D., & Bindman, A. (1993). Primary care and public emergency department overcrowding. *American Journal of Public Health, 83,* 372–378.

Health Insurance Portability and Accountability Act of 1996, P.L. 104–191, 110 Stat. 1936 (1996).

Health Security Act, H.R. 3600, 103d Cong., 1st Sess. (1993).

Hillary's new strategy [Editorial]. (1996, July 24). *Wall Street Journal,* p. A19.

Hoechstetter, S. (1996). Taking new directions to improve public policy [Editorial]. *Social Work, 41,* 343–346.

Holahan, J., Winterbottom, C., & Rajan, S. (1995, Winter). A shifting picture of health insurance coverage. *Health Affairs, 14,* 253–263.

Iglehart, J. K. (1995). A conversation with Leonard D. Schaeffer. *Health Affairs, 14*(4), 131–142.

Johnson, H., & Broder, D. S. (1996). *The system: The American way of politics at the breaking point.* Boston: Little, Brown.

Judis, J. B. (1995). Abandoned surgery: Business and the failure of health care reform. *American Prospect, 21,* 65–73.

Kassirer, J. P. (1995). Managed care and the morality of the marketplace. *New England Journal of Medicine, 333,* 50–52.

Knox, R. A. (1994, March 26). Studies challenge view of US as world leader in medicine. *Boston Globe,* p. 3.

Knox, R. A. (1996, July 31). Poll finds protection of Medicare ranks high inmost voters' minds. *Boston Globe,* p. A8.

Kogan, R. (1996, August 13). *Budget reductions under the Dole plan: Where and how much.* Washington, DC: Center on Budget and Policy Priorities.

Krugman, P. (1994). *Peddling prosperity: Economic sense and nonsense in the age of diminished expectations.* New York: W. W. Norton.

Levit, K. R., Lazenby, H. C., & Sivarajan, L. (1996). Health care spending in 1994: Slowest in decades. *Health Affairs, 15*(2), 130–144.

Managed Competition Act of 1993, H.R. 3222, 103d Cong., 2d Sess. (1993).

Marannis, D., & Weisskopf, M. (1996). *Tell Newt to shut up!* New York: Simon & Schuster.

Mark, T., & Mueller, C. (1996). Access to care in HMOs and traditional insurance plans. *Health Affairs, 15*(4), 81–87.

McClure, L. (1994). Labor and health care reform. *Z Magazine, 7*(1), 52–55.

McKenzie, N., & Bilofsky, E. (1993). Pay and pray? *Health/PAC Bulletin, 23*(3), 3.

Mizrahi, T. (1995). Health care: Reform initiatives. In R. L. Edwards (Ed.-in-Chief), *Encyclopedia of social work* (19th ed., Vol. 2, pp. 1195–1197). Washington, DC: NASW Press.

Moon, M. (1996, January 17). *Proposed changes in the structure of Medicare under the Balanced Budget [sic] Act of 1995* (104th Cong., 1st Sess.). Testimony.

National Association of Social Workers (1993a, October 1). *An analysis of the Clinton health care [sic] in relation to the five basic principles of health care reform* [Issue Brief]. Washington, DC: Author.

National Association of Social Workers. (1993b, November 1). *NASW members urged to contact senators and representatives to shape message of the health care reform debate* [Government Relations Alert]. Washington, DC: Author.

National Association of Social Workers. (1997). National health care. In *Social work speaks: NASW policy statements* (4th ed., pp. 228–234). Washington, DC: NASW Press.

National Association of Social Workers. (1996, October 4). *The Health Insurance Portability and Accountability Act P.L. 104l–191. Mental Health Parity. Title VII, VA-HUD Appropriations Bill. P.L. 104–204* [Government Relations Update]. Washington, DC: Author.

National Health Care Act, S. 684, 103d Cong., 1st Sess. (1993).

Nichols, S. (1996). PNHP calls for banning for-profit health delivery. *Action for Universal Health Care, 5*(1), 3.

Osborne, D., & Gaebler, T. (1993). *Reinventing government: How the entrepreneurial spirit is transforming the public sector.* New York: Plume.

Pellett, G. (Producer). (1994). *The great health care debate with Bill Moyers.* New York: Public Broadcasting System.

Preston, J. (1996, April 14). Hospitals look on charity care as unaffordable option of past. *New York Times,* p. A1.

Quadagno, J. (1994). *The color of welfare: How racism undermined the War on Poverty.* New York: Oxford University Press.

Rachlis, M., & Kushner, C. (1994). *Strong medicine: How to save Canada's health care system.* Toronto: HarperCollins.

Rasell, E., & Lillie-Blanton, M. (1994). The Clinton plan: Hazardous to our health? *Z Magazine, 7*(1), 45–51.

Reinhardt, U. E. (1995). Turning our gaze from bread and circus games. *Health Affairs, 14*(1), 33–36.

Reinhardt, U. E. (1996). Spending more through cost control: Our obsessive quest to gut the hospital. *Health Affairs, 15*(2), 145–154.

Relman, A. S. (1992, August). *The choices for health care reform.* Camp Hill: Pennsylvania Blue Shield Institute.

Robinson, J. C. (1996). Dynamics and limits of corporate growth in health care. *Health Affairs, 15*(2), 155–169.

Rosenthal, E. (1995, June 26). Two hospitals charging poor for medicine. *New York Times,* p. B1.

Rothstein, R. (1995). Friends of Bill? Why liberals should let up on Clinton. *American Prospect, 20,* 32–41.

Schwartz, W. B. (1994). In the pipeline: A wave of valuable medical technology. *Health Affairs, 13*(3), 70–79.

Seven-Year Balanced Budget Reconciliation Act of 1995, H.R. 2491, 104th Cong., 1st Sess.

Skocpol, T. (1995). The rise and resounding demise of the Clinton plan. *Health Affairs, 14*(1), 66–85.

Skocpol, T. (1997). *Boomerang: Health care reform and the turn against government.* New York: W. W. Norton.

Social Security and Medicare Boards of Trustees. (1996). *Status of the Social Security and Medicare programs.* Washington, DC: Author.

Starr, P. (1995). What happened to health care reform? *American Prospect, 20,* 21–31.

Starr, P. (1996). *Twice bitten* (Health policy and politics in the second Clinton administration). Available http://www.princeton.edu/~starr/article/twicebit. html.

Therapy parity in Senate bill wins backing. (1996, June). *NASW News,* p. 1.

Thorpe, K. (1995). Medical savings accounts. *Health Affairs, 14*(3), 254–259.

Thorpe, K. E., Shields, A. E., Gold, H., Altman, S. H., & Shactman, D. (1995, November). *The combined impact on hospitals of reduced spending for Medicare, Medicaid and employer sponsored insurance.* Unpublished study, Brandeis University, Waltham, MA.

U.S. General Accounting Office. (1996). *Health insurance for children: Private insurance continues to deteriorate: Report to the ranking minority member, Subcommittee on Children and Families, Committee on Labor and Human Resources, U.S. Senate.* Washington, DC: U.S. Government Printing Office.

Ware, J. E., Jr., Bayliss, M. S., Rogers, W. H., Kosinski, M., & Tarlov, A. R. (1996). Differences in 4-year health outcomes for elderly and poor, chronically ill patients treated in HMO and fee-for-service systems: Results from the Medical Outcomes Study. *JAMA, 276,* 1039–1048.

Wencour, S., & Reisch, M. (1989). *From charity to enterprise: The development of American social work in a market economy.* Urbana: University of Illinois Press.

White House. (1997, March 26). Remarks of the president on the Advisory Commission on Consumer Protection and Quality in the Health Care Industry [Press Release]. http://library. whitehouse.gov/Retrieve.cgi?db type=8056&query=Adv.

Worker Transition Initiative. (1996). *Clinton/Gore reelection campaign.* Washington, DC: Author.

Yankelovich, D. (1995). The debate that wasn't: The public and the Clinton plan. *Health Affairs, 14*(1), 7–23.

Zelman, W. A. (1994). The rationale behind the Clinton health reform plan. *Health Affairs, 13*(1), 9–29.

Zwanziger, J., & Melnick, G. (1996). Can managed care plans control health care costs? *Health Affairs, 15*(2), 185–199.

ABOUT THE AUTHOR

Stephen Gorin, PhD, *is professor, Social Work Program, Plymouth State College, 17 High Street, Plymouth, NH 03264.*

Accepted January 23, 1997

Safe to Talk: Abortion Narratives as a Rite of Return

Helen Susan Edelman

"I now understand why women have died from abortions—it was the secrecy that killed them."

(from personal correspondence with D.M.)

Defamiliarizing Assumptions[1]

America's worst-kept secret is its 1.5 million women who annually choose to abort their babies.[2] Worst-kept, because everybody knows and everybody is talking about it; secret, because everybody knows and nobody's talking about it.

"I was secretive about it, only telling a very close woman friend of mine from high school. I did not tell the man until after the abortion. I told my boyfriend that I had minor surgery and couldn't have sex for two weeks. I did feel secretive about it at the time."

(from personal correspondence with M.P.)[3]

"I did not tell many people about this abortion. I was deeply ashamed to be in this situation for a third time. How could a bright independent woman be in this predicament AGAIN?? I spiraled into a deep depression. I contemplated suicide and engaged in self-destructive behavior."

(from personal correspondence with K.C.)

"I was 22 years old, eight-and-a-half years ago. At the time, there didn't seem to be any safe environments for speaking about it. My doctor knew, and my two closest friends. I never told the father, as we weren't in a relationship. I'm not sure if this was a smart thing to do or not, but I went through it by myself."

(from personal correspondence with C.J.)

"I filled out an insurance claim just to see if they might pay it, and of course, they didn't. I wish I hadn't filed that claim. I hate knowing that some huge organization knows such personal information about me. I don't feel good about it. I certainly don't feel safety in their knowledge."

(from personal correspondence with S.V.)

Many women experience abortion without remorse or guilt; indeed, they celebrate it as a motivator to get on with the business of life as usual.[4] For others, the subject of this study (in which I asked women to speak about their abortions in terms of contributing factors to their decision; pregnancy loss; secrecy and silence[5]; trust; subsequent sexuality, self-esteem; and relationship with the baby's father), an abortion signifies multiple sacrifices. Among them, women cited: a potential child; youthful innocence; parenting or familial fantasy; relationship with the baby's father; trust; and the sense of control or security. These varied responses depend on personally constructed meanings and expectations of loss, death, parenthood, womanhood and pregnancy (Madden, 1994: 87) and whether the fetus had been considered a "child."

"In the small Idaho ranching community where I grew up there was an old woman, the matriarch of one of the wealthier ranching families, who had had a number of illegal abortions in addition to several children. When she was dying in the hospital, her last words, whispered to one of the nurses, were 'Oh, all those little babies! I'm so sorry. What can I tell them? Will they forgive me?'"

(from personal correspondence with V.M.)

"I still cry at the thought of the ordeal, but I am still confused as to whether it is grief over the loss or grief over the becoming of what everyone said I would."

(from personal correspondence with M.K.)

Though a woman may perceive her abortion as an occasion of profound loss, she is deprived of the opportunity to publicly grieve in our high-tech pronatalist culture where death is never an acceptable peri-natal outcome. As a not-mother, the woman who has an abortion is marginalized. "Our lives remain untheorized" (Morell, 1994: xv). The not-mother is unspeakable, unknowable and uninteresting in a world where "sources for gratification are denied women if they are pursued in lieu of children" (Morell, 1994: 39), and where "feminist culture has not produced alluring images or thinkable identities for the childless" (Snitow, 1993: N145).

Often, a woman who has an abortion conceals her actions, and may never find a safe venue for mourning. Almost always, women who experience abortion choose secrecy expressed as

 From *Journal of American Culture*, Winter 1996, pp. 29-39. © 1996 by the American Culture Association. Reprinted by permission.

silence, choose not to speak about it except with a small, select group of intimate family members or friends. Many never tell even the father of the aborted fetus. In addition to the stress of deciding whether to have an abortion, their angst is compounded by emotional isolation and the burden of secrecy which contributes to alienation (Buttenweiser and Levine in Fried, 1990: 121).

> "This is not something I talk about. Sometimes it's still a politicized issue. I have told some friends and I can see their disapproval. It made me angry and wary about careless revelation."
>
> (from personal correspondence with A.G.)

Abortion narratives, as a category of feminist folklore, represent in metaphor and microcosm the abortion experience, mythologizing it, imbuing it with symbolism and ritual, and creating of abortion as accessible an arena for women as any other exclusively female experience (childbirth, menstruation, menopause, lactation, etc.). "By looking at disparate narratives and finding common themes, we seek a structure and unity of narrative in our experiences of the world, within both our own lives, and the larger human community" (Field and Marck, 1994: 87).

Escape from the Margins

In "Motherhood Lost: Cultural Dimensions of Miscarriage and Stillbirth in America," Layne (1990: 70) examines the "veil of silence" that surrounds pregnancy loss for those who miscarry or have stillborn babies. She points out that incomplete pregnancies trap women in a "liminal state" between pregnancy and birth (Layne, 1990: 74). When term pregnancy is not achieved, the woman who lost a baby can neither retreat to the absolute status of not-mother prior to her pregnancy, nor advance to motherhood. However, Layne points out, community-based grief and loss groups; medical attention; family, social and spiritual support; and cultural focus on death acknowledge the woman's grief and loss, repairing the disrupted continuum connecting not-mother to mother. Although her status remains ambiguous (she has experienced pregnancy but not birth), the women who has lost a baby to miscarriage or stillbirth can access the "rite of return" to prepregnancy status (Layne, 1990: 74).

Women who have abortions are less likely to navigate that safe return to pre-pregnancy status; often silenced, their pregnancy is never acknowledged, the loss never mourned. In the absence of conventional forums for women mourning aborted fetuses, I suggest that their narratives, considered as a body of folklore,[6] function as their "rite of return," mobilizing the possibility of reconciliation of their losses and revisioned female identity that does not require women to give birth to every baby they conceive. By disclosing her abortion story, a woman attempts to forge and formalize a common bond with forgiving listeners and achieve reincorporation into the community-at-large. She also distances herself from the event and circumstances that surrounded it by creating an opportunity to demonstrate how much she's changed and how far she's come from the situation that made it impossible to carry a baby to

term. Turning the abortion into a story brings it out of the shadow of the margins:

> "I think the telling asks something of the listener, some understanding of the issue of choice, some empathy for the younger self."
>
> (from personal correspondence with N.K.)

> "I did not feel safe talking about it at all at the time. I felt safe in my own house, and mostly in my friend Brooke's house. I didn't write about it in my journal at all for over a year, and that is unusual for me. Now I feel safer talking about it. I've sort of decided my life isn't all that extraordinary, it isn't so terribly shocking that the world would end if everyone found out."
>
> (from personal correspondence with S.V.)

Such confession is "part of a symbolic system in which, after suitable expiation, the repentant 'sinner' may return to the community" (Hepworth and Turner, 1982: 37). Confessional narratives are remedial, restitutive devices which restate and uphold the social order.

> "Thank you for the opportunity to tell my story. It was healing to write it down."
>
> (from personal correspondence with D.M.)

> "I would be willing to respond to a questionnaire about my abortion experiences. This sounds like an important and necessary project."
>
> (from personal correspondence with B.S.)

> "I hated having to do this again (have a fourth abortion) but there was a feeling of resignation that prevailed. Writing my dissertation on abortion was very therapeutic."
>
> (from personal correspondence with K.C.)

Women's ability to articulate the abortion experience is "crucial for psychic well-being" (Cornell, 1993: 145). Nevertheless, because of cultural ambivalence towards abortion, most narratives are generated covertly and maintained in secret. (I believe the anonymity of my survey made it a "safe place to talk," and contributed to the high number of candid responses I received.)

> "I have told the story to only a handful of people. *This is the first time in 29 years that I have written it down.*"
>
> (from personal correspondence with N.K.)

> "I didn't have to think about who I would tell. I was much more concerned about who *not* to tell. I guess I could say I decided not to tell anyone. I only feel safe talking about my abortion to my sister and boyfriend (now partner) who already knew. I feel fairly safe writing about it now although *I plan to save only one copy of this under lock and key.*"
>
> (from personal correspondence with D.M.)

When a woman is unexpectedly pregnant, the decision to have an abortion becomes a pivotal moment in her life trajectory disrupted by "disjunction between expectation and conditions" (Ginsburg, 1989: 138). Her retrospective interpretation of her abortion provides opportunity to reorder events and motivations, and to make sense of them for herself and her listener, possibly for the first time. "One step towards (their healing) could be allowing women to fully experience and name their actions in a fashion that feels authentic to them.

Abortion must be acknowledged for a woman to begin to re-construct her life" (Rabuzzi, 1994: 52).

> "I am looking forward to the chance to process some of this personal baggage in a more systematic way."
>
> (from personal correspondence with K.C.)

> "I have been hoping for a while to hear about such a call for information, because I have wanted someone to ask me how I felt. Thanks for asking. I've been waiting to do this. I really have. Thanks for asking."
>
> (from personal correspondence with S.V.)

Breaking the silence taboo to speak about their abortions connects women to others who shared the experience—and the information. "As women share their life experiences, their personal stories take on greater meaning . . . views of self in a larger context operate to validate the individual experience and to make it part of the collective experience of all women . . .(thus) the individual becomes politically significant" (Fried, 1990: 124).

With few exceptions, the women in this study who did seek support sought it from other women, rejecting men as confidants or companions throughout their experiences. Women "embody potential empathy" for each other (Fried, 1990: 125) because of their universal ability to experience pregnancy. When women are unable to speak about their abortions to other women, especially their mothers, it "shakes the foundations of their specific relationships, and the general promise of shared trust" (Fried, 1990:125).

> "I decided to limit the people I talk to. I just didn't want to go into it. I think that several of my friends who I've told since then have been hurt that I didn't tell them when I was going through it. My mother would feel terrible pain that I didn't tell her. It was not their business. I wanted someone who I knew wouldn't judge me. I told my mentor at graduate school. I told another woman I used to work with. They are both older than me. I knew they would be able to compassionately listen and they would know my telling them was an indication of the depth of my trust. In fact they both told me very personal things about themselves in our conversations. I only wanted to tell women. To this day I haven't told a single man about my experience."
>
> (from personal correspondence with S.V.)

> "A girlfriend picked me up and we went out to lunch afterwards. She and her roommate were the only people I told, they weren't my closest friends. Even when, later, women friends told me about their abortions, I kept mine to myself. It's only been in the last 10 years or so, since my second divorce, that I've talked about it. My mother still doesn't know, though my daughter does. My second husband never knew, and I honestly don't know if I've ever told Joe who's closer to me than any man has ever been."
>
> (from personal correspondence with V.M.)

On the other hand, being unable to share the abortion experience with the male partner creates anger and ambivalence towards the individual and the relationship:

> "(Between December 29 when I got pregnant, and January 20 when I called Planned Parenthood) I didn't tell anybody. I had cried deeply for days and nights before. I felt like everything within me had collapsed, had tightened up and settled into a compact core. I felt dense and full of deep and sorrowful meaning. I felt intensely within my body. I remember caring for my body. This is one of the saddest memories I have. I ate more vegetables. I drank more juice. I held my own body. I was so careful with me. I never considered telling my ex-partner. I guess I am afraid he will find out. I felt like just by looking at me people knew I was going to have an abortion. It's funny how I think I'm completely over it and then I find out I'm not. What I want to do is figure out how to compassionately accept it. I think that part of my abortion mourning is also part of my mourning the end of my relationship. I never mourned or yearned for the child. It was like I mourned the possibility. I never regretted the decision. It was the deepest sadness I ever felt. It permeated my whole being. But regret was not a part of that sadness. I did regret the sex play that led to the pregnancy."
>
> (from personal correspondence with S.V.)

Speaking from the margins, the narrator discloses her "crime" to escape liminality. The very act of concealment is her acknowledgment of the "social badness" of her abortion. The confessional narrative "buries the wrong, and erases the actual memory, replacing it with the growth of 'right' feeling in a rite of reconciliation" (Douglass, 1966: 136).

The dialectic between the need for privacy and the discomfort of liminality is played out in the folklore as it simultaneously protects the speaker (by reinterpreting her abortion to confirm current life status), and satisfies the public demand for contrition. Stillbirth and miscarriage are involuntary; abortion is elective pregnancy loss. To compensate for her unmaternalist thinking the woman must don a cloak of sadness for her missed opportunity for nurturance. Though her reasons for having an abortion may have been to remove an impediment to social or career mobility, or financial stability, the contrite abortion narrative restates the focus from the mother's needs to the potential baby's. Selfishness is reframed as selflessness when the narrator's rhetoric shifts from having an abortion to improving or maintain her own status quo, to being having an abortion because she is unwilling to bring a baby into the world whose quality of life would be compromised by her inability to properly care for it. In this re-interpretative life script, a woman may free herself from both the external sanctions of isolation and stigma, and the internal sanctions of guilt and shame. Folklore provides a vast stock of nearly interchangeable supporting details for both narrator and listener as it reveals and resolves the tension between individual action and community order.

Trying Hard to Hear You: Penetrating the Silence

The silence surrounding abortion has multiple meanings and roles which adapt in context. Silence's tactical function is to prevent attracting stigma attached to women who become "structural males" by denying their "natural obligation" to bear children (Ginsburg, 1989: 216). Increasing violence at abortion clinics, which has escalated from vandalism to murder (Judges, 1993: 43), and public discussion of whether or not abortion "should" be legal and when personhood begins also deter open discussion. Women may "go underground" with their needs and concerns to protect their physical and social well-being.

Silence defends against disclosure as well. Just as gay men conceal their grief and rage over repeated losses of friends and lovers to AIDS (Blincoe and Forrest, 1993: 1) to hide the fact of their own homosexuality, women who choose abortions deny themselves the experience of mourning to protect that secret.

Symbolically, silence reflects the sexual shame (Cornell, 1993: 145), stripped-down powerlessness, and vulnerability many women feel during abortion. Many women spoke of self-loathing and anger at themselves for being unexpectedly pregnant. Secrecy—empowered and operationalized by silence—exacerbates an already-painful withdrawal from the social order, shrouding it "with guilt and shame" (Fried, 1990: 121).

> "My abortion lowered my self-esteem considerably, and for a long time caused me to feel—and act—like 'used goods' in male/female relationships."
>
> (from personal correspondence with G.M.)

> "I never even told my college roommates, with whom I was very close, I guess because of shame, until many years later. And I lied to them about the reason for my absence from school. The worst part of the entire abortion was the degradation that went with it. I simply couldn't handle the total secrecy. It was so degrading. The trip to Puerto Rico was my mother's first plane flight—and she couldn't talk about it."
>
> (from personal correspondence with G.M.)

> "The details of my three abortions have been suppressed for so long, that I do not remember my exact age at the time, the clinic it was performed at or the costs of same. However, the shame and fear are quite clear in my memory. I can only share the details with intimate friends—however, I have never discussed it with my own siblings. My abortions were secret until I was an adult. It's still painful."
>
> (from personal correspondence with S.E.)

> "I wanted to have that baby. I 'knew' it was a girl. I 'knew' she wanted to be born. I miss her, to this day I miss her. I was crying and very upset but assured the clinic workers that this was my choice and that I wanted to go through with the abortion. I wish they had refused to believe my lies. I did not allow myself to get angry very much. I was afraid of the power of that anger. I was depressed for nearly a year after that abortion. I felt like a failure as a human being. I had failed my daughter. I had failed to protect her. I hated myself for that."
>
> (from personal correspondence with K.C.)

Silence also creates and maintains social boundaries, excluding those who might disapprove of abortion (Tefft, 1980: 63), by controlling the flow of personal information. Some women expressed that their silence reflected respect for the privacy of the "dead baby."

Silence disenfranchises, disavows and renders invisible the woman and her experience. Most women report that there was no counseling available to them before or after their abortions, confirming the taboo against talking. When a woman is pregnant unexpectedly, "ads, billboards, pro-choice and pro-life voices debate" what she should do about it. She is "surrounded by others' thoughts on their experiences, but few women are asked to voice their own" (Field and Marck, 1994: 82).

> "The discourse around abortion, pro-life and pro-choice, don't leave much space for genuine grief (especially if you still think you did the right thing)."
>
> (from personal correspondence with A.B.)

Finally, silence may be emblematic of civil disobedience and embody a vigorous feminist counter-discourse to the moral code promoting subjugation of female independence to a tra-

ditional focus on "motherhood as the only permissible social role in which all women could command respect" (Gordon, 1976: 130). As Martin notes: "Many women express a connection between being in control of the uterus and being in control of the mouth." This is particularly interesting juxtaposed with Douglas' (1966) views on pollution and body margins. Like birth, abortion violates the uterus (internal margin) and vagina (external margin), making the woman who undergoes it a social polluter who must be purified. Narration also involves matter (speech) violating a margin (the mouth). It is worth remarking that pollution implies women controlling these ports of entry from her body into the world, but purification appears to require the social body to assume control over her margins. Silence, in which no matter traverses a body margin, is consistent with the prevailing discourse describing female compliance. The counter-discourse of unverbalized noncompliance (abortion) challenges that demand.

> "I kept it private because I wanted to keep it under some sort of control, because, again, this was the most intensely private decision I've ever had to make."
>
> (from personal correspondence with S.V.)

Women broke silence to share their abortion narratives with me for as many articulated reasons as there were responses. Some hoped to help others by their candor:

> "I decided before the test came back to have the abortion, and told my husband and brother-in-law. Years later, I told my mother. Since then, I've told lovers and friends. Even classes, if it seemed relevant."
>
> (from personal correspondence with G.G.)

Others wished to bare their souls:

> "I would like to tell my story. There does not seem to be a good place to tell it—I do not want to go to a consciousness meeting; I am not anxious for others to find out."
>
> (from personal correspondence with J.V.)

A few answered simply because they were asked and felt neither cathartic nor altruistic impulses. One aims at demystifying the experience by speaking about it publicly, even to her classes. "The individual woman's opportunity to transform experience into a story both provides continuity between the past and the current action, expectations, or belief" (Ginsburg, 1989: 137). Generally, women expressed genuine pleasure at being asked to tell their stories.

> "I would be happy to answer a questionnaire or discuss this further with you. And YES, we need to support each other through this badly maligned but very necessary option."
>
> (from personal correspondence with J.M.)

> "Thanks so much for asking these questions. I don't know if I've given you any real help, but you helped me. It was positive to think about this in a focused way."
>
> (from personal correspondence with C.J.)

Uncharted Territory

Abortion deconstructs motherhood, separating it from womanhood as an ascribed status, even for pregnant women. Lack of consensus surrounding these fundamental images in our culture (woman, mother, pregnancy) threatens understanding of life's (and the body's) thresholds and mysteries: birth, copulation (and its implications for adulthood and family) and death. With choice comes reshaped life scripts where narrators re-view and achieve closure on their experiences by manipulating old symbols and actions with intent to reinvent a world that accommodates their vision. A narrative connects the speaker to the listener, and both speaker and listener to the narrator's past and present, "unifying inner and outer histories" (Ginsburg, 1989: 137).

The folklore of abortion brings together disparate personal histories of women seeking community in shared experience. At the same time, as interpretation folklore distorts and collapses socially (re-)constructed cognitive, sentient and experiential categories as reinterpretations of the abortion experience incorporate political, social and technological change: Sex no longer (necessarily) leads to pregnancy, pregnancy no longer (necessarily) leads to motherhood, pregnancy resulting from lack of control has been eclipsed by pregnancy resulting from vigilance, privacy is open to public scrutiny, structurally female obligations (to reproduce) give way to the structural male option to be sexual without reproducing, mother-baby unity is reframed as antagonism by fetal rights discourse, and abortion shifts from desperate reaction to unexpected life circumstances to affirmative action to maintain carefully constituted life circumstances. The narrator is telling a story about an event in the past, but reconstituting it to reflect her current status and values. The story does not represent the event so much as it explains her actions and behaviors in the present.

> "A month later, another friend of mine from college lost her two-year-old daughter to a brain tumor. Her death and funeral became my grief, and I wept for days for the loneliness of loss."
>
> (from personal correspondence with N.K.)

> "It felt safer to talk then than now. I only talk about my abortion with people who seek me out for counseling or who I am certain of in terms of their position on reproductive rights."
>
> (from personal correspondence with C.M.)

> "I've learned to talk about it more over the years. I'm not ashamed of what I did, or the decision I made, so I don't have any reason not to tell people. However, it was a highly personal experience so I don't tell everyone. I don't flaunt it. And I don't open myself up for criticism or ridicule. Basically, if it's appropriate for the conversation, I tell."
>
> (from personal correspondence with C.J.)

Individual voices reflect particular histories; as a continuous text, the conflated narratives as a body of folklore articulate an environment for reconsidering the meanings of womanhood, motherhood, pregnancy, abortion, choice, heterosexuality, childbirth and childrearing by resisting and resituating the cultural parameters that define these ambiguous arenas, their malleable meanings and functions. Metamorphosing definitions arise from reframed memories shared through storytelling as a generation of feminists encounter and reject standards for behavior set for their grandmothers. It is through experiencing the interpretation, not the event, that such standards are recreated.

> "This abortion of mine is so much like history, it's a legend."
>
> (from personal correspondence with A.G.)

Unpacking the Baggage

While themes and symbols emerging from abortion narratives may appear familiar and universal, many are ambiguous and polysemous (for example, abortion may represent both loss [of control] and gain [of mobility], or fertility and childlessness; silence may expose fear of disclosure, or power over the dissemination of information). Symbols and images are constituted first at the level of individual experience, reconstructed in the public imagination, and ultimately deconstructed as they become conditions and starting points for personal and social action (Fox in Hollis, Pershing and Young, 1993: 30). The narratives embed personal conflict in the body politic. Personal symbols become cultural ones (Layne, 1990: 90).

> "I am extremely grateful for the choice I had in terminating three pregnancies. However, I believe they are morally wrong."
>
> (from personal correspondence with S.E., mother of three)

> "I suppose I could say that if anything, my abortion made me even more adamant about the need to defend this right."
>
> (from personal correspondence with S.N., no children)

> "I can never get over what a miracle birth is. I think the decision to abort is extremely personal and I'm thankful I was allowed to make that decision."
>
> (from personal correspondence with M.F., mother of three)

> "I will have to reconsider my response as a grieving process, and one that has never ended. I made the absolute right choice to have an abortion, and I was relieved, even happy at the time. I have never once regretted the decision, yet there are feelings surrounding the loss of a potential child that remain with me."
>
> (from personal correspondence with M.P.)

Part of their folklore about themselves is women's resistance to suppression; the act of telling the story represented significant power for these women.

> "I told others as they needed to know. My lover who impregnated me, the man I lived with and later married, a friend who loaned me money, women who help me locate a clinic, and finally, in an only-on-the-left-moment, the entire steering committee of a strike I was involved in during the course of an argument about who should get arrested—I couldn't risk civil disobedience and miss the clinic appointment."
>
> (from personal correspondence with C.M.)

Narratives are a spacious arena for negotiating meanings and expectations. As new values are assigned to events and human beings, malleable narratives accommodate themselves to embrace the appropriate role. Narrative folklore about abortion is a medium through which reprocessed knowledge travels for exchange among women, or among women who have had abortions and whoever they choose to tell. The stories encode the experience so that others may know what to expect, how to act, how to react. Narratives allow and encourage ambiguity, embodying both passive and active resistance to moral codes, and a vehicle for self-management. By linking meaning and action in ways that revise and transform both, the narrative also disambiguates male/female, passive/active, pregnancy/motherhood, motherhood/womanhood, private/public, life/death, mother-child unity/disunity, selfish/selfless and other polar cultural elements evinced in abortion stories.

Narratives are a call to action as well as a window on the past. These narratives call for an end to hypocrisy in a culture that claims to support both reproduction and females in workplace, but makes women's roles as mother incompatible with the marketplace. This ambivalence forces a woman to choose abortion over personal gain, when she should be able to choose both parenting and satisfying work. If American women were offered superior subsidized daycare, cash benefits for time taken off to parent, guaranteed paid maternity and newborn insurance, and extended leave time from work, abortion would be more of a real choice and less of a symptom of "contradictory social expectations for women" in a culture that claims to value "self-management and productivity" but only rewards compliance (Rodman, Sarvis, Bonan, 1987: 78).

As a feminist strategy, creating abortion folklore reframes and mobilizes silence, calling for visibility and active resistance that endow women who choose abortion with a voice—and a safe place to shout.

An Afterword: My Own Story

When I began to ask women about their abortions, I was surprised at the generosity of their responses. Relatives, friends, friends of friends, and even strangers offered a range of deeply personal, candid, often anguished, provocative, and always thoughtful replies. Clearly, the story is one waiting to be told.

Women I know personally, I spoke with face-to-face; many others responded to an e-mail request for abortion narratives. As the responses came back to me one-by-one, a surprising number of women asked me to tell my own story in return. A fair exchange. "One of the distinctive features of feminine inquiry is insistence that the researcher appear not as an invisible, anonymous voice of authority, but as a real, historical individual with concrete, specific desires and interests" (Harding, 1987: 9). (In fact, several respondents actually were unwilling to participate in this work until they had heard my own abortion narrative, to know where I stood politically and personally. To these women I responded promptly and in writing.) To respect the expectation of those who asked me to include my own story in this work, I offer this afterword before:

It was 1983 and I was 31, married and the mother of two daughters, ages 6 and 1. I was beginning graduate school and had a teaching assistantship; I also earned money as a freelance journalist. Essentially, I was financially dependent on my husband, an attorney. My own earnings covered child care expenses.

I realized I was pregnant in the beginning of March. Because I had been pregnant twice before, I recognized the symptoms immediately. I can't remember now if I did a home pregnancy test, but I did have an "official" one at university health services. My marriage was faltering badly at the time and my husband was furious and depressed when I told him I was pregnant. He told me he didn't want anything to do with raising another child. When I realized he was serious and how at-risk I was as an unemployed mother of two young children, I agreed to have an abortion, though it was not a choice I would have made if the marriage had been stable. First, I contacted my regular obstetrician who had delivered my youngest

daughter; he did not perform abortions, his secretary told me. I was on my own. Fortunately, a woman I knew at school recently had talked to me about her abortion. I called her for the name of her doctor, which she shared. I called his office and was scheduled for an abortion the following week. Once I was committed to having an abortion, I almost couldn't stand knowing a baby was growing inside me. My mother-in-law gave us the $500 cash we needed (she is an unequivocal prochoice advocate). I went through the time between making the appointment and the appointment itself like an automaton, doing everything exactly, thoughtlessly, numbed. I don't believe I allowed myself to consider my own feelings about abortion until it was over.

Ironically (everything seems ironic in retrospect), my sister's wedding was the day before the abortion—in Colorado. I flew out there knowing I was pregnant, knowing my marriage was failing, knowing I was having an abortion Monday morning. I refused to go through the security gates at the airport because I was pregnant. Despite my plan for an abortion 72 hours later, I was protecting my baby. The guards were compliant. I sat and talked with my father for hours in the lobby of the hotel, saying nothing. I said nothing to my sister, either, not wanting to ruin her day or focus any attention on my own needs. Another irony: many years later, she confided in me that she had had an abortion also—and had never told me because it was during my first pregnancy and she didn't want to undermine my joy. And another irony: the baby was due in November—as my other two had been.

A moment of panic came at the airport when the plane was overbooked and some of us had to stay behind. I had to be at the abortion at 7 a.m. the next day. I was ready at that point to announce this to the crowd, but ended up with a seat at the last moment. By then I realized I absolutely didn't want to have an abortion, but since I was having one, I wanted it over with.

It is interesting to me that I can no longer remember why I wasn't using birth control when I became pregnant. I was still breastfeeding my 1-year old, so the Pill would have been out of the question, but I did have a diaphragm in my night table drawer. At some level I was willing to risk pregnancy—and the risk in my case is a high one; every time I have gotten pregnant it has been within two months of "trying." Maybe I was "trying" to complicate the marriage even more. Maybe I was "trying" to conceive the boy my husband was disappointed not to have the second time around. Maybe I was just not thinking at all.

I had made elaborate child care arrangements for my daughters and they were well-tended while I was aborting their sibling. I remember being anxiety-ridden over what to wear to the abortion; I didn't want to appear comfortable, as if this were too casual an outing; and I didn't want to dress too well, as if I were going to a party. I don't remember now what I finally wore. On the way to the abortion, my husband finally turned to me and said if I didn't want to go, he'd back off. But it was too late for me. I was on automatic pilot—and besides, I didn't want a baby so unwelcomed by the father. It never occurred to me then that the fact that I wanted the baby was sufficient reason to continue the pregnancy.

The doctor who performed my abortion was one of the kindest human beings I have ever met. I remember crying and feeling it was painful, but I can't say I remember pain. I remember asking if he could see if it were a girl or a boy. He said "no." He said he could usually tell whether the woman having an abortion was a parent because it seemed harder for someone already a mother to have an abortion than it was for those without children. I remember the doctor holding my hand at the end of it, saying, "You have to forgive yourself." I remember asking for some sleeping pills because I hadn't been sleeping at all. He gave me enough for a week. I remember the nurse getting my husband who kept saying, "Can we leave yet?" He was in the middle of a big trial, impatient. He took me home and left me there alone. I didn't see him again until he came home for dinner with the girls.

I stayed home for two days, in bed. Physically I was fine. I just wanted to wallow; I wanted to be "sick." I wanted to acknowledge what I had experienced with something concrete—and being bedridden worked for me at the time. I had told my closest friends at school and home what was going on. One was experiencing infertility problems with her husband and was supportive at the time, but later admitted to being furious at me for "wasting a life." One was unconditional in her support, but shocked me by saying she had passed the information to her Mormon husband, who found what I was doing unforgivable. (My unmarried friend at school, on the other hand, was concerned and non-judgmental.)

I knew it was the end of the marriage, then. I stopped having sex with my husband, became actually repulsed at the sight of him naked, moved into the guest room. I had an affair. I stopped breastfeeding and went on the Pill and became a fanatic about having control of my own fertility. (This never changed.) I transferred my medical records to the doctor who had done the abortion, sent him a huge waiting room plant, a tree, and began to bring him bag lunches and sit with him to eat. At the time I remember thinking I was "returning to the scene of the crime," though I am not sure whose crime it was; now I think I was reassuring myself that this person accepted me despite what I had made him an accomplice to. It was a strange collusion. I took a leave of absence from school and went to work full-time so I could support myself and never have to rely on the charity of a husband again. I never have.

My husband and I hardly talked about the abortion; it certainly didn't come up when we named our reasons for considering divorce. But on what would have been the baby's birthday, I brought home a puppy (I didn't realize this until months later). I frequently imagined what it would have been like to have three children. I started seeing a psychiatrist, but didn't tell him for months I had had an abortion. I actually didn't consciously connect that event to my unhappiness. He was shocked that I had withheld this for so long. Incredibly, though I would sit there and expound on my sexual exploits in my by-now obsessive affair, I considered the abortion too personal to talk about. My husband moved out. I sold the house, which was in my own name. The most verbally violent fight I had with my ex-husband came in 1989 when he was dating a very young woman and told me: "And the best part is, she's still in her child-bearing years." He was baffled by my eruption. He didn't get it.

Flash forward. 1991. I am pregnant by my second husband, a very carefully planned pregnancy. My former husband called to say he's been noticing how happy I am; he believes we would have salvaged our marriage if he hadn't insisted on the abortion. He is sorry. I am bleeding during this pregnancy and I am crazy with worry my body is punishing me for the abortion, that I am going to lose this baby. The obstetrician tells me "no," he has heard this fear expressed before and the bleeding is not related to the abortion. The baby is born perfect.

Flash forward. 1993. I am pregnant again, and sadly, again, my marriage is mangled. But this pregnancy was deliberate; I don't blame it on ignorance. I don't want my three-year old son to grow up without a sibling. On the other hand, as the reality of what being a single mother again all these years later might mean, I seriously consider an abortion. I talk about it to my husband (who is categorically opposed) and to close friends. I don't even feel it's very private. I talk about it to the rabbi, my daughters, my doctor. I think about it every day. My ex-husband calls to vote against it. He thinks I've never recovered from the first one and would have an even harder time reconciling another. In the end, I decide to carry the pregnancy to term and am not sorry now I did. Another perfect baby born in 1994. But at this fourth Cesarean section delivery, at my request, the obstetrician tied my fallopian tubes and removed the fimbria that draw eggs up from the ovaries and deposit them in the uterus. I feel like the poster child for Planned Parenthood—planning gone awry.

A breakthrough: I decide to do research as an anthropologist in the area of abortion. I tell my 18-year old daughter that I've had an abortion and why. She astonishes me by telling me she's known this for years; she heard the horrendous fight I had with her father about his young fertile girlfriend. She is pro-choice, she tells me. My daughter is my ally. I am hers. I bring her to the obstetrician who delivered my last baby and make sure she's on the Pill. Her doctor makes sure that in addition to being on the Pill, she's supplied with condoms. We have different, but compatible, agendas, the doctor and I.

It would be fair to say I mourned my aborted baby, not in an immediate outburst of grieving, but in a long, slow process of unraveling and rebuilding, understanding my choice and using it to fuel advice I give now to my oldest daughter, and will surely give to the next one as she grows into the need for it. The baby I aborted was never "replaced" by the two I've had since, but I was relieved to know the abortion didn't impair my reproductive health. And, the experience, if not the actual baby, has become an emblem for me of that murky period in my life, my struggle to outgrow the parameters of a broken-down marriage, my recognition of the paralyzing consequences of dependency, my subsequent insistence on being in control of my fertility. And finally, quite obviously and unabashedly, that abortion informs my work today.

Notes

1. A "defamiliarized assumption" is defined in Ginsburg, (1990: 142) as the "strain" between the arrangement of events according to cultural

norms and the actual plot's "strange twists" that draws attention to the difference between expectation and experience.

2. This statistic was reported in its 1994 "Facts in Brief On Abortion in the United States" by the Alan Guttmacher Institute, a not-for-profit reproductive health research, policy analysis and public education corporation located in New York and Washington, p. 1.

3. The excerpts from personal correspondence in this essay are the responses I received in writing or conversation from women who answered my e-mail call for abortion narratives. I have promised anonymity in this paper; however, this file is available in my personal archives for review to confirm its contents. For the sake of consistency, both written and spoken communications are designated "personal correspondence."

4. As Layne surmises and Madden confirms (1994: 85), emotions following pregnancy loss are varied, and, Madden adds "less uniformly negative than accounts imply" (1994: 85). To present a balanced view of women's responses to abortion, I include here the equally compelling and valid narratives of women who did not experience grief after their abortions though they were not the subject of this research.

"I do not recall grieving at all; I can remember feeling mostly intense relief."

(from personal correspondence with J.C.)

"I had an abortion in Mexico in 1965 when it was illegal to have one in the U.S. and had no regrets then or since."

(from personal correspondence with N.K.)

"I would like to respond as someone who has not felt grief (or guilt) but is conscious that such a decision changes one's feelings about how much control is possible in any life, and that facing such a decision does not happen to everyone, and no doubt changes everyone who has to make that decision, whatever is decided."

(from personal correspondence with J.C.)

5. My inquiry about secrecy apparently was uninteresting or irrelevant to respondents. No one spontaneously addressed it and, when I asked about secrecy directly, most rephrased the issue as "privacy," and noted substantive differences between secrecy and privacy. Secrecy is the withholding of information to avoid punishment or censure; privacy is the withholding of information because of its intimate nature.

6. More than 50 percent of all pregnancies among American women are unintended—and half of these are terminated by abortion. Nearly three out of every 100 American women aged 15–44 has an abortion—43 percent of whom has had at least one before. Unmarried American women have more abortions than live births (Francke, 1978: 44). Since its legalization in the early 1970s, according to the Alan Guttmacher Institute (see note 3, above) approximately 30 million American women have had abortions.

The value of these demographics is to demonstrate that the American abortion experience is sufficiently common to have by now generated an extensive body of abortion folklore as counter-discourse to the maternalist ideology that links womanhood with inevitable motherhood (and motherhood with adulthood), and in opposition to the popularized belief that women who have abortions are by definition emotionally unstable (Rodman, Sarvis and Bonan, 1987: 71).

These demographics also demonstrate that women having abortions are not a marginalized few, but a significant proportion of those 5.5 million Americans who become pregnant each year. Though popular pro-natalist folklore promotes only mothers as "real women" (Morell, 1994: 6), and women who abort as "anti-mothers" whose bodies are "increasingly a source of danger for developing fetuses" (Tsing in Ginsburg and Tsing, 1990: 282), in fact, a large number of women choose to fulfill their female identities without giving birth to every baby they conceived. Many already have, or plan to have, children; for some, the act of having an abortion is inconsistent with their self-concept.

Works Cited

Benfield-Barker, G.J. *The Horrors of the Half-Known Life.* New York: Harper and Row, 1976.

Blincoe, Deborah and John Forrest. "The Dangers of Authenticity." In *New York Folklore, Prejudice and Pride: Lesbian and Gay Traditions in America,* Vol. XIX, No. 1–2, 1993.

Bok, Sissela. *Secrets.* New York: Pantheon Press, 1982.

Buttenweiser, Sarah and Reva Levine. *Breaking Silences. A Post-Abortion Support Model.* Fried, 1990.

Cornell, Drucilla. *Transformations.* New York: Routlege & Kegan Paul, 1993.

Douglas, Mary. *Purity and Danger.* London: Routledge & Kegan Paul, 1966.

Field, Peggy Anne and Patricia Beryl Marck, eds. *Uncertain Motherhood.* Thousand Lakes, CA: Sage, 1994.

Fine, Michelle. *Possibilities of Feminist Research.* Ann Arbor: U of Michigan P, 1992.

Francke, Linda Bird. *The Ambivalence of Abortion.* New York: Random House, 1978.

Fried, Marlene Gerber. *From Abortion to Reproductive Freedom.* Boston: South End Press, 1990.

Ginsburg, Faye D. *Contested Lives.* Berkeley: U of California P, 1989.

Ginsburg, Faye and Anna Lowenhaupt-Tsing. *Uncertain Terms.* Boston: Beacon Press, 1990.

Gordon, Linda. *Woman's Body, Woman's Right.* New York: Penguin, 1976.

Gregg, Robin. "Choice as a Double-Edged Sword." *Women and Health,* Vol. 20 (3), 1993: 53–73.

Harding, Sandra. *Feminism and Methodology.* Bloomington: U of Indiana P, 1987.

Hepworth, Mike and Bryan S. Turner. *Confession.* London: Routledge & Kegan Paul, 1982.

Hollis, Susan Tower, Linda Pershing and M. Jane Young. *Feminist Theory and the Size of Folklore.* Chicago: U of Illinois P, 1993.

Hoshiko, Sumi. *Our Choices.* New York: Harrington Park Press, 1993.

Judges, Donald P. *Hard Choices, Lost Voices.* Chicago: Ivan R. Dee, 1993.

King, Charles R. "Calling Jane: The Life and Death of a Woman's Illegal Abortion Service." *Women and Health,* Vol. 20 (3), 1993: 75–91.

Layne, Linda. "Motherhood Lost: Cultural Dimensions of Miscarriage and Stillbirth in America." *Women and Health,* Vol. 16 (3/4), 1990: 69–98.

Lowenhaupt-Tsing, Anna. "Monster Stories" in Ginsburg and Tsing, *Uncertain Terms.* 1990: 282–305.

Madden, Margaret. "The Variety of Emotional Reactions to Miscarriage." *Women and Health,* Vol. 21 (23), 1994: 85–104.

Martin, Emily. *The Woman in the Body.* Boston: Beacon Press, 1987.

Morell, Carolyn M. *Unwomanly Conduct.* New York: Routledge & Kegan Paul, 1994.

Nathanson, Constance A. *Dangerous Passages.* Philadelphia: Temple UP, 1991.

Pincus, Lily and Christopher Dare. *Secrets in the Family.* Boston: Faber and Faber, 1978.

Propp, V. *Morphology of the Folktale.* Austin: U of Texas P, 1968.

Rabuzzi, Kathryn Allen. *Mother with Child.* Indianapolis: Indiana UP, 1994.

Rodman, Hyman, Betty Sarvis and Joy Bonar. *The Abortion Question.* New York: Columbia UP, 1987.

Russo, Nancy Felipe, Jody D. Horn and Shannon Tromp. "Childspacing Intervals and Abortion Among Blacks and Whites." *Women and Health,* Vol. 20 (3), 1993: 43–51.

Snitow, Ann. "Feminist Analyses of Motherhood." *Encyclopedia of Childbearing: Critical Perspectives.* Barbara Katz Rothman, ed. Phoenix, Az: Onyx Press, 1993. 145–47.

Tefft, Stanton K. ed. *Secrecy.* New York: Human Services Press, 1980.

Thompson, Sharon. "Drastic Entertainments." In Ginsburg and Tsing, *Uncertain Terms.* 1990: 28–269.

Van Gennep, Arnold. *The Rites of Passage.* Chicago: U of Chicago P, 1960.

Helen Sue Edelman, MA, is a healthcare marketing communications professional currently serving as Director of Corporate Communications for Northeast Health, a regional, not-for-profit, integrated system of primary, acute, emergency, rehabilitative, long-term, chronic, community-based, and homecare healthcare and human services headquartered in Troy, New York. She has a master's degree in anthropology from the State University of New York at Albany.

The Chasm in Care

IN THE UNITED STATES, AIDS deaths dropped 47 percent from 1996 to 1997—thanks mostly to expensive drug treatments. Though such therapies have reduced AIDS fatalities in the United States and Western Europe, elsewhere the picture is almost uniformly bleak. Rates of HIV infection are soaring in impoverished African and Asian countries—the nations least prepared to prevent and treat the disease.

More than 30 million people are now infected with HIV, and almost 90 percent of them live in the developing countries of Asia and sub-Saharan Africa. Worldwide, 16,000 people are newly infected Africa. India, with 4 million cases, is now the world leader in absolute numbers. Infection rates are also rising with blinding speed in Ukraine, a country that was largely free of HIV before the 1991 breakup of the Soviet Union. It now has 110,000 people infected with HIV. That is nearly four times as many as in all of Eastern Europe just four years ago.

Poor countries can't afford expensive drugs to treat the disease. But last year brought a bit of Ivory Coast—were given a placebo, despite results from a 1994 study showing that the drug reduced maternal HIV transmission. Still, the CDC persisted, noting that the 26-week treatment the

In Zimbabwe, one-quarter of the adult population is now thought to be infected with HIV.

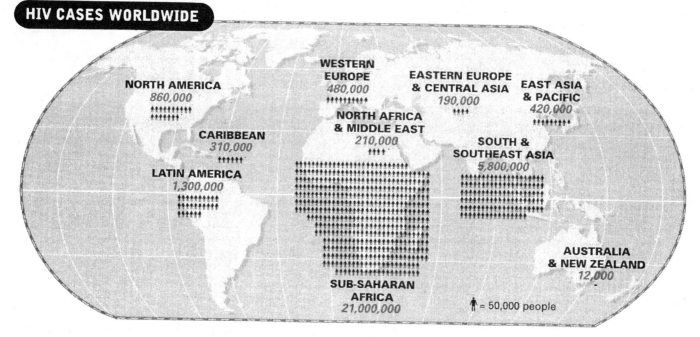

HIV CASES WORLDWIDE

NORTH AMERICA
860,000

CARIBBEAN
310,000

LATIN AMERICA
1,300,000

WESTERN EUROPE
480,000

NORTH AFRICA & MIDDLE EAST
210,000

EASTERN EUROPE & CENTRAL ASIA
190,000

EAST ASIA & PACIFIC
420,000

SOUTH & SOUTHEAST ASIA
5,800,000

SUB-SAHARAN AFRICA
21,000,000

AUSTRALIA & NEW ZEALAND
12,000

= 50,000 people

ILLUSTRATION BY IAN WORPOLE

with the virus every day—a figure twice as large as previous estimates, which were modeled in part on the infection rate in Uganda, where the epidemic has recently begun to plateau. In some countries, the extent of infection is nothing short of horrifying. In Zimbabwe, for example, one-quarter of the adult population is now thought to be infected with HIV. But the ravages are not limited to good news. In February the Centers for Disease Control and Prevention announced that a short, four-week course of the anti-AIDS drug AZT during late pregnancy and delivery halved the transmission rate of the virus from HIV-positive women to their babies. The trial had been heavily criticized as unethical because half its subjects—pregnant HIV-positive women in Thailand and the earlier study tested costs $800—roughly 80 times the annual health budget per person in many poor, developing countries. Only a second trial could test whether a shorter, less expensive course of drug treatment could work, too.

When positive results came from Thailand last February, the trial was halted, and the Ivory Coast women on the placebo were switched to the drug.

But even the cost of the short, four-week course of AZT—$50—is far beyond the reach of many women in developing countries. The good news is that the Joint United Nations Program on HIV/AIDS, based in Geneva, agreed to pay for the treatment of 30,000 HIV-positive pregnant women in 11 developing countries. Glaxo Welcome, the maker of AZT, will supply the drug at a 60 to 75 percent discount.

Though the United States can generally afford such preventive strategies, there are still substantial gaps. For example, 40 percent of all U.S. AIDS cases occur among injecting drug abusers, and the majority of pediatric AIDS cases occur among children born to injecting drug users or their partners. Yet despite results from a recent government inquiry demonstrating that needle-exchange programs can reduce HIV transmission among injecting drug users by 30 percent, the Clinton administration in April refused to lift a ban on federal funding for such programs, stating that the programs send the wrong message to children.

This past year also saw new findings illuminating the early history of the AIDS virus. In February, researchers led by David Ho of the Aaron Diamond AIDS Research Center in New York announced that they had isolated fragments of the HIV genome from a blood sample drawn in 1959 from a man living in what was then Léopoldville, Belgian Congo (now Kinshasa in the Democratic Republic of Congo). By comparing genetic sequences of these segments with sequences from more recent strains of HIV, they created a family tree and traced elements in the 1959 sample to a common ancestor of three present-day HIV subtypes. The 1959 virus, it turned out, closely resembles the ancestral virus, which is believed to have hopped from an animal host into humans. Based on that resemblance, the researchers suspect the hop probably occurred in the early 1950s or mid-1940s—soon after the end of World War II and the collapse of European colonialism in Africa.

The timing of those events supports the observation that the spread of HIV accelerates in conditions of social turmoil and poverty. Simon Wain-Hobson, a British virologist and AIDS researcher at the Pasteur Institute in Paris, believes that the disruption and migration that characterized post-colonial Africa may have played a key role in the spread of HIV. "The English and the French kept people ruthlessly under control," says Wain-Hobson. "They didn't let them move; they didn't let them travel. And what happened finally when the English pulled out was a free-for-all. There were pogroms, there was corruption, there was blackmail, there were movements of populations, the introduction of the motorcar. There was the beginning of

IN THE SENEGALESE capital of Dakar, the HIV infection rate has stayed below 2 percent. The reason is Senegal's HIV-prevention program, which includes sex education in schools, clinics for treating sexually transmitted diseases (which increase the susceptibility to HIV infection), and promotion of condom use. Condom distribution in Senegal rose from 800,000 in 1988 to more than 7 million in 1997.

HIV INFECTS more than 10 percent of adults in nine African countries: Botswana, Kenya, Malawi, Mozambique, Namibia, Rwanda, South Africa, Zambia, and Zimbabwe. If AIDS did not exist, the average life expectancy in these countries would be 58 years. AIDS has reduced that to 48 years. Because those infected with HIV tend to die in the prime of life, the loss devastates families and may weaken these nations' economies.

IN CAMBODIA, 1 in 30 pregnant women, 1 in 16 soldiers, and nearly 1 in 2 prostitutes test positive for HIV.

the urbanization of Africa, which is a postwar event." These developments, he believes, may have helped HIV expand beyond the narrow range it occupied after it first emerged. "It's a plausible hypothesis," says Wain-Hobson, "but we might never get beyond that."

—Josie Glausiusz

Recovery or Resistance?

WITH THE ADVENT OF POWERFUL DRUG combinations, HIV infection is no longer a death sentence—at least for those with health insurance. Triple-drug therapies, which combine three classes of drugs, so disable the viral machinery that HIV levels in the blood can, in many cases, drop to imperceptible levels. This is especially true for those treated early in the course of infection. But even those with advanced cases can benefit. Immunologist Brigitte Autran, of the Pitié-Salpêtriére Hospital in Paris, studied 320 late-stage AIDS patients who had been on triple therapy for two years. In June she reported that not only had the amount of HIV in their blood plummeted but their CD4 cell counts rose from an average of 50 cells per cubic millimeter of blood to 300 and above (500 to 1,000 is normal). That's welcome news, because CD4 cells orchestrate the immune response to infection. "This is probably the first time that we've shown a potential for true regeneration in the immune systems of adults," says Autran.

Sadly, however, patients cannot reduce the drug regimen to minimize side effects. In October two large studies showed that cutting back to one or two drugs permits the virus to rebound. Even worse, triple therapy doesn't work for everyone. Robert Shafer, an infectious-diseases physician at Stanford Medical Center, encountered the problem in four long-term patients who had been referred to his clinic after tests showed that triple therapy wasn't curbing viral replication. Most had started treatment in the 1980s on AZT, the first commonly used anti-AIDS drug, then added newer drugs as each became available—including the powerful protease inhibitors, which disable an enzyme involved in the formation of infectious virus. But HIV reproduces quickly and makes many mistakes in copying its genetic information. So if drug therapy doesn't shut down viral replication completely—and before triple therapy was available, it seldom did—viral mutations conferring resistance can easily emerge in step with each new drug. Tests of viral samples from these patients, says Shafer, proved the virus to be impervious to as many as nine different drugs—including the protease inhibitors.

Multiple-drug resistance is already turning up among many other HIV-infected patients on long-term drug therapy. But even more worrisome is the possibility that multiple-drug-resistant strains might become common among newly infected HIV patients. "I definitely believe that they can," says Shafer. Indeed, shortly after his study was published in June, a case came to light of a gay man infected with a multi-drug-resistant strain by his HIV-infected partner.

—Josie Glausiusz

Religion/Spirituality and Health Among Elderly African Americans and Hispanics

Jacqueline M. Stolley, PhD, RN, CS; and Harold Koenig, MD, MHSc

The significance of the cultural dimension in aging is extremely important for the psychiatric nurse, primarily because the "myth" of the "melting pot" is not valid. Although it is important to view elders in a multicultural sense, it is also paramount to understand that there may be great heterogeneity within cultural or ethnic groups (Tripp-Reimer, Johnson & Rios, 1995).

The Function of Religion

One of the most important support systems for ethnic groups in America is spirituality or the religion (religiosity) in which spirituality is expressed. Religion can provide support in common aspects of everyday living, and comfort in times of distress (Tripp-Reimer et al, 1995).

Religion has served to buffer psychological stressors and enable humans in general and the ethnic elder in particular to adapt or cope with life's events (Courtenay, Poon, Martin, Clayton, & Johnson, 1992; Idler & Kasl, 1992; Koenig, Cohen, & Blazer, 1992; Williams, 1994).

Jacqueline M. Stolley, PhD, RN, CS, is an Associate Professor at The Trinity College of Nursing in Moline, IL, and a Doctoral Candidate at the University of Iowa, Iowa City, IA. Harold Koenig, MD, MHSc, is an Associate Professor of Psychiatry and of Internal Medicine and the Director of the Program on Religion, Aging, & Health at Duke University Medical Center, Durham, NC.

Address all correspondence to Dr. Jacqueline M. Stolley, PhD, RN, CS, Trinity College of Nursing, 501 10th Ave., Moline, IA 61265.

Knowledge of the effects of religious beliefs on ethnic groups can help health care professionals provide care that is culture specific and sensitive to the beliefs of individuals. It is imperative for the psychiatric nurse to be aware of spiritual and religious influences that may contribute to behaviors of elders that may be misinterpreted as healthy or unhealthy to the uninformed practitioner.

The influence of spirituality or religiosity in the lives of elderly African Americans and Hispanics is presented here to describe the importance of this phenomenon in these groups.

An Effort to Increase Cultural Sensitivity

The significance of both culture and spirituality has not escaped the attention of the American Psychiatric Association, which has included a new category in the fourth edition of the *Diagnostic and Statistical Manual of Mental Disorders* (DSM-IV, American Psychiatric Association, 1994). This category is incorporated under Other Conditions That May Be a Focus of Clinical Attention (V Code) Religious or Spiritual Problems.

This change is the result of a debate by a variety of experts that a more culturally sensitive diagnostic classification system was needed (Lukoff, Lu, & Turner, 1992; Turner, Lukoff, Barnhouse & Lu, 1995). There has been criticism of early versions of the DSM because of the lack of sensitivity to culture contained within diagnoses. As a result of this insensitivity, conditions that may

have been culturally bound were diagnosed as a pathology (Lukoff et al.; Turner et al.).

In response to these problems, the DSM-IV Task Force collaborated with the Workgroup on Culture and Diagnosis of the National Institute of Mental Health (NIMH) to consider cultural and spiritual components in the assessment and diagnosis of mental disorders (Turner et al.).

The psychiatric nurse should use these criteria to examine the relationship between the syndrome and relevant DSM-IV categories, including various Axis I disorders, as well as the new nonpathological category of religious or spiritual problem.

The change in the DSM enables the mental health professional to diagnose on the basis of other conditions, and for the psychiatric nurse to intervene appropriately, recognizing a previously unaddressed clinical reality (Turner et al., 1995). It is not surprising that the American Psychiatric Association developed more culturally and spiritually sensitive criteria in view of the growing body of research that links spirituality or religiosity to mental and physical health.

Spirituality/Religiosity Among Elderly African Americans

In the 1990 census, 31.1 million persons were aged 65 or older, composed of 27.0 million (87%) Caucasians and 2.5 million African Americans (Bureau of Census and National Institute on Aging, 1993). African Americans represent the second largest racial or ethnic group of elders, and that proportion is expected to increase from 8% in 1990 to 10% in 2050 (Bureau of Census and National Institute on Aging, 1993). Additionally, geographic location of African Americans is the most diverse of all the major ethnic groups (Tripp-Reimer et al., 1995). It is not surprising, then, that the majority of research on spirituality/religiosity within a major ethnic group has been conducted on African Americans.

A key component

Most research that has investigated spirituality or religiosity among elderly African Americans suggests that religion and religious organizations are central to their lives (Chatters & Taylor, 1989; Taylor & Chatters, 1991). In particular, the importance of religion for elder African Americans is prominent. Levin and Taylor (1997) found that African Americans tend to pray more often than their Anglo counterparts. Furthermore, compared with younger African Americans, older African Americans are more likely to be affiliated with a religion, attend religious services as an adult, and be a church member (Chatters & Taylor, 1989; Taylor & Chatters, 1991).

Older African Americans participate in nonorganizational and private religious activities such as viewing religious broadcasts, reading religious materials, and praying more frequently than their younger counterparts (Chatters & Taylor, 1989). They also report a greater degree of subjective religious involvement.

Examination of denominational affiliation among older African Americans found that over half of older African Americans are Baptists (54.7%), with smaller proportions being Methodist (13.6%) and Roman Catholic (5.7%); the remainder are distributed over 25 divergent religious affiliations (Taylor & Chatters, 1991). More than 75% of all elderly African Americans are church members and at least half attend religious services at least once a week.

The use of nonorganized religious activity among elderly African Americans is pronounced. In fact, more than 93% of African Americans report that they pray nearly every day and this activity tends to increase with age (Chatters, Levin, & Taylor, 1992; Levin, Taylor & Chatters, 1994; Levin & Taylor, 1993). It is interesting to note that frequent religious participation is greater in black females than black

males, and that lower levels of religious involvement has been noted in divorced and widowed African Americans when compared with those who are married (Chatters et al.; Levin et al.)

Religion, Social Support, and Health

Religion and the church have been powerful sources of social support for elderly African Americans. Historically, the African American church has been the central institution in the community, serving a broad range of religious and

More than 75% of all elderly African Americans are church members; at least half attend religious services at least once a week.

▬

nonreligious functions, and evidence exists that religion may be more central in the lives of African Americans than Anglos (Princeton Religion Research Center, 1987). In fact, frequency of church attendance is the most significant predictor of both frequency and quantity of support received.

The most common form of reported aid is socioemotional support received during times of ill health (Levin et al., 1994).

Enforces a sense of well-being

Church support plays a major role in an individual's feelings of life satisfaction, with a higher feeling of well-being associated with greater level of contact with church friends. In fact, this contact seems to be more important than involvement with nonchurch friends or family (Walls & Zarit, 1991).

Even in nursing homes the importance of religiosity can be found. Cline (1992) studied the relationship between social support, health, and religiosity in a nursing home population of 80 sub-

jects. Results showed that there were strong effects for social support on health and ratings of religiosity and that African Americans had significantly higher religiosity than Anglos. However, there was no significant relationship between religiosity and health ratings.

Further evidence for the importance of the church for African Americans was found in a study by Ferraro and Koch (1994), who reported that although the effects of social support on health appeared similar for African Americans and Anglos, the link between religion and health was stronger for African Americans than Anglos. This was particularly true for those persons who practiced their religion and for those who turned to religion as a coping resource in times of poor health. Similar results have been reported in other studies.

Levin et al. (1995) found statistically significant associations among organizational religiosity and both health and life satisfaction. Furthermore, they found that the relationship between health and participation in nonorganizational religious activity was strong and that organizational religiosity has a strong, significant association with life satisfaction. These data suggest that the association between religion and well-being is consistent over the life course and not merely an accident resulting from confounding of measures of organizational religiosity and health status (Levin et al.).

Religion/Spirituality and Psychological Variables

Coping mechanisms

Even though religion and spirituality are most commonly reported as important sources of social support for black Americans, they can also be used for dealing with negative life events in a more positive way. Rosen (1982) examined spontaneously mentioned coping behaviors and found that religious coping behaviors were the most common response, occurring in 51% of African Americans and 28% of Anglos.

These findings are not surprising. Women, the less educated, and people of lower social class have been consistently associated with greater religious activity (Princeton Religion Research Center, 1987). Similarly, Krause and Van Tran (1989) found that although life stress tended to erode feelings of self-worth and mastery, these negative effects were offset or counterbalanced by increased religious involvement. Likewise, Handal, Black-Lopez, & Moergen (1989) found that black women who scored low on religious attachment have the highest psychological distress when compared with those with moderate or high scores.

Religion and depression

On the other hand, Nelson (1989) found little relationship between religion and coping with depression. However, she did find that elderly African Americans were more intrinsically oriented to religion, tended to "live their religion" and had religion play a major role in their day-to-day activities. African-American elderly indicated that religion provided comfort in times of stress and used prayer in times of stress, more so than Anglos. For Anglos, religion was not the focal point that provided meaning, but it was a resource for meeting social interests.

Even so, the African American subjects as a total group were more depressed and their use of religion had not been a successful coping resource. In any event, the findings of this study suggest that African-American and Anglo elderly persons differ in religious orientation and their religious orientation does not necessarily determine their success in coping with depression (Nelson, 1989). However, it may be that African Americans turn to religion more frequently when depressed, reflecting a positive association between depression and intrinsic religiosity.

An example is provided by Ellison (1995) who found that an inverse relationship existed between the frequency of church attendance and depressive symptoms among Anglos, but not among African Americans. Additionally, findings indicate that the absence of denominational affiliation is positively associated with depressive symptoms among African Americans, but not in Anglos.

Another interesting finding was that the frequency of private devotional activities (e.g., prayer) is positively associated with depressive symptoms among both racial groups, again pointing to a possible tendency to use prayer to cope during depressive episodes (Ellison, 1995). Not surprisingly, Bearon and Koenig (1990) found that African Americans tended to use prayer more frequently than Anglos for intervention of symptoms of illness.

Counteracting detrimental effects

In the same vein, Krause (1992) reported that religiosity tended to counterbalance or offset the deleterious effects of physical health problems and deaths (stressors) by bolstering feelings of self-worth. Additionally, Brown and Gary (1994) found that for African Americans, having a denominational affiliation was associated with fewer depressive symptoms.

> For African Americans, religion is seen as an important social support and mechanism for coping with stressful life events.

This study showed a direct and positive association between religious involvement and mental health, and underscored the importance of religious affiliation. It should be noted, however, that African-American males tend to have disproportionately lower religious participation than other groups (Brown & Gary, 1994).

Nevertheless, in their study, Ferraro and Koch (1994) noted that African Americans were more likely to turn to religion for coping than Anglos, lending strength to results of previous research that marked religion as a coping resource for African Americans.

In summary, studies generally show a heavy reliance on religion for African Americans, particularly females. Religion is seen as an important social support and a mechanism for coping with stressful life events and serves as more than a spiritually oriented purpose. Although not all studies support the positive effect of religiosity, the preponderance of studies do.

Spirituality/Religiosity Among Hispanics

Study of religious/spiritual influences in the lives of older Hispanics has been sparse. Recently, interest has been kindled in this area, along with the influence of religion/spirituality in other ethnic groups. This is encouraging, because Hispanics (consisting of Mexican Americans, Puerto Ricans, Cubans, and other South Americans), account for about 1.1 million (4%) of the elderly, according to the 1990 census (Bureau of Census, National Institute of Aging, 1993). This group is expected to increase to 9% by the year 2020 and 16% by 2050.

Additionally, although the preponderance of Mexican Americans reside in the Southwest (Tripp-Reimer et al., 1995), a large number can be found in the farming areas of the Midwest. Puerto Ricans tend to settle in the New York and Northeast, and Cubans in Florida. Acknowledging the growing numbers of Hispanics in the United States, it is important that research involving this ethnic group including the influence of spirituality/religiosity be done.

Studies have shown that the vast majority of this population is Christian with 85% to 89% Roman Catholic, a fact not surprising in view of the critical role the Catholic Church has had in the development of this population in their respective countries of origin (Andrews, 1989; Gallego, 1988; Markides & Martin, 1983). However, these studies also report that from 9% to 13% of all Hispanics are Protestant, reflecting a recent phenomenon in this country and in Latin America (Maldonado, 1995).

A high percentage of Hispanics reported that they engaged in weekly church attendance (Maldonado, 1994, 1995). In a sample surveyed in San Antonio, 75% reported that they attended a religious activity weekly, with women reporting higher rates of attendance, and a high proportion of men reporting that they never attend (Maldonado, 1994, 1995). Interestingly, prayer meetings, one form of religious activity, were attended more frequently by women (46%) than men (39%), and church school is more commonly attended by men (54%) than women (23%).

This same study reported that older Hispanics were more active in religious activities in older years, and in fact one third, especially women (42%), would like to be even more active. Health and transportation are the major problems that prevent regular church attendance. These data suggest that religious activities are more noteworthy among Hispanic women than men, similar to findings of studies of black Americans.

Religion/Spirituality and Social Support

Hispanic elders play prominent roles in the religious support system, both as clergy and as members of the congregation, especially in Pentecostal and Seventh Day Adventist groups. In this role, they are likely to express cultural values (including religion) from generation to generation (Delgado, 1982). Additionally, several religious institutions provide child care, with elders staffing such programs. Because they are most available, retired Hispanic elders may be asked to assist sick members of the congregation, serving an important social function (Delgado, 1982).

The subgroup of Mexican-Americans has perhaps been the most studied of Hispanics, generally comparing them with their Anglo counterparts. The importance of religion for Mexican-Americans has been studied by several researchers. For example, the relationships between church attendance, self-rated religiosity, and private prayer with aging were investigated with longitudinal data on older Mexican-Americans and Anglos.

Church attendance and practice of private prayer remained relatively stable over time as well as self-rated life satisfaction for both ethnic groups. Among Anglos, the effect of church attendance on life satisfaction increased significantly during the study interval but only church attendance was significantly related to life satisfaction for both groups (Markides, 1983).

In another study, Levin and Markides (1988) found that church attendance was significantly correlated with life satisfaction in women, but was unrelated to life satisfaction in men. These results may point to the fact that many Hispanic women, particularly those new to America, obtain most of their social support through religious activities.

Religion and life satisfaction

Hispanics have been the object of discrimination in the United States, tending to form their own organizations, such as churches. Although men may participate in religious activities, they have other vehicles for obtaining social support, such as work activities, and so-cial activities in the local tavern, so often taboo for Hispanic women. Further, religious participation may tend to prohibit activities for men that may be viewed as nonreligious, such as going to the local tavern. Thus, religious participation may not contribute to the life satisfaction of men who believe they must adhere to religious rules (Levin & Markides, 1988).

More recently, Angel and Angel (1992) reported that elder Hispanics (Cuban, Mexican, and Puerto Ricans) who have frequent contact with family and friends and participate in church activities manage better than Hispanic elders who are more socially isolated.

F or Hispanic elders, the dying process is enhanced by having a doctor who has respect for the person's spirituality and religion.

■

The importance of religion and its association with well-being is further illustrated in a study conducted by Owens, Mills-Bowling, and Arana (1994). They found that Hispanic older adults perceived their religion to be more important to them than did the European American adults. Additionally, religion was reported to be more important to those who were less acculturated. This finding is not surprising in view of the fact that religion and church can be the primary source of contact for many who are relatively new to this country.

Support for caregivers

Further evidence that supports the importance of religion and spirituality in social and emotional support can be found in a study of mental illness and caregiving in Hispanic families. It was found that religion plays an important role in providing support to caregivers. In addition, both religious institutions and religious healings were found to be major sources of solace (Guarnaccia, Papra, Deschampes, Milstein, & Argiles, 1992). The importance of the church as a mechanism providing psychological and social support is communicated in these studies.

The importance of attention to religious and spiritual needs of the patient by health care professionals can be seen throughout the process of life. In a discussion of factors that enhance the dying process for Hispanic elders it was reported that having a doctor who is considered one of the family, who focuses on the inner importance of the person, and who has respect for the person's spirituality and religious beliefs is of major importance (Siefken, 1993). The implications of this finding are important to busy health care providers and should be considered not only by physicians, but also by psychiatric nurses who care for this and other ethnic groups.

Religion/Spirituality and Health

The relationship among religiosity/spirituality and health practices and outcomes for Hispanics has been studied. In a longitudinal study, Levin and Markides (1986) found a positive relationship between church attendance and subjective health among young and older female participants only. This association held even when controlling for non-religious social participation, implying that the relationship could not be explained entirely in terms of the positive effects of social interaction. However, when self-perceived "physical capacity" was controlled for, the relationship between attendance and health became nonsignificant.

It is possible that religious attendance is not the only explanation for high ratings of subjective health; rather, the physical capacity to attend church chiefly clarifies this association.

A link with hypertension

Interestingly, Levin and Markides (1985) found that hypertension was more prevalent among older Mexican-Americans who rated themselves "highly religious" compared with those "less than very religious" (30%). Church attendance was unrelated to blood pressure. The authors speculate that guilt arising from pressures to conform to high behavioral standards may contribute to hypertension. Another explanation is that persons with hypertension may have sought religion is a response to their health predicament or the finding may be due to elimination of the least religious subjects from the study because of mortality due to hypertension. This may have created a deceptive relationship (Levin & Vanderpool, 1989). Because the sample was in the Southwest (Texas), it is important to determine if these results hold true for other areas of the country.

The importance of acknowledging religious and spiritual issues when dealing with disease and health in this population is evident. For instance, a survey conducted by Zaldivar and Smolowitz (1994) examined whether religious, spiritual, and folk medicine beliefs determine the patient's belief about diabetes and choices of treatment.

Survey participants included 104 non-Mexican-American Hispanic adults with diabetes. Of patients surveyed, 78% believed it was God's will that they had diabetes, and 17% of patients reported using herbs to treat their diabetes. This points to the potential necessity of involving clergy and folk healers in treatment to assure optimum interventions and outcomes (Zaldivar & Smolowitz, 1994).

In summary, the relationship between religion and spiritual support among Hispanics is well documented as is the relationship with black Americans. However, the relationship between religion and physical health is ambiguous and needs further study. In any event, the significance of spirituality/religiosity and physical and mental health is evident in these studies.

Implications and Conclusion

The majority of studies regarding African Americans and Hispanics indicates the importance of religion, and particularly the church, for social support and coping. Although not all research supports this assertion, most studies do. Evidence exists that religion has a positive impact on health. Multivariate measurement of religiosity and spirituality must be included in the study of the relationship between these variables and health. It is not enough to merely ask questions about affiliation or attendance, but to include questions about types of participation (organizational,

nonorganizational), and the meaning of religious beliefs (intrinsic religiosity or beliefs).

Awareness of the spiritual dimension

With the growing awareness of cultural and religious differences that can affect physical and mental health, the psychiatric nurse must be aware of the spiritual/religious dimension and the impact on mental and physical and mental health across cultures. Because the American Psychiatric Association (1994) has formulated outlines that encompass cultural and religious differences and similarities, these principles can readily be incorporated into psychiatric nursing practice not only in mental health, but also in physical health arenas using a holistic model.

> I t is not enough to merely ask questions about affiliation or attendance, but to include questions about types of participation and the meaning of religious beliefs.

Nursing has always been sensitive to individualized care of patients, but more recently has begun to focus attention on culturally defined issues and how they affect physical and mental health outcomes. Because the population of the United States is culturally and spiritually diverse, individualistic care must embrace this diversity to achieve optimum outcomes.

Maintain an accepting attitude

Patients may be reluctant to share their spiritual or religious beliefs, attitudes and practices for fear of chastisement by others who do not share these attributes. An attitude of acceptance by the psychiatric nurse can be paramount

in incorporating the spiritual and religious dimension in care to ease the healing process, and perhaps find meaning in life's stresses and strains.

Psychiatric nurses can design interventions that embrace culturally related religious and spiritual beliefs, attitudes and practice of patients. Including this information in initial assessment and ongoing interactions with patients conveys a feeling of acceptance and respect for these very personal attributes.

Seek assistance

Additionally, the psychiatric nurse can enlist the services of clergy and church members who experience similar beliefs to participate in the healing process. In any event, the psychiatric nurse is in a unique position to encourage the patient to use healthy religious practices to deal with their illness, whether mental or physical, rather than denying or avoiding this human dimension that may be so pivotal to their lives.

References

American Psychological Association. (1994). *Diagnostic and statistical manual of mental disorders, 4th ed.* Washington, DC: American Psychiatric Press.

Andrews, J. (1989). *Poverty and poor health among elderly Hispanic Americans.* New York: Commonwealth Fund Commission on Elderly People Living Alone.

Angel, J. L., & Angel, R. J. (1992). Age at migration, social connections, and well-being among elderly Hispanics. *Journal of Aging and Health, 4,* 480–499.

Bearon, L. B., & Koenig, H. G. (1990). Religious cognitions and use of prayer in health and illness. *The Gerontologist, 30,* 249–253.

Brown, D. R., & Gary, L. E. (1994). Religious involvement and health status among African-American males. *Journal of the National Medical Association, 86,* 825–831.

Chatters, L. M., Levin, J. S., & Taylor, R. J. (1992). Antecedents and dimensions of religious involvement among older African American adults. *Journal of Gerontology, 47,* S269–278.

Chatters, L. M., & Taylor (1989). Age differences in religious participation among Black adults. *Journal of Gerontology, 44,* S183–189.

Cline, D. J. (1992). *The effects of social support on health and religiosity in nursing home elderly.* Chicago: Illinois Institute of Technology.

Courtenay, B. C., Poon. K. W., Martin, P., Clayton, G. M., & Johnson, M. A. (1992). *International Journal of Aging and Human Development. 34*(1), 47–56.

Delgado, M. (1982). Ethnic and cultural variations in the care of the aged: Hispanic elderly and natural support systems. A special focus on Puerto Ricans. *Journal of Geriatric Psychiatry, 15,* 239–251.

Ellison, C. G. (1995). Race, religious involvement, and depression in a southeastern U.S. community. *Social Science and Medicine, 40,* 1561–1572.

Ferraro, K. F., & Koch, J. R. (1994). Religion and health among black and white adults: Examining social support and consultation. *Journal for the Scientific Study of Religion, 33,* 362–375.

Gallego, D. T. (1988). Religiosity as a coping mechanism among Hispanic elderly. In M. Sotomayer and H. Curiel (Eds.), "Hispanic Elderly: Cultural Signature" (pp. 117–135). Edinburg, Texas: University of Texas–Pan American Press.

Guarnaccia, P. J., Parra, P., Deschamps, G., Milstein, G., & Argiles, N. (1992). Si dios quiere: Hispanic families' experiences of caring for a seriously mentally ill family member. *Culture, Medicine and Psychiatry, 16,* 187–215.

Handal, P. J., Black-Lopez, W., & Moergen, S. (1989). Preliminary investigation of the relationship between religion and psychological distress in black women. *Psychological Reports, 65,* 971–975.

Idler, E. L., & Kasl, S. V. (1992). Religion, disability, depression, and the timing of death. *American Journal of Sociology, 97,* 1052–1079.

Koenig, H. G., Cohen, H. J., & Blazer, D. G. (1992). Religious coping and depression among elderly, hospitalized medically ill men. *The American Journal of Psychiatry, 149,* 1693–1700.

Krause, N., & Van Tran, T. (1989). Stress and religious involvement among older African Americans. *Journal of Gerontology, 44,* S4–13.

Krause, N. (1992). Stress, religiosity, and psychological well-being among older African Americans. *Journal of Aging and Health, 4,* 412–439.

Levin, J. S., & Markides, K. S. (1985). Religion and health in Mexican Americans. *Journal of Religion and Health, 24,* 60–69.

Levin, J. S., & Markides, K. S. (1986). Religious attendance and subjective health. *Journal for the Scientific Study of Religion, 25,* 31–40.

Levin, J. S., & Markides, K. S. (1988). Religious attendance and psychological well-being in middle-aged and older Mexican-Americans. *Sociological Analysis, 49,* 66–72.

Levin, J. S. & Taylor, R. J. (1993). Gender and age differences in religiosity among Black Americans. *The Gerontologist, 33*(1), 16–23.

Levin, J. S., & Taylor, R. J. (1977). Age differences in patterns and correlates of the frequency of prayer. *The Gerontologist, 37*(1), 75–88.

Levin, J. S., Taylor, R. J., & Chatters, L. M. (1994). Race and gender differences in religiosity among older adults: Findings from four national surveys. *Journal of Gerontology, 49,* S137–145.

Levin, J. S., Chatters, L. M., & Taylor, R. J. (1995). Religious effects on health status and life satisfaction among Black Americans. *Journal of Gerontology, 50B,* S154–163.

KEYPOINTS

Religion/Spirituality

Religion/Spirituality and Health Among Elderly African Americans and Hispanics. Stolley, J., Koenig, H. Journal of Psychosocial Nursing and Mental Health Services 1997;35(11):32–38.

1 It is important to view elders in a multicultural sense and also understand that there may be great heterogeneity within cultural or ethnic groups.

2 Knowledge of the impact of religion and spiritual beliefs for ethnic groups can help health care professionals design interventions that are culture-specific to the beliefs of individuals.

3 The psychiatric nurse is in a unique position to encourage the patient to use healthy religious practices to deal with their illness, whether mental or physical.

Levin, J. S., & Vanderpool, H. Y. (1989). Is religion therapeutically significant for hypertension? *Social Sciences and Medicine, 29,* 69–78.

Lukoff, D., Lu, F., & Turner, R. (1992). Toward a more culturally sensitive DSM-IV. Psychoreligious and psychospiritual problems. (Review). *Journal of Nervous & Mental Disease, 180,* 673–682.

Maldonado, D. (1994). Religiosity and religious participation among Hispanic elderly. *Journal of Religious Gerontology, 9*(1), 41–60.

Maldonado, D. (1995). Religion and persons of color. In M. A. Kimble, S. H. McFadden, J. W. Ellor, and J. J. Seeber, *Aging, spirituality, and religion, A handbook.* Minneapolis: Fortress Press.

Markides, K. S. (1983). Aging, religiosity, and adjustment: A longitudinal analysis. *Journal of Gerontology, 28,* 621–625.

Markides, K., & Martin, H. W. (1983). *Older Mexican Americans.* Austin, Tex: Center for Mexican American Studies.

Nelson, P. B. (1989). Ethnic differences in intrinsic/extrinsic religious orientation and depression in the elderly. *Archives of Psychiatric Nursing, 3,* 199–204.

Owens, S. A., Mills-Bowing, C., & Arana, C. (1994, November). *Ethnicity, religiosity, health, and well-being: A comparison of Hispanic and European American older adults.* Poster presented at the 47th Annual Scientific Meeting of the Gerontological Society of America, Atlanta, Ga.

Princeton Religion Research Center. (1987). 1987 *Religion in America.* Princeton, NJ: The Gallup Poll.

Rosen, C. C. (1982). Ethnic differences among impoverished rural elderly in use of religion as a coping mechanism. *Journal of Rural Community Psychology, 3,* 27–34.

Siefken, S. (1993). The Hispanic perspective on death and dying: A combination of respect, empathy, and spirituality. *Pride Institute Journal of Long-Term Home Health Care, 12*(2), 26–28.

Taylor, R. J. & Chatters, L. M. (1991). Non-organizational religious participation among elderly black adults. *Journal of Gerontology, 46,* S103–11.

Tripp-Reimer, T., Johnson, R. & Rios, H. (1995). Cultural dimensions in gerontological nursing. In M. Stanley & P. G. Beare (Eds.). *Gerontological nursing* (pp. 28–36). Philadelphia: J. B. Lippincott.

Turner, R. P., Lukoff, D., Barnhouse, R. T., & Lu, F. G. (1995). Religious or spiritual problem. A culturally sensitive diagnostic category in the DSM-IV. *Journal of Nervous and Mental Disease, 183,* 435–44.

Walls, C. T., & Zarit, S. H., (1991). Informal support from black churches and the well-being of elderly African Americans. *The Gerontologist, 31,* 490–495.

Williams, D. R. (1994). Measurement of religion. In J. S. Levin (Ed.), *Religion, aging, and health.* Thousand Oaks, California: Sage.

Zaldivar, A., & Smolowitz, J. (1994). Perceptions of the importance placed on religion and folk medicine by non-Mexican-American Hispanic adults with diabetes. *The Diabetes Educator, 20,* 303–306.

The Managed Care Experience: The Social Worker's Perspective

Holly A. Riffe, PhD

ABSTRACT. The noise surrounding managed care is deafening. Clinicians all over America are gearing up for the worst. But what are the implications for social workers? A survey drawn from the NASW Clinical Social Worker Registry reveals that the influence managed care practices have on social work activities is perceived to be increasing and that social workers are experiencing ethical conflicts when dealing with primary insurers. This article explores the experience of managed care in a sample of 442 social worker clinicians and discusses the implications for ethics and social work. *[Article copies available for a fee from The Haworth Document Delivery Service: 1–800–342–9678. E-mail address: getinfo@haworthpressinc.com]*

Social workers are now experiencing the impact of dwindling resources in virtually all direct practice arenas (Weisman, Curbow, & Khoury, 1996; Brown, 1994; Bursztajn & Brodsky, 1994; Lazarus, 1994; Broskowski, 1991). Not only are insurance companies regulating the length and type of treatments that are available (Graham, 1995; Sabin, 1994); hospitals are merging with other hospitals and states are cutting mental health budgets through the transfer of responsibilities to "local control" (Shera, 1996). These types of systemic changes have the potential for creating havoc in the daily lives of social work practitioners as well as in their work with clients (Perloff, 1996; Sabin, 1994; Stern, 1993).

Managed care has increased substantially since the 1973 approval of the Health Maintenance Organization Act (Garnick et al., 1994; Winegar, 1992; Newman & Bricklin, 1991; Shayne & Kinney, 1986). In social service

Holly A. Riffe is an Assistant Professor at the University of Kentucky.

Address correspondence to Holly A. Riffe, College of Social Work, University of Kentucky, 671 Patterson Office Tower, Lexington, KY 40506–0027.

The author wishes to gratefully acknowledge the editorial assistance of David Royse, PhD, and Vernon Wiehe, PhD, in the preparation of this manuscript.

agencies, cost containment strategies such as peer review of services and intensive individual case management are being used to restrict the use of insurance dollars (Garnick et al., 1994; Hoge et al., 1994; Broskowski, 1991). These approaches to cutting costs have influenced the relationships between social workers and their clients by limiting forms of acceptable treatment (Riffe & Kondrat, 1997; Shapiro, 1995; Kuhl, 1994). For instance, social workers and other medical professionals may recommend that a client be hospitalized to avoid endangering self or others while the case manager for the insurance company denies reimbursement for inpatient treatment. Another scenario could be when the client and social worker feel that the course of treatment for a particular problem requires a certain length of time (e.g., six months) but the insurance company deems an acceptable duration to be five sessions. The insurer's time estimate is based on actuarial data that summarizes the average length of time to treat a particular diagnosis. These examples point out the concern over the ethical and legal liability of social workers in a managed care environment as well as a disregard for the self-determination of clients.

Although there are an increasing number of articles being published about managed care (e.g., Graham, 1995; Kane, 1995; Herron, 1992), no social work articles to date have attempted to explore the practitioner's experience

From *Social Work in Health Care*, Vol. 28, No. 2, 1998, pp. 1-9. © 1998 by The Haworth Press, Inc., Binghamton, New York. Reprinted by permission.

with managed care. This lack of research is disappointing when managed care has become such an important and timely issue. Newspaper and magazine articles abound, detailing the toll that managed care has taken in the health field. For example, an Act of Congress was required to allow mothers and their newborn babies to stay in the hospital until physicians deemed it safe for them to return home (Laino, 1997). In women's health care, there is a move on the part of insurers to require that mastectomies be performed on an outpatient basis.

The illustrations described above provide evidence that there are problems with managed care; however, capturing a valid measure for the incidence of managed care poses a significant challenge. Anecdotally, there seems to be some agreement about the meaning of managed care for practitioners, but there is no single measure or concise definition of this concept. Managed care typically takes two forms for mental health benefits. First, there are limitations, typically on number of sessions, that are imposed by the insurance company (Haas & Cummings, 1991). These treatment limitations were defined in this research as brief treatment (5–10 sessions).

Second, case management or some other influence by the funding source is commonly experienced by practitioners (Broskowski, 1991; Arches, 1989). This type of oversight typically requires a case manager, who is employed by the insurer, to guide treatment activities for each insured case. Both treatment session limitations and funding source influence were used in this study as indications of managed care.

Many of the changes that have emerged with managed care have developed rapidly, sometimes leaving the front line workers unprepared and perplexed. It is imperative that, in research and in the education of future social workers, we begin to scrutinize the impact of social and fiscal policy on the lives of practicing social workers and their clients. This study begins that process by examining the experience of clinical social workers with managed care and the impact of current fiscal restrictions on social work practice.

METHODS

Sample

The sample was chosen from social workers employed in either Ohio or Michigan who were members of the National Association of Clinical Social Workers. Social workers who had voluntarily joined this organization were thought to be the most likely group to be engaged in direct practice and therefore most knowledgeable about managed care. The sample was limited to Ohio and Michigan in order to select a geographically homogeneous group. Seven hundred surveys were mailed to randomly selected social workers. Thirty-two of those surveys were undeliverable, reducing the actual sample size to 668. Of those, 512 questionnaires were returned which resulted in a re-

sponse rate of 76.6 percent. However, some of the respondents were unable to complete the questionnaires due to retirement or other employment changes; thus, the results of the research are based on a final sample of 442 completed surveys.

Sample Characteristics

The sample was composed of 284 female (64.3%) and 145 male (32.8%) social workers (13 subjects did not respond). The mean age was 51.6 with a range of 27 to 87 (s.d. = 9.1). Ninety percent of the subjects (n = 398) were European American and the remaining ten percent were a combination of African American (2%), Asian American (0.9%), Latino (0.5%), Native American (2%), and "other" (1.1%) persons (3.5% of subjects did not respond). The respondents had an average of 21.2 years of experience in mental health services (range: 1.8 years to 51 years; s.d. = 8.38 years) and had been employed in their current setting for a mean of 11.3 years (range: 1 month to 40 years; s.d. = 7.39 years). Forty-six percent (n = 204) were employed in a private practice setting while the rest of the respondents worked primarily in outpatient or hospital settings.

Measurement

Two questions were included on the survey to quantify the number of cases where brief treatment was the primary method of intervention. In one question the respondents were asked to specify, in a forced choice format of 25% intervals, the percentage of cases in which they engaged in brief treatment. Since some practitioners prefer brief treatment techniques to longer treatment and because some psychosocial difficulties (e.g., acute grief reactions) warrant a briefer approach, a second question was asked to determine if this was a recent change in the use of brief treatment. This question asked respondents if their use of brief treatment had increased, decreased, or stayed the same over the last three years.

The questionnaire contained four items adapted from Arches (1989) that were designed to measure the influence of private insurance funding sources on social workers' practice.

The items were:

1. Funding sources specify the type of client I can work with;
2. Funding sources influence the length of time I treat a client;
3. Funding sources limit the types of treatment activities to the detriment of my clients;
4. I find the demands of the funding sources conflict with professional ethics.

The respondents were asked to indicate answers on a Likert-type scale (1 = completely, 2 = often, 3 = occasionally, 4 = rarely, 5 = not at all).

FINDINGS

Managed Care and Brief Treatment

On the survey, respondents were asked "In what percentage of your cases do you engage in brief treatment (5–10 sessions)?" Thirty-three percent of the 442 respondents indicated that they used brief treatment in 0 to 24% of their cases. Twenty-nine percent utilized this protocol in 25 to 49% of their cases, 22% reported use in 50 to 74% of their cases, and 16% responded that brief treatment was used in 75 to 100% of their cases. Notably, thirty-eight percent of the respondents used brief treatment with more than half of their caseload.

Since the rise in the use of brief treatment is assumed to be an indicator of the expansion of managed care, respondents were asked if the amount of brief treatment used in their caseload had increased, decreased, or remained the same over the last three years. The majority of the respondents reported that their use of brief treatment techniques had increased over the past three years (52.5%). Forty-four percent reported that their use of brief treatment had stayed the same. Only 14 respondents (3.2%) indicated that their use of brief treatment had decreased.

Managed Care and Funding Source Influence

More than half of the sample (54.9%) reported that funding sources either occasionally or completely specified the type of client the respondents saw in practice while 45% experienced very little influence in this area.

As predicted by managed care's philosophy of utilizing briefer approaches to treatment, nearly half (49.5%) of the respondents stated that funding sources were perceived as "often" influencing the length of time the client was in treatment while an astonishing 16.1% reported funding sources "completely" influenced the length of treatment. Twenty-one percent experienced "occasional" influence and the remaining 13.5% responded that managed care representatives "rarely" or "never" influenced the length of time they treated clients.

Nearly 70% of the respondents indicated that funding sources limited treatment to the detriment of clients at least "occasionally" while the remaining 30% "rarely" or "never" felt that clients' treatment was dangerously limited.

As the National Association of Social Workers revises its Code of Ethics (NASW, 1996), the social work profession should be greatly concerned that 76% of the respondents reported that the demands of the funding sources conflicted with their professional ethics. Specifically, 11% felt that managed care "completely" conflicted with their ethics, 30% reported "often" feeling conflicts, and 35% stated that they "occasionally" experienced these ethical conflicts. Only 24% of the respondents stated that they "rarely" (15%) or "never" (9%) perceived an ethical conflict.

DISCUSSION

The data showed that the use of brief treatment increased with more than half of the respondents in the last 3 years. This raises some interesting questions. For instance, what was the impetus for the increase in the use of brief treatment? Given that the mean age of the sample was approximately 50 years and the focus of most social work programs 20 to 30 years ago was psychoanalytic, it is probably safe to conclude that the expansion in the use of brief treatment was not driven by social work educators. If insurance reimbursement for mental health services began dictating lengths of treatment on a large scale during a certain time period, such as the 1980s, and there was a corresponding increase in the use of briefer approaches, one could conclude with some measure of certainty that the change in practice was driven solely from constraints in resources. If the latter scenario is the case, then one inference is that insurance companies are determining treatments based on fiscal concerns. This is a disturbing prospect indeed. In hindsight, it would have been interesting to inquire if there was a dramatic increase in the use of brief treatment techniques after a specific point in time or if respondents thought that continuing education was extraordinarily influential. It is important to note that in more recent years, social work education has been at the forefront of incorporating time-limited models of treatment such as task-centered and strength-based approaches (see e.g., Cowger, 1994; Gomez, Zurcher, Farris, & Becker, 1985; Reid, 1992).

Agency directors should note that the autonomy of social workers was dramatically impacted by their interaction with managed care representatives. Specifically, interaction with funding sources decreased the autonomy of clinical social workers by impacting treatment decisions such as the type of client seen, the length of treatment, and limitations in treatment that had detrimental impacts on the client. Since research indicates that autonomy is directly related to job satisfaction (see, e.g., Poulin & Walter, 1992; Buffum, 1987; Buffum & Ritvo, 1984) and professional productivity (Colarelli, Dean, & Konstans, 1987), one might expect social workers practicing in a managed care environment to be less satisfied with their jobs. This decrease in job satisfaction may have outcomes such as less productive therapeutic relationships or higher agency turnover (e.g., Riffe & Kondrat, 1997).

The finding that funding sources are influencing the length of treatment also translates into a significant ethical dilemma for social workers. The National Association for Social Workers Code of Ethics (1996) states that "[s]ocial workers should take reasonable steps to avoid abandoning clients who are still in need of services" (1.16 b). What happens to clients who are terminated prematurely either by ending treatment or by transferring the client to another practitioner? Precipitous termination of treatment could contribute to the reemergence of the presenting problem or could inhibit the client from seeking future treatment for the same or other difficulties. For instance, if a client entered treatment for depression caused by situational stress, then stress management training could provide some relief. However, if there were underlying causes of the depression, of either a biological or a psychosocial nature, one might argue that stress management would provide only temporary alleviation of the symptom. More important, the practitioner may have lost the only chance to conduct an adequate assessment since clients often have great difficulty entering and remaining in treatment.

The transfer of clients is an option in lieu of termination of treatment; however, this alternative may impact the level of trust needed to develop a therapeutic relationship. If the client must be transferred, this could result in the client feeling as if his or her problems were "too big" for the clinician to handle. That a trained social worker cannot handle a client's problem is a dramatic statement to make to clients who have sought treatment due to their difficulties with managing daily activities.

The purpose of this research was not to argue that managed care is not appropriate or needed. It was intended to assist agency directors and private practice practitioners in refocusing energies on the experience of the social worker and by extension, on the client. In this era of downsizing and shifting of fiscal resources it is easy to lose sight of the front line social workers who may be suffering personally and professionally. Attending to basic professional needs during this period may involve training social workers to negotiate with managed care companies through new assessment and documentation techniques (see e.g., Callahan, 1996; Corcoran & Vandiver, 1996; Kagle, 1993) or more recent therapeutic models such as a strengths-focused model (e.g., Saleebey, 1992). Attentive listening may be one of the most important supervisory techniques to support clinicians as they negotiate this latest challenge in service provision.

Accepted for Publication: 11/21/97

REFERENCES

Arches, J. (1989). *Structural components contributing to burnout and job satisfaction in social workers.* Unpublished doctoral dissertation. Boston University, Boston.

Broskowski, A. (1991). Current mental health care environments: Why managed care is necessary. *Professional Psychology: Research and Practice, 22*(1), 6–14.

Brown, F. (1994). Resisting the pull of the health insurance tarbaby: An organizational model for surviving managed care. *Clinical Social Work Journal, 22*(1), 59–71.

Buffum, W. E. (1987). Professional autonomy in community mental health centers. *Journal of Sociology and Social Welfare, 14*(1), 117–132.

Buffum, W. E. & Ritvo, R. A. (1984). Work autonomy and the community mental health professional: Guidelines for management. *Administration in Social Work, 8*(4), 39–54.

Bursztajn, H. J. & Brodsky, A. (1994). Authenticity and autonomy in the managed-care era: Forensic psychiatric perspectives. *The Journal of Clinical Ethics, 5*(3), 237–242.

Callahan, J. (1996). Documentation of client dangerousness in a managed care environment. *Health and Social Work, 21*(3), 202–207.

Colarelli, S. M., Dean, R. A., & Konstans, C. (1987). Comparative effects of personal and situational influences on job outcomes of new professional. *Journal of Applied Psychology, 72*(4), 558–566.

Corcoran, K., & Vandiver, V. (1996). *Maneuvering the maze of managed care: Skills for mental health practitioners.* New York: Free Press.

Cowger, C. D. (1994). Assessing client strengths: Clinical assessment for client empowerment. *Social Work, 39*(3), 262–267.

Garnick, D. W., Hendricks, A. M., Dulski, J. D., Thorpe, K. E., & Horgan, C. (1994). Characteristics of private-sector managed care for mental health and substance abuse treatment. *Hospital and Community Psychiatry, 45*(12), 1201–1205.

Gomez, E., Zurcher, L. A., Farris, B. E., & Becker, R. E. (1985). A study of psychosocial casework with Chicanos. *Social Work, 30,* 477–482.

Graham, M.D. (1995). The American academy of child and adolescent psychiatry's managed care strategy. *Psychiatric Services, 46*(7), 659, 660.

Haas, L. J. & Cummings, N. A. (1991). Managed outpatient mental health plans: Clinical, ethical, and practical guidelines for participation. *Professional Psychology: Research and Practice, 22*(1), 45–51.

Herron, W. G. (1992). Managed mental health care redux. *Professional Psychology: Research and Practice, 23,* 163–164.

Hoge, M. A., Davidson, L., Griffith, E. E. H., Sledge, W. H., & Howenstine, R. A. (1994). Defining managed care in public-sector psychiatry. *Hospital and Community Psychiatry, 45*(11), 1085–1089.

Kane, C. F. (1995). Deinstitutionalization and managed care: Deja Vu? *Psychiatric Services, 46*(9), 883–884.

Kagle, J. D. (1993). Record keeping: Directions for the 1990's. *Social Work, 38,* 190–196.

Kuhl, V. (1994). The managed care revolution: Implications for humanistic psychotherapy. *Journal of Humanistic Psychology, 34*(2), 62–81.

Laino, C. (1997). New laws protect patient rights. CNBC Internet site: http://www.msnbc.com/news

Lazarus, A. (1994). Managed care: Lessons from community mental health. *Hospital and Community Psychiatry, 45*(4), 301.

National Association of Social Workers (1996). *Code of Ethics.* Washington, DC: Author.

Newman, R. & Bricklin, P. M. (1991). Parameters of managed mental health care: Legal, ethical, and professional guidelines. *Professional Psychology Research and Practice, 22*(1), 26–35.

Perloff, J. D. (1996). Medicaid managed care and urban poor people: Implications for Social Work. *Health and Social Work, 21*(3), 189–195.

Poulin, J. E. & Walter, C. A. (1992). Retention plans and job satisfaction of gerontological social workers. *Journal of Gerontological Social Work, 19*(1), 99–114.

Reid, W. J. (1992). *Task Strategies.* New York: Columbia University Press.

Riffe, H. A. & Kondrat, M. E. (1997). Social worker alienation and disempowerment in a managed care setting. *Journal of Progressive Human Services, 8*(1), 41–55.

Sabin, J. E. (1994). Caring about patients and caring about money: The American Psychiatric Association code of ethics meets managed care. *Behavioral Sciences and the Law, 12*(4), 317–330.

Saleebey, D. (1992). *The strengths perspective in social work practice.* New York: Longman.

Shapiro, J. (1995). The downside of managed mental health care. *Clinical Social Work Journal, 23*(4), 441–451.

Shera, W. (1996). Managed care and people with severe mental illness: Challenges and opportunities for Social Work. *Health and Social Work, 21*(3), 196–201.

Stern, S. (1993). Managed care, brief therapy, and therapeutic integrity. *Psychotherapy, 30* (1), 162–175.

Weisman, C. S., Curbow, B., & Khoury, A. J. (1996). Women's health centers and managed care. *Women's Health Issues, 6*(5), 255–263.

Winegar, N. (1992). *The clinician's guide to managed mental health care.* Binghamton, NY: The Haworth Press, Inc.

Lobotomy's Back

In 1949 lobotomy was hailed as a medical miracle. But images of zombielike patients and surgeons with ice picks soon put an end to the practice. Now, however, the practitioners have refined their tools.

BY FRANK T. VERTOSICK, JR.

LAST YEAR A TEAM OF HARVARD INVESTIGA-tors headed by neurosurgeon G. Rees Cosgrove published a technical report bearing the ponderous title "Magnetic Resolution Image—Guided Stereotactic Cingulotomy for Intractable Psychiatric Disease." Although steeped in medical jargon, the report's central thesis—that psychiatric diseases can be treated by the selective destruction of healthy brain tissue—dates back to a much earlier, less sophisticated age when the search for a surgical cure for mental illness spawned an entire medical specialty known as psychosurgery.

Psychosurgery enjoyed a brief period of global acceptance around the time of World War II but was quickly driven from the medical mainstream with the advent of better, nonsurgical methods of treating the mentally ill. Now, almost half a century after psychosurgery's demise, the Harvard Medical School and a handful of other centers are hoping that new and improved surgical techniques can revive it. Today's neurosurgeons are also trying to rename the field "psychiatric surgery," presumably to avoid the Hitchcockian overtones of the older moniker. But, as rock star Prince discovered, shedding the name that made you famous isn't easy.

In their 1996 paper that appeared in the respected journal *Neurosurgery,* Cosgrove and his co-workers described a brain operation designed to relieve emotional distress and reduce abnormal behavior. Between 1991 and 1995, they performed cingulotomies—which means, essentially, that they burned dime-size holes in the frontal lobes of the brain—on 34 patients suffering from one of the following afflictions: severe depression; bipolar disorder, or manic-depression; obsessive-compulsive disorder (OCD); and generalized anxiety disorder. The target of their operations, the cingulate gyrus, is a thin ribbon of gray matter believed to play a role in human emotional states. The authors used a computer-guided technique known as stereotaxis to advance an electrode into the cingulate gyrus, then cooked the tissue with electric current.

Cingulotomy produced major clinical improvement, as judged by psychiatrists, in a little over a third of the patients; another quarter of them had a "possible response" to surgery. Not stellar results, to be sure, but the Harvard patients all had severe disease that had proved resistant to all other available therapies. Any good outcomes in this population might be significant, and the investigators believed that their results were good enough to warrant a larger trial of cingulotomy.

Despite its high-tech approach, however, the Harvard paper still looks anachronistic, to say the least. Finding a paper extolling the virtues of psychosurgery in today's medical literature is rather like finding one advocating bloodletting. Modern neurosurgeons destroying normal brain to treat mental illness? To borrow from Samuel Johnson, this is akin to a dog walking on its hind legs—the question is not how well the act can be done but why it's even attempted.

In spite of its elevated reputation, neurosurgery is a crude business, even—or especially—to a neurosurgeon, and I've been in practice for ten years. When confronted with an exposed brain at the operating table, I feel as if I'm about to repair a computer with a chain saw. The living brain has a surreal fragility; its porcelain surface is laced with delicate arteries that begin as thick cords but quickly branch into finer and finer threads. Looking at the surface of the brain is like looking at a satellite photo of a large city—one immediately senses a function far more complex than what is visible.

The idea that a sophisticated derangement in brain function, like OCD, can be cured by frying holes in the frontal lobe looks as patently absurd as recovering a lost file from a floppy disk by burning it with a curling iron. But experience suggests that such lesions can work, *if* they are done correctly and on the right patients.

PSYCHOSURGERY GOT ITS START back in 1890 when Gottlieb Burckhart, a Swiss psychiatrist and surgeon, tried removing portions of the cerebral cortex from schizophrenic brains. His victims, previously agitated and tormented by violent hallucinations, became more "peaceful" after the operation. Burckhart's operation didn't impress his colleagues, though, and an angry outcry from the European medical community prevented its further use.

Psychosurgery surfaced again with a vengeance in Portugal, during the mid-1930s; shortly thereafter, neurologist Walter Freeman enthusiastically imported it to the United States. Psychiatrists started to believe Freeman's proselytizing hype, and desperate families of the mentally ill began seeking surgery for their loved ones. During World War II the United States saw an increased demand for mental health care as thousands of combat-fatigued veterans crowded already overburdened hospitals. In this setting, psychosurgery became established as a standard therapy. Over the 20-odd years that psychosurgery held the attention of the medical mainstream, perhaps as many as 35,000 patients underwent psychiatric operations of one form or another.

But as Burckhart had discovered decades earlier, the medical community could not long ignore the ethical quagmire surrounding psychiatric brain operations. In the 1950s the rising use of psychosurgery ignited a national debate over the morality of inflicting irreversible brain injuries on the most emotionally vulnerable patients. While this debate smoldered among academics right up to the 1970s, the introduction of the tranquilizer chlorpromazine in 1954 rendered many of the concerns about psychosurgery moot.

Armed with effective chemical therapies, psychiatrists soon turned to pills instead of the knife and quit referring their patients for surgery. A few centers continued to use modified forms of psychosurgery on very small numbers of patients, both here and in Europe, well into the 1980s, so psychosurgery as a specialty never died—although psychosurgery as an industry did.

Should psychosurgery be brought back from the realm of the experimental and made a mainstream treatment once again? Should we reopen this ethical can of worms? As Cosgrove's report shows,

there are those who think we should. Hundreds of severely incapacitated people fail all other treatments, including drugs, electroshock, and psychotherapy, leaving surgery their only option. The illness most helped by cingulotomy—major depression—can be life-threatening. If psychosurgery works, shouldn't it be used?

The successful resurrection of extinct brain operations has a recent precedent: pallidotomy for parkinsonism. In this procedure, parts of the globus pallidus, a clump of tissue in the core of the brain controlling limb coordination, are surgically destroyed. The operation is technically similar to cingulotomy, and in the past few years it has enjoyed a renaissance. Before the discovery of L-dopa—a chemical substitute for the brain chemical dopamine—surgeons carried out pallidotomies and a number of other destructive procedures to ease the tremor and rigidity of Parkinson's disease. After the introduction of L-dopa, the role of the surgeon in the treatment of Parkinson's lessened, and the operations soon fell into relative disuse.

While L-dopa did revolutionize the treatment of Parkinson's, the drug proved ineffective in a small number of patients. Still others responded to medical therapy only to become resistant to it months or years later. As neurologists accumulated more experience with drug treatments for Parkinson's, they realized that medical therapy alone could not keep the disease at bay. A growing demand for alternative treatments renewed interest in pallidotomy, and several medical centers began trying it again. Since today's image-guided pallidotomy can be done with far greater accuracy than was ever possible before, modern surgical results have been excellent, and pallidotomy is currently available nationwide.

But bringing back pallidotomy, an operation with no historical baggage, was a piece of cake. To achieve a similar comeback in their own field, modern neurosurgeons must overcome psychosurgery's dark past—a considerably more difficult task.

Looking back today, psychosurgery is seen as nothing short of a mental health holocaust perpetrated by mind-stealing hacks in the dimly lit clinics of public psychiatric hospitals. It will always be synonymous with the flagship operation of its heyday, the dreaded prefrontal lobotomy. In the conventional

form of the operation, a neurosurgeon poked holes in the patient's skull just above and in front of the ear canals on both sides of the head and plunged a flat knife, called a leucotome, into the frontal lobes to a depth of about two inches. By sweeping the leucotome up and down within the brain, the surgeon amputated the anterior tips of the frontal lobes, the so-called prefrontal areas, from the rest of the brain. In contrast to the half-inch lesions of pallidotomy and cingulotomy, the lobotomist sliced an area of brain equal to the cross section of an orange.

This technique soon gave way to a quicker, albeit somewhat grislier, version of prefrontal lobe destruction. Before World War II, brain surgeons—not exactly a dime a dozen even today—were quite scarce; this lack of surgical expertise hindered the wider use of psychosurgery. To rid himself of the need for a surgeon, Freeman began tinkering with the transorbital approach invented by Amarro Fiamberti in Italy. (At this point, James Watts, Freeman's surgical colleague in conventional lobotomies, ended their collaboration, saying the transorbital procedure was too risky.)

In Freeman's modification of the procedure, the lobotomist inserted an ice pick (yes, an ice pick) under the upper eyelid and drove it upward into the frontal lobe with a few sharp raps of a mallet. The pick was then twisted and jiggled about, thus scrambling the anterior frontal lobes. The ice-pick lobotomy could be done by anyone with a strong stomach, and, even better, it could be done anywhere. Freeman carried his ice pick in his pocket, using it on one occasion to perform a lobotomy in a motel room. A cheap outpatient procedure, the ice-pick lobotomy became a common psychosurgical choice in state hospitals across the country.

In the late 1950s lobotomy's popularity waned, and no one has done a true lobotomy in this country since Freeman performed his last transorbital operation in 1967. (It ended in the patient's death.) But the mythology surrounding lobotomies still permeates our culture. Just last year the operation surfaced on the television show *Chicago Hope*. Few of us have ever met a lobotomized patient, but we all know what to expect—or at least we think we do. Who can forget the vacant stare of the freshly knifed Jack Nicholson in *One Flew Over the*

Cuckoo's Nest? At best, according to the popular conception, the luckier victims recovered enough to wander about like incontinent zombies.

Although some patients ended up this way, or worse, the zombie stereotype derives more from Hollywood fiction than from medical reality. Lobotomy peaked in the 1950s, not during the Middle Ages. While we may have been a little more bioethically challenged back then, we weren't Neanderthals either. Lobotomy could never have survived for 20 years if it yielded a lot of cretins. In fact, intelligence, in those cases where it was measured pre- and postoperatively by formal testing, remained unaffected by a competent lobotomy, and in some cases it even improved.

Not surprisingly, the operation did have disturbing side effects. Patients often suffered major personality changes

put into the context of the era: in the 1940s brain surgery for any disease was very risky.

It's easy for us to forget that the media first hailed psychosurgery as a medical miracle. Lobotomy's reputation once ran so high that the Nobel committee awarded the prize in Medicine and Physiology to its inventor, the Portuguese neurologist Egas Moniz, in 1949. But less than a decade after this endorsement, lobotomy was dead and its memory vilified.

The operation's descent into disgrace had many causes. For one thing, lobotomy never had a scientific basis. Moniz got the idea for it in a flash after hearing a presentation by Fulton and Jacobsen, two Yale physicians, during a 1935 neurological conference in London. The Americans described two chimpanzees, Becky and Lucy, that had become remarkably calm after frontal lobe ablation.

mals are vanishingly tiny; even chimps and apes have fairly small ones. In humans, on the other hand, the frontal lobes make up nearly two-thirds of the cerebrum, or higher brain. Since mental illnesses are uniquely human afflictions, a therapeutic surgical assault on the frontal lobes seemed quite plausible.

Moniz subsequently created a fanciful theory of "abnormally stabilized pathways" in the brain to justify his operation. He reasoned that cutting brain fibers might interrupt the abnormal brain circuitry of psychiatric patients, freeing them from a cycle of endless rumination. Since then, no better rationale for lobotomy has been advanced. Nevertheless, a lack of scientific justification doesn't doom an operation as long as the operation works. Many good operations, pallidotomy included, can trace their origins to pseudoscience or serendipity. But was lobotomy ever a

The living brain has a surreal fragility; the porcelain surface is

UPI/Corbis Bettmann

Neurologist Walter Freeman made lobotomies simple; he used an ice pick.

and became apathetic, prone to inappropriate social behavior, and infatuated with their own toilet habits. They told pointless jokes and exhibited poor hygiene. Postoperative deaths, although uncommon, occurred and could be gruesome. But all these problems must be

This single, almost casual observation prompted Moniz to return home and begin human trials immediately. Further animal work would not be useful, he argued, since no animal models of mental illness existed. Why he rejected the thought of further animal experimentation while still viewing Fulton and Jacobsen's tiny report as a virtual epiphany remains a mystery. Moniz, who had just endured a nasty priority fight concerning his invention of cerebral angiography, may have rushed into human trials in order to stake the earliest claim to lobotomy.

The association of the frontal lobes with emotional and intellectual dysfunction was hardly a radical idea, even in 1935. The frontal lobes of lower mam-

good operation? We've had half a century to study it and we're still not sure.

Unfortunately, lobotomists showed no great talent for comprehensive, long-term analysis of their data. The esteemed Moniz often followed his patients for only a few weeks after their surgery. The peripatetic Freeman drove about the country doing hundreds of ice-pick procedures, but only near the end of his life did he find out how the majority of them fared. Even then, his assessments proved vague and unconvincing.

Only a single certain conclusion emerged from the dozens of lobotomy studies that have appeared over the years: schizophrenics don't get better after surgery. This is ironic, given that they were the first to undergo psychosurgery. We now have an inkling as to why the treatment doesn't work. Unlike depression and mania, which are disorders of mood, schizophrenia is a disorder of thought. And what a lobotomy alters is emotional state, not cognitive abilities.

Most lobotomists had vague and paternalistic ideas of what constituted a "good" result. Results were typically judged by psychiatrists, families, or institutional custodians; detailed surveys of what the patients thought rarely appear in the psychosurgery literature. This seems strange, since a cure, as judged by outsiders, may not be viewed that way by the patient. Is the patient, although inwardly miserable, cured because he no longer assaults the nursing staff, or because he can now sit quietly for hours without screaming? A careful reading of Freeman's more detailed case histories shows that a few patients didn't even see themselves as ill in the first place, although they realized that their behavior disturbed others.

Probably the most important factor in lobotomy's demise was its deep physical and metaphysical ugliness. More than one seasoned professional vomited or passed out while watching Freeman crack through a patient's orbital bone with his ice pick. Moreover, prospective

It's doubtful that many real families ever had such fanciful motives behind their surrogate assents for lobotomy, although even mundane motives can be illegitimate. Was it right to authorize a lobotomy to make an argumentative person a quiet one? Or to stop behaviors repugnant to everyone—everyone, that is, except the patient?

I N RETROSPECT, THE REAL QUESTION isn't why lobotomy died, but why it survived for so long. The answer is simple: Walter Freeman. Lobotomy became his career, his crusade, and he spread psychosurgery's gospel with boundless enthusiasm. His elegant bearing and Freudian goatee gave him the look of a world-renowned healer of minds. In the end, his force of will could no longer counter lobotomy's growing ethical opposition and pharmaceutical competition. Freeman did

tients closely for years and test them exhaustively.

But two problems remain. First, Cosgrove's report, like earlier psychosurgery studies, makes no mention of the patients' perception of their operations; it details only what their psychiatrists thought. Patients can't even request this surgery on their own; an operation is offered only if the psychiatrist agrees. In other "quality of life" operations—facelifts, surgical removal of herniated spinal disks, elective joint replacements—the patient approaches the surgeon directly, requests surgery, and then personally decides if the postoperative outcome is satisfactory. An orthopedic surgeon doesn't ask an internist if a knee replacement has alleviated a patient's pain. So why must we rely on psychiatrists to tell us if a patient no longer feels depressed after cingulotomy?

laced with arteries that begin as thick cords but branch into finer threads.

patients often had to be dragged to an operating room or clinic. In *Psychosurgery,* the textbook he coauthored with Watts, Freeman frankly describes his unorthodox methods of obtaining "consent" for lobotomy. Occasionally, forcible sedation was needed to keep the patient from backing out at the last minute.

Freeman's landmark treatise also notes that if the patient was "too disturbed" to sign a consent, a close relative could give permission instead. He didn't elaborate on how disturbed a person needed to be to abdicate his right to refuse lobotomy. Freeman never considered the possibility that relatives might have less than honorable motives for agreeing to the dissection of their loved one's frontal lobes. Tennessee Williams, however, had no trouble envisioning such a nasty scenario. In his play *Suddenly Last Summer,* Mrs. Venable orders her young niece, Catharine, to be lobotomized. Catharine knew a little too much about the deviate practices of Mrs. Venable's late son, Sebastian. Who would believe the poor child after she had the appropriate "therapy" at Lion's view asylum?

his best to carry on, but it was no use.

Modern psychosurgery has no evangelist equal to Freeman to spread its message, and so it must survive only on its merits. Time will tell whether it can.

There are good reasons to think the field can be revived. For starters, modern procedures like magnetic resonance-guided cingulotomy bear little resemblance to the ugly lobotomies of the past. Computer-guided electrodes the thickness of pencil lead that can inflict minute injuries with millimeter precision have replaced ice picks and leucotomes. Procedures now take place only in sophisticated operating theaters, not in motel rooms or in the back rooms of county hospitals.

Modern neurosurgeons like Cosgrove approach their operations not as true believers but as skeptical scientists. Freeman's arm-twisting consents are also gone; today multidisciplinary committees review each patient on a rigorous case-by-case basis. And no one but the patient can give consent for cingulotomy—there were no Mrs. Venables involved in the Harvard study. Unlike the itinerant lobotomists of Freeman's time, modern psychosurgeons follow their pa-

Second, the cingulotomy rests on no firmer scientific foundation than lobotomy did. First performed in 1952 as a modified version of the lobotomy, cingulotomy was based on Freeman's observations that lobotomy patients seemed to have less "psychological tension" when fibers near the cingulate gyrus were severed. This ribbon of brain tissue is thought to be a conduit between the limbic region, a primitive area involved in emotional behavior, and the frontal lobes, the seat of reason and judgment. But we lack any more detailed understanding of how the cingulate gyrus functions. As such, cingulotomy can trace its intellectual heritage right back to the chimps Becky and Lucy.

Psychosurgery will never become as routine as it was in the 1940s and 1950s. The most refractory of the chronically disabling mental illnesses, schizophrenia, can't be treated surgically. Depression, while quite common, usually responds to one of the many excellent medical therapies that must be tried first, leaving few patients as candidates for surgery. And patients with OCD often respond to non-surgical treatments. Thus, the pool of patients likely to benefit from cingulotomy will always be fairly small. In addition, few major medical centers can muster the psychiatric, bioethical, and surgical resources to perform and evaluate the procedure correctly.

Then there is that sticky public relations problem. No matter how refined their surgeries, modern psychosurgeons will still be perceived as lobotomists. An unfair label, perhaps, but one that will prove difficult to shed.

A greater concern may be that the public won't care at all. In Freeman's day, society paid to house and care for great numbers of the mentally infirm, making psychiatric disease a public health problem of the first order. This may be why no one bothered to ask the patients what they thought of surgery—the lobotomists weren't treating patients, they were treating a national crisis. Since lobotomy did make patients easier to care for, and even got many

out of institutions and off the public dole, psychosurgeons served the national interest well. Freeman acknowledged that the lobotomist often put the needs of society over those of the individual, arguing that it was better for a patient "to have a simplified intellect capable of elementary acts than an intellect where reigns disorder of subtle synthesis. Society can accommodate itself to the humble laborer, but it justifiably mistrusts the mad thinker."

The goal of lobotomy wasn't to control disease but to control patients. Some would argue that our present heavy use of psychotropic drugs is just as flawed, in that we don't make the patients better—we just succeed in preventing them from bothering us.

As a nation, we could seriously question all our recent efforts in the mental health arena. During the last three dec-

ades, mental illness has been literally cast into the streets. Asylums have vanished and many private health plans now refuse to pay for psychiatric treatment. Before we judge the lobotomists of old too severely, we should go to the nearest street grate and see how we are dealing with our mental health crisis today. High-profile diseases like AIDS and breast cancer dominate the headlines and the federal research budgets, leaving many victims of mental illness to suffer in silent solitude.

Modern psychosurgeons are thus courageous in seeking to address a difficult problem. By trying to bring the best neurosurgical technologies to a group of patients who have run out of hope, they risk the scorn of those who see only what psychosurgery was and not what it can be. I wish them luck. Given the lessons of history, they'll surely need it.

Cultural diversity and mental health: The Haudenosaunee of New York State

The purpose of this study was to determine if there are differences between American Indian and white, non-Hispanic recipients of mental health services that indicate the need for a modified treatment approach with Native Americans. Findings were that 38 American Indian recipients differed from a matched sample of 38 white, non-Hispanic participants in diagnosis, time since last mental health visit, education, and religion. This study raises further questions for study and provides some limited information for people who treat American Indian clients.

Key words: **American Indian; cultural diversity; Haudenosaunee; Iroquois; mental health**

Kathleen A. Earle

Until 1970 it was widely thought that American Indians had no mental health needs or resources (Attneave, 1984). Mental health care for native people was not officially addressed until the Mental Health Office of the Indian Health Service was established in 1965 (Nelson, McCoy, Stetter, & Vanderwagen, 1992). Meanwhile, despite the encroachment of European settlers on native lands and psyche, native people apparently managed to deal with problems of adjustment or serious mental disorder within their own society. Many of these traditional approaches, including the use of indigenous healers, or "medicine men" (Attneave, 1984; LaFromboise, 1988; Lejero,

Kathleen A. Earle, PhD, LMSW is assistant professor of social work, University of Southern Maine, Box 9300, 96 Falmouth Street, Portland, ME 04104; e-mail: kearle@usm.maine.edu. *The author thanks Alan Ackley, director, Zoar Valley Clinic, for his assistance in completing this study.*

Antone, Francisco, & Manuel, 1988; Williams & Ellison, 1996) have recently been revived.

Among the Iroquois of New York State, traditional healing rituals such as the "False Face" ceremony are still used for mental health problems (Earle, 1996). This ceremony has been described by anthropologist Wallace (1959) as a ritualized purging of an individual's mental illness and by Fenton (1987) as a public or private ceremony to rid a community, household, or individual of disease.

Although the literature suggests that American Indians need a unique mental health approach based on different cultural norms, research supporting this hypothesis is rare (Blount, Thyer, & Frye, 1992; Manson, Tatum & Dinges, 1982). The research presented in this article is a necessary precursor to comparative studies of different approaches with indigenous people. The hypothesis of this study was that American Indian and white, non-Hispanic mental health care recipients differ in demographic characteristics, services received, and attitudes toward mental health. If so, this may indicate the need for an alternative therapeutic approach for Native Americans.

APPROPRIATE THERAPEUTIC APPROACH

Various elements of an appropriate therapeutic approach have appeared in the literature. The need to assess degree of acculturation is a crucial part of the treatment of American Indians (Trimble, Manson, Dinges, & Medicine, 1984; Williams & Ellison, 1996). Growing up or being educated on or near a reservation, having social activities primarily with other American Indians, being involved in religious or tribal activities, having an extended family orientation, and knowing about native culture are indications of cultural identification with a native group (Sue & Sue, 1990).

Once an identification with a native culture is found a nondirective, facilitative approach is advocated by Blount et al. (1992) and by Greene, Jensen, and Jones (1996). This approach was defined even more narrowly by Good Tracks (1973) as one of "noninterference." Good Tracks stated that overzealous social workers who want to "rescue" their clients are overstepping a boundary they may not even know exists.

According to Sue and Sue (1990), native cultures do not emphasize self-revelation, making face-to-face individual treatment difficult. As Laine (WICHE, 1993) noted in reference to her brother, diagnosed with schizophrenia: "Our people are taught to keep feelings to themselves or within the family, so typical day programs are not conducive to helping him be as well as he can be" (p. 18).

Many authors stress the need for a family or group approach for American Indians (Blount et al., 1992; Edwards & Edwards, 1984; Lefley, 1990). An American Indian whose personal experience has been primarily as part of a group may appear passive or hostile when seen for individual counseling because he or she does not know what is expected (Blount et al., 1992). Group treatment (Owan, 1982; Red Horse, 1980), or family treatment (Joe & Malach, 1992; Red Horse, 1980, 1982) are more in keeping with the existing tribal structure.

A therapist may consider the optional use of Native American healers, a preference for some (LaFromboise, 1988), when counseling a Native American person or family (Jilek, 1971; Joe & Malach, 1992). This must be done with caution, respecting the privacy of ceremonies that are frequently closed to outsiders (Joe & Malach, 1992).

Some authors address specific aspects of Indian culture that may affect a therapeutic encounter. These include differences in conceptions of time for many American Indians (Joe & Malach, 1992; McShane, 1987; Sue & Sue, 1990). Respecting this difference may require waiting for what the client or family perceives is a good time for a meeting rather than sticking to rigid schedules. Differences in body language, such as reluctance to make eye contact (Sue & Sue, 1990) or a preference for periods of silence (Joe & Malach, 1992) also need to be accepted. Readers are cautioned, however, against generalizing these traits to all American Indians. There are wide discrepancies between tribes and within tribes (Gross, 1995; Jarvenpa, 1985; Williams & Ellison, 1996).

BACKGROUND

There are between 1 and 2 million American Indians living in the United States, making up less than 1 percent of the population (Joe & Malach, 1992; Nelson et al., 1992). The National Plan for American Indian Mental Health Services (U.S. Department of Health and Human Services [HHS], 1989) reported that American Indians have much more serious and numerous mental health problems than the general population, although rates were not included.

Apart from small-scale studies of specific populations, data on actual prevalence of mental illness among American Indians is difficult to find. This may be partially the result of problems of diagnosis among Western therapists and of definition among American Indians.

Problems of Diagnosis

O'Nell (1989) reported that styles of presentation such as "flat affect," "hallucinations involving spirits," and "prolonged mourning" are more frequent among Native Americans than among the general population. However, symptoms such as these do not necessarily indicate psychopathology (Manson, Shore, & Bloom, 1985; Price-Williams, 1987). For example, episodes of prolonged, ardent, and emotionally fraught mourning, which are part of a ritual ceremony prescribed by the Iroquois Constitution (Parker, 1968; Wallace, 1959), can be misdiagnosed as signs of severe depression requiring psychiatric hospitalization (Perkins, 1927).

Problems of Definition

In addition, there are reports of emotional difficulties among American Indians that are not defined in the general culture (Johnson & Johnson, 1965; Lewis, 1975; Manson et al., 1985; Matchett, 1972; O'Nell, 1989; Trimble et al., 1984). These disorders include, for example, *pibloktoq* (arctic hysteria [Trimble et al., 1984, p. 209]), *iich'aa* (moth sickness, which is said to be caused by brother–sister incest [Trimble et al., 1984, p. 204]), *windigo* (delusion of tranformation into a *witiko* who has a fear of ice [Trimble et al., 1984, p. 202]), *wacinko* (when people pout when they do not get what they want or when the situation is unbearable [Lewis, 1975, p. 754]) and *tawatl ye sni* (O'Nell, 1989). *Tawatl ye sni*, translated as "totally discouraged," was reported by Johnson and Johnson (1965) among the Dakota Sioux on the Standing Rock reservation. The authors identified a specific syndrome among members of the tribe that included "(1) conditions of present deprivation; (2) the traveling of one's thoughts to the dwelling place of dead relatives, the ghost camp; (3) an orientation to the past as the best time; (4) thoughts of death; (5) facilitating a move to the death camp by willing death, threatening or committing suicide, or drinking to excess; (6) being preoccupied with ideas of ghosts or spirits; and (7) expression that present actions are blocked, like in the statement 'There's nothing he can do. It's hopeless.' " (O'Nell, 1989, p. 59). Although these symptoms would appear to fit Western definitions of depression, O'Nell stated that "it is clear that the cultural meanings of these categories are sufficiently different from depressive disorder . . . to warn against drawing facile equations across these systems of thought" (p. 60).

Definition of an American Indian

The definition of who is an American Indian may also affect the accuracy of data regarding prevalence of mental illness. The U.S. Constitution describes American Indian tribes as sovereign nations who deal directly with the federal government. Specific Indian nations must apply to the U.S. government to be recognized as such. Individual tribal membership, or "enrollment" in an Indian tribe or nation, is based on percentage of American Indian blood and either patrilineal or matrilineal descent (Prucha, 1990). On the basis of earlier history, many American Indian people do not trust the U.S. government and are not federally enrolled (Schaaf, 1990). Also, many people who are biracial but who do not meet enrollment criteria may identify themselves as American Indian on standard surveys and official records, and in census data.

The Haudenosaunee

The Iroquois Indians of New York State were chosen as a population for analysis. The Haudenosaunee, also called Iroquois, consist of six nations (Mohawk, Oneida, Onondaga, Cayuga, Seneca, and Tuscarora) allied into a confederacy. In September 1994 there were approximately 18,000 enrolled members of the Iroquois Confederacy. These included 6,469 Seneca, 1,050 Tonawanda Seneca, 462 Cavuga, 6,140 St. Regis Mohawk, 1,200 Tuscarora, 1,694 Onondaga, and 1,109 Oneida (personal communication with the Eastern Area Office of the U.S. Bureau of Indian Affairs [BIA], Buffalo, NY, November, 1994). About half of the Iroquois live on or near one of the seven reservations located in central, western, and northern New York State. Members of the Confederacy may be found anywhere in the United States and Canada.

METHOD

Using New York State data, two research questions were addressed: First, do American Indian recipients differ in demographic and service variables from white, non-Hispanic recipients of mental health services? And second, do American Indian recipients of services have different attitudes toward mental health than white recipients? A multisite descriptive design using two comparisons between two groups was undertaken.

Comparison of Demographic and Services Variables

The first part of the study compared American Indian and white, non-Hispanic people who received mental health services (outpatient, inpatient, or residential) from the New York State Office of Mental Health (OMH) between January and October 1994. Counties in upstate, central, and western New York, which contained or were adjacent to the seven Iroquois reservations were included in the study. Information was obtained from the OMH's Department of Mental Hygiene Information System (DMHIS).

The DMHIS is based on data from forms completed when a person is admitted to, released from, or transferred within an OMH-operated program. It includes information such as age, gender, ethnicity, education, religion, legal status, county of residence, marital status, diagnosis, household composition, type of residence, source of referral, veteran status, type of income, presence of a significant problem (for example, alcohol, substance abuse, mental health, mental retardation or developmental disability, physical disability), time since last service, program site, and type of service received.

Initial analyses compared all available data for the two groups using chi-square tests. After differences among white, non-Hispanic, and American Indian recipients were identified, logistic regression was used to predict native ethnicity based on these differences. Of 90 Native Americans receiving mental health services, one-half were treated by OMH clinics attached to prisons. These 45 recipients were dropped from the study because of the unavailability of data from the DMHIS in crucial areas. For example, the DMHIS lists under "county of residence" the county where the prison is located rather then the county where the person lived before he or she was in prison. Adult respondents were the focus of the study.

To control for gender, program, and age when performing the logistic regression analysis, the 45 American Indians were matched to 45 white, non-Hispanic recipients. Although there were over 6,000 white recipients of services on which to match, matches by specific program site, age, and gender yielded at most two possible matches, in which case the first one was chosen.

Comparison of Attitudes

The second part of the study compared attitudes toward mental health of American Indian and white recipients of mental health care. Copies of the Mental Health Values Questionnaire (MHVQ) (Tyler, Clark, Olson, Klapp, & Cheloha, 1983; Tyler & Suan, 1990) were left to be anonymously completed by a convenience sample of people at or near an outpatient site identified in the first part of the study as serving 14(31 percent) of the 45 American Indians.

The MHVQ (Tyler & Suan, 1990; Tyler et al., 1983) was developed at the University of North Dakota to measure attitudes toward mental health. The authors first defined the domain of good mental health by asking groups of patients, professionals, mental health workers, and college students to generate a pool of traits indicative of good mental health. Factor analysis was used to construct a questionnaire using these traits, and the in-

strument was administered to groups of respondents with other standard scales to determine reliability and validity of the instrument (Tyler et al., 1983).

The MHVQ asks respondents to rate statements such as "The person is happy most of the time" as indicating good or poor mental health on a five-point scale, where 1 = very poor mental health, 2 = poor mental health, 3 = neutral, not related to mental health, 4 = good mental health, and 5 = very good mental health. The reliability coefficients of the eight factor subscales (self-acceptance, negative traits, achievement, affective control, good interpersonal relations, untrustworthiness, religious, and unconventional reality) ranged from .76 to .88.

The authors later administered the MHVQ to 93 white and 66 American Indian undergraduates at the University of North Dakota and found that the "unconventional reality" subscale discriminated between the two groups. The most important finding of the study was that white students were significantly more likely to associate unconventional experiences (having visions, communicating with spirits of the dead, guiding one's life according to spirits, seeing things others do not see, and hearing things others do not hear) with poor mental health than were the American Indian students. The American Indian students reported a neutral relationship of such experiences to mental health (Tyler & Suan, 1990).

We distributed 180 copies of the MHVQ to clinic, continuing treatment, or residential clients from October 1995 through February 1996. Each form had a dollar bill attached and a stamped envelope addressed to the researcher. The majority of forms were handed out randomly to white clients and specifically to Native American clients by receptionists or staff of the programs. During the last month of the study, some forms were distributed to American Indians by an American Indian who was a member of the consumer advisory board, at the suggestion of the primary site director. All forms were handed out with no instructions other than those written on the first page. Demographic data such as gender, age group, ethnic type of white (French, German, and so forth) or American Indian identity (specific tribe or nation), and federal enrollment (yes or no) for American Indian respondents were included. As shown in Table 1, the respondents in part 1 of the study and respondents in part 2 were similar in gender and age breakdown, the only two variables that the two samples had in common.

TABLE 1—Comparison of American Indian Respondents from Part 1 and Part 2 of Study

Characteristic	Part 1:DMHIS (N = 38)		Part 2:MHVQ (N = 14)	
	n	%	n	%
Gender				
Male	18	47	6	43
Female	20	53	8	57
Age (years)				
18–20	1	3	2	14
21–30	7	18	1	7
31–40	14	37	4	29
41–50	8	21	4	29
51–60	6	16	2	14
61–70	0		1	7
70 or older	2	5	0	

NOTE: DMHIS = Department of Mental Hygiene Information System (New York). MHVQ = Mental Health Values Questionnaire (Tyler, Clark, Olson, Klapp, & Chelona, 1983; Tyler & Suan, 1990).

RESULTS

Differences in Demographic and Services Variables

Initial analyses found that the 45 American Indian recipients of services differed significantly from the 6,064 white non-Hispanic recipients on average age; the average was 40 for white clients and 33 for American Indians [$F(1, 6,108) = 9.447, p < .005$]. Nearly half (49 percent) of the American Indians specified a religion other than Catholic or Jewish, compared with 18 percent of white people (χ^2 (3, $N = 6,109$) = 23.01, $p < .001$]. American Indians had higher reported rates of an alcohol-related diagnosis: 27 percent of American Indians and 9 percent of white clients [$\chi^2(1, N = 6,109) = 13.49, p < .001$]. Over four-fifths (84 percent) of American Indians and 69 percent of whites were single or divorced or separated [$\chi^2(3, N = 6,109) = 8.27, p < .05$]. Forty-two percent of American Indians and 23 percent of white clients were seen for outpatient admission rather than for inpatient admission, screening, or termination [$\chi^2(6, N = 6,109) = 23.56, p < .001$].

The 45 cases were then matched with 45 white, non-Hispanic cases by age, gender, and specific program site. Dropping from the analysis six children under 18 and one case with too few data elements to match yielded 38 white and 38 American Indian adult respondents. To increase the power of the logistic regression analysis, all variables of interest

were dichotomized into characteristic "yes" or characteristic "no/unknown." Lumping "unknown" with "no" is the most rigorous approach, as some of the unknowns may be a desirable "yes" for these variables.

After the groups were matched by age, gender, and program, the only variables that differed significantly using chi-square analysis were time since last visit and significant alcohol problem; American Indians were less likely to have been last seen over a year ago [$\chi^2(1, N = 76) = 3.71, p < .05$] and more likely to report a significant alcohol problem [$\chi^2(1, N = 76) = 3.71, p < .05$]. (The DMHIS allows people completing Form OMH 725 to check under significant problems any of the following that apply: mental illness, alcohol, mental retardation/developmental disability, substance abuse, significant physical impairment, or other specified problem.) Data on diagnosis for this study showed proportionately fewer American Indians (89.5 percent) had diagnoses of severe mental illness (defined as "significant mental illness" on OMH Form 725) compared with whites (97.4 percent) although these results were not statistically significant. Other variables that were not significant but yielded relatively high chi-square values were included in the logistic regression analysis—education less than high school and significant substance abuse problem.

Religion other than Christian or Jewish, living with relatives, and unemployment were included as well. Religion had a high chi-square value in the original comparison of white people and American Indians [x^2(3, N = 6,109) = 23.01, p < .01] and was felt to be related to the second half of the study in that "having visions," and so forth, may be related to religion. Living with relatives, an indication of a possible extended family, was included because it is considered by many authors as central to American Indian lifestyle (Joe & Malach, 1992; Red Horse, 1980, 1982; Wilkinson, 1980). Lack of employment was included both because it has been found to be a fact of life for many American Indians (Blount et al., 1992; Nelson et al., 1992; HHS, 1989) and because it may be related to lack of success as defined by the dominant culture, also described as characteristic of American Indians (Dykeman, Nelson, & Appleton, 1995; Joe & Malach, 1992; Sue & Sue, 1990). A "yes" response was expected for the American Indian clients to all of these dichotomized variables except for "last visit over one year ago." (Because the desired response for this variable was no, lumping "no" with "unknown" weakens the analysis.) Marital status and type of visit were not entered into the model because their chi-square values were low when the groups were matched.

Logistic regression analysis allows the researcher to determine the combined influence of several variables on an independent variable and to use these variables to predict membership in a dichotomized group. The group in this case was American Indian: yes–no. The following variables were chosen by the model as predictors of membership in the Indian/yes group: alcohol problem/yes; last seen over one year ago/no; education less than high school/yes; specific religion other than Christian or Jewish/yes. This model correctly predicted ethnicity 63.2 percent of the time.

Using Cohen's kappa yields a value of r = .26. This statistic and its level of significance [χ^2(71, N = 76) = 94.7, p = .03], indicate the variables chosen by the model (time since last service, alcohol problem, education level, and religion) are responsible for 26 percent of the difference above chance between the two groups. This is a moderate-to-strong effect size. Although power is difficult to calculate in a logistic regression, by using regression as a proxy measure, we find this analysis had a power of 80 percent (Cohen, 1988).

Differences in Attitude

Of the 180 copies of the Mental Health Values Questionnaire (MHVQ) distributed, 47 were returned. Seven were not completed correctly or were missing demographic information, leading to a return rate of 22 percent. Those which were complete were from 26 white and 14 American Indian respondents.

The low response rate to the survey may have been affected by two unexpected occurrences at the time of the study: (1) The primary outpatient program's parent office began a major reorganization in 1995–96 in which many outpatient programs were told they might be closed. (2) There was a major internal disruption at the Iroquois reservation adjacent to the study site right before the beginning of data collection. Several months after this study was completed the outpatient program director was laid off as part of OMH's downsizing of state operated programs.

The disruption at the reservation was the result of differences between members of the traditional, clan-based culture and the elected leaders and led to a fatal shooting. There was a resulting lack of communication with people or agencies outside the reservation for a number of months while the tribal members attempted to restore unity and internal order. These unrelated factors may have affected both the numbers of people attending the state mental health programs and the willingness of people to complete the survey.

Because of both the low response rate and the implausibility of assumptions regarding normality, the Mann-Whitney U and Kruskal-Wallis statistical tests for ordinal data were used (Kenny, 1987). Initial comparisons (using t test and chi-square analysis) between 26 white and 14 American Indian anonymous respondents to the survey were made on demographic variables (age, gender) to ensure the two groups were equivalent. The Mann-Whitney U test was then used to compare responses of the two groups on each of the 99 questions and the eight subscales designed by the authors of the questionnaire (Tyler et al., 1983).

Most white respondents checked membership in more than one ethnic group. The most commonly checked groups were German (46 percent), English (46 percent), and Irish (35 percent). American Indian respondents included eleven people (79 percent) who were federally enrolled members of the Seneca Na-

TABLE 2—Differences in Responses between White and American Indian Respondents to the Unconventional Reality Subscale of the MHVQ: 1995–96

| | Average Score | | | |
Response on Subscale	White	Native American	Z Score	Mann-Whitney two-tailed p
Unconventional reality	2.2	2.8	−2.4095	.02
The person has visions.	2.0	3.0	−2.5224	.01
The person sees things that others do not see.	1.8	2.9	−2.4741	.01
The person guides his/her life according to spirits.	2.2	3.0	−2.3813	.02
The person views things differently at different times	3.0	3.7	−1.9675	.05
The person is bored most of the time	2.0	2.8	−2.3234	.02
The person attempts to improve himself or herself.	4.5	4.1	−2.134	.03
The person communicates directly and honestly with others	4.5	4.1	−2.7055	.01

NOTES: MHVQ = Mental Health Values Questionnaire (Tyler, Clark, Olson, Klapp, & Chelona, 1983; Tyler & Suan, 1990). 1 = very poor mental health, 2 = poor mental health, 3 = neutral, not related to mental health, 4 = good mental health, 5 = very good mental health.

tion and three persons, a Cherokee, a Shoshone, and a white/Mohawk/Blackfoot/ Cheyenne, who were not enrolled in their tribe/nation. The white/Indian person was treated as an American Indian in the analysis.

Attitudes toward what constitutes good or poor mental health differed significantly between white and American Indian respondents on seven specific items, and on one of the subscales, "unconventional reality," as shown in Table 2. The first four items after the "unconventional reality" subscale are part of this scale, as defined by the original authors (Tyler et al., 1983). The American Indian respondents reported that having visions, seeing things others do not see, and guiding one's life according to spirits are not related to either poor or good mental health (Table 2). White recipients reported these statements were indicative of poor mental health. These responses were similar to those of the students at the University of North Dakota for these items in the original study using the MHVQ.

In the original study the importance to mental health of "viewing things differently at different times" did not differ significantly between the two groups (Tyler & Suan, 1990). In this study, white recipients reported that viewing things differently at different times was not related to good or poor mental health, whereas the American Indian response was closer to "good mental health." The flexibility of response indicated by the assignment of "good" mental health to the ability to change

one's mind may be a reflection of the importance of individual decision making among the Haudenosaunee. This was chronicled as early as 1884 in the *Annual Reports of the Trustees of the Peabody Museum* as follows:

Ostensibly the supreme power of the tribe was vested in a council composed of chiefs and elders, though there is reason to believe that in all they did they acted as attorneys for the women rather than independently and of their own volition. As a rule their decisions were respected though this was not always the case; and in the event of opposition on the part of any individual, he was at liberty to follow the bent of his own inclination. (Carr 1984, p. 30)

Responses to three items not included in the "unconventional reality" subscale were also found to differ significantly between the two groups. As with the first three statements, being bored showed "poor" mental health for white respondents but was closer to neutral for American Indians. Making attempts to improve oneself and communicating directly and honestly with others were rated as showing "good" mental health by American Indians but rated closer to "very good" mental health by whites. Similar results to these were not found in the original study by Tyler and Suan (1990).

Differences among Native American Responses to the MHVQ

Federal enrollment in the Seneca Indian Nation was used as a proxy for lack of assimi-

TABLE 3—Differences in Responses between White (Group 1), Nonenrolled American Indian (Group 2), and Enrolled American Indian (Group 3) Recipients of Mental Health Services (1995–96 (Kruskal-Wallis analysis of variance).

| | Mean Rank | | | | |
Variable	Group 1	Group 2	Group 3	χ^2	p
Unconventional reality subscale	15.33	23.67	24.25	5.813	.05
Has visions	15.81	16.33	27.45	8.976	.01
Sees things others do not see	17.31	20.33	28.09	7.268	.03
Guides life according to spirits	17.06	26.00	25.85	5.671	NS
Views things differently at different times	17.94	17.33	27.41	5.778	NS
Is bored most of the time	17.17	32.27	23.55	7.059	.03
Makes attempt to improve himself or herself	23.02	9.83	17.45	5.877	.05
Communicates directly and honestly	23.75	9.00	15.95	8.384	.02

NOTE: NS = not significant.

lation into the mainstream culture. The use of enrollment as a proxy for lack of acculturation is based on discussion in the literature indicating that ties of location and kinship to an American Indian reservation community connote adherence to American Indian cultural tradition. Eleven of the 14 Indian respondents were federally enrolled Seneca Indians living on or near the Seneca Cattaraugus Reservation. Analysis of variance was undertaken using the Kruskal-Wallis test to gauge the effects of Seneca enrollment (see Table 3 for results). The results of the Kruskal-Wallis test for the direction and relative size of mean rank indicate the effect of enrollment in the Seneca Nation on the variable of interest. These data show that the enrolled Seneca Indians were largely responsible for differences from whites on statements related to having visions and seeing things others do not. The nonenrolled Indians from other tribes were most responsible for the differences from whites on statements related to being bored, improving self and communicating directly and honestly.

These results suggest the possibility that the three nonenrolled American Indians fit the "pan-Indian" profile. Among pan-Indians the lines dividing specific native cultures are blurred and traits attributed primarily to the plains Indians become symbolic of a generic Indian identity (Jarvenpa, 1985; Nagel & Snipp, 1993). According to Williams and Ellison (1996) pan-Indians are likely to avoid activities of the dominant culture and to adopt the traditions of various American Indian

groups. In so doing, it is possible that many of the American Indian stereotypes as described by Mander (1991) and others (Joe & Malach, 1992; Sue & Sue, 1990) may be evident. These include a de-emphasis on time or schedules (being bored is not a problem), sharing rather than acquiring (personal success is less important), and primary allegiance to the American Indian group (communicating directly and honestly is less important with members of the dominant culture) (Mander, 1991).

Limitations of the Study

Each part of this study had its own limitations. Part 1 was affected by the limitations of the DMHIS database. They include lack of information that may have been important to the study as well as gaps in information that was available. Part 2 was limited because participation was voluntary. The convenience sample of people who completed the forms may have differed in terms of motivation, mental disability, education, and other traits from people who did not take part in the survey. The lack of consistency in distribution of the questionnaires may also have affected the results.

Sampling is an issue for both parts of the study. Because part 1 was used to identify a site for part 2 of the study, some of the participants for the two parts of the study may be the same, further limiting an already small sample size. The small sample size limits the generalizability of the findings to other Native American groups.

IMPLICATIONS FOR PRACTICE

To be effective with American Indian clients, a social worker must first decide which culture the client belongs to. Williams and Ellison (1996) quoted the following factors as indications that a client is acculturated to Western norms: high level of formal education, generations of removal from a reservation, low family affiliation, lack of current contact with a reservation, and previous personal or family experience with Western health care.

The results of this study support earlier literature regarding the possible effects of traditional Native American religious beliefs on attitudes toward mental health (Lejero et al., 1988; LaFromboise, 1988; O'Nell, 1989; Tyler & Suan, 1990). For the Seneca Indian clients, such attributes as having visions and guiding one's life according to spirits may incorrectly appear to be symptoms of a serious mental disorder such as schizophrenia.

If identification with a Native American culture has been ascertained, the worker may want to use American Indian healers as an adjunct to treatment. Although some authors suggest joint treatment, many attempts at collaboration fail because of confusion about issues of billing, credibility, and expectations of both the therapist and client (LaFromboise, 1988). Among the Haudenosaunee, involvement of a clinician in a traditional rite such as those performed by the False Face Society would be prohibited. The referral to traditional ceremonies has been successfully used by at least one director of a mental health program that serves members of the Iroquois Confederacy (personal communication with Rob Higgens, director, St. Regis Mohawk Mental Health Services, St. Regis Reservation, Hogansburg, NY, May 1997).

This study found that American Indians were less likely to have been seen at an outpatient program over a year ago and more likely to have an alcohol problem when compared with white clients. These factors may be related because people appearing at a New York State–operated mental health clinic with a primary alcohol diagnosis would be referred to another program, and people with a chronic mental illness would be seen over a period of years. With an American Indian client who has a dual mental health/alcohol abuse diagnosis, the skilled therapist must be attuned not only to standard treatment for alcohol abuse but also to cultural aspects of intervention. The clinician should know, for example, that among many groups of Native Americans, including the Haudenosaunee, the adherence to a traditional religion requires abstention from alcohol (Choney, Berryhill-Paapke, & Robbins, 1995; Earle, 1996).

When setting goals with a Native American client, a therapist needs to be aware that the client's goals may not be those of members of the dominant culture. One implication of this study, found in the literature as well, is that American Indians may be less likely than members of the general population to have achieved educational success (Blount et al., 1992; LaFromboise, 1988; Marshall, Martin, Thomason, & Johnson, 1991; McShane, 1987) or to value individual success as defined by the dominant culture (Dykeman et al., 1995; Sue & Sue, 1990; Wilkinson, 1980). Rather than attending a conventional college, for example, a more relevant goal for a traditional American Indian client may be to learn his or her own native language or to attend a tribal college or American Indian Studies program (Wollock, 1997).

AVENUES FOR FURTHER STUDY

This study raised some intriguing and important questions. To expand information found about mental health services provided by New York State, this study used an additional database. Data from all (federal, state, local, private, and proprietary) mental health programs in the identified counties were compared to census data to obtain a comparative rate of service. Program data were from the Patient Characteristics Survey completed every two years by OMH and accessible to the author. The rates, which included data from four federal mental health clinics operated on Iroquois reservations by the Indian Health Service, were one service per 100 population for American Indians and 11 services per 100 population for white people during a two-week period.

Because Native Americans in these areas of New York State are receiving standard services at a much lower rate than white people, where, if at all, are American Indians getting mental health services? Are people receiving traditional American Indian mental health healing rituals in lieu of standard services? It is not known, for example, how many members of the Haudenosaunee use traditional healing for personal problems.

The clinic that was the primary site for part 2 of the study served about one-third of the Native Americans receiving services from OMH in part 1. It thus differs from other services in upstate, central, and western New York. The next highest number of American Indian clients seen at one site was five.

Visits to the study site found that it was adjacent to an Iroquois reservation and that the program director had grown up in a white family on the grounds of another Iroquois reservation. At the program director's initiative, clinic staff had received ongoing training from experts in American Indian culture from a nearby university.

Another question raised is "Why were half the Native Americans who received OMH services in these areas of New York receiving them in prison?" According to Bloom, Manson, and Neligh (1980), the difficulties of obtaining emergency psychiatric commitment of American Indians when needed for "danger to self or others" may lead to the inappropriate use of jails, a common response of a community to disruptive or aberrant behavior. The difficulty of commitment is the result primarily of the unique relationship of Native American tribes with the federal government rather than the state governments, leading to possible disagreements about jurisdiction in matters of psychiatric commitment for American Indians (Bloom et al., 1980; Lejero et al., 1988).

CONCLUSION

This study suggests there may be important differences between these white and American Indian clients in demographic and service variables and attitudes toward mental health that require a different therapeutic approach for American Indians. I hope that this analysis of the primarily Iroquois people of New York State will provide some direction for future study and some limited assistance to any social worker who treats American Indian clients. The need for additional research is indicated in this difficult but interesting area.

REFERENCES

Attneave, C. L. (1984). Themes striving for harmony: Conventional mental health services and American Indian traditions. In S. Sue & T. Moore (Eds.), *The pluralistic society: A community mental health perspective* (pp. 149–191). New York: Human Services Press.

Bloom, J. D., Manson, S. M., & Neligh, G. (1980). Civil Commitment of American Indians. *Bulletin of the American Academy of Psychiatry and the Law, 8,* 1–10.

Blount, M., Thyer, B. A., & Frye, T. (1992). Social work practice with Native Americans. In D. F. Harrison, J. S. Wodarski, & B. A. Thyer (Eds.), *Cultural diversity and social work practice* (pp. 107–134). Springfield, IL: Charles C Thomas.

Carr, L. (1984). On the social and political position of women among the Huron–Iroquois tribes. In W. G. Spittal (Ed.), *Iroquois women: An anthology* (pp. 9–36). Ontario, Canada: Iroqrafts.

Choney, S. K., Berryhill-Paapke, E., & Robbins, R. R. (1995). The acculturation of American Indians: Developing frameworks for research and practice. In J. G. Ponterotto, J. M. Casas, L.A. Suzuki, & C. M. Alexander (Eds.), *Handbook of multicultural counseling* (pp. 73–92). Thousand Oaks, CA: Sage Publications.

Cohen, J. (1988). *Statistical power analysis in the behavioral sciences.* Hillsdale, NJ: Lawrence Erlbaum.

Dykeman, C., Nelson, J. R., & Appleton, V. (1995). Building working alliances with American Indian families. *Social Work in Education, 17,* 148–158.

Earle, K. A. (1996). Working with the Haudenosaunee: What social workers should know. *New Social Worker, 3,* 27–28.

Edwards, E. D., & Edwards, M. E. (1984). Group work practice with American Indians. *Social Work with Groups, 7,* 7–21.

Fenton, W. N. (1987). *The false faces of the Iroquois.* Norman: University of Oklahoma Press.

Good Tracks, J. G. (1973). Native American noninterference. *Social Work; 18,* 31–35.

Greene, G. J., Jensen, C., & Jones, D. H. (1996). A constructivist perspective on clinical social work practice with ethnically diverse clients. *Social Work, 41,* 172–180.

Gross, E. R. (1995). Deconstructing politically correct practice literature: The American Indian case. *Social Work, 40,* 206–213.

Jarvenpa, R. (1985). The political economy and political ethnicity of American Indian adaptations and identities. *Ethnic and Racial Studies, 8,* 29–48.

Jilek, W. G. (1971). From crazy witch doctor to auxiliary psychotherapist—The changing image of the medicine man. *Psychiatria Clinica, 4,* 200–220.

Joe, J. R., & Malach, R. S. (1992). Families with Native American roots. In E. W. Lynch & M. J. Hanson (Eds.), *Developing cross-cultural competence: A guide for working with young children and their families* (pp. 89–115). Baltimore: Paul H. Brookes.

Johnson, D. L., & Johnson, C. A. (1965). Totally discouraged: A depressive syndrome of the Dakota Sioux. *Transcultural Psychiatric Research Review, 2,* 141–143.

Kenny, D. A. (1987). *Statistics for the social and behavioral sciences.* Boston: Little, Brown.

LaFromboise, T. D. (1988). American Indian mental health policy. *American Psychologist, 47,* 388–396.

Lefley, H. P. (1990). Culture and chronic mental illness. *Hospital and Community Psychiatry, 41,* 277–285.

Lejero, L., Antone, M., Francisco, D., & Manuel, J. (1988). An indigenous community mental health service on the Tohono O'odham (Papago) Indian reservation: Seventeen years later. *American Journal of Community Psychology, 16,* 369–379.

Lewis, T. (1975). A syndrome of depression and mutism in the Ogala Sioux. *American Journal of Psychiatry, 132,* 753–755.

Mander, J. (1991). *In the absence of the sacred: The failure of technology and the survival of the Indian Nations.* San Francisco: Sierra Club Books.

Manson, S. M., Shore, J. H., & Bloom, J. D. (1985). The depressive experience in American Indian communities: A challenge for psychiatric theory and diagnosis. In A. Kleinman & B. Good (Eds.), *Culture and depression: Studies in anthropology and cross-cultural psychiatry of affect and disorder* (pp. 331–368). Berkeley: University of California Press.

Manson, S. M., Tatum E., & Dinges, M. G. (1982). Prevention research among American Indian and Alaskan natives. In S. M. Manson (Ed.), *New directions in prevention with American Indians* (pp. 11–62). Portland: Oregon Health Services.

Marshall, C. A., Martin, W. E., Thomason, T. C., & Johnson, M. J. (1991). Multiculturalism and rehabilitation counselor training: Recommendations for providing culturally appropriate counseling services to American Indians with disabilities. *Journal of Counseling and Development, 70,* 225–234.

Matchett, W. F. (1972). Repeated hallucinatory experiences as part of the mourning process among Hopi Indian women. *Psychiatry, 35,* 185–194.

McShane, D. (1987). Mental health and North American Indian/native communities: Cultural transactions, education, and regulation. *American Journal of Community Psychology, 15,* 95–115.

Nagel, J., & Snipp, M. (1993). Ethnic reorganization: American Indian social, economic, political, and cultural strategies for survival. *Ethnic and Racial Studies, 16,* 203–235.

Nelson, S. H., McCoy, G. F., Stetter, M., & Vanderwagen, W. C. (1992). An overview of mental health services for American Indians and Alaska natives in the 1990s. *Hospital and Community Psychiatry, 43,* 257–261.

O'Nell, T. D. (1989). Psychiatric investigations among American Indians. *Culture, Medicine and Psychiatry, 13,* 51–87.

Owan, T. C. (1982). Neighborhood-based mental health: An approach to overcome inequities in mental health services delivery to racial and ethnic minorities. In D. E. Biegel & A. J. Naperstek (Eds.), *Community support systems and mental health: Practice, policy, and research* (pp. 282–300). New York: Springer.

Parker, A. C. (1968). *Parker on the Iroquois.* Syracuse, NY: Syracuse University Press.

Perkins, A. E. (1927). Psychoses of the American Indians admitted to Gowanda State Hospital. *Psychiatric Quarterly, 1,* 335–343.

Price-Williams, D. (1987). Summary: Culture, socialization, and mental health. *Journal of Community Psychiatry, 15,* 357–361.

Prucha, F. P. (1990). *Documents of United States Indian Policy.* Lincoln: University of Nebraska Press.

Red Horse, J. (1980). Family structure and value orientation in American Indians. *Social Casework 61,* 462–467.

Red Horse, J. (1982). Clinical strategies of American Indian families in crisis. *Urban and Social Change Review, 15,* 17–19.

Schaaf, G. (1990). *Wampum belts and peace trees.* Golden, CO: Fulcrum.

Sue, D.W., & Sue, D. (1990). *Counseling the culturally different: Theory and practice.* New York: John Wiley & Sons

Trimble, J. E., Manson, S., Dinges, G., & Medicine, B. (1984). American Indian concepts of mental health: Reflections and directions. In P. B. Pederson, N. Sartorius, & A. J. Marsella (Eds.), Mental health concepts: *The cross cultural context* (pp. 199–220). Beverly Hills, CA: Sage Publications.

Tyler, J., Clark, J. A., Olson, D., Klapp, D. A., & Cheloha, R. S. (1983). Measuring mental health values. *Counseling and Values, 27,* 20-31.

Tyler, J. D., & Suan, L. V. (1990). Mental health values differences between Native American and Caucasian American college students, *Journal of Rural Community Psychology, 11,* 17–29.

U.S. Department of Health and Human Services, U.S. Indian Health Service. (1989). *National plan for Native American mental health services* (Draft document).

Wallace, A.F.C. (1959). The institutionalization of cathartic and control strategies in Iroquois religious psychotherapy. In M. K. Opler (Ed.), *Culture and mental health: Cross-cultural studies* (pp. 63–96). New York: Macmillan.

Western Interstate Commission for Higher Education. (1993). *The journey of Native American people with serious mental illness.* Boulder, CO: WICHE Publications.

Wilkinson, G. T. (1980). On assisting Indian people. *Social Casework, 61,* 451–454.

Williams, E. E., & Ellison, F. (1996). Culturally informed social work with American Indian clients: Guidelines for non-Indian social workers. *Social Work, 41,* 147–151.

Wollock, J. (1997). Protagonism emergent: Indians and higher education. *Native Americans, 14,* 12–23.

Pay Per Plea

Public defenders come at a price

BY ERIN MIDDLEWOOD

Five women sit around a table in a stark, cement-walled holding room at the Rock County Jail in Janesville, Wisconsin. The women, recently arrested and dressed in jailhouse orange, talk with a paralegal, who is evaluating their eligibility for public defense.

One of the women receives welfare benefits. Two have no means of support. One works part-time and pulls in only $30 a week. Another sells her plasma. All of them qualify for public defense. And all of them will have to pay for it.

Paralegal Amy Kelber explains to them that Wisconsin started a new program in August 1995 requiring poor people to pay for their public representation. Defense costs $200 for a misdemeanor, Kelber tells the women, and $400 for a felony—unless the defendant pays $50 within thirty days. Kelber emphasizes that even if they never pay, the women will still get a lawyer, but their accounts will be turned over to a collection agency.

At the end of the interview, Kelber gives each woman an envelope for her nonrefundable payment.

"Will I pay in the next thirty days? No," says Laureanette Ingram, twenty-nine, who has been living with her brother and has no job. "I can't. I got to find something to eat with. I got to put shoes on my feet."

Wisconsin is one of a growing number of states, including Kansas and Virginia, that now charge indigent defendants for public representation. Many states charge those seeking a public defender an evaluation fee ranging from $10 to $100. Last fall, California passed a law allowing its counties to charge $25. On January 1, 1997, Florida will implement a $40 fee.

Colorado, Connecticut, Massachusetts, New Jersey, New Mexico, and South Carolina have all implemented fees in the last several years.

None of these states deny representation to those who can't pay. Even so, public-defender fees represent a small but significant erosion of the Sixth-Amendment right to legal counsel. The fees could drive away potential public-defender clients. And, as public-defender offices begin to rely on their indigent clients for funding, they are likely to encounter major cashflow problems.

Justice Hugo Black wrote in the unanimous 1963 *Gideon* Supreme Court decision that "any person haled into court who is too poor to hire a lawyer cannot be assured a fair trial unless counsel is provided for him."

More than thirty years later, some state legislatures are asking public-defender offices to fudge on that assurance.

Waring Fincke argued in a March 1996 *Wisconsin Lawyer* article that imposing payment of fees on those who aren't convicted may be unconstitutional.

"The public-defender office was assailed by rightwingers in the Legislature who fail to see a need for state public defenders in the first place," he says. Fincke is a board member of the Wisconsin Association of Criminal Defense Lawyers and former staff lawyer for the public defender. "They see money going to the public-defender office and wonder, 'Why spend so much money on criminals?' They make the leap that if you are accused, you have to be guilty. In a budget crunch, that makes the public-defender budget ripe for the picking."

Facing shrinking budgets, some public-defender offices have embraced the idea of raising a few dollars from their clients.

"Lack of revenue prompted our support of the fee," says J. Marion Moorman, one of twenty elected public defenders in Florida. "Funding wasn't keeping pace with growth in caseload."

But charging the indigent hasn't been fruitful. The Wisconsin Public Defender's September 1996 Budget Forecasting Report showed that the agency had sent $12.7 million in accounts to collections, and recouped only $38,800.

The negligible financial return is only the mildest of the program's problems. In fact, the new program amounts to a hidden budget cut for the Wisconsin Public Defender. The office predicts it will bring in only about $2.5 million of the $7.5 million the state says it ought to collect from defendants over the next two years.

Wisconsin is the only state that charges poor defendants for representation no matter what the outcome of their cases. Convicted and acquitted alike must pay. If indigent defendants don't shell out $50 up front, they must pay a steeper price later. And if they don't pay later, State Collection Service, Inc., a firm contracted by the state of Wisconsin, will go after them.

It's hard to tell how many people are warded off by the fee. The state public defender doesn't keep a count of who declines representation because of the payment requirement. The best count the office offers is in its monthly Budget Forecasting Report, which includes reports from around Wisconsin of defendants who have turned down a public defender because of cost.

Paralegal Amy Kelber sees about forty defendants a week, and of those, she estimates two decline public representation and plead no contest.

"Most turndowns are in person, but some people with prior experience shy away from applying [for public defense]," says Michael Tobin, director of

Erin Middlewood is the Associate Editor of the Progressive Media Project.

the Wisconsin Public Defender trial division. "We don't turn anyone away because they can't pay. If they are turning us down, it's because they found out they would have to pay in the future."

Defendants who wind up without representation find themselves in courtrooms alone and confused. "All of the criminal judges are seeing an increase in defendants without an attorney," says Stuart A. Schwartz, a Dane County, Wisconsin, circuit-court judge. "Most are intimidated by the process. When I ask them questions, they don't know what to say. ... Some defendants don't appreciate the seriousness of the crime. They think that if they come into court, they'll just be able to talk to someone."

People who qualify for public-defender representation are, by definition, very poor, and throughout the nation indigency standards are getting stricter.

According to new standards in Florida, a person's income must be below the federal poverty level to be considered indigent. For a single person, that's $7,740 per year, and for a family of four, $15,600 per year.

In Wisconsin, the indigency standard is complicated, but the state calculates cost-of-living for a single person to be $1,488 over six months. That's $62 a week. A single person accused of a felony who doesn't have expenses beyond this amount (such as child-support payments or health insurance) could earn as little as $2,938 over six months and be ineligible for public defense. Judges can appoint counsel at county expense for those who are very poor yet not deemed indigent, but, because of the effect on county budgets, they tend to do so only for those accused of serious felonies.

These standards keep more people out of the public-defender's office than the new fees. "More people don't receive public defense because of indigency standards themselves than because of the collections policy implemented in 1995," says Tobin.

But both policies—fee collection and miserly definitions of poverty—are part of the same trend toward recouping defense costs from the poor who use public representation. Behind this trend are a number of factors, including shrinking state budgets, a desire to appear tough on crime, and, more fundamentally, contempt for the poor.

"It's an expression of society's dislike for indigent defendants and a desire to squeeze everything possible out

of them. It's an expression of frustration—not an expectation of getting money," says Ira Mickenberg, a training coordinator for the Washington, D.C., public defender.

Mickenberg knows Wisconsin's system well. In October 1995 he was training director for the Wisconsin Public Defender, but left because he didn't like the direction the agency was taking.

"There is, in general, political animosity toward poor people who are receiving any government benefits," Mickenberg says.

> **T**he idea is, if public defenders can't get enough funding from their state, they'll get it from squeezing the poor people who seek representation.

Peter Erlinder, president of the National Lawyers Guild, takes it further. He calls imposing fees on indigent defendants another salvo in generalized class warfare.

"The majority of people who get arrested for criminal acts are people who have little or no resources," says Erlinder, a constitutional-law professor at William Mitchell College of Law in St. Paul, Minnesota. "It's a piece of a class attack. There is a racial dimension as well. In a state like Minnesota, for example, an African-American working-class male is twenty-three times more likely to be in prison than a white working-class male. In California, 40 percent of the African-American population is in the criminal-prosecution system or involved in some fashion—on probation, in jail, in prison."

According to the most recent U.S. Bureau of Justice Statistics figures, compiled in a 1992 report called "Justice Expenditure and Employment," the government spent $5.5 million on prosecution and related legal costs in 1990, while public defenders spent only about $1.7 million.

The Bureau's 1996 report "Indigent Defense" says that 80 percent of those

charged with felonies in the nation's seventy-five largest counties relied on a public defender or on assigned counsel for legal representation.

Erlinder thinks the disadvantage is greater. "Even though government must bear the cost of all prosecutions, it's also true that somewhere in the range of 90 percent of all defendants have to rely on government-supplied attorneys, and yet funding for criminal-defense systems across the country is far less than 90 percent of prosecution," he says.

That's where public-defender application fees and cost-recoupment measures such as Wisconsin's come in. The idea is, if public defenders can't get enough funding from their state, they'll get it from squeezing the poor people who seek representation.

"The worst thing about it is not the immediate financial consequences, but the enormous amount of resources that could be better used in actually defending people," Mickenberg says. "Public defenders are required to set up a bureaucracy to screen people, evaluate whether they qualify [for court-appointed counsel], and enforce collections—all resources that could be used to defend people. Public defenders are frequently strapped for cash, and courts are crowded as it is."

Judge Schwartz fears the consequences. "Unrealistic fiscal guidelines do not lend themselves to the smooth administration of justice," he says.

The real problem is underfunding of public defense, says Robert Burke, a staff attorney for the National Legal Aid and Defender Association. He's concerned that states are using these new fees to avoid fully funding public-defender offices. "If fees are used to replace other funding," he reckons, "that's a mistake."

Given Wisconsin's low rate of collection, these fees won't solve anything.

"Nobody with any brains at all has any real expectation of collecting a significant amount of money," Mickenberg chides. "They know they'll never really be able to collect the 400 bucks. It's a way for politicians to go to the public and say, 'We're being tough on crime.' It's smoke and mirrors and cheap politics—a way for politicians to trick the public into thinking they're doing something when they don't have a clue."

But fees aren't likely to go away. "The people who are affected—the accused or convicted—don't have a constituency besides the public defenders who represent them, who lack the funding to do so effectively," Burke concludes. "There's no one to stand up for them."

UNEQUAL JUSTICE

Preserving the Rights of the Mentally Retarded in the Criminal Justice System

by Fred Pelka

I t can happen quickly," writes advocate Robert Perske. A brutal crime is committed, outraging an entire community. Local police, under pressure to solve the case, latch onto a suspect, perhaps someone tangentially related to the victim, someone seen as "peculiar" or "retarded" and considered by police to be "fringe" or "abnormal." The suspect is brought to a police station, persuaded to waive the right to remain silent and to have an attorney present, and signs a confession. Even though the suspect might subsequently recant, a jury, confronted with a signed confession, votes to convict.

Perske has made it his mission to defend people with mental disabilities whom he feels are being railroaded by the criminal justice system. Leigh Ann Reynolds, project associate at the National Arc (formerly the Association for Retarded Citizens), calls him "the only person, that I'm aware of, who's been tracking this problem on a national level." Perske has collected data on more than 100 cases of people with mental retardation who have been convicted of capital crimes. In some of these cases, the defendants have been convicted of crimes they did not commit; in others, while the defendants may have been involved in the crimes, they may have had no conception of the harm they were committing or were under the influence of a nondisabled career criminal. Either way, the bottom line for Perske is: Did that person receive equal justice? Whether guilty or innocent, did the system treat that person as other citizens are treated when charged with the same crime? Often the answer appears to be "no."

Take, for example, the case of Richard Lapointe, convicted of the 1987 rape and murder of his wife's eighty-eight-year-old grandmother, Bernice Martin. There was no physical evidence linking Lapointe to the crime. The sole basis of his conviction was a confession, written by the police, that Lapointe signed in the early morning hours of July 5,1989, after a nine-and-a-half-hour interrogation. Lapointe waived his *Miranda* rights, but Perske doubts that he understood what this meant. Lapointe has Dandy-Walker syndrome, a congenital brain malformation affecting his ability to think abstractly, as well as his eyesight, his hearing in both ears, and his balance.

According to the detective in charge of the investigation, Lapointe was targeted as a suspect—a full two years after the crime—because he acted "strange," asking police officers he saw if they'd solved the case and if he was a suspect. "People who know him," comments Perske, "say that's just the way he is. He was concerned about what happened to his wife's grandmother and was friendly with the police who came into the places where he worked as a dishwasher." In addition, Lapointe's denial when asked if he had committed the murder was, according to the police, "passive," instead of the "very strong affirmative objection you would expect."

Lapointe's style, however, has never been "affirmative." In school he was taunted by classmates as "Mr. Magoo" because of his thick glasses and bumbling manner. The diminutive, five-foot-four-inch Lapointe also uses a hearing aid and is incapable of strenuous activity because of a shunt surgically implanted into his skull to remove excess brain fluid. Whoever murdered Bernice Martin bound her tightly around the neck and wrists with strips of torn clothing, sexually assaulted her, stabbed her, and then set fire to her cottage apartment. Perske calls the crime "a raging, athletic murder," while Lapointe has been described as "short, chubby, weak, and awkward."

To obtain Lapointe's confession, police perpetrated what journalist Tom Condon, in an article for the *Hartford*

From *The Humanist,* November/December 1997, pp. 28-32. Portions of this article appeared in the April 1997 issue of *Mainstream: Magazine of the Able-Disabled.* © 1997 by Fred Pelka. Reprinted by permission.

Advocates point out that many people with mental retardation are taught to trust and obey authority figures: parents, teachers, and the police.

Courant, calls "an elaborate ruse." Condon recounts how, on July 4, 1989, Lapointe was taken to the Manchester, Connecticut, police station for "a chat":

> Two rooms in the station were festooned with props—pictures, charts, lists, and diagrams—that portrayed Lapointe as the killer. A chart said his fingerprints were found on the knife used in the crime. Another linked him to the crime through DNA testing. There was a list of detectives [including "Detectives Friday and Gannon"] who were on the "Bernice Martin Homicide Task Force." None of this was true.

There were no fingerprints and no DNA evidence, while the "task force" consisted of one detective, Paul Lombardo, new to the case and eager to use his recent FBI training in "criminal profiles."

Most of us, brought into a police station for questioning about a murder, would ask to see an attorney. Certainly, we'd be skeptical of a homicide task force including *Dragnet* detectives Friday and Gannon. Lapointe, however, trusted authority figures and considered the police to be his friends. At any rate, his poor eyesight prevented him from seeing much of the placards. Told that there was conclusive evidence linking him to the murder, he asked if it were possible for someone to commit such a crime but not remember. He was told it was. After several hours, Lapointe signed a statement that read: "On March 8 I was responsible for Bernice Martin's death and it was an accident. My mind went blank." Afterward, Lapointe said he signed this confession in exchange for being allowed to use the bathroom. He retracted this first confession, but over the next several hours signed two more, each written by the police and each more detailed than the last.

"There is nothing illegal about the police lying to a suspect," says Perske. Indeed, Timothy J. Sugrue, executive assistant state's attorney for Connecticut, acknowledges that misleading suspects "is a common investigative technique." Nor is there any requirement that the police make video or audio tapes, or even keep written notes, when conducting an interrogation. Oddly enough, having obtained a confession from Lapointe, police allowed this supposed perpetrator of a brutal rape and murder to leave the station and return home to his disabled wife and small child. He wasn't arrested until late the next day.

Perske heard about the case from someone familiar with his work. "I got a call about somebody being rail-roaded in Manchester, Connecticut, which is my own state. So I called the public defender in charge of the case, read some of the early motions, and became convinced that it was very much like the other cases I'd observed. I showed up for the first day of the trial and stayed for forty-eight court days, watching it all transpire." At first, Perske was the only spectator sitting behind Lapointe on the left side of the courtroom. "Everybody else was sitting on the right side, behind the prosecutor," he said. "I suffered a lot of panic after the first week because the prosecution was asking for the death penalty, and it looked like they were going to kill this guy." He began making phone calls, "getting onto everybody's answering machine, saying you have to come and see what's happening here; you have to be a witness."

Perske and the others in the newly formed Friends of Richard Lapointe were hopeful that the jury would acquit. Instead, it found Lapointe guilty. "Basically, the jurors took the word of the police, that Ritchie knew what he was doing when he confessed," Perske said. "Juries tend to believe that no one would confess to a crime they didn't commit." Lapointe was sentenced to life in prison plus sixty years, with no possibility of parole.

Why would someone confess to a crime that someone else committed? Advocates point out that many people with mental retardation are taught to trust and obey authority figures: parents, teachers, and the police. Dick Sobsey, author of *Violence and Abuse in the Lives of People with Disabilities,* describes how institution staff, for example, use behavior modification techniques to make residents easier to manage. According to Sobsey, the resulting "learned helplessness," in which compliance to authority becomes second nature, is one reason why people with cognitive and developmental disabilities are more at risk for sexual abuse and exploitation. Dennis Heath of People First, a national advocacy organization of people with mental disabilities, puts it another way: "Under pressure, our people often knuckle under. They're generally not taught to stand up for their rights."

"Most of my clients confess, whether they did it or not," says Suzanne Lustig, director of the Developmentally Disabled Offenders Program in North Brunswick, New Jersey, a state-funded advocacy program that designs "personalized justice plans" for people with mental retardation who are convicted of a crime, as an alternative to serving time in prison. She says most of her clients are on the third-grade reading level and the fourth-grade math level. "The only thing they know how to write is their name," Lustig says, just enough to sign a confession or a waiver of their *Miranda* rights. "They want to confess, they want to make people happy. They're also good at sensing what it is that authority figures want from them and then providing it." Lustig and others maintain that this willingness to please, together with the leading manner in which some interrogations are conducted, can result in detailed confessions from people who are entirely innocent.

An example of this dynamic at work can be found in the transcript of the interrogation of David Vasquez, found in Perske's book, *Unequal Justice: What Can Happen When Persons with Retardation or Other Developmental Disabilities Encounter the Criminal Justice System.* Vasquez was picked up by police in Arlington, Virginia, on January 4, 1984, for questioning about the murder of a woman who had been raped in her home and then strangled with the cords of a Venetian blind:

Interrogator: Did she tell you to tie her hands behind her back?
Vasquez: Ah, if she did, I did.
Interrogator: Whatcha use?
Vasquez: The ropes?
Interrogator: No, not the ropes. Whatcha use?
Vasquez: Only my belt.
Interrogator: No, not your belt. . . . Remember . . . cutting the Venetian blind cords?
Vasquez: Ah, it's the same as rope.
Interrogator: Yeah.

Later, Vasquez is asked how he committed the murder. He starts to say that he stabbed the victim. The police interrogator, losing his temper, screams, "You hung her!" Vasquez replies, "What?" "You hung her!" the interrogator repeats. "Okay," says Vasquez, "so I hung her." Vasquez was convinced by his public defender to accept a plea bargain and was given a forty-year sentence for second-degree murder. He was pardoned in 1989—after being incarcerated for five years—when the real perpetrator was finally apprehended.

A further example is Johnny Lee Wilson. On April 18, 1986, the twenty-year-old Wilson, diagnosed with "organic brain damage and mental retardation," was brought into the police station in Aurora, Missouri, for questioning about the murder of seventy-nine-year-old Pauline Martz. *Unequal Justice* contains portions of the transcript of a police interrogation which, unlike Richard Lapointe's, was taped:

Interrogator: You can swear to God or whoever you like, that ain't going to get you out of trouble.
Wilson: Uh huh.
Interrogator: For you are in serious trouble right now. Murder is what you're in. Murder! Premeditated, willful, malicious, burning up an old lady in her house! That's what you're in on Wilson. Ain't no sense kidding around it!

Wilson: I wasn't near that house, though.
Interrogator: I think it's despicable!

Later in the questioning, the interrogator asks about the color of the victim's blouse:

Wilson: I'll say it was white, kind of white or bluish blouse.
Interrogator: Okay, how about bluish? I'll go for that.
Wilson: Yeah.
Interrogator: How about bluish-green, maybe.
Wilson: Yeah.

The questioning then turns to the way the victim was tied:

Wilson: I'm thinking.
Interrogator: What are some of the things that could be used?
Wilson: Handcuffs, I think.
Interrogator: No. No. Wrong guess. [The victim was tied with duct tape.]

It's important to note here that, during trial, prosecutors often point to details in the defendant's description of the crime that "only the perpetrator could know" as evidence of the validity of the confession.

On April 30,1987, Wilson appeared in court to plead guilty to first-degree murder:

Judge Elliston: Why are you pleading guilty, Johnny?
Wilson: I don't know.
Elliston: You don't know why you're pleading guilty?
Wilson: Just for first-degree murder.
Elliston: Well, that's what you're pleading to, but why are you wanting to enter the plea?
Wilson: I don't know. . . .

Elliston: Do you know that the death penalty is a possibility in this case?
Wilson: Yes.
Elliston: Do you want the death penalty?
Wilson: No.
Elliston: Do you want to avoid the death penalty?
Wilson: Yes.
Elliston: Are you admitting that you committed this murder?
Wilson: Yes.

On the basis of his "confession" and plea, Wilson was sentenced to life in prison without the possibility of parole. In 1991, convicted murderer Chris Brownfield, serving time in a Kansas prison, admitted that he and an accomplice had committed the murder for which Wilson was convicted. Nevertheless, motions to reopen the case were denied. Missouri Governor Mel Carnahan pardoned Wilson on September 29, 1995.

One factor contributing to these kinds of scenarios is the crushing isolation often endured by people with mental retardation or brain injury. Like Lapointe, they are often taunted as "retards" and "morons" and made the butt of cruel jokes. This leaves them vulnerable to those who pretend to be their friends, whether it be police detectives looking to snare a confession or criminals hoping to ex-

In their pursuit of a confession, the police are not above using threats to a suspect's family or friends—threats to which individuals with mental disabilities may be particularly vulnerable.

ploit them. For this reason, some of the cases Perske has investigated involve a developmentally disabled person who has been maneuvered into taking the blame for a nondisabled criminal mastermind. "The criminal befriends the person, and then involves them in their criminal activity" Perske says. "Then, when it comes time for charges and trials, the nondisabled criminal makes a deal with the prosecutor, agreeing to testify against the disabled defendant for a reduced sentence." An example of this would be the case of Jerome Bowden, sentenced to death for the 1976 murder of Kathryn Stryker. According to Perske, "The so-called normal accomplice really was the solo perpetrator, but he managed to bring in Jerome Bowden. Jamie Graves, the guy who fingered him, did not get the death penalty. I can name three or four more cases like that."

In their pursuit of a confession, the police in some instances are not above using threats to a suspect's family or friends—threats to which individuals with mental disabilities may be particularly vulnerable. Disabled parents, for example, because of the social prejudice against them, often have a heightened fear of losing custody of their children. "Ritchie told me," says Perske, "that the police said that if he didn't confess they'd take his kid away from him." This part of Lapointe's story is seemingly confirmed by a tape recording secretly made by police during an interrogation of his wife, Karen, which took place at their home while Lapointe was at the police station. "Richard is going to be arrested, okay?" says Detective Michael Morrissey to Karen Lapointe, who has cerebral palsy. Morrissey, like Lombardo, also lied to her about the existence of DNA evidence and fingerprints implicating her husband, saying, "I don't want that to happen to you, because you're going to have to deal with somebody else taking care of your son. Do you know that?" When Lapointe's family came to the station asking to see him, they were told his "interview" could not be interrupted.

Lapointe's public defender tried to convince the jury that his client's confession should not be taken at face value. Unfortunately, many jurors (as well as police, attorneys, and judges) have a limited understanding of mental disability. According to Timothy Sugrue, the trial record shows that Lapointe "has a normal range IQ [100 is considered "normal"; Lapointe scored 92]. There was no evidence produced that demonstrated that he suffered from any thought disorder or mental deficiency." Perske, Lustig, and others respond by saying that IQ scores are not a reliable measure of mental impairment, particularly not a person's ability to withstand psychological coercion.

"People think they know what mental retardation is," Lustig said, "but what they think is mental retardation is generally Down's syndrome, where there are obvious physical characteristics." The vast majority of people with mental retardation have no discernible physical characteristics, nor is their demeanor obviously "retarded." According to Lustig, "Our biggest problem is ignorance, and getting [mentally disabled defendants] identified." In addition, even when the police and the courts know that a defendant is disabled, as in the Lapointe case, they may know little or nothing about the impact of that individual's particular disability. "We've learned a lot more about the effects of Dandy Walker since the trial," Perske says, knowledge that might have made a difference in the verdict. Unfortunately, such new evidence is irrelevant in any appeal, unless an entirely new trial is ordered.

Another complicating factor is that people with mental retardation will often go to great lengths to cover their difficulties in understanding and communicating, even denying that they have a disability. "Police officers don't know how to pick up on this," Lustig said. "Attorneys and judges don't know the right questions to ask. [People with mental retardation] don't want to tell anyone that they have mental retardation. There's a stigma attached."

Indeed, simply being seen as retarded (or mentally ill) is often all it takes to turn someone from a functioning member of the community into a "suspicious character." In *Unequal Justice*, Perske recalls an interview with a "patrolman turned investigator" who described his job as keeping an eye "on the garbage of humanity"—the "fringe people." Perske writes that these turned out to be

> any "strange-acting" people—usually retarded, or poor, or ethnic, or any combination of the three. [The detective] understood that "some of the better people" had family members with retardation as well. He did not doubt, however, that if they ever moved away from the control of their families, they too would become part of the criminal element in town.

But efforts to "pass" can have disastrous consequences. Jerome Bowden often denied that he was retarded. In his last conversation with his attorneys, Bowden told them, "I did the best I could" on the IQ test the state administered to determine whether he was competent to be executed. (At his trial, he testified that he signed a confession after being told it was the only way he could avoid the death penalty.) Bowden was sent to the Georgia electric chair on June 24, 1986. Asked for his final words, he told the assembled audience: "I am Jerome Bowden and I would like to say my execution is about to be carried out. I would like to thank the people of this institution. I hope that by my execution being carried out, it will bring some light to this thing that is wrong."

Perske is currently pressing for changes in the law to minimize the potential for the abuses he's seen. One recommendation is that all police interrogations be videotaped, so that juries have access to the process of confession and not just a typed end-product. He also sees DNA testing, where possible, as a way of helping to ensure that only the guilty are punished. And both Perske and Lustig believe that police, attorneys, and judges need to be educated about mental disability.

"In every neighborhood there's a case like this," Perske said. "What I hope is that people will become involved, will show up at the courtroom, will organize into citizens' groups to ensure that the prosecution isn't browbeating someone into making a confession, and that we don't pun-ish people who clearly have no understanding of the crime they committed or the punishment to which they may be subjected." To this end, Dennis Heath reports that People First will take up the Lapointe case in particular, and this entire issue in general, at the organization's next annual convention in November.

In the meantime, things do not look good for Richard Lapointe. In July 1996, the Connecticut Supreme Court rejected his appeal, and in November 1996 the U.S. Supreme Court refused even to hear it. The final hope of the Friends of Richard Lapointe is a habeas corpus suit that was filed in federal district court this past June.

"Rich has one bite of the apple on this," Perske said. "If this fails, I'm afraid we'll be visiting him in prison for the rest of our lives." Connecticut law does not permit the state's governor to grant pardons.

Fred Pelka is a freelance writer and the author of The ABC-CLIO Companion to the Disability Rights Movement. *Those interested in finding out more about the Lapointe case and others like it can contact Robert Perske, 54 Burn-colt Road, Florence, MA 01062; fax (413) 586-1852.*

PRIVATE PRISONS

Over the next 5 years analysts expect the private share of the prison "market" to more than double.

by Eric Bates

A few hours after midnight one August evening last year, Walter Hazelwood and Richard Wilson climbed a fence topped with razor wire at the Houston Processing Center, a warehouse built to hold undocumented immigrants awaiting deportation. Once outside, the two prisoners assaulted a guard, stole his car and headed for Dallas.

When prison officials notified the Houston police that the men had escaped, local authorities were shocked. Sure, immigrants had fled the minimum-security facility near the airport a few times before. But Hazelwood and Wilson were not being detained for lacking the papers to prove their citizenship. One was serving time for sexual abuse; the other was convicted of beating and raping an 88-year-old woman. Both men, it turned out, were among some 240 sex offenders from Oregon who had been shipped to the Texas detention center months earlier—and local authorities didn't even know they were there.

The immigration center is owned and operated by Corrections Corporation of America, which manages more private prisons than any other company worldwide. While C.C.A. made nearly $14,000 a day on the out-of-state inmates, the company was quick to point out that it had no legal obligation to tell the Houston police or country sheriff about their new neighbors from Oregon. "We designed and built the institution," explained Susan Hart, a company spokeswoman. "It is ours."

Yet like a well-to-do rancher who discovers a couple of valuable head of cattle missing, C.C.A. expected Texas rangers to herd the wayward animals back behind the company's fence. "It's not our function to capture them," Hart told reporters.

Catching the prisoners proved easier, however, than charging them with a crime. When authorities finally apprehended them after eleven days, they discovered they could no more punish the men for escaping than they could lock up a worker for walking off the job. Even in Texas, it seemed, it was not yet a crime to flee a private corporation.

"They have not committed the offense of escape under Texas law," said district attorney John Holmes. "The only reason at all that they're subject to being arrested and were arrested was because during their leaving the facility, they

assaulted a guard and took his motor vehicle. *That* we can charge them with, and have."

The state moved quickly to pass legislation making such escapes illegal. But the Texas breakout underscores how the rapid spread of private prisons has created considerable confusion about just what the rules are when a for-profit company like Corrections Corporation seeks to cash in on incarceration. Founded in 1983 with backing from the investors behind Kentucky Fried Chicken, C.C.A. was one of the first companies to push the privatization of public services. The selling point was simple: Private companies could build and run prisons cheaper than the government. Business, after all, would be free of red tape—those inefficient procedures that waste tax dollars on things like open bidding on state contracts and job security for public employees. Unfettered American capitalism would produce a better fetter, saving cash-strapped counties and states millions of dollars each year.

Sooner or later, people realize that "the government can't do anything very well," Thomas Beasley, a co-founder of C.C.A. and a former chairman of the Tennessee Republican Party, said near the start of prison privatization. "At that point, you just sell it like you were selling cars or real estate or hamburgers."

Not everyone is quite so enthusiastic about the prospect of selling human beings like so many pieces of meat. By privatizing prisons, government essentially auctions off inmates—many of them young black men—to the highest bidder. Opponents ranging from the American Civil Liberties Union to the National Sheriffs Association have argued that justice should not be for sale at any price. "The bottom line is a moral one," says Ira Robbins, who wrote a statement for the American Bar Association opposing private corrections. "Do we want our justice system to be operated by private interests? This is not like privatizing the post office or waste management to provide services to the community. There's something meaningful lost when an inmate looks at a guard's uniform and instead of seeing an emblem that reads 'Federal Bureau of Prisons' or 'State Department of Corrections,' he sees one that says 'Acme Prison Corporation.' "

Eric Bates is a staff writer with The Independent *in Durham, North Carolina. Research support was provided by the Investigative Fund of The Nation Institute.*

But such moral concerns have gone largely unheeded in all the excitement over how much money the boys at Acme might save taxpayers. There's only one problem: The evidence suggests that the savings reaped from nearly fifteen years of privatizing prisons are more elusive than an Oregon convict in a Texas warehouse.

In 1996 the General Accounting Office examined the few available reports comparing costs at private and public prisons. Its conclusion: "These studies do not offer substantial evidence that savings have occurred." The most reliable study cited by the G.A.O. found that a C.C.A.-run prison in Tennessee cost only 1 percent less to operate than two comparable state-run prisons. The track record also suggests that private prisons invite political corruption and do little to improve quality, exacerbating the conditions that lead to abuse and violence.

Although private prisons have failed to save much money for taxpayers, they generate enormous profits for the companies that own and operate them. Corrections Corporation ranks among the top five performing companies on the New York Stock Exchange over the past three years. The value of its shares has soared from $50 million when it went public in 1986 to more than $3.5 billion at its peak last October. By carefully selecting the most lucrative prison contracts, slashing labor costs and sticking taxpayers with the bill for expenses like prisoner escapes, C.C.A. has richly confirmed the title of a recent stock analysis by PaineWebber: "Crime pays."

A Corrections Corp. co-founder said of the move to private prisons, 'You just sell it like you were selling cars or real estate or hamburgers.'

"It's easier for private firms to innovate," says Russell Boraas, who oversees private prisons for the Virginia Department of Corrections. As he inspects a medium-security facility being built by C.C.A. outside the small town of Lawrenceville, Boraas notes that the prison has no guard towers—an "innovation" that saves the company $2.5 million in construction costs and eliminates twenty-five full-time positions. "Think about it," Boraas says. "A state corrections director who eliminates guard towers will lose his job if a prisoner escapes and molests a little old lady. The president of the company won't lose his job, as long as he's making a profit."

Although corrections officials like Boraas initially viewed the drive to privatize prisons with skepticism, many quickly became converts. The crime rate nationwide remains well below what it was twenty-five years ago, but harsher sentencing has packed prisons and jails to the bursting point. There are now 1.8 million Americans behind bars—more than twice as many as a decade ago—and the "get tough" stance has sapped public resources and sparked court orders to improve conditions.

With their promise of big savings, private prisons seemed to offer a solution. Corporate lockups can now hold an estimated 77,500 prisoners, most of them state inmates. Over the next five years, analysts expect the private share of the prison "market" to more than double.

Corrections Corporation is far and away the biggest company in the corrections business, controlling more than half of all inmates in private prisons nationwide. C.C.A. now operates the sixth-largest prison system in the country—and is moving aggressively to expand into the global market with prisons in England, Australia and Puerto Rico. That's good news for investors. *The Cabot Market Letter* compares the company to a "a hotel that's always at 100% occupancy . . . and booked to the end of the century." C.C.A. started taking reservations during the Reagan Administration, when Beasley founded the firm in Nashville with a former classmate from West Point. Their model was the Hospital Corporation of America, then the nation's largest owner of private hospitals. "This is the home of H.C.A.," Beasley thought at the time. "The synergies are the same."

From the start, those synergies included close ties to politicians who could grant the company lucrative contracts. As former chairman of the state G.O.P. Beasley was a good friend of then-Governor Lamar Alexander. In 1985 Alexander backed a plan to hand over the entire state prison system to the fledgling company for $200 million. Among C.C.A.'s stockholders at the time were the Governor's wife, Honey, and Ned McWherter, the influential Speaker of the state House, who succeeded Alexander as governor.

Although the state legislature eventually rejected the plan as too risky, C.C.A. had established itself as a major player. It had also discovered that knowing the right people can be more important than actually saving taxpayers money. The company won its first bid to run a prison by offering to operate the Silverdale Work Farm near Chattanooga for $21 per inmate per day. At $3 less than the county was spending, it seemed like a good deal—until a crackdown on drunk drivers flooded the work farm with new inmates. Because fixed expenses were unaffected by the surge, each new prisoner cost C.C.A. about $5. But the county, stuck with a contract that required it to pay the company $21 a head, found itself $200,000 over budget. "The work farm became a gold mine," noted John Donahue, a public policy professor at Harvard University.

When the contract came up for renewal in 1986, however, county commissioners voted to stick with Corrections Corporation. Several enjoyed business ties with the company. One commissioner had a pest-control contract with the firm, and later went to work for C.C.A. as a lobbyist. Another did landscaping at the prison, and a third ran the moving company that settled the warden into his new home. C.C.A. also put the son of the county employee responsible for monitoring the Silverdale contract on the payroll at its Nashville headquarters. The following year, the U.S. Justice Department published a research report warning about such conflicts of interest in on-site monitoring—the only mechanism for insuring that prison operators abide by the contract. In addition to being a hidden and costly expense of private prisons, the report cautioned, government monitors could "be co-opted by the contractor's staff. Becoming friendly or even beholden to contract personnel could lead to the State receiving misleading reports."

But even when problems have been reported, officials often downplay them. The Justice Department noted "substantial staff turnover problems" at the Chattanooga prison, for instance, but added that "this apparently did not result in major reductions in service quality." The reason? "This special effort to do a good job," the report concluded, "is probably due to the private organizations finding themselves in the national limelight, and their desire to expand the market."

The same year that federal officials were crediting C.C.A. with "a good job" at the undermanned facility, Rosalind Bradford, a 23-year-old woman being held at Silverdale, died from an undiagnosed complication during pregnancy. A shift supervisor who later sued the company testified that Bradford suffered in agony for at least twelve hours before C.C.A. officials allowed her to be taken to a hospital. "Rosalind Bradford died out there, in my opinion, of criminal neglect," the supervisor said in a deposition.

Inspectors from the British Prison Officers Association who visited the prison that year were similarly shocked by what they witnessed. "We saw evidence of inmates being cruelly treated," the inspectors reported. "Indeed, the warden admitted that noisy and truculent prisoners are gagged with sticky tape, but this had caused a problem when an inmate almost choked to death."

The inspectors were even more blunt when they visited the C.C.A.-run immigration center in Houston, where they found inmates confined to warehouselike dormitories for twenty-three hours a day. The private facility, inspectors concluded, demonstrated "possibly the worst conditions we have ever witnessed in terms of inmate care and supervision."

Reports of inhumane treatment of prisoners, while deeply disturbing, do not by themselves indicate that private prisons are worse than public ones. After all, state and federal lockups have never been known for their considerate attitude toward the people under their watch. Indeed, C.C.A. and other company prisons have drawn many of their wardens and guards from the ranks of public corrections officers. The guards videotaped earlier this year assaulting prisoners with stun guns at a C.C.A. competitor in Texas had been hired despite records of similar abuse when they worked for the state.

Susan Hart, the C.C.A. spokeswoman, insisted that her company would never put such people on the payroll—well, almost never. "It would be inappropriate, for certain positions, [to hire] someone who said, 'Yes, I beat a prisoner to death,' " she told *The Houston Chronicle*. "That would be a red flag for us." She did not specify for which positions the company considers murder an appropriate job qualification.

In fact, C.C.A. employs at least two wardens in Texas who were disciplined for beating prisoners while employed by the state. And David Myers, the president of the company, supervised an assault on inmates who took a guard hostage while Myers was serving as warden of a Texas prison in 1984. Fourteen guards were later found to have used "excessive force," beating subdued and handcuffed prisoners with riot batons.

The real danger of privatization is not some innate inhumanity on the part of its practitioners but rather the added financial incentives that reward inhumanity. The same economic logic that motivates companies to run prisons more efficiently also encourages them to cut corners at the expense of workers, prisoners and the public. Private prisons essentially mirror the cost-cutting practices of health maintenance organizations: Companies receive a guaranteed fee for each prisoner, regardless of the actual costs. Every dime they don't spend on food or medical care or training for guards is a dime they can pocket.

As in most industries, the biggest place to cut prison expenses is personnel. "The bulk of the cost savings enjoyed by C.C.A. is the result of lower labor costs," PaineWebber assures investors. Labor accounts for roughly 70 percent of all prison expenses, and C.C.A. prides itself on getting more from fewer employees. "With only a 36 percent increase in personnel," boasts the latest annual report, "revenues grew 41 percent, operating income grew 98 percent, and net income grew 115 percent."

Like other companies, C.C.A. prefers to design and build its own prisons so it can replace guards right from the start with video cameras and clustered cellblocks that are cheaper to monitor. "The secret to low-cost operations is having the minimum number of officers watching the maximum number of inmates," explains Russell Boraas, the private prison administrator for Virginia. "You can afford to pay damn near anything for construction if it will get you an efficient prison."

At the C.C.A. prison under construction in Lawrenceville, Boraas indicates how the design of the "control room" will enable a guard to simultaneously watch three "pods" of 250 prisoners each. Windows in the elevated room afford an unobstructed view of each cellblock below, and "vision blocks" in the floor are positioned over each entranceway so guards can visually identify anyone being admitted. The high-tech panel at the center of the room can open any door at the flick of a switch. When the prison opens next year, C.C.A. will employ five guards to supervise 750 prisoners during the day, and two guards at night.

Another way to save money on personnel is to leave positions unfilled when they come open. Speaking before a legislative panel in Tennessee in October, Boraas noted that some private prisons in Texas have made up for the low reimbursement rates they receive from the state "by leaving positions vacant a little longer than they should." Some C.C.A. employees admit privately that the company leaves positions open to boost profits. "We're always short," says one guard who asked not to be identified. "They do staff fewer positions—that's one way they save money." The company is growing so quickly, another guard explains, that "we have more slots than we have people to fill them. When they transfer officers to new facilities, we're left with skeletons."

At first glance, visitors to the South Central Correctional Center could be forgiven for mistaking the medium-security prison for a college campus. The main driveway rolls through wooded hills on the outskirts of Clifton, Tennessee, past picnic benches, a fitness track and a horse barn. But just inside the front door, a prominent bulletin board makes clear that the prison means business. At the top are the words "C.C.A. Excellence in Corrections." At the bottom is "Yesterday's Stock Closing," followed by a price.

In addition to employing fewer guards, C.C.A. saves money on labor by replacing the guaranteed pensions earned by workers at state-run prisons with a cheaper— and riskier—stock-ownership plan. Employees get a chance to invest in the company, and the company gets employees devoted to the bottom line. "Being a stockholder yourself you monitor things closer," says Mark Staggs, standing in the segregation unit, where he oversees prisoners confined for breaking the rules. "You make sure you don't waste money on things like cleaning products. Because it's your money you're spending."

Warden Kevin Myers (not related to C.C.A. president David Myers) also looks for little places to cut costs. "I can save money on purchasing because there's no bureaucracy," he says. "If I see a truckload of white potatoes at a bargain, I can buy them. I'm always negotiating for a lower price."

But what is thriftiness to the warden is just plain miserly to those forced to eat what he dishes out. "Ooowhee! It's pitiful in that kitchen," says Antonio McCraw, who was released from South Central last March after serving three years for armed robbery. "I just thank God I'm out of there. You might get a good meal once a month. The rest was instant potatoes, vegetables out of a can and processed pizzas. C.C.A. don't care whether you eat or not. Sure they may cut corners and do it for less money, but is it healthy?"

The State of Tennessee hoped to answer that question when it turned South Central over to C.C.A. in 1992. The prison was built at roughly the same time as two state-run facilities with similar designs and inmate populations, giving officials a rare opportunity to compare daily operating costs—and quality—under privatization.

The latest state report on violence at the three prisons indicates that South Central is a much more dangerous place than its public counterparts. During the past fiscal year, the C.C.A. prison experienced violent incidents at a rate more than 50 percent higher than state facilities. The company also posted significantly worse rates for contraband, drugs and assaults on staff and prisoners.

"If that doesn't raise some eyebrows and give you some kind of indication of what the future holds, I guess those of us who are concerned just need to be quiet," says John Mark Windle, a state representative who opposes privatization.

Corrections officials note that understaffing can certainly fuel violence, which winds up costing taxpayers more money. The state legislature has heard testimony that employee turnover at South Central is more than twice the level at state prisons, and prisoners report seeing classes of new recruits every month, many of them young and inexperienced. "The turnover rate is important because it shows whether you have experienced guards who stick around and know the prisoners," says inmate Alex Friedmann, seated at a bare table in a visitation room. "If you have a high turnover rate you have less stability. New employees come in; they really don't know what's going on. That leads to conflicts with inmates."

Internal company documents tell a similar story. According to the minutes of an August 1995 meeting of shift supervisors at South Central, chief of security Danny Scott "said we all know that we have lots of new staff and are constantly in the training mode." He "added that so many employees were totally lost and had never worked in corrections."

A few months later, a company survey of staff members at the prison asked, "What is the reason for the number of people quitting C.C.A.?" Nearly 20 percent of employees cited "treatment by supervisors" and 17 percent listed "money."

Out of earshot of their supervisors, some guards also say the company contributes to violence by skimping on activities for inmates. "We don't give them anything to do," says one officer. "We give them the bare minimum we have to."

Ron Lyons agrees. "There's no meaningful programs here," says Lyons, who served time at state-run prisons before coming to South Central. "I can't get over how many people are just laying around in the pod every day. I would have thought C.C.A. would have known that inmate idleness is one of the biggest problems in prisons—too much time sitting around doing nothing. You definitely realize it's commercialized. It's a business. Their business is to feed you and count you, and that's it."

Given all the penny-pinching, it would seem that C.C.A. should easily be able to demonstrate significant savings at South Central. Instead, a study of costs conducted by the state in 1995 found that the company provided almost no savings compared with its two public rivals. The study—cited by the General Accounting Office as "the most sound and detailed comparison of operational costs"—actually showed that the C.C.A. prison cost *more* to run on a daily basis. Even after the state factored in its long-term expenses, C.C.A. still spent

At its heart, privatizing prisons is really about privatizing tax dollars, transforming public money into private profits.

$35.38 a day per prisoner—only 38 cents less than the state average.

The study contradicted what is supposed to be the most compelling rationale for prison privatization: the promise of big savings. But the industry champion dismissed its defeat by insisting, much to the amazement of its challengers, that it hadn't tried very hard to save tax dollars. "When you're in a race and you can win by a few steps, that's what you do," said Doctor R. Crants, who co-founded C.C.A. and now serves as chairman and chief executive officer. "We weren't trying to win by a great deal."

The comment by Crants, as remarkable as it seems, exposes the true nature of privatization. When it comes to savings, the prison industry will beat state spending by as narrow a margin as the state will permit. To a prison company like C.C.A., savings are nothing but the share of profits it is required to hand over to the government—another expense that cuts into the bottom line and must therefore be kept to a minimum, like wages or the price of potatoes. At its heart, privatizing prisons is really about privatizing tax dollars, about transforming public money into private profits.

That means companies are actually looking for ways to keep public spending as high as possible, including charging taxpayers for questionable expenses. The New Mexico Corrections Department, for example, has accused C.C.A. of overcharging the state nearly $2 million over the past eight years for operating the women's prison in Grants. The company fee of $95 a day for each inmate, it turns out, includes $22 for debt service on the prison.

Last summer, a legislative committee in Tennessee calculated that state prisons contribute nearly $17.8 million each year to state agencies that provide central services like printing, payroll administration and insurance. Since company prisons usually go elsewhere for such services, states that privatize unwittingly lose money they once counted on to help pay fixed expenses.

The "chargebacks," as they are known, came to light last spring when C.C.A. once again proposed taking over the entire Tennessee prison system. This time the company offered to save $100 million a year—a staggering sum, considering that the annual budget for the system is only $270 million.

Like many claims of savings, the C.C.A. offer turned out to be based on false assumptions. Crants, the company chairman and C.E.O., said he derived the estimate from comparing the $32 daily rate the company charges for medium-security prisoners at South Central with the systemwide average of $54. But the state system includes maximum-security prisons that

The track record suggests that private prisons save little, invite political corruption and exacerbate the conditions that lead to violence.

cost much more to operate than South Central. "It's almost like going into a rug store," says State Senator James Kyle, who chaired legislative hearings on privatization. "They're always 20 percent off. But 20 percent off what?"

Yet the sales pitch, however absurd, had the intended effect of getting Kyle and other lawmakers into the store to look around. Once there, the prison companies kept offering them bigger and better deals. Given an opportunity to submit cost estimates anonymously, firms offered fantastic savings ranging from 30 percent to 50 percent. Threatened by the competition, even the state Department of Corrections went bargain basement, offering to slash its own already low cost by $70 million a year. Despite opposition from state employees, legislators indicated after the hearings that they support a move to turn most prisoners over to private companies—a decision that delighted C.C.A. "I was pretty pleased," Crants said afterward. The governor and legislators are wrangling over the details, but both sides have agreed informally to privatize roughly two-thirds of the Tennessee system. A few prisons will be left in the hands of the state, just in case something goes wrong.

Lawmakers didn't have to look far to see how wrong things can go. South Carolina decided last February not to renew a one-year contract with C.C.A. for a juvenile detention center in the state capital. Child advocates reported hearing about horrific abuses at the facility, where some boys say they were hogtied and shackled together. "The bottom line is the staff there were inexperienced," said Robyn Zimmerman of the South Carolina Department of Juvenile Justice. "They were not trained properly."

Once again, though, such stark realities proved less influential than the political connections enjoyed by C.C.A. The chief lobbyist for the company in the Tennessee legislature is married to the Speaker of the state House. Top C.C.A. executives, board members and their spouses have contributed at least $ 110,000 to state candidates since 1993, including $1,350 to Senator Kyle. And five state officials—including the governor, the House Speaker and the sponsor of the privatization bill—are partners with C.C.A. co-founder Thomas Beasley in several Red Hot & Blue barbecue restaurants in Tennessee.

The political clout extends to the national level as well. On the Republican side, Corrections Corporation employs the services of J. Michael Quinlan, director of the federal Bureau of Prisons under George Bush. On the Democratic side, C.C.A. reserves a seat on its seven-member board for Joseph Johnson, former executive director of the Rainbow Coalition. The *Nashville Tennessean* points to Johnson as evidence that the company "looks like America. . . . Johnson is African-American," the paper observes, "as are 60% of C.C.A.'s prisoners."

Johnson played a pivotal behind-the-scenes role earlier this year, using his political connections to help C.C.A. swing a deal to buy a prison from the District of Columbia for $52 million. It was the first time a government sold a prison to a private company, and C.C.A. hopes it won't be the last. Earlier this year, with backing from financial heavyweights like Lehman Brothers and PaineWebber, the company formed C.C.A. Prison Realty Trust to focus solely on buying prisons. The initial stock offering raised $388.5 million from investors to enable C.C.A. to speculate on prisons as real estate.

Why would cities or states sell their prisons to the C.C.A. trust? PaineWebber cites the lure of what it calls "free money." Unlike many public bond initiatives earmarked for specific projects like schools or sewage systems, the broker explains, "the sale of an existing prison would generate proceeds that a politician could then use for initiatives that fit his or her agenda, possibly improving the chances of re-election." Companies building their own prisons certainly receive friendly treatment from officials. Russell Boraas invited companies bidding on a private prison to a meeting and asked what he could do to help. "I said, 'Guys, I know quite a bit about running construction projects, but I don't know much about private prisons. What are you looking for? What can I do to make this user-friendly for you?' They said it would be nice if they could use tax-exempt bond issues for construction, just like the state." So Boraas allowed companies to finance construction with help from taxpayers, and a local Industrial Development Authority eventually aided C.C.A. in getting $58 million in financing to build the prison.

Such deals raise concerns that private prisons may wind up costing taxpayers more in the long run. Although governments remain legally responsible for inmates guarded by public companies, firms have little trouble finding ways to skirt public oversight while pocketing public money. Instead of streamlining the system, hiring corporations to run prisons actually *adds* a layer of bureaucracy that can increase costs and reduce accountability. Prison companies have been known to jack up prices when their contracts come up for renewal, and some defer maintenance on prisons since they aren't responsible for them once their contract expires.

Even more disturbing, private prisons have the financial incentive—and financial influence—to lobby lawmakers for harsher prison sentences and other "get tough" measures. In the prison industry, after all, locking people up is good for business. "If you really want to save money you can lock prisoners in a box and feed them a slice of bread each day," says Alex Friedmann, the prisoner at South Central. "The real question is, Can you run programs in such a way that people don't commit more crime? That should be the mark of whether privatization is successful in prisons—not whether you keep them locked up but whether you keep them out."

C.C.A. officials dismiss such concerns, confident the current boom will continue of its own accord. "I don't think we have to worry about running out of product," says Kevin Myers, the warden at South Central. "It's unfortunate but true. We don't have to drum up business."

Perhaps—but Corrections Corporation and other company prisons already have enormous power to keep their current prisoners behind bars for longer stretches. Inmates generally lose accumulated credit for "good time" when they are disciplined by guards, giving the C.C.A. stockholders who serve as officers an incentive to crack the whip. A 1992 study by the New Mexico Corrections Department showed that inmates at the women's prison run by C.C.A. lost good time at a rate nearly eight times higher than their male counterparts at a state-run lockup. And every day a prisoner loses is a day of extra income for the company—and an extra expense for taxpayers.

Some C.C.A. guards in Tennessee also say privately that they are encouraged to write up prisoners for minor infractions and place them in segregation. Inmates in "seg" not only lose their good time, they also have thirty days added to their sentence—a bonus of nearly $1,000 for the company at some prisons. "We will put 'em in seg in a hurry," says a guard who works at the Davidson County Juvenile Detention Facility in Nashville.

The prison holds 100 youths—"children, really," says the guard—most of them teenage boys. "They may be young, but they understand what's going on," he adds. One day, as a 14-year-old boy was being released after serving his sentence, the guard offered him some friendly advice.

"Stay out of trouble," he said. "I don't want to see you back here."

"Why not?" the kid responded. "That's how you make your money."

AE Article Review Form

We encourage you to photocopy and use this page as a tool to assess how the articles in **Annual Editions** expand on the information in your textbook. By reflecting on the articles you will gain enhanced text information. You can also access this useful form on a product's book support Web site at **http://www.dushkin.com/online/.**

NAME: _____ DATE: _____

TITLE AND NUMBER OF ARTICLE: _____

BRIEFLY STATE THE MAIN IDEA OF THIS ARTICLE: _____

LIST THREE IMPORTANT FACTS THAT THE AUTHOR USES TO SUPPORT THE MAIN IDEA:

WHAT INFORMATION OR IDEAS DISCUSSED IN THIS ARTICLE ARE ALSO DISCUSSED IN YOUR TEXTBOOK OR OTHER READINGS THAT YOU HAVE DONE? LIST THE TEXTBOOK CHAPTERS AND PAGE NUMBERS:

LIST ANY EXAMPLES OF BIAS OR FAULTY REASONING THAT YOU FOUND IN THE ARTICLE:

LIST ANY NEW TERMS/CONCEPTS THAT WERE DISCUSSED IN THE ARTICLE, AND WRITE A SHORT DEFINITION:

ANNUAL EDITIONS revisions depend on two major opinion sources: one is our Advisory Board, listed in the front of this volume, which works with us in scanning the thousands of articles published in the public press each year; the other is you—the person actually using the book. Please help us and the users of the next edition by completing the prepaid article rating form on this page and returning it to us. Thank you for your help!

ANNUAL EDITIONS: Social Welfare and Social Work 00/01

ARTICLE RATING FORM

Here is an opportunity for you to have direct input into the next revision of this volume. We would like you to rate each of the 42 articles listed below, using the following scale:

1. Excellent: should definitely be retained
2. Above average: should probably be retained
3. Below average: should probably be deleted
4. Poor: should definitely be deleted

Your ratings will play a vital part in the next revision.
So please mail this prepaid form to us just as soon as you complete it.
Thanks for your help!

RATING

ARTICLE

1. Bethlem/Bedlam: Methods of Madness?
2. Roslyn's Mutual Aid Lodges: Between Assimilation and Cultural Continuity, 1887–1940
3. "Hallelujah, I'm a Bum"
4. Every Picture Tells a Story
5. When the Laws Were Silent
6. Poverty 101: What Liberals and Conservatives Can Learn from Each Other
7. D.C.'s Indentured Servants
8. Government Can't Cure Poverty
9. Counting Race and Ethnicity: Options for the 2000 Census
10. Of Race and Risk
11. In Defense of Affirmative Action
12. Service Redlining: The New Jim Crow?
13. The War between Men and Women
14. Homosexuality across Cultures: Sensitizing Social Workers to Historical Issues Facing Gay, Lesbian and Bisexual Youth
15. Missed Opportunity
16. A Critique of the Case for Privatizing Social Security
17. Don't Go It Alone
18. Welfare Reform Legislation Poses Opportunities and Challenges for Rural America
19. Why Welfare Reform Is Working
20. Welfare to Work: What Happens When Recipient Meets Employer?
21. Welfare's Fatal Attraction
22. Beyond the Welfare Clock
23. Welfare and the "Third Way"

RATING

ARTICLE

24. Left Behind
25. Welfare to Work: A Sequel
26. Now, the Hard Part of Welfare Reform
27. Q: Are Single-Parent Families a Major Cause of Social Dysfunction?
28. Father's Day Every Day
29. Youth at Risk: Saving the World's Most Precious Resource
30. Weapon-Carrying and Youth Violence
31. Measuring and Monitoring Children's Well-Being across the World
32. Beyond the Boundaries of Child Welfare: Connecting with Welfare, Juvenile Justice, Family Violence and Mental Health Systems
33. Universal Health Care Coverage in the United States: Barriers, Prospects, and Implications
34. Safe to Talk: Abortion Narratives as a Rite of Return
35. The Chasm in Care
36. Religion/Spirituality and Health among Elderly African Americans and Hispanics
37. The Managed Care Experience: The Social Worker's Perspective
38. Lobotomy's Back
39. Cultural Diversity and Mental Health: The Haudenosaunee of New York State
40. Pay per Plea: Public Defenders Come at a Price
41. Unequal Justice: Preserving the Rights of the Mentally Retarded in the Criminal Justice System
42. Private Prisons

(Continued on next page)

We Want Your Advice

ANNUAL EDITIONS: SOCIAL WELFARE AND SOCIAL WORK 00/01

ABOUT YOU

Name

Date

Are you a teacher? ☐   A student? ☐
Your school's name

Department

Address

City

State

Zip

School telephone #

YOUR COMMENTS ARE IMPORTANT TO US !

Please fill in the following information:
For which course did you use this book?

Did you use a text with this *ANNUAL EDITION*? ☐ yes ☐ no
What was the title of the text?

What are your general reactions to the *Annual Editions* concept?

Have you read any particular articles recently that you think should be included in the next edition?

Are there any articles you feel should be replaced in the next edition? Why?

Are there any World Wide Web sites you feel should be included in the next edition? Please annotate.

May we contact you for editorial input? ☐ yes ☐ no
May we quote your comments? ☐ yes ☐ no